Front Projection of a Schoolhouse, with Trees, Shrubbery, &c.

THE SCHOOL

AND

THE SCHOOLMASTER

A MANUAL

FOR THE USE OF

TEACHERS, EMPLOYERS, TRUSTEES, INSPECTORS, &c., &c.
OF COMMON SCHOOLS.

IN TWO PARTS.

PART I.

BY ALONZO POTTER, D.D.,

OF NEW-YORK.

PART II.

BY GEORGE B. EMERSON, A.M.,

OF MASSACHUSETTS.

Entered, according to Act of Congress, in the year 1842, by
HARPER & BROTHERS,
In the Clerk's Office of the Southern District of New-York.

ADVERTISEMENT.

It is proper to state, that this volume has been prepared at the request of a friend of Common Schools, and is now published through his instrumentality. He has directed a copy of it to be placed in each of the School Districts, incorporated Academies, and County Clerks' Offices of the State of New-York, as well as in the hands of the Governors of the several states, and of the Deputy Superintendents of Common Schools in the several counties of this state.

Though prepared with special reference to the condition and wants of Common Schools in the State of New-York, its general principles and most of its details will be found applicable to similar schools in other parts of the country, and, indeed, to all seminaries employed in giving elementary instruction.

State of New-York.

Secretary's Office,
Department of Common Schools.

Albany, August 15, 1842.

THE following volume, entitled "The School and the Schoolmaster," has been specially prepared for the benefit of the Common Schools of this State. The first part of the work, commencing with "The Education of the People," was written by PROFESSOR A. POTTER, D.D., of Union College, Schenectady. The second part, commencing with "The Schoolmaster," was written by GEORGE B. EMERSON, A.M., of Boston, who has long been a celebrated practical teacher of youth.

The approbation of this volume by the Superintendent of Common Schools was made a condition of its publication. I have therefore attentively examined, in manuscript, both parts of the work, and have been much gratified with the plan and the execution of the respective parts; and under the confident expectation that this volume will be an important acquisition to our Common Schools, as well as to parents, teachers, and all the friends of Education, I hereby award to it my unqualified commendation.

S. YOUNG,
Superintendent Common Schools

Perspective of Schoolhouse, Outbuildings, and Grounds.

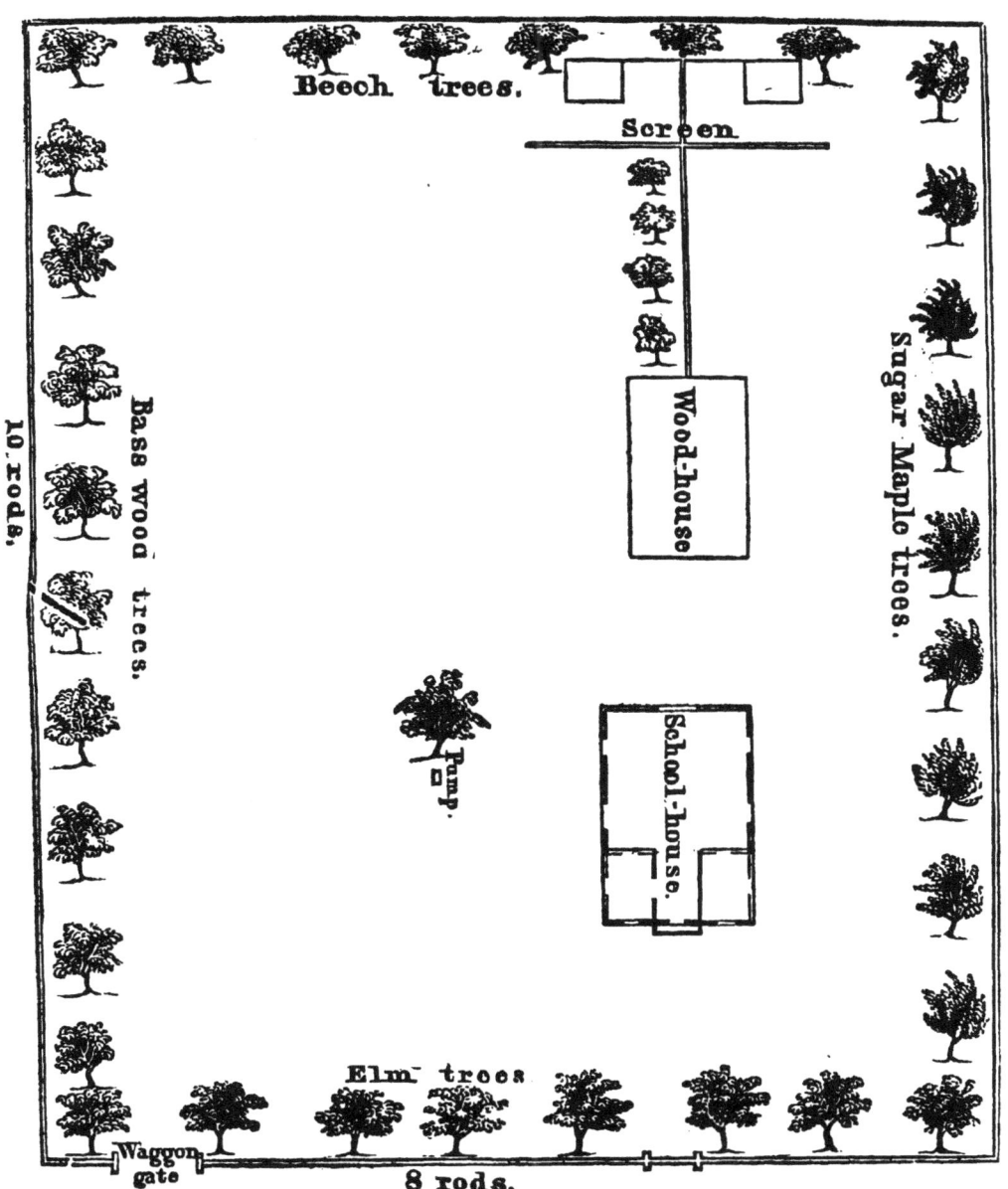

Plan of Grounds, &c.

PART I.

THE SCHOOL:

ITS OBJECTS, RELATIONS, AND USES.

WITH A SKETCH

OF THE

EDUCATION MOST NEEDED IN THE UNITED STATES, THE PRESENT STATE OF COMMON SCHOOLS, THE BEST MEANS OF IMPROVING THEM,

AND THE CONSEQUENT

DUTIES OF PARENTS, TRUSTEES, INSPECTORS, &c

BY

ALONZO POTTER, D.D.,

PROFESSOR OF MORAL PHILOSOPHY IN UNION COLLEGE.

NEW-YORK:

HARPER & BROTHERS, 82 CLIFF STREET.

1846.

CONTENTS.

INTRODUCTION . . . . Page 1

CHAPTER I.
EDUCATION OF THE PEOPLE.

SEC. I. What is Education? 19
   II. Prevailing Errors in regard to the Nature and End of Education 28
   III. The same Subject continued 35
   IV. Same Subject continued 50
   V. What is the Education most needed by the American People? 64
   VI. The Importance of Education, 1. To the Individual . 91
   VII.   "   "   2. To Society . . 111

CHAPTER II.
COMMON SCHOOLS.

SEC. I. Relation of Common Schools to other Means of Education 154
   II. *Present State of Common Schools.*—1. Schoolhouses. 2. Manners. 3. Morals 168
   III. *Same Subject continued.*—4. Intellectual Instruction. 5. Irregular Attendance 180
   IV. *How can Common Schools be improved?*—1. Discussion. 2. Female Teachers. 3. Union or High Schools. 4. Consolidation of Districts 197
   V. *The Improvement of Common Schools (continued). Organization in Cities.*—1. District System. 2. Monitorial. 3. Fächer System. 4. American System. 5. Diversity of Class-books 218
   VI. *Same Subject continued.*—Education of Teachers . 236

INTRODUCTION.

"Were the benefits of civilization to be partial, not universal, it would be only a bitter mockery and cruel injustice."—DUCHATEL.

A LATE writer (Lamartine) has spoken of the *cross* and the *press* as the instruments of the two greatest movements ever made in behalf of human civilization. To these may be added two other agents of mighty power: the *steam-engine* and the *common school*. The *moral* nature of man can be permanently raised and transformed by nothing short of the benignant influence of Christianity. His *intellectual* powers can be duly developed and wisely applied only under the guidance of knowledge; and of knowledge the press is now the grand expositor and representative. To promote his *physical* well-being, we need industry; and of that industry which subdues the earth, vanquishes time and space, and makes all things tributary to man's convenience, the steam-engine is unquestionably the most proper symbol.

It is worthy of remark, that as each of these great powers is necessary to the improvement of mankind, so each of them becomes more efficient in proportion as it co-operates with the rest. Christianity needs the press, the press needs the steam-engine; and these, in their turn, are safe and beneficent agents only when they who wield them are animated and controlled by Christian principle. It is still more to our purpose, however, to observe, that no one of them can exert its appropriate influence, or dispense its proper benefits without the aid of the *school*. Minds, for instance, besotted by ignorance and unaccustomed to thought, can hardly be reached by the more lofty and spiritual appeals which are sent forth from the cross of Christ. The press must speak in vain to those who cannot read, or who, to the mechanical art of interpreting its mysterious symbols, have never added habits of inquiry, or a desire for knowledge. And even industry, although it always brings some blessings to those whom it employs, can still do comparatively little for men who alienate their higher natures when they labour, or who waste its fruits in sensual indulgence, or in mental vacancy. It is only in proportion as minds are awakened by early education, that they can share in the fruits of an improved civilization. To shut them out from the school, is to deny them access to a large proportion of the best and noblest influences, which are supplied by Christianity, and by science and the arts.

But if the school is an essential agent of civilization, it is the *Common* School, that forms the appropriate agent of modern and democratic civilization—of that civilization which aims at the greatest good of the greatest number. As this end is peculiar to the social movements of modern times, so is the instrument which it employs. Schools have always been found in the train of civilization, as the only means by which her blessings could be preserved and perpetuated; but the idea of schools which should secure to every human being, by improving his mind, a substantial share in the triumphs of Learning, Liberty, and Religion, this, it is believed, was an idea unknown to the wisest of ancient sages and states. They wrote and speculated much about education; but it was an education denied to more than four fifths of the people, who, being barbarians, were born, according to Aristotle, to be slaves, and who, as slaves, were denied all spiritual as well as civil rights. It was an education, too, by which the citizen was to be moulded for the exclusive service of the commonwealth, rather than one which was to unfold in due proportion all his powers, and prepare him for a course of free and generous self-culture.

In the Middle Ages, when education was dispensed in monastic establishments, and enjoyed, for the most part, only by the clergy, we are not to wonder that the people were in ignorance. Even after the revival of letters, and when the art of Printing had awakened the slumbering intellect of Europe, little progress was made in *popular* education until the Bible had been translated into living languages, and the privilege of reading it had come to be reckoned as one of the most precious, among the rights of the Christian and the man. The rule which was then extensively adopted in the Continental churches, of admitting no one to his first communion who could not read the Scriptures, coupled with another rule, which made this first communion necessary in order to qualify him for marriage or any civil employment—these regulations naturally served to make a certain degree of instruction universal throughout the north of Europe.

The same religious and enlightened spirit presided over the legislation of the early settlers of New-England. Both in Massachusetts and Connecticut, it was ordained by law, almost immediately after their settlement,* that the selectmen of the towns should see that " every parent or master instructed the young members of his family (whether children, apprentices, or servants) in so much learning as would enable them perfectly to read the English tongue and have a knowledge of the capital laws; that once a week he should catechise them in the grounds and principles of religion; and that every young person should be carefully bred and brought up to some honest, lawful calling, labour, or employment." It will be observed that these regulations are, in

---

* In Massachusetts in 1642, in Connecticut in 1650.

truth, more enlightened and comprehensive than those which had been adopted in Europe at the era of the Reformation. In the latter, *religious* culture seems to have been almost the only object; in the former, it was also an object to make enlightened citizens capable of self-government, and trained to habits of regular industry.

Not satisfied, however, with these provisions for *domestic* education, the inhabitants soon proceeded to lay the foundation of that *Common School system* which has been so long the pride and strength of New-England. As early as 1647, only twenty-seven years after the landing of the Mayflower at Plymouth, it was enacted in Massachusetts, in order that "learning," to use the language of the statute, "might not be buried in the graves of their forefathers both in church and commonwealth—that (the Lord assisting their endeavours) in every township containing fifty householders or more, one should forthwith be appointed to teach such children as should resort to him to read and write; and that, in any township containing one hundred householders, they should set up a grammar-school to fit youth for the University." This law, planting elementary schools at the door of every family, was the first, it is presumed, adopted by any Christian state,* and may claim to be the parent of much

---

* It is somewhat humiliating to reflect, that the earliest law on record, providing for the universal diffusion of school education, was the work of a people whom we are pleased to style barbarians (the Chinese), and was in existence two thousand years ago. According to a late writer (Davis), it required that every town and village, down even to a few families, should have a Common School. He also states that one of their works, of a date anterior to the Christian era, speaks of the "*ancient* system of instruction." It is proper, however, to add, that it does not seem to have been the object of the Chinese, as of the New-England system, to favour a free and full development of man's nature. The studies are confined by authority to one unvarying routine; science, properly so called, is excluded; the spirit of spontaneous inquiry is repressed, and the whole aim

of the legislation on the subject of Popular Instruction which has distinguished the last half century.*

To maintain and perpetuate *religious* knowledge among the people was evidently the chief object with the framers of these early school-laws, both in the Old World and in the New. With some notion of the importance, as well to the state as to the individual, of a comprehensive and generous culture, which should awaken and train all the powers of the soul, it is still clear that they failed to recognise all its value in these respects. In Europe it is now admitted that the elementary education given in obedience to these regulations contributed but little to raise the character of the

is to make an orderly and industrious servant of the state as now constituted. To use the language of another, "the whole channel of thought and feeling for each generation is *scooped out* by that which preceded it, and the stream always fills, but rarely overflows its embankments." It is also questionable whether the Chinese schools succeed in making the whole population capable, as is sometimes said, of reading. According to some missionaries, many of the inhabitants are unable to read at all, and others do it mechanically, and without any perception of the meaning of the author.

* The system of parochial schools in Scotland is sometimes appealed to, as the earliest example of a legal provision for universal education. The law, however, establishing these schools, was not passed till 1696, nearly 50 years after the enactment of the one in Massachusetts; and the preamble of that law clearly shows that the previous efforts of the General Assembly of the Kirk of Scotland, and of the civil government in behalf of Education, had failed to make it general. This preamble states that "Our Sovereign Lord, considering how prejudicial the *want of schools in many places* had been, and how beneficial the establishing and settling thereof will be to this church and kingdom, therefore his majesty, with advice and consent," &c., and then the act proceeds to order that a school be established and a schoolmaster appointed in *every parish*, and that the landlords be obliged to build a schoolhouse and a dwelling-house for the use of the master, and that they pay him a certain salary, exclusive of the fees of the scholars.

mass of the people. In New-England, much was probably ascribed to schools which resulted from other causes, such as the animating influence of a New World, with all its tempting prizes, its numberless incentives to enterprise and forecast, and the opportunities which it afforded, in its political and ecclesiastical institutions, for the cultivation and gradual development of knowledge and power.*

That these schools have exercised a vast and most happy influence, not only over New-England, but over all parts of our country, is unquestionable; yet it is evident that even in Massachusetts itself, the very cradle of the system, their unspeakable importance has not been duly appreciated. While wealth and population were increasing, and education, of course, was growing more and more necessary, the statute-books of that state show for a long period only a declining interest in schools. The salutary rigour of the primitive laws was gradually relaxed, till in 1789 it was ordained that common schools need be maintained but six months in the year, and grammar-schools only when there were two hundred householders in a town; and in 1824 it was declared, that in towns having less than FIVE *thousand* inhabitants, none but a teacher of English need be provided.† It is grateful to add, however, that during the last five years this downward course of legislation has been arrested,‡ and

---

* The influence which our institutions exert (especially as they unfold themselves in New-England) in developing intelligence, self-control, and activity, has been explained with great clearness and accuracy by De Tocqueville. See his Democracy in America.

† There was also a provision in the colony charter of Massachusetts, that towns of more than 500 families should support *two* grammar-schools and *two* writing-schools. This provision disappeared in the later, commonly called the province, charter.

‡ The testimony of the present enlightened secretary of the Board of Education (in Massachusetts) indicates how much the schools had failed to accomplish their ends. Speaking of their state at the time of his appointment (1837), he says, "The Common School system

that the most enlightened and liberal efforts are now making to raise the standard of public instruction in that ancient and honoured commonwealth.

In our own state, the Common School—as part of a system of public instruction, maintained and encouraged by law—is of recent origin. The act establishing the Common School Fund, which has formed the basis of the system, was passed in 1805;* but no revenue was distributed

---

of Massachusetts has fallen into a state of general unsoundness and debility; a great majority of the schoolhouses are not only ill adapted to encourage mental effort, but in many cases are absolutely perilous to the health and symmetrical growth of the children; the schools are under a sleepy supervision; many of the most intelligent and wealthy of our citizens have become estranged from their welfare; and the teachers of the schools, although, with very few exceptions, persons of estimable character and of great private worth, yet, in the absence of all opportunities to qualify themselves for the performance of the most delicate and difficult task which, in the arrangements of Providence, is committed to human hands, are necessarily, and therefore without fault of their own, deeply and widely deficient in the two indispensable prerequisites for their office, viz., a knowledge of the human mind as the subject of improvement, and a knowledge of the means best adapted wisely to unfold and direct its growing faculties."

* Ten years earlier, a temporary appropriation ($50,000 annually for five years) was made "for the encouragement of schools." Owing to the state of the treasury, but about $150,000 of this appropriation was realized. The statute was in many respects imperfect, and was suffered to expire; but it contained one important principle, which was afterward incorporated with the Common School system of the state. This was, that the supervisors of the counties should distribute the amount of the grant among the several towns, and that these towns should raise equal amounts by tax. By the existing law, however, the money is apportioned *according to the whole population*; by the law of 1795 it was distributed *according to the number of taxable inhabitants*. The former is evidently the more equitable and benevolent provision; and it may be doubted whether the principle of it ought not to be extended. The moneys granted from the state treasury are intended both to *encourage* and to *assist*

nor was any system organized, till ten years later. But twenty-seven years have now elapsed since the organization was completed, and it is most cheering to consider, that within that brief space, ten thousand and five hundred schools have been established and supplied with school-houses; that nearly three millions of dollars are now annually expended in their support; and that more than five hundred thousand children are reported as being under instruction.

A fund, amounting in all to more than five millions of dollars, is held sacred by the state for their use, and the annual revenue of this fund, together with an equal sum raised by taxation, is dispensed each year among all the School Districts of the state, in proportion to the number of children within the bounds of each, and on condition, that the school is kept open four months in the year, by a teacher who has been duly examined and licensed. That these schools have exerted a great and beneficial influence can hardly be doubted. In 1816,* when the first returns were

the people in educating their children. In both respects, it is often more needed, and would prove more useful, in sparsely settled districts, where the inhabitants are generally poor, than in districts which are rich and populous. It may be doubted, too, whether the distribution should not be so regulated as *to stimulate improvement*, both in the attendance of scholars and in the qualifications of teachers. By the present law, the amount apportioned to a town depends on the whole population; the amount apportioned to a district depends *on the number of children in said district over five and under sixteen years of age.* Would it not be an improvement if, leaving the apportionment to the towns as it is, the *amount allowed to the districts* were according to the *actual attendance* at school for any given period?

* The present Common School system owes its organization to a law passed in 1811, authorizing the governor to appoint five commissioners, to report to the next Legislature a system for the establishment of Common Schools, and the distribution of the interest of the School Fund. These commissioners reported on the 4th of

made, one fifth of all the children in the state, between the ages of 5 and 16, were not in attendance; whereas, in 1839, but one *eightieth* part of the whole were in that condition.*
And while this system has been thus rapidly extending in our own state, similar systems have been rising, both in the new states of the West, and in several of the older ones on the Atlantic coast. By law, one thirty-sixth part of all lands owned by the General Government, within the limits of the new states, is reserved for the support of common schools, besides large tracts which are appropriated to academies and colleges; and thus provision is made that population, as it moves westward, shall carry education in its train, and be kept in constant contact with the genial influences of knowledge and civilization.

A similar movement in favour of the universal diffusion of knowledge by means of schools, has been made throughout a large part of Europe. Systems which had been gradually maturing for the last two centuries—some under the auspices of governments, and some through private beneficence—but which were still incomplete and unorganized, have at length been thoroughly digested, and have become more or less incorporated with the state. In Europe, the whole subject of education—from that dispensed in the primary school to that which is imparted in the university—is placed under the supervision of some public functionary; and by such means, the powerful aid of the government is employed in sustaining, directing, and stimulating the energies of the people, and the liberality of the benevolent. At

February, 1812; and on the 19th of the following June an act was passed, providing for the appointment of a superintendent, and the organization of a system substantially the same as the one now in force.

* See the able report of the superintendent for 1840—Table marked D.

this moment, provisions adequate to the elementary instruction of all the children in the land, exist not only in Prussia, but also in Holland, in Saxony, Austria, and all the other states of Germany; in France, Switzerland, Denmark, Sweden, and Norway. Even in Russia, so long the abode of barbarism, and associated now, in most minds, with little of refinement or civilization, a system of universal education is in the course of construction; and already the genial influence of the District School is enjoyed in unhappy Poland, in the dreary wastes of Siberia, and in the wild and inhospitable regions beyond Mount Caucasus.* Indeed, the time seems to have arrived—let the Christian and the philanthropist hail it with joy—when the great truth, so long overlooked by statesmen and philosophers, is to be universally recognised throughout the most enlightened parts of Christendom—the truth that *all* are entitled to a share in the great heritage of knowledge and thought—that the development of his faculties by scholastic culture is a *right* which belongs to every human being, and that it is not more the duty of governments to recognise and protect this right, than it is their interest to cherish and extend it.

Nor is this all. The last fifty years have witnessed another movement in regard to popular education, scarcely less cheering. It was once thought sufficient, if schools were established and maintained. But it is now known that all this may be accomplished, and yet little be really achieved for the cause of human improvement. That schools may, in some cases, be substantially useless and inoperative—that in others, they may be employed by a despotic government as convenient agents for keeping aloof the spirit of change and advancement—and that in others, again, they may, by a too exclusive cultivation of the intellect and by

* See the report of Prof. Stowe on the *State of Education in Europe.*

ministering to the lower propensities, train up a factious and disorganizing spirit—these are sad but momentous truths, which have at last forced themselves on the attention of the friends of humanity. It has been discovered, too, that everything human tends to degenerate, and that a system of public instruction, however perfect, can be upheld in its vigour and excellence, only by unceasing vigilance. A profound conviction of all this has led to the cultivation of a new art, and, it may be added, to the formation of a new science.

Elementary teaching, which, it was once supposed, might be intrusted to any one, and which was, in fact, usually committed (would that such were no longer the case) only to those whom physical infirmity had rendered unequal to every other employment, is now beginning to be regarded as an art requiring skill and address, and as implying, also, an active exercise of the *moral* sentiments and affections. It is discovered that *pedagogy* (as the Germans, by whom its principles have been most thoroughly investigated, term it) is a science founded on the nature of man, and to be deduced as well from the study of that nature as from the collective experience of mankind; that if it be absurd for a man to practise medicine or law, without any special instruction and training preparatory to his profession, so is it absurd in itself—fraught with danger to the subject, and with presumption in the operator—for one to attempt to develop, inform, and guide the faculties of a child without previous preparation. In connexion with improved methods of training teachers, there have been adopted more effectual means of supervising their labours, and of securing for them the co-operation of the public as well as the powerful aid of the government. Thus has arisen, in most of the countries of central Europe, a new branch of social science—one which occupies a prominent place in the eyes of the statesman, as well as in those of the philosopher.

The end of public instruction is no longer merely to have schools, but to have *good* schools; schools which shall be sure to awaken mind and cultivate good principles—which shall be imbued with the spirit alike of progress and of conservatism—which shall contain within themselves the elements of permanent improvement, and be the perennial sources of a healthy and powerful influence to those whom they train.

In this great and benignant reform the people of the United States have shared but partially. Though we are more dependant on education for our welfare than any other nation, it is still a melancholy truth that some of the most arbitrary governments of Europe have done more, within the last half century, to provide good schools and good teachers for their subjects, than has been done by the free people of this land, to make a similar provision for themselves. We are not left, however, without some grounds of encouragement. In Massachusetts and Connecticut, where the Common School system first saw the light, Central Boards have been instituted under the eye of the State Governments, and have been charged with the duty of awakening a new and more general interest on the subject of primary education among the people, and of leading them to the adoption of more uniform and efficient methods. A gentleman of ardent zeal and enlightened views has also been appointed in each of those states, as well as in others, to carry out these plans by personal visitation and addresses, as well as through the medium of the press, and by assembling the people of different districts for mutual conference. In New-York—besides measures, recently adopted for training teachers and establishing School District Libraries, which have been productive of the happiest results—a new element of vigour and improvement has been introduced within the last year, in the appointment of a Deputy Superintendent of Common Schools for each county. In the mean time, the press ev erywhere teems with the most earnest and searching discussion of all subjects which have a bearing on the welfare of schools;* and though the experienced observer may see much in these discussions which is crude and visionary, they still show that the public mind is awake, and that it is bent on improvement.

It would seem, then, that we have reached a most interesting era in the progress of *popular education*. With us, the people are now addressing themselves to the work of regenerating and perfecting their own schools. What, in other countries, has been accomplished mainly by the strong arm of law, is to be accomplished here (if at all) by the voluntary action of parents and citizens, aided and superintended by the state; and in no work more important, or fraught with more eventful consequences, were we ever called to enlist. Did our fathers assert successfully and triumphantly our national independence, it was chiefly because they had been fitted for the arduous and high task by the nurturing influence of schools and churches. Did they and their successors lay deep and broad the foundations of our freedom and prosperity, and rear with surpassing skill and prudence the structure of constitutional law, it must be attributed, in great part, to the same causes. An uneducated, undisciplined people, leave no such monuments of wisdom and patriotism behind them. Is it to be expected,

---

* More has probably been written on the subject of education within the last fifty years, than during all previous time. Another fact is also worthy of notice, as significant of the change which has passed over the opinions of mankind on this subject. Formerly, when writers treated of education, they had reference only to "our noble and gentle youth," as Milton terms them; to those who were intended for the higher walks of life. This was the case with Locke, Fenelon, Ascham, and with Milton himself. It is only within the last century that we find education proper, *i. e.*, *the education of the whole people*, made the subject of prominent discussion.

then, that a people uneducated and undisciplined can long preserve these monuments,* or can ever reap the appropriate fruits of our institutions and our privileges? Nothing is now needed to make our heritage as blessed in reality as it is in promise but refined habits, stern principles of virtue, and an enlightened appreciation, diffused among all our people, of our responsibilities and powers. It is superfluous to add, that such principles are not to be developed except by culture. To expect that men will become wise, virtuous, or happy by mere accident, or without specific exertions directed to these ends, is to expect that this world's history is to be reversed, and that its future will give the lie to all its past. "Vice," says Seneca, "we can learn ourselves, but virtue and wisdom require a tutor."

This volume is a contribution to the great work of school regeneration which is now in progress. It is offered with a deep sense, not only of the importance, but also of the difficulty of the undertaking. It is offered in the humble but earnest hope of being able to afford some suggestions which will prove useful, not only to teachers, but also to parents, inspectors, school commissioners, and other officers, as well as to the friends of education generally. During the last thirty years there has been much discussion, as well as experiment, in regard to different systems of public instruction. The best methods of providing well-qualified teachers, the relative efficacy of different modes of teaching and discipline, and the surest means of maintaining schools in a healthy and efficient state, have all been subjects of examination. It will be the object of this volume, avoiding mere

---

* William Penn, himself a scholar, legislator, and philanthropist, thus announces, in his "Frame of Government," the fundamental principle of a free people: "That which *makes* a good government," says he, "must *keep* it so, viz., men of wisdom and virtue *propagated* by a *virtuous education of youth*."

conjecture or speculation, to collect such results and principles, as may seem to have been *settled* by the experience of the past. It will also aim at the cultivation, among all who are connected with schools, of a more adequate sense of their importance, and of a spirit of improvement and reform at once active and chastened.

It consists of Two Parts.

The First Part will treat of,

I. The Education of the People; its nature, object, importance, practicability, means, &c.

II. The Common School; its relation to other means of education, and to civilization.

III. The Present State of Common Schools.

IV. Means of Improvement.

Schenectady, July, 1842.

THE

EDUCATION OF THE PEOPLE.

PART I.

CHAPTER I.

THE EDUCATION OF THE PEOPLE.

SECTION I.

WHAT IS EDUCATION?

"I call that education which embraces the culture of the whole man, with all his faculties—subjecting his senses, his understanding, and his passions to reason, to conscience, and to the evangelical laws of the Christian revelation."—DE FELLENBERG.

THE term *Education*,* when employed in its primitive and literal signification, means the drawing out or development of the human faculties. When we look on a child, we perceive at once that, besides corporeal organs and powers, he has a spiritual nature. In these organs themselves, with their ceaseless but not unmeaning activity, we see evidence that this little being has intelligence, sensibility, and will. Such powers exist in early infancy but as germes, which are destined, however, to burst forth, and which, like the vegetating powers of the seed that we have planted, are ready to be directed and controlled by us, almost at our will. As we can train up to a healthy and graceful maturity the young plant, which, if neglected, would have proved unsightly and sterile, so can we train up in the way he should go that child, who, if left to himself, would have been almost certain to be vicious and ignorant. It is the peculiar pliability and impressibility of this early period of life, that give it such claims on the educator.† When

---

* From the Latin words *e* and *duco*, to lead or draw out of.

† "Certainly," says Lord Bacon, "custom is most perfect when

habit has once fastened itself on the intellect and the heart, appeals and influences are comparatively powerless. In whatever degree, then, it may be our interest and duty to promote the welfare of our fellow-creatures, and especially of our own children, in the same degree does it become important, that we lose no portion of that which is the precious seedtime of their lives. Hardly any season is too early for the culture of this soil; and if it would be reckoned the height of guilt to refuse food or raiment to the body of a helpless little one, what must we think of that cruel neglect which leaves its nobler nature to pine, and finally to perish, for lack of knowledge? Educated in one sense this child will be—if not for weal, then for wo!

> "For nature, crescent, does not grow alone
> In thews and bulk; but as this temple waxes,
> The inward service of the mind and soul
> Grows wide withal."

It is for the parent and guardian to decide what character this development shall take.

The power of education we are not disposed to overrate. It has sometimes been described, even by wise men, as an all-prevailing agent, which can "turn the minds of children as easily this way or that, as water itself,"* and before

---

it beginneth in young years; *this we call education, which is, in effect, but an early custom.* So we see in languages, the tongue is more pliant to all expressions and sounds; the joints are more supple to all feats of activity and motions in youth than afterward; for it is true, that late learners cannot so well take the ply, except it be in some minds that have not suffered themselves to fix, but they kept their minds open and prepared to receive continual amendment, which is exceeding rare."

* This is the language of Locke in his Treatise on Education. In another passage he says, "I think I may say, that of all the men we meet with, nine parts out of ten are what they are, good or evil, useful or not, by their education. It is this which makes the great difference in mankind, and in their manners and abilities."

which all original differences may be made to disappear. It seems to us, that a slight acquaintance with children is sufficient to refute this theory. Even when reared in the same family and subjected to the same course of physical and moral training, children exhibit, amid a general resemblance in manners and principles, the greatest diversity in endowments and disposition. It is evidently not to be desired, that all men and women should be cast in the same intellectual more than in the same corporeal mould; and hence, though compounded of the same primitive elements, these elements have been so variously mingled and combined, that each individual has his own peculiar and indestructible nature, as well as his own sphere of action—that thus every place and calling can be filled. As this variety, then, exists, and can never be entirely effaced, it ought to be respected in education.

But does it follow that the work of education is therefore slight or unimportant? While we are bound to take the individual as he is, and having ascertained his peculiar type of character and measure of capacity, to keep these ever in view, is there not still a vast work to be accomplished? It is the business of education, to watch the dormant powers and foster their healthy and well-proportioned growth, restraining and repressing where their natural activity is too great, and stimulating them when they are too feeble. To respect each one's individuality is not only consistent with

In a practical work, which aimed at convincing men that much greater care ought to be taken in the education of youth, this was an error on the right side. It is not likely that the bulk of mankind will, in practice, ever exaggerate the efficacy of care and culture. But, among theorists and philanthropists, the error is fraught with bad consequences. It leads them to undervalue the experience of the past, and to expect too much from new plans of training and instruction, and to vary those plans too frequently.

this great work, but is indispensable to its highest success Doing so, we can effect vast changes and improvements in character. The sluggish we may not be able to inspire with great vivacity, nor subdue the ardent and enthusiastic to the tone of a calm and calculating spirit. But we can arrest in each dangerous tendencies; in each we can correct mental obliquities and distortions, and cultivate a healthy and self-improving power. We can study the purposes of the Creator in framing such a mind, and strive wisely, as well as unceasingly, to fulfil those purposes. In one word, we can labour to rear this child, yet without fixed character or compacted energies, to the stature of a perfect man or woman. As one star differeth from another star in magnitude and splendour, though each in its appointed place be equally perfect, so in the intellectual and spiritual firmament one mind may outshine another, and yet both alike be perfect in their sphere, and in fulfilling the mission assigned them by God.

Milton has called that " a complete and generous education which fits a man to perform justly, skilfully, and magnanimously, *all the offices, both private and public, of peace and of war.*" It is evident that such an education can be enjoyed by few; and that, though enjoyed by all, it would bestow, on but a limited number, the lofty capacities indicated by the great poet. A vast proportion of the walks of human life are humble and sheltered. Let us be grateful, however, that while in such walks we escape the fiery trials which await those who tread the high places of earth, they still afford scope and opportunity for the exercise of the most manly and generous qualities. He may be great, both intellectually and morally, who has filled no distinguished " office," either " of peace or of war." Let it rather be our object, then, in rearing the young, to form a *perfect character*—to build up a spirit of which all must say, as was said of Brutus by Antony,

"His life was gentle, and the elements
So mixed in him, that Nature might stand up,
And say to all the world, *This was a man !*"

Such, then, in general, is the object of education. Let us be more particular. The child comes into life *ignorant* and *imbecile*. With faculties which, duly trained, fit him to traverse the universe of truth, he yet begins his course a helpless stranger. To him, this universe is all a mighty maze, without a plan. He is a stranger alike to himself, to the world, and to God. But daily his faculties open; his intellectual eye begins to turn towards the light of truth, as his organic eye turns towards the sunbeam that falls across his chamber. His senses, those fleet messengers, carry to him constant intelligence from the world without. Soon he comes to remember and compare these reports—to reason and resolve. His mind now yearns after more knowledge. Through the livelong day, save when tired nature claims repose, he is busy seeking, or receiving with unexpected delight, new accessions of truth. All the while his faculties of memory and comparison—of judgment and abstraction—of generalization and inference, are in exercise; and, though no book opens its mysterious light upon his understanding, nor living voice pours into his ear the fruits of another's experience and knowledge, he is still for himself a learner.

Yet such a progress—which is only instinctive and spontaneous—plainly needs direction, and will, if left to itself, soon reach its utmost limit. The forlorn condition of the untutored deaf mute shows how meager and deceptive are the attainments of every unaided mind; and, even where such a barrier has not been interposed by nature, we find that those who have been left without formal instruction soon become stationary, and that their minds are crowded with errors and prejudices. It is the province of education (*i. e.*, of a system of training and tuition conducted by rule) to take this restless spirit, rejoicing in the consciousness of its awakened powers and thirsting for knowledge, and to conduct it, for a time, along the straight path of true wisdom. For, why was that spirit, in the very outset of its course, made so helpless? Why was it deprived of those instincts which conduct the inferior animals, infallibly, to their being's end and aim? Why attached for months to a mother's breast, and afterward sheltered and kept in life and health only by unceasing vigilance and care? Why, but to engage all a parent's energies in its nurture and full development; or, rather, why, but to engage them in fitting it for the unending work of self-development? The brute needs but a few powers, for it has but few wants, and they are to last but a few years. Man has wants and desires as boundless as his own immortality.

To educate the *intellect*, then, is to so unfold, direct, and strengthen it, that it shall be prepared to be, through all its future course, a zealous and successful *seeker after truth*. It is to give it control of its own powers, and to teach it towards what those powers should be directed. It is to endow it by practice with the ability to collect its energies at will, and to fix them long on one point. It is to train the *senses* to observe accurately; the *memory* to register carefully and recall readily; the *reason* to compare, reflect, and judge without partiality or passion. It is to infuse into the soul a principle of enduring *activity* and curiosity, such that it shall ever be awake in quest of light, never counting itself to have apprehended, but pressing continually forward towards higher truths and a larger knowledge.

Again, man begins life *without virtue*. He has *propensities* that urge him to self-gratification, *affections* that impel him to gratify others, and *moral instincts* that incline him to duty. But, left to himself and without culture, his propensities predominate; the affections spend themselves in capricious acts of kindness or charity; and the moral instincts raise, without effect, their solemn and monitory voice. It is the office of *moral education* to harmonize these contending and irregular powers, by restoring conscience to its rightful authority, and by replacing unreflecting impulses with fixed and enlightened principles. It is its business to cultivate habits which make man master of himself, and which enable him, even when pressed by fierce temptation, to prefer loss, disgrace, and death itself, before dishonour. "The great principle and *foundation* of *all* virtue," says Locke, "lies in this: that a man is able to deny himself his own desires, cross his own inclinations, and purely follow what reason directs as best, though the appetite lean the other way."

Again, man begins life *without taste*. Through his senses, he is early attracted and charmed by what he terms beautiful. As he advances in years, these impressions, made by outward objects, blend themselves with remembrances of the past, and with creations of the mind itself. The result is seen in conceptions which bear away the soul from the imperfections and trials of actual life, to a world of imagined purity, beauty, and bliss. Now, in the untutored mind, these conceptions are rude and often uncouth. It is the province of education to give them form and symmetry—to teach the true difference between beauty and deformity—to inspire a love for simple excellence in literature and art, as well as a taste for the beauties and sublimities of nature—and, finally, to awaken a profound reverence for moral grandeur, and thus kindle aspirations after glory, honour, and immortality.

Finally, man begins life *without physical vigour*. Neither his intellectual nor his moral powers can hold intercourse with, or act upon the world without, except through material organs. And in our present state, these organs are also necessary to the soul, even in its more spiritual operations; and they weigh it down to imbecility whenever they become greatly diseased or enfeebled. Mark how a Cæsar quails before this foe!

> "He had a fever when he was in Spain,
> And when the fit was on him, I did mark
> How he did shake; 'tis true, this *god did shake:*
> *His coward lips did from their colour fly;*
> And that same eye, whose bend doth awe the world,
> Did lose his lustre: I did hear him groan;
> Ay, and that tongue of his, that bade the Romans
> Mark him, and write his speeches in their books,
> Alas! it cried, *Give me some drink*, Titinius,
> As a sick girl."

Hence the unspeakable importance of *physical education*, which teaches us how to guard against many diseases, how to maintain and improve the vigour of our bodies, and how to develop and perfect the delicacy of our senses.

Do we ask, then, *What is Education*, or what, in the language of Milton, is a "*virtuous and noble education?*" The answer is ready. It is, whatever tends to train up to a healthy and graceful activity our mental and bodily powers, our affections, manners,* and habits. It is the business, of

---

* The cultivation of *manners* is not sufficiently regarded in our systems of *popular* education. The following remarks of an English manufacturer, who devoted great care to the education of the families employed by him, are full of truth, and are applicable to our own country. "The importance of good manners among this class of people, as among all others, appeared to me to be very great, more so than is generally acknowledged; for though every one approves and admires them when met with, little attention is paid to their cultivation in the systems of instruction for the labouring

course, of all our lives, or, more properly, of the whole duration of our being. But since impressions made early are the deepest and most lasting, that is, above all, education which tends in childhood and youth to form a manly, upright, and generous character, and thus to lay the foundation for a course of liberal and virtuous self-culture. "*The education*," says an able writer, "*required for the people*, is that which will give them the full command of every faculty, both of mind and body; which will call into play their powers of observation and reflection; which will make thinking and reasonable beings of the mere creatures of impulse, prejudice, and passion; that which, in a *moral* sense, will give them objects of pursuit and habits of conduct, favourable to their own happiness, and to that of the community of which they will form a part; which, by multiplying the means of rational and intellectual enjoyment, will diminish the temptations of vice and sensuality; which, in the social relations of life, and as connected with objects of legislation, will teach them the identity of the individual with the general interest; that which, in the physical sciences—especially those of Chemistry and Mechanics—will make them masters of the secrets of nature, and give them powers which even now tend to elevate the moderns to a higher

classes. I wish to see our people distinguished by their good manners, not so much for the sake of those manners, as because they indicate more than they show, and they tend powerfully to nourish and protect the growth of the virtues which they indicate. What are they, indeed, when rightly considered, but the silent though active expression of Christian feelings and dispositions? The gentleness, the tenderness, the delicacy, the patience, the forbearance, the fear of giving pain, the repression of all angry and resentful feelings, the respect and consideration due to a fellow-man, and which every one should be ready to pay and expect to receive—what is all this but the very spirit of courtesy? What is it but the very spirit of Christianity? And what is there in this that is not equally an ornament to the palace and the cottage, to the nobleman and the peasant?"

rank than that of the demigods of antiquity. All this, and more, should be embraced in that scheme of education which would be worthy of statesmen to give, and of a great nation to receive; and the time is near at hand when the attainment of an object thus comprehensive in its character, and leading to results, the practical benefits of which it is almost impossible for even the imagination to exaggerate, will not be considered a Utopian dream."*

SECTION II.

PREVAILING ERRORS IN REGARD TO THE NATURE AND END OF EDUCATION.

"Locke was not like the pedants of his own or other ages, who think that to pour their wordy book-learning into the memory is the true discipline of childhood."—HALLAM.

IF the sketch which we have thus drawn of the nature and ends of education be correct, it must be evident that it is a subject in regard to which great misconception prevails. We apprehend, indeed, that hardly one cause so much contributes to maintain existing evils and imperfections in our educational system as the prevalence of these misconceptions. "*The improvement of education,*" says another, "*will alone lead to its extension;*" and we add, that a clearer comprehension of its nature will alone lead to its improvement. Changes may be multiplied, but they will rarely prove to be improvements, unless they proceed on a clear and definite understanding of the end to be attained. Means are wisely chosen only when they are precisely adapted to the object sought, and they are thus adapted, only when that object stands out clearly and boldly before the mind. Let us, then, look at some of these prevailing misconceptions.

* Westminster Review.

By many, education is regarded simply as the means of communicating to the young certain *mechanical accomplishments,* which, in the progress of society, have become essential to our comfort and success. Thus, in the opinion of one, a child is educated when he can read, write, and cipher.* To these, others would add certain higher scholastic attainments, more or less in number; and a third party hold no child to be educated, unless to what they term

---

* The influence of this misconception on the state of popular instruction in England is thus noticed by a late writer: "In the number of schools and of pupils, our account, on the whole, is extremely satisfactory. Where, then, do we fail? Not in the schools, but in the instruction that is given there: a great proportion of the poorer children attend only the Sunday-schools, and the education of once a week is not very valuable; but generally, throughout the primary schools, nothing is taught but a little spelling, a very little reading, still less writing, the Catechism, the Lord's Prayer, and an unexplained, unelucidated chapter or two in the Bible; add to these the nasal mastery of a hymn, and an undecided conquest over the rule of Addition, and you behold a very finished education for the poor. The schoolmaster and the schoolmistress, in these academies, know little themselves beyond the bald and meager knowledge that they teach, and are much more fit to go to school than to give instructions. Now the object of education is to make a reflective, moral, prudent, loyal, and healthy people. A little reading and writing of themselves contribute very doubtfully to that end. Just hear what Mr. Hickson, a most intelligent witness (in his evidence on the Poor Laws), says on this head:

"'*Query.* Are you of opinion that an efficient system of national education would materially improve the condition of the labouring classes?

"'*Answer.* Undoubtedly; but I must beg leave to observe, that something more than mere teaching to read and write is necessary for the poorer classes. Where books and newspapers are inaccessible or not used, the knowledge of the art of reading avails nothing. I have met with adults who, after having been taught to read and write when young, have almost entirely forgotten those arts for want of opportunities to exercise them.'"—*England and the English,* vol. i., p. 186.

"school learning" is added some trade or employment by which he can make a living. The great and all-important fact that a child has powers and sentiments which predestine him to advance forever in knowledge and virtue, but powers which will be stifled or perverted in their very infancy without proper culture—this fact is overlooked. It is not considered that he has a moral and intellectual *character* to be formed, and that this character will never reach the required excellence, unless wise principles are instilled, and good habits formed.

A child leaves school without having contracted either a desire for knowledge, or a love of good books. He knows as little of his own frame, of the laws of his intellectual and moral nature, of the constitution of the material world, and of the past history of his country and race, as if on these subjects books were silent—and yet he is said *to be educated!* What is still more important, he has been subjected to no early, constant, and efficient *training* of his disposition, manners, judgment, and habits of thought and conduct. The sentiments held to be appropriate to the adult have not been imbibed with the milk of infancy, and iterated and reiterated through the whole of subsequent childhood and youth; the manners considered becoming in men and women have not been sedulously imparted in early years; nor have the habits regarded as conducive to individual advancement, social happiness, and national prosperity, been cultivated with the utmost diligence; and yet—the child is said *to be educated!* He knows little, and yet he imagines that he knows all or enough!

"Well!" exclaimed a young lady just returned from school, "my education is at last finished; indeed, it would be strange if, after five years' hard application, anything were left incomplete. Happily, that is all over now, and I have nothing to do but to exercise my various accomplishments.

"Let me see! as to French, I am mistress of that, and speak it, if possible, with more fluency than English. Italian I can read with ease, and pronounce very well—as well, at least, and better, than any of my friends; and that is all one need wish for in Italian. Music I have learned till I am perfectly sick of it; but, now that we have a grand piano, it will be delightful to play when we have company. I must still continue to practise a little; the only thing, I think, that I need now improve myself in. And then there are my Italian songs! which everybody allows I sing with taste; and as it is what so few people can pretend to, I am particularly glad that I can.

"My drawings are universally admired, especially the shells and flowers, which are beautiful, certainly; besides this, I have a decided taste in all kinds of fancy ornaments.

"And then my dancing and waltzing! in which our master himself owned that he could take me no farther! just the figure for it, certainly; it would be unpardonable if I did not excel.

"As to common things, Geography, and History, and Poetry, and Philosophy, thank my stars, I have got through them all! so that I may consider myself not only perfectly accomplished, but also thoroughly well-informed.

"Well, to be sure! how much I have fagged through; the only wonder is, that one head can contain it all."

With this picture—a picture but too just of most of the subjects, not only of what is called a fine education, but of education of every degree—the lively writer* contrasts the revery of "a silver-headed sage," who, after passing in review all his profound attainments in science and letters, and comparing them with the vast field still unexplored, exclaims, "Alas! how narrow is the utmost extent of human knowledge! how circumscribed the sphere of intellectual

---

* Jane Taylor.

exertion! What folly in man to glory in his contracted powers, or to value himself upon his imperfect acquisitions."

Akin to the error just noticed is another, which makes education consist in *acquiring knowledge*. That no education is complete or sufficient which leaves the subject of it *in ignorance* is plain; and there is a certain amount of knowledge which, as it seems absolutely needful to man's highest welfare, and is, moreover, within the reach of all, so should it be considered as an indispensable part of the education of the whole people. Such in addition to reading, writing, and arithmetic, and a proper knowledge of the Scriptures, is an acquaintance with the criminal laws of the government under which we live, with general geography and history, and, to some extent, with our own physical, intellectual, and moral constitution. The grand error is, that that is called *knowledge*, which is mere rote-learning and word-mongery. The child is said to be educated, because it can repeat the text of this one's grammar, and of that one's geography and history; because a certain number of facts, often without connexion or dependance, have, for the time being, been deposited in its memory, though they have never been wrought at all into the understanding, nor have awakened, in truth, one effort of the higher faculties. The soil of the mind is left, by such culture, nearly as untouched, and as little likely, therefore, to yield back valuable fruit, as if these same facts had been committed to memory, in an unknown tongue. It is, as if the husbandman were to go forth and sow his seed by the way-side, or on the surface of a field which has been trodden down by the hoofs of innumerable horses, and then, when the cry of harvest home is heard about him, expect to reap as abundant returns as the most provident and industrious of his neighbours. He forgets that the same irreversible law holds in mental as in material husbandry: *Whatever a man soweth, that shall he also reap.*

The first duty of the teacher, whether he be a parent, or hired instructer, is to enrich and turn up the soil* of the mind, and thus quicken its productive energies. Awaken a child's faculties; give him worthy objects on which to exercise them; invest him with proper control over them, and let him have tasted often the pleasure of employing them in the acquisition of truth, and he will gain knowledge for himself. Yet it is worthy of remark, that this cannot be done effectually and thoroughly, without imparting, at the same time, much knowledge. It is in the act of apprehending truth, of perceiving the evidence on which it rests, of tracing out its relations to, and dependance on other truths, and then of applying it to the explanation of phenomena and events—it is by such means that we excite, invigorate, and discipline the faculties. It has been much disputed, whether it be the primary object of education, to discipline and develop the powers of the soul, or to communicate knowledge. Were these two objects distinct and independent, it is not to be questioned, that the first is unspeakably more important than the second. But, in truth, they are inseparable. That training which best disciplines and unfolds the faculties will, at the same time, impart the greatest amount of real and effective knowledge; while, on the other hand, that which imparts thoroughly, and for permanent use and possession, the greatest amount of knowledge, will best develop, strengthen, and refine the powers. In proportion, however, as intellectual vigour and activity are more important than mere rote-learning, in the same proportion ought we to attach more value to an education

---

* Berkeley, in one of his *queries*, asks, "Whether the mind, like the soil, does not by disuse grow stiff, and whether reasoning and study be not like dividing the glebe."—*Querist*, p. 140.

which, though it only teaches a child to read, has, in doing so, taught him also to THINK, than we should to one which, though it may have bestowed on him the husks and shells of half a dozen of the sciences, has never taught him to use with pleasure and effect his reflective faculties.* He who *can think*, and *loves to think*, will become, if he has a few good books, a wise man. He who knows not how to think, or who hates the toil of doing it, will remain imbecile, though his mind be crowded with the contents of a library.

This is, at present, perhaps the greatest fault in intellectual education. The new power, with which the scientific discoveries of the last three centuries have clothed civilized man, renders knowledge an object of unbounded respect and desire; while it is forgotten, that that knowledge can be mastered and appropriated only by the vigorous exercise and application of all our intellectual faculties. If the mind of a child, when learning, remains nearly passive—merely receiving knowledge as a vessel receives water which is poured into it—little good can be expected to accrue. It is as if food were introduced into the stomach which there is no power to digest or assimilate, and which will therefore be rejected from the system, or lie a useless and oppressive load upon its energies.

* "At the first," says Erasmus, "it is no great matter *how much* you learn, but *how well* you learn it."—*Colloquies*, p. 607.

SECTION III.

THE SAME SUBJECT CONTINUED.

"The exaltation of talent, as it is called, above virtue and religion, is the curse of the age. Education is now chiefly a stimulus to learning, and thus men acquire power without the principles which alone make it a good. Talent is worshipped; but if divorced from rectitude, it will prove more of a demon than a god."—CHANNING.

ANOTHER and not less pernicious error, is to mistake for education *a partial, narrow culture*, which operates on but a part of the mind. In some instances, the moral nature is addressed, to the exclusion or neglect of the intellectual; but much more frequently, the intellectual powers are fostered, to the grievous neglect of the spiritual and moral. The child is dealt with, not only as though these two classes of powers were separate and independent of each other, which is a great mistake, but as if one class could be safely roused and enlisted in action, while the other remains dormant.

Under the reign of the scholastic philosophy, a discipline which developed the reasoning faculty and cultivated the study of theology, took sole possession of places dedicated to education. In our own age, we have passed to the opposite extreme. Unbounded pains are now taken, to enlighten a child in the first principles of science and letters, and also in regard to the business of life. At a time, too, when an intellectual has been substituted for a physical supremacy, and results are produced almost entirely by talent and address, it is thought an object of vast consequence, to develop mental energy and activity. In the mean time, the culture of the heart and conscience is often sadly neglected; and the child grows up a shrewd, intelligent, and influential man, perhaps, but yet a slave to his lower propensities. Talent and knowledge are rarely blessings either to their possessor or to the world, unless they are placed under the control of the higher sentiments and principles of our nature. Better that men should remain in ignorance, than that they should eat of the fruit of the tree of knowledge, only to be made more subtle and powerful adversaries of God and of humanity.*

In this respect, "much," to borrow the language of Dr. Morrison, "may be learned from the Chinese. They not only make education universal, but they place that which is moral above that which is physical." With a system of philosophy, and religious faith, which is eminently deficient in large and comprehensive views, they still succeed, to a degree, perhaps, unparalleled in the history of the world, in inculcating certain social and political duties. The great object of their policy, is to maintain industry, subordination, and social order; and their chief instrument for attaining this object, is the *training* of the young, as distinguished from mere *instruction*. With us, the latter is the chief part of education; with them, the former. We, too, talk much to the young of their " rights ;" the Chinese dwell principally, and, we may add, only, on their *duties*. They rely on the "*habitual* and universal inculcation of obedience and deference, in unbroken series, from one end of society to the other; beginning in the relation of children to their parents, continuing through that of the young to the aged, of

* "In the Celestial Hierarchy," says a late writer, "according to Dionysius Areopagita, the Angels of Love hold the first place, the Angels of Light the second, and Thrones and Dominations the third. Among Terrestrials, the intellects which act through the imagination upon the heart may be accounted the first in order, the merely scientific intellects the second, and the merely ruling intellects—those which apply themselves to mankind without the aid of either science or imagination—will not be disparaged if they are placed last."

the uneducated to the educated, and terminating in that of the people to their rulers."*

This topic occupies the whole of the first four books of Confucius; and twice in every moon, sixteen discourses of one of their wisest and most virtuous monarchs, which treat of these and kindred social duties, are read to the whole Empire.† The results of such precepts constantly repeated—to which conformity is rigidly exacted, and which are enforced by the examples of parents, instructers, and all classes of citizens—may be foreseen. "They are apparent," says Davis, "on the very face of the most cheerfully industrious and orderly, and the most wealthy nation of Asia." The people are contented; there is little abject poverty; age is reverenced more than wealth; and the subjects are devoted,

---

* See Davis's China, chap. vi.

† The texts of these discourses will illustrate the spirit of Chinese economy and education. "1. Be strenuous in filial piety and paternal respect, that you may thus duly perform the social duties. 2. Be firmly attached to your kindred and parentage, that your union and concord may be conspicuous. 3. Agree with your countrymen and neighbours, in order that disputes and litigation may be prevented. 4. Attend to your farms and mulberry-trees, that you may have sufficient food and clothing. 5. Observe moderation and economy, that your property may not be wasted. 6. Extend your schools of instruction, that learning may be duly cultivated. 7. Reject all false doctrines, in order that you may duly honour true learning. 8. Declare the laws and their penalties, for a warning to the foolish and ignorant. 9. Let humility and propriety of behaviour be duly manifested, for the preservation of good habits and laudable customs. 10. Attend each to your proper employments, that the people may be fixed in their purposes. 11. Attend to the education of youth, in order to guard them from doing evil. 12. Abstain from false accusing, that the good and honest may be in safety. 13. Abstain from the concealment of deserters, that others be not involved in their guilt. 14. Duly pay your taxes and customs, to spare the necessity of enforcing them. 15. Let the tithings and hundreds unite for the suppression of thieves and robbers. 16. Reconcile animosities, that your lives be not lightly hazarded."

with a loyalty the most ardent and inflexible, to their government. If all this can be accomplished under a system so imperfect, merely by the use of wise means, what might not be expected in a free, enlightened, and Christian land, if we would but give to *moral* education its proper prominence, and substitute thorough *training* for mere instruction?

This error of postponing moral to intellectual culture has, like all other errors, engendered its opposite. Perceiving its danger and deploring its prevalence, good and thoughtful men are led, in some cases, to doubt altogether the expediency of educating the people; in others, they maintain, in their zeal for religious education, that that alone is necessary or desirable. It must be remembered, however, that a moral and religious culture which does not awaken and develop the faculties of the understanding, and build itself upon clear and rational convictions, can have little value. It will neither regulate the life, nor sustain the fortitude and confidence of the believer. The powers of thought must be so far unfolded and strengthened, that the mind can seize upon truths and moral motives, and hold them with a steady, unyielding grasp, before moral or religious lessons can make a deep and lasting impression. "It is the same spirit and principle," says South, "that purifies the heart and clarifies the understanding;" and we have no more right to suppose that the heart can be enlightened while the understanding is left in darkness, than we have to suppose that the intellectual part of man can be healthy while his moral nature is unsound. So long as the heart is neglected, passions and prejudices will gather before the intellectual eye, and darken or distort all its perceptions of truth. On the other hand, a torpid and unenlightened intellect reduces religious faith to a mere blind assent, which makes no distinction between the substance and accidents of truth, and substitutes its tithe of mint, anise, and cummin for the weightier matters of the law.*

That the great truths of Christianity, when properly taught, form one of the best means of rousing and improving the intellect, is a delightful fact. But in connexion with this fact, we cannot be reminded, too often, that what is *called* religious education, frequently fails in this respect; that too much faith is apt to be reposed in the mere name and form of it, when the spirit is wanting; and hence that hopes are excited by the bare circumstance that children are in attendance at a Sunday-school, or are members of a Bible or catechetical class, or by the fact that the Bible and

---

* Confirmations of this truth may be found in every neighbourhood. A remarkable one has been afforded recently by the peasantry in the county of Kent (Eng.). An impostor appeared among them in 1838, named Thoms, who, with no other advantages than a handsome person and a slender education, succeeded in persuading great numbers to receive him, first, as Baron Rothschild; then as the Earl of Devon; afterward as King of Jerusalem; and, finally, after one or two other transformations, as the Saviour of mankind. He gave them the sacrament, anointed himself and them with oil, and inspired them with the belief that no bullet could touch them. This was not only in a beautiful country in which there was no hostility to the poor laws, and where the peasantry had good wages and were lightly taxed, but it was under the very spires of the Canterbury Cathedral, and amid a population accustomed to go to church, possessing hardly any but religious books, and of whom a majority had, in their youth, gone to Sunday-schools. These facts show that religious instruction will be powerless in most cases, unless the mind has been developed by general culture. Truth must not only be presented to the mind; there must be capacity to apprehend and disposition to act upon it. In the case just referred to, the Bible or Testament, the Catechism, and a few religious tracts, were the only books known in the houses or used in the schools. The consequence had been, that these were read without interest or intelligence, and children who could read in the Testament with fluency, instantly began to spell and hesitate when desired to read out of another book.

other religious books are used in schools, which hopes prove, in the end, to be utterly fallacious. No plan of education is entitled to confidence, because none is founded upon a just view of the nature and wants of man, which does not recognise the importance of both intellectual and moral culture, and which does not cultivate a taste for every branch of liberal and useful knowledge.

I cannot dismiss the subject of *moral* education, without adverting to the great insensibility which seems to prevail among us, *in regard to the power of example*. What meets the eye, always sinks deeper into the mind than what only falls upon the ear. This is peculiarly the case with *moral* instructions. When imbodied in action, and illustrated and adorned by the daily life of a parent, teacher, or friend, they become surpassingly impressive and attractive. On the other hand, when our precepts are glaringly contradicted by our practice, they are worse than useless. " Parents," says Paley, and the remark may be extended to teachers, " parents, to do them justice, are seldom sparing in lessons of virtue and religion; in admonitions which cost little, and profit less; while their *example* exhibits a continual contradiction of what they teach. A father, for instance, will, with much solemnity and apparent earnestness, warn his son against idleness and extravagance, who himself loiters about all day without employment, and wastes the fortune, which should support or remain a provision for his family, in riot, or luxury, or ostentation. Or he will discourse gravely before his children of the obligation and importance of revealed religion, while they see the most frivolous and oftentimes feigned excuses detain him from its reasonable and solemn ordinances. Or he will set before them, perhaps, the supreme and tremendous authority of Almighty God; that such a being ought not to be named, or even thought upon, without sentiments of profound awe and veneration. This may be the lecture he delivers to his family one hour; when the next, if an occasion arise to excite his anger, his mirth, or his surprise, they will hear him treat the name of the Deity with the most irreverent profanation, and sport with the terms and denunciations of the Christian religion, as if they were the language of some ridiculous and long exploded superstition. Now even a child is not to be imposed upon by such mockery. He sees through the grimace of this counterfeited concern for virtue. He discovers that his parent is acting a part; and receives his admonitions as he would hear the same maxims from the mouth of a player. And when once this opinion has taken possession of the child's mind, it has a fatal effect upon the parent's influence in all subjects, even those in which he himself may be sincere and convinced. Whereas a silent, but observable regard to the duties of religion, in the parent's own behaviour, will take a sure and gradual hold of the child's disposition, much beyond formal reproofs and chidings, which, being generally prompted by some present provocations, discover more of anger than of principle, and are always received with a temporary alienation and disgust."*

Another, and, at present, much neglected branch of education, is *the culture of taste and imagination*. These are leading principles of the human mind, which must always exert great influence over its operations and its welfare. If duly cultivated, they aid and quicken the understanding, exalt the aspirations of the heart, and lend grace and dignity to manners. Truth is never more readily apprehended, nor does it ever lay stronger hold upon the memory and affections, than when illustrated and embellished by fancy. High purposes to honour God and benefit man, are by none conceived with so much force, nor by any maintained with such indomitable firmness, as by those whose imagina-

* Paley's Moral Philosophy, b. iii., pt. iii., chap. ix.

tions bring the far distant future near, and transform possible into actual achievements. To children, the creations of fancy or imagination are a principal source, both of pleasure and of activity. In youth, they inspire ardour and generosity of purpose; and through life, men are stimulated to exertion by the promises with which they clothe the future, and by that irrepressible yearning after a higher excellence to which they give birth.

It must be evident, then, to every one, that much of our happiness and dignity will depend on the direction given to these faculties by culture. If allied to virtue, and placed under the guidance of reason, they must become fruitful sources of enjoyment, and contribute most efficiently to our intellectual and moral progress; whereas they must become equally efficient in inducing wretchedness and corruption, when they usurp the place which belongs to reason, and form an alliance with our vicious or malevolent feelings.

One of the means of securing to these faculties a healthy and perfect development, is to employ them in aid of intellectual education. In selecting text-books for the young, as well as books for ordinary reading, always prefer those which portray truth with vivid and rich illustrations, and which conform, in style and method, to the rules of good taste.

Another and most important means of cultivating imagination and taste is found in the study of the *fine arts, including poetry and eloquence.* In contemplating the works of a great master in any art, we substitute regular efforts of imagination, for those wild and eccentric movements, to which it is so prone, and by this means we gradually gain control over it. Instead of surrendering our minds to its capricious guidance, and wasting on dreams the time which ought to be given to duty or improvement, we learn to subordinate it to specific ends and uses. In this way, too, our conceptions of beauty and sublimity are enlarged and perfected. If careful to study none but works conceived in the spirit of truth and virtue, our hearts are made better; taste is refined; the soul learns to breathe freely in an atmosphere above the world, and yet not so remote, but it can return refreshed and invigorated, to meet the claims of life. An innocent and elegant resource is also provided against seasons of leisure and recreation. We close the avenues through which many gross temptations assail the heart, and remedy, in part, the disproportioned development of our powers which is occasioned by our profession, or by the spirit of the age.

In our age, there is special occasion for this kind of culture. The social condition of most civilized nations is such that intelligence and activity are awakened to a degree unparalleled in history; but they have been hitherto, directed, too exclusively, to material or political interests. Imagination is too much employed on dreams of a golden prosperity for the individual, or on visions of a national greatness which is to be the wonder of the world. Everything is apt to be measured by the standard of palpable utility, and whatever does not tend to swell the credit side of the balance sheet, or to add to reputation and influence, is held of little account. The essential dignity of the mind—its independence on the outward world—these are lost sight of; while we regard ourselves too much as ciphers without intrinsic value, and dependant for our consideration and importance on position, or property; on connexion with the state, or on relation to a party. Might not the cultivation of the arts contribute to recall us to a sense of our proper worth?

By affording to imagination a more tranquil and elevating employment, might it not serve, also, to allay, in some degree, the excessive fervour of our activity, and thereby render us more contented and happy?

And by promoting a more delicate and refined taste,

would it not be likely to lessen the rage for display which is the vice of the times, and contribute to substitute grace of manners for vulgar pretension—the chaste embellishments of art, for extravagance and ostentation in dress and furniture?

We shall learn, moreover, in this way, that there is a utility which does not admit of being estimated by material standards; that, though the arts called useful minister to wants more urgent and obvious than those supplied by the fine arts, the latter are equally real; and that the civilization of any people may be estimated by the degree of importance which is ascribed to one of them as compared with the other.

And, finally, we may hope that, by recalling men to a clearer consciousness of their inward powers and capacities, the culture of these arts will serve, in some degree, to arm them against the encroachments of society, and to save them from a moral and spiritual bondage, which is worse, than any political servitude.

I will advert to but one other branch of education before closing this subject. This is *physical* culture; the great importance of which seems to have been much more thoroughly appreciated by the ancients than it is by us. Education was by them reduced to four heads: grammar, music, drawing, and *gymnastics;* the object of the last being, according to Aristotle, to invigorate the body and fortify the mind. It was a settled principle with them, that moral education ought to precede the intellectual, and that the culture of the body ought to precede that of the mind. "Until children have completed their fifth year," says Aristotle, "no painful task should be imposed and no violent exertion required from the mind or body, lest health might be injured and growth obstructed. All that utility demands is to keep the faculties awake and to prevent them from contracting any habits of sloth; which will be best effected by such plays and sports as are neither illiberal, nor fatiguing, nor sedentary." He adds, in another passage, "Before the eighth year the school for children ought to be the father's house; but during this early period they must be strictly guarded against the infectious communication of servants, no illiberal gesture is to be presented to their sight; no il liberal image is to be suggested to their fancy. Lewd in decency of language ought to be reprobated in every well-regulated city; for, from using filthy expressions without shame, there is an easy transition to the practising of filthy actions without disgust."* And again: "Till the age of puberty the lighter gymnastic exercises only should be enjoined and practised; athletic exertions and a forced regimen ought to be proscribed and prohibited; for such artificial violence would mar the work of nature, disfigure the

* There can be no doubt that the neglect of physical, as connected with moral culture, is often *the cause of insanity*. Says one of the ablest physicians who has devoted himself to the treatment of this fearful malady, "A defective and faulty education, through the period of infancy and childhood, may perhaps be found to be the most prolific cause of insanity; by this, in many, a predisposition is produced, in others it is excited, and renders incontrollable the animal propensities of our nature. Appetites indulged and perverted, passion unrestrained, and propensities rendered vigorous by indulgence and subjected to no salutary restraint, bring us into a condition in which both moral and physical causes easily operate to produce insanity, if they do not produce it themselves." He adds in another report, "The first principles of physical education, which teach us how to avoid disease, are all-important to all liable to insanity from hereditary predisposition. The physical health must be attended to, and the training of the faculties of the mind be such as to counteract the active propensities of our nature, correct the disposition of the mind to wrong currents and too great activity, by bringing into action the antagonizing powers. Neglect of this early training entails evils upon the young which are felt in all after life."—*See Dr. S. B. Woodward's Seventh and Eighth Reports as Superintendent of the State Lunatic Asylum (Mass.).*

shape, impede the growth, and forever prevent the attainment of manly strength. During the three years immediately following puberty, the application of youth should be directed to those branches of education which form and invigorate the mind. They will then, at the age of seventeen, be capable of submitting to a regulated diet, and of sustaining the fatigue of athletic exercises."*

This system of physical training was not, with the ancients, a mere theory. It was rigidly observed, and the result was seen in the vigour of their health, and the gracefulness of their carriage. The moderns have made many discoveries in regard to the laws of life and health; but these laws are strangely neglected when we come to practical education. To borrow the words of Spurzheim, "Many parents are anxious to cultivate the mind, though at the expense of the body. They think they cannot instruct their offspring early enough to read and to write, while their bodily constitution and health are overlooked. Children are shut up, forced to sit quiet, and to breathe a confined air. This error is the greater, the more delicate the children and the more premature their mental powers are. The bodily powers of such children are sooner exhausted; they suffer from dyspepsy, headache, and a host of nervous complaints; their brain is liable to inflammation and serous effusion; and a premature death is frequently a consequence of such a violation of nature. It is, indeed, to be lamented that the influence of the physical on the moral part of man is not sufficiently understood. There are parents who will pay masters very dearly, in hope of giving excellence to their children, but who will hesitate to spend the tenth part to procure them bodily health. Some, by an absurd infatuation, take their own constitutions as a measure of those of their children, and because they themselves, in advanced life, can support confinement and intense application with

* Aristotle's Politics, book v.

little injury to health, they conclude that their young and delicate children can do the same. Such notions are altogether erroneous; bodily deformities, curved spines, and unfitness for various occupations, and the fulfilment of future duties, frequently result from such misunderstood mismanagement of children. The advantages of a sound body are incalculable for the individuals themselves, their friends, and their posterity. Body and mind ought to be cultivated in harmony, and neither of them at the expense of the other. Health should be the basis, and instruction the ornament of early education. The development of the body will assist the manifestations of the mind, and a good mental education will contribute to bodily health.

"Young geniuses often descend, at a later age, into the class of common men. Indeed, experience shows, that among children of almost equal dispositions, those who are brought up without particular care, and begin to read and write when their bodily constitution has acquired some solidity, soon overtake those who are dragged early to their spelling-books at the detriment of their bodily frame. No school education, strictly speaking, ought to begin before seven years of age. We shall, however, see, in a following chapter on the laws of exercise, that many ideas and notions may be communicated to children by other means than books, or by keeping them quiet on benches. When education shall become practical and applicable to the future destination of individuals, children will be less plagued with nothings, but they will be made answerable not only for their natural gifts of intellect, but also for the just employment of their moral powers and the preservation and cultivation of their bodily constitution, since vigour in it is indispensable to enjoyment and usefulness. They will be made acquainted with the natural laws of nutrition and all vital functions, and with their influence on health."*

* Spurzheim on Education, p. 80.

I have thus insisted on the necessity of a *comprehensive culture* which aims at the education of the whole man. It is a subject which claims, at this time, particular attention. The causes which operate on the formation of human character are extremely numerous and diversified, and studies whicn, in the estimation of many, are useless or of trifling importance, may still be essential to a perfect development of our powers and susceptibilities.* This truth, and the consequent responsibility which rests on all classes of citizens in regard to education, is forcibly illustrated in the following passage from a sermon of Dr. Ramsden, formerly assistant Professor of Divinity at Cambridge (Eng.). He is showing the tendency of all knowledge to *form the heart of a nation.*

"We will venture to say how, in the mercy of God to man, *this heart comes to a nation*, and how its exercise or affection appears. It comes by priests, by lawyers, by philosophers, by schools, by education, by the nurse's care, the mother's anxiety, the father's severe brow. It comes by letters, by silence, by every art, by sculpture, painting, and poetry; by the song on war, on peace, on domestic virtue, on a beloved and magnanimous king; by the Iliad, by the Odyssey, by tragedy, by comedy. It comes by sympathy, by love, by the marriage union, by friendship, generosity, meekness, temperance; by virtue and example of virtue. It comes by sentiments of chivalry, by romance, by music, by decorations and magnificence of buildings; by the culture of the body, by comfortable clothing, by fashions in dress, by luxury and commerce. It comes by the

---

* Bishop Berkeley asks, "Whether an early habit of reflection, *though obtained by speculative sciences, may not have its use in practical affairs.*" Also, "Whether those parts of learning which are forgotten may not have improved and enriched the soil, like those vegetables which are raised, not for themselves, but are ploughed in for a dressing of the land."—See *Querist*, p. 140.

severity, the melancholy, the benignity of countenance; by rules of politeness, ceremonies, formalities, solemnities. It comes by rights attendant on law, by religion, by the oath of office, by the venerable assembly, by the judge's procession and trumpets, by the disgrace and punishment of crimes, by public fasts, public prayer, by meditation, by the Bible, by the consecration of churches, by the sacred festival, by the cathedral's gloom and choir. *Whence the heart of a nation comes*, we have, perhaps, sufficiently explained. And it must appear to what most awful obligation and duty we hold all those from whom this heart takes its nature and shape — our king, our princes, our nobles, all who wear the badge of office or honour, all priests, judges, senators, pleaders, interpreters of law, all instructers of youth, all seminaries of education, all parents, all learned men, all professors of science and art, all teachers of manners. Upon them depends the fashion of the nation's heart. By them it is to be chastised, refined, and purified. By them is the state to lose the character and title of the beasts of prey. By them are the iron scales to fall, and a skin of youth, beauty, freshness, and polish to come upon it. By them it is to be made so tame and gentle, as that a child may lead it."

SECTION IV.

SAME SUBJECT CONTINUED.

"A skilful master, who has a child placed under his care, must begin by sounding well the character of his genius and natural parts."—QUINTILIAN.

ANOTHER fault in prevailing systems of education is, that *they do not sufficiently adapt themselves to the different characters, capacities, and circumstances of children.* We are far from holding, with some, that a free and unregulated development is all that is needed for a child; and hence that the sole province of parents and teachers is to remove unfriendly influences, and leave him to himself. This was the theory of Rousseau, as expounded in his *Emile;** and

* This may be regarded, says a late writer, as the principal work of Rousseau. It is a moral romance, which appeared in 1762, and treats chiefly of education. The plan of instruction which it inculcates is to allow the youthful mind to unfold itself without restraint, and rather to protect it against bad impressions than to attempt to load it with positive instruction. The objects of Nature are to be gradually presented to it. Necessity alone is to regulate and restrain it, till reason, unfettered by prejudice and previous habits, is able to weave the drapery in which it is afterward to be swathed. The child of reason, thus thrown into a mass of human beings, actuated by different motives, guided by different principles, and pursuing different objects from itself, like a skilfully-constructed bark without its rudder, and stripped of its canvass and cordage, can have no other fate than that of being dashed against the cliffs or sunk beneath the waves. In discussing the subject of religious education, he exhibited the same inconsistency and absurd views. The French savants were displeased with his glowing sentiments of piety, with his impassioned admiration of the morality of the Gospel and of the character of its Founder; while the friends of religion and social order were shocked with his attacks upon miracles and prophecy, with his insidious and open objections to Christianity, and with the application of human reason to subjects beyond its sphere and above its power. The French parliament not only condemned the Emile,

how little faith he himself had in it, may be inferred from the answer, which he is said to have given, to a gentleman who introduced to him his son, whom he said he had educated according to the principles of the *Emile*. " So much the worse," quickly replied Rousseau, " for you and your son too."

It is by no means to be assumed that each child is an angel in disguise, and that those who have the care of him are to welcome, as a necessary part of his being, every development which he may present of feeling and disposition. With much that requires regulating and directing, they will also find much in him, that needs to be repressed, with a stern hand. But does it follow, therefore, that we are to disregard the peculiarities of talent and temper in children, and subject them all to the same inflexible rule? " Some," says Quintilian,* " are indolent unless spurred on, others cannot bear imperious treatment; some are kept to their duty by fear, others are discouraged by it; some need continual pains, others proceed by fits and starts." Are all these to be passed through precisely the same process, and reduced, if possible, to the same type and level? Is it to be forgotten that the world is greatly benefited by the material diversities which appear among men in respect to character, capacity, and taste, and that no discipline is to be desired which would obliterate such diversities? It must be evident, too, that such a discipline offers violence to nature, and, what is more to be lamented, that it fails altogether to reach some minds, while on others it inflicts incurable injury.

In addition to this prevailing disregard of *individual* peculiarities, there is, perhaps, still greater inattention to peculiarities of *sex and condition in life*. One cannot look at the

but compelled Rousseau to retire precipitately from France, by commencing a criminal prosecution against him.

* Lib. i., cap. iii.

female—with less muscular vigour and more nervous sensibility than the other sex; with more timidity and gentleness; with deeper affections and more acute sensitiveness—without perceiving, that she has been appointed to a sphere very different from that of man. Her appropriate empire is over the family, where she not only lays the foundation of society by laying the foundation, during childhood, of individual character, but where she ever exerts, through her acquaintance, and especially through her husband and children, a humanizing influence over the world. Her heart does not, like man's, become indurated or alloyed by intercourse with business, and by collision with sordid passions. She retains, if properly educated, her generous and virtuous instincts in greater vigour, and continues more keenly alive to the wants and woes of suffering humanity. How salutary and powerful, then, is her ministry, when, in the sanctuary of home, she breathes gentleness and kindness into the sterner natures of the other sex; when, in the spirit of a Roman, or, rather, of a Christian matron, she summons her husband, brothers, and sons, to do valiantly, and yet meekly, for God and the right.

But, to fit her for such a noble ministry, she needs a training, quite different from that given to the other sex. Her delicacy and purity must remain untarnished. Her diffidence and even bashfulness, at once a grace and a protection, should be cherished as a peculiar treasure. She is to have all accomplishments which lend a charm to her person and manners; but these must be held as insignificant, when compared with those which qualify her for the duties of a wife and mother, and which tend to inspire a taste for the privacy of domestic life, for its pleasures and privileges. If she has no more urgent duties, her graceful pen may well be employed in the service of truth and virtue; and her presence and assiduities are always like sunshine in the dark abodes of poverty and sorrow, and even in the retreats of guilt and shame. But she cannot too studiously shun the gaze of the multitude. The strifes and tumults of the senate-house and the platform are too rude even for her eye to rest upon, much more for her voice to mingle in. Her chastity is her tower of strength, her modesty and gentleness are her charm, and her ability to meet the high claims of her family and dependants, the noblest power she can exhibit to the admiration of the world.

Such being her destination, it is obvious that she requires a corresponding education. Instead of needing, as seems to have been the opinion of Locke and Fenelon,* but little intellectual culture, she should have a mind well disciplined, and stored with knowledge. She ought, also, to be thoroughly versed in whatever belongs to domestic life and occupations. She should have, on the one hand, such a taste for books and study, that she will never willingly remit the work of self-culture; and, on the other, she should be so imbued with a sense of the dignity and responsibility of woman's mission in life, and so instructed in its duties, that she will always be ready for the humblest and most arduous of its claims. Above all things, that feminine grace, which results from the possession of delicate feelings and gentle thoughts and manners, should be preserved, and she should be taught to shrink from noise and notoriety.

* In his work on Female Education, entitled *Sur l'Education des Filles*, Fenelon has this passage: "Keep their minds as much as you can within the usual limits, and let them understand that the modesty of their sex ought to shrink from science with almost as much delicacy as from vice." This doctrine is afterward somewhat qualified, and the treatise itself is full of wise suggestions in regard to the moral training of childhood, which were then new. It has been beautifully said of it by Hallam, that its author " May, perhaps, be considered the founder of that school which has endeavoured to dissipate the terrors and dry the tears of childhood."

That such training is not as general as it ought to be, is but too evident. Though destined, especially in this country, to enter early on the duties of a wife and mother, she is rarely qualified for those duties in youth. Much of the time which might have sufficed to give her knowledge and practical skill, in respect to household affairs, is wasted in a manner injurious alike to health, habits, and taste. In her intellectual training, vast consequence is attached to accomplishments, which, in most instances, are learned imperfectly at first, and then entirely laid aside in after life, while the foundation of a robust, intellectual character is seldom laid. At the same time, she grows up, in too many cases, with a feeble constitution of body, and with little relish for substantial acquirements in literature, or even for the more elegant pursuits which embellish the life of woman.* In the absence, too, of proper restraint and of a discipline sufficiently domestic and private, she does not always exhibit the diffidence and the maidenly reserve so appropriate to her age and sex. To borrow, from a private letter lately received, the words of a distinguished foreigner, who has

---

* That man is worthily despised who does not qualify himself to support that family of which he has voluntarily assumed the office of protector. Nor, surely, is that woman less deserving of contempt, who, having consumed the period of youth in frivolous reading, dissipating amusement, and in the acquisition of accomplishments which are to be consigned, immediately after marriage, to entire forgetfulness, enters upon the duties of a wife with no other expectation than that of being a useless and prodigal appendage to a household, ignorant of her duties and of the manner of discharging them, and with no other conceptions of the responsibilities which she has assumed, than such as have been acquired from a life of childish caprice, luxurious self-indulgence, and sensitive, feminine, yet thoroughly finished selfishness. And yet I fear that the system of female education at present in vogue is, in many respects, liable to the accusation of producing precisely this tendency.—WAYLAND's *Moral Science* (1835), p. 342.

spent some years in this country, "There is a class of girls, unfortunately very large in the United States, who are weaned from the delicate influence of strict domesticity, who think that pert boldness and freedom make them ladies, who go all sorts of lengths in bantering with young men, and who pride themselves more upon taking, on board a steamboat, the seat of an old man, without thanking him, than upon the glorious character of a meek, pure, and kindly sister, daughter, or friend."

Even when great pains are taken with the education of females, and the avowed object is to give a thorough, substantial course of instruction, the methods adopted are not always judicious. A prevailing fault, in all education, at present, is a too free use of *stimulants*; and this fault is, perhaps, most prevalent—where it is most injurious—in the training of girls. Teachers aim too much at immediate and striking results; and when this is the case with enthusiastic and accomplished instructers—operating on minds which, from age, sex, and mutual emulation, are intensely excitable—there is much danger that paroxysms of study may be occasioned, not only unfavourable to health, but also to that calm and steady love for books, and that spirit of self-culture, which form the only sure guarantee for ultimate and great excellence. Nothing is more common, than to find youth who have distinguished themselves for ardent application at school, but who carry from it no habits of judicious reading, and no very evident love for knowledge. They have been confined over the desk, when their health imperiously required exercise and sports in the open air; they have been encouraged to exhibit themselves as prodigies of acquirement, before they could either relish or digest the studies so prematurely pursued; and they too frequently leave school, at an early age, with shattered constitutions, undisciplined characters, and minds in which memory and judgment have been severely taxed, at the expense of taste, and, perhaps, too, of that modest delicacy, which forms the highest grace of the female character.

This error, doubtless, springs, in part, from the very early age, at which school education commences with us. In Prussia, children are rarely placed at school before *seven*. Here, they usually begin at *four*. Another cause, which also has its effect, is the active emulation maintained among our seminaries, and which, with the mistaken ambition of parents to have their children taught many branches in the shortest possible space of time, renders it almost necessary, that an institution which aims at a large share of public patronage, should strive rather to teach *much*, than to teach *well*, and to lay more stress upon the acquisition of knowledge, than upon the due cultivation and development of all the faculties of the soul. Still the error is a serious one, and ought to be avoided.

The length to which these remarks have already extended, preclude me from dwelling on another species of adaptation, which ought to characterize our systems of training and instruction, *i. e.*, adaptation to *the future condition and pursuits of a child*. It is not held, that early in life the boy or girl should be educated, as if their specific destination were already fixed, and they could therefore be profitably employed in acquiring the peculiar skill and knowledge which belong to their adopted profession. But there is one common destination, to which all the people of this country seem appointed, and this is a life of useful, and, in most cases, laborious occupation. Our children, therefore, need to be taught early, by example and by precept, that there is respectability and happiness, in a life of labour. Instead of being dealt with, as if industry were a great hardship, they should be taught, practically, that it is the appropriate business, in some form, of all mankind, and that to labour with the hands is no more necessarily a degradation, than to labour with the pen. They should be taught, that there is scope for talent, and for a generous ambition, elsewhere, than in the professions usually called learned or liberal, and that it is high time that every pursuit should be made liberal, by being prosecuted in a liberal and enlightened spirit. And in a nation, where a vast proportion of the people must be employed in husbandry, the affections of children ought to be won early towards rural life. A taste for horticulture, and for the beautiful and picturesque in nature; some knowledge of the principles of rural economy, and a proper sense of the independence, security, and happiness, which attach to the life of a well-educated cultivator of the soil: these ought to be instilled into the minds of children; and those who live in the country, instead of being left to think that the path to happiness and success leads to the city or the village, should be encouraged to seek enjoyment, in the due improvement of their own opportunities and privileges. It would be well, also, if some knowledge of the *application* of the first principles of science to the other industrial arts, were generally cultivated among the young; that, thus, they might not only be better prepared for the life of a mechanic or artisan, but might be accustomed to regard all these pursuits of industry, in their connexion with science and liberal studies.

The last misconception in regard to education which I shall notice is one, in some respects, more important than any or all others; since it involves them all, and is apt to result in the greatest evils, both to individuals and to society. It consists in supposing, that the great *end and use of education is to give us worldly success and consideration*. It is first assumed, that these are our greatest good, and then education is recommended, as the most certain means of obtaining them. Now it is not to be denied, that a good education does materially aid us in acquiring property, reputation, and influence; but it will do this quite as much, and, indeed, more, for those whose aims are higher than property or reputation, as it will for those, who regard these as the ultimate end of life. He, who is bent most earnestly on discharging his duty, and on the improvement of his own nature, will almost invariably prosper in business, and will become to others the object of respect and confidence. He will not be less industrious than others; he will generally be more prudent in selecting means, and more skilful and persevering in applying them. He moves in harmony with those great and inflexible laws of the Creator which make wealth and dignities *means rather than ends*, and which render it impossible, that such objects should ever satisfy our nobler desires. In disregarding these laws, lies the grand mistake of most of us. We look for happiness, to outward estate. We forget that "the mind is its own place, and can make a hell of heaven—a heaven of hell." Happiness can dwell, where there is neither wealth, nor pomp, nor power. Indeed, it rarely dwells where these are. It is not to be bought with money. It cannot be won, in the strifes, and heart-burning rivalries of the fashionable or ambitious. It is the reward only of inward effort—of self-control. It calls for that supreme reference to the interests of the mind, and that independence of outward events, which form the principle of faith, and which can be found, only in subordinating the sensual to the spiritual element of our nature. It is to be found in that peace which passeth understanding—that contentment which is inspired, not by sloth or sensuality, but by a calm and wise estimate of the true ends of life; which, though employed in acquiring, still holds it more blessed to give than to receive, and which, in all its efforts for public or private weal, leaves the issue to Infinite Wisdom and Mercy. To attain such a spirit is to *succeed* in life; all other success will prove baseless and unsubstantial.

An eloquent writer* has well exposed this great and per-

* Mrs. Austin, translator of Cousin's Report on Public Instruction in Prussia.

nicious error of many friends of popular education. "It seems to me, too, that we are guilty of great inconsistency as to the ends and objects of education. How industrious have not its most able and zealous champions been continually instilling into the mind of the people, that education is the way to advancement, that knowledge is power, that a man cannot 'better himself' without some learning! And then we complain, or we fear, that education will set them above their station, disgust them with labour, make them ambitious, envious, dissatisfied! We must reap as we sow: we set before them objects the most tempting to the desires of uncultivated men; we urge them on to the acquirement of knowledge by holding out the hope that knowledge will enable them to grasp these objects; if their minds are corrupted by the nature of the aim, and imbittered by the failure which *must* be the lot of the mass, who is to blame?

"If, instead of nurturing expectations which cannot be fulfilled, and turning the mind on a track which must lead to a sense of continual disappointment, and thence of wrong, we were to hold out to our humbler friends the appropriate and attainable, nay, unfailing ends of a *good* education; the gentle and kindly sympathies; the sense of self-respect and of the respect of fellow-men; the free exercises of the intellectual faculties; the gratification of a curiosity that 'grows by what it feeds on,' and yet finds food forever; the power of regulating the habits and the business of life, so as to extract the greatest possible portion of comfort out of small means; the refining and tranquillizing enjoyment of the beautiful in nature and art, and the kindred perception of the beauty and nobility of virtue; the strengthening consciousness of duty fulfilled, and, to crown all, 'the peace which passeth all understanding;' if we directed their aspirations this way, it is probable that we should not have to complain of being disappointed, nor they of being deceived.

Who can say that wealth can purchase better things than these? and who can say that they are not within the reach of every man of sound body and mind, who, by labour not destructive of either, can procure for himself and his family food, clothing, and habitation?

"It is true, the same motives, wearing different forms, are presented to all classes. 'Learn' that you may 'get on' is the motto of English education. The result is answerable. To those who think that result satisfactory, a change in the system, and, above all, in the spirit of education, holds out no advantages."

I have thus dwelt, at much greater length than I intended, on prevailing misconceptions, in regard to the nature and end of education. My apology is, that all wise efforts, for the improvement of schools and of domestic education, must be founded on a clear perception of the object to be attained. The most grievous mistakes which are made in the management and tuition of the young, can be traced directly back to erroneous or inadequate notions on this subject. In dismissing it now, I do not know that I can, in any way so clearly or forcibly set forth the views which I am anxious to impress on the reader, as by presenting an example. It is an example furnished by our own history; and, most happily, it is found in the person of him whom we all most delight to honour. It seems, indeed, a providential fact, that the individual, who draws towards his name and memory a profounder reverence than any other American, who is most closely identified with the establishment both of our national independence and of the permanent union of the States, and who presents, in his life and character, the most perfect model of the man and the citizen, should also have received only such an education, as ought to be within the reach of every child among us.

The school education of Washington was only what is usually termed a common one. Reading, writing, arithmetic, and keeping accounts, with the addition of Geometry and Surveying, formed the whole of his scholastic attainments; and, like a large portion of American youth, he left school before he reached the age of sixteen. But was he, therefore, uneducated or badly educated? He had already, even at that early age, given evidence that his character was moulding under the influence of discipline and culture, and that the foundation was laid for those moral and intellectual habits, which formed the secret of his power and eminence through life. With great fondness for athletic amusements, and even for military sports, he combined a probity and self-control, which made him the object of universal respect among his companions, and which led to his being almost invariably selected as the arbiter of their disputes. To show, how early he cultivated habits of diligence, regularity, and neatness, and how deeply he was impressed with the importance of controlling his own passions, and discharging every social and relative duty, Mr. Sparks gives extracts from one of his manuscript schoolbooks, written before he was thirteen years old. Besides various *forms* for the transaction of business, such as notes of hand, receipts, indentures, bonds, &c., and selections of poetry pervaded by a religious spirit, this book contains what he called *Rules of Behaviour in Company and Conversation*, compiled by himself from various sources, and of which, many are admirably calculated to soften and polish the manners, to keep alive the best affections of the heart, to inculcate a reverence for every moral duty, and especially to cultivate habits of self-control.*

---

* "One hundred and ten rules," Mr. Sparks says, "are here written out and numbered. The source from which they were derived is not mentioned. They form a minute code of regulations for building up the habits of morals, manners, and good conduct in a very young person. A few specimens will be enough to show their general complexion; and whoever has studied the character of Wash-

Here, then, at the early age of thirteen, we see in this boy's education, the germes of that patriot, statesman, and chief, who was always to be "without fear and without reproach." Proper prominence was assigned, in his training, to moral culture. The greatest pains were taken, to form habits of diligence, and persevering application. Though much knowledge was not conveyed to him at school, yet an active curiosity was awakened, and a spirit of self-culture and self-reliance developed, which always enabled

ington, will be persuaded that some of its most prominent features took their shape from these rules thus early selected and adopted as his guide." In the Appendix (No I.) of the second volume of Washington's Writings, *fifty-seven* of these rules are given. I extract a few of them:

"1. Every action in company ought to be with some sign of respect towards those present.

"2. Be no flatterer.

"3. Show not yourself glad at the misfortune of another, though he were your enemy.

"4. Strive not with your superiors in argument, but always submit your judgment to others with modesty.

"5. Take all admonitions thankfully, in what time or place soever given; but afterward, not being culpable, take a time or place convenient to let him know it that gave them.

"6. Use no reproachful language against any one, neither curse, nor revile.

"7. Let your conversation be without malice or envy, for it is a sign of a tractable and commendable nature; and in all causes of passion, admit reason to govern.

"8. Gaze not on the marks or blemishes of others, and ask not how they came.

"9. When you deliver a matter, do it without passion and with discretion, however mean the person be you do it to.

"10. In disputes, be not so desirous to overcome, as not to give liberty to each one to deliver his opinion.

"11. When you speak of God or his attributes, let it be seriously in reverence. Honour and obey your natural parents, although they be poor.

"12. Labour to keep alive in your breast that little spark of celestial fire called conscience."

him, even under the most difficult and untried circumstances, to meet the claims of his station. In his case, education was made to perform its great and most important office, by training its subject to habits of ardent and generous self-improvement. It is true, doubtless, that education has rarely had so noble a subject to operate on. Still, it is to be remembered, that Washington seems to have had originally no very splendid endowments, and that his strength lay chiefly in that fine balance of powers, and in that unblenching perseverance of labour and purpose, which are the gift rather of education than of nature. Hence we maintain, that his life does present a most cheering example to his young countrymen. A sphere so exalted, and duties so eventful as his, will probably never devolve on any of the generation of his countrymen now rising into life. But every walk of life affords scope for energy, diligence, self-control, and a lofty public spirit. In every sphere, if we would be men and live as men, we shall be called to master great difficulties, and in all we may make vast progress in knowledge and virtue, and may render vast service to our country and race. Let us, then, remember what Washington was, and what, by the faithful use of his powers and opportunities, he became, and let us listen to the monitory and inspiring summons which comes forth from his life—" GO THOU and *do likewise.*"*

---

* Hume has shown, in the following passage, that he appreciated the great and salutary power of good example when combined with proper efforts on our own part. "The prodigious effects of education," he says, "may convince us that the mind is not altogether stubborn and inflexible, but will admit of many alterations from its original make and structure. Let a man propose to himself the model of a character which he approves; let him be well acquainted with those particulars in which his own character deviates from this model; let him keep a constant watch over himself, and bend his mind, by a continual effort, from the vices towards the virtues, and I doubt not but in time he will find *in his temper an alteration for the better.*"

SECTION V.

WHAT IS THE EDUCATION MOST NEEDED BY THE AMERICAN PEOPLE?

"In proportion as the structure of a government gives force to public opinion, it is essential that public opinion should be enlightened."—WASHINGTON.

"In vain would that man claim the tribute of patriotism who should labour to subvert these great pillars of human happiness"—religion and morality—"these firmest props of the duties of men and citizens."—*Ibid.*

I HAVE already intimated, that education is a *right* of every human being, and in the previous sections of this chapter, I have endeavoured to explain, what kind and degree of education is called for, everywhere, by the condition of *man as man*. It is important to determine, farther, in what way the education of the people ought to be modified, *by the spirit of the age*, and especially *by the condition of our own country*. Every state of society, and every form of government has its dangers as well as advantages, and we should never forget, that it is through education, which incorporates principles and habits with the very nature of children, that we can most effectually avert the one, and secure the other. What, then, are the dangers and advantages of our condition? It is believed, that a slight examination of them will satisfy us that special and most anxious attention ought, now, to be given to

1. *Moral and Religious Education.* Moral motives and restraints, which are always necessary, have become, in this age and land, of the last importance. "Where is the security," asks Washington, in his farewell address, "for property, for reputation, for life, if the sense of religious obligation *desert* the oaths which are the instruments of in-

vestigation in courts of justice," and which bind, it may be added, incumbents of office to the faithful discharge of their duties? Moral ties once dissolved, those of a political nature would be utterly powerless. And if this is the case, everywhere and at all times, it must be especially so with us, and at this time. Men are, now, less patient than they once were, of the restraints of authority and even of law, and are more bent on change. They are excited, and sometimes almost maddened, by the vast revolutions which are accomplished, with magical celerity, in the physical relations of nations and individuals. Constantly they are tempted, to grasp at glittering prizes held out by a material and sensual civilization, and to substitute hazardous and gambling speculation for industry, frugality, and virtue. A gross and outward success occupies, in the minds of the people, that place which ought to be given only to worth; and a man is thought to be nothing unless he is rich, or popular, or installed in office. In this country, with immense general industry and activity, there is still a great want of regular occupation—which the individual adopts for life, and which he pursues in a contented and cheerful spirit. Each one seems to be struggling for something other, and, as he vainly imagines, better than his own; yet, though rarely satisfied with his lot, he is apt to be abundantly satisfied with himself. Politicians find it expedient to flatter the people grossly, in order to lead them; and the people, while glorying in their collective liberty, exhibit, too often, the sad spectacle of being, as individuals, overawed by public opinion or enslaved by faction. In such a state of things, there may be a high degree of outward refinement, much of the show of virtue, and even brilliant advances in what styles itself civilization. The danger is, lest, under this fair exterior, the soul of true virtue be eaten out—lest the lower passions and propensities, by becoming everywhere predominant, gradually sap the very foundation of the social edifice, and leave it to perish through its own weight and rottenness.* Situated as the people of this country are, they cannot too vigilantly guard against the approach of that era of dark and fatal degeneracy, when, according to the ironical definitions of Fielding, *patriot* comes to mean a candidate for place; *worth*, power, rank, and wealth; *wisdom*, the art of getting all three.

I am well aware, that these evils and dangers are counterpoised by signal advantages, both in our institutions, and in our position. But with all these, we shall still need the utmost aid of moral and religious culture. We need that, in the absence of positive laws, the people shall be able to restrain and direct themselves; and that, when laws are established, they shall be objects of profound respect and submission. We need that our youth should be taught, in their earliest years, to entertain the deepest horror of fraud and falsehood, and to resolve that, through life, their faith, when once plighted, whether in private or public contracts, whether in affairs of a personal or political nature, shall be sacred

---

* A great poet points out the fatal defect of this species of civilization.

>   " Egyptian Thebes,
> Tyre, by the margin of the sounding waves,
> Palmyra, central in the desert, fell,
> And the arts died by which they had been raised.
> Call Archimedes from his buried tomb
> Upon the plain of vanished Syracuse,
> And feelingly the sage shall make report
> How insecure, how baseless in itself,
> Is the philosophy whose sway depends
> On mere material instruments; how weak
> Those arts and high inventions, if unpropped
> By Virtue! He, with sighs of pensive grief
> Amid his calm abstractions, would admit
> That not the slender privilege is theirs
> To save themselves from rank forgetfulness!"
>   WORDSWORTH.

and irrevocable. We need to build up a force of character, and a strength of principle, which will enable men to breast themselves against the corrupt influences of fashion, party, and prevailing immorality; and to lift their protest, when necessary, with meekness, but yet without fear, against the encroachments of an unhallowed public opinion. We need, too, a training which shall inspire the young with deep reverence for parents and for old age, with proper deference towards the judgment of the wise and good of all ages, and with that graceful diffidence in their own sagacity and power, which will lead them, without surrendering their own independence, to have due respect for the recorded wisdom and experience of the past.*

* By reverence I mean "that earnestness in contemplating things, which strives to know their real character and connexion, and the absence of arrogant forwardness and self-sufficiency, which considers everything silly, useless, or unmeaning, because not agreeing with its own views, or not showing its character at once to the superficial observer; or not conforming to custom. We have seen that it is the high prerogative of man to acknowledge superiors and inferiors, to have laws, and to obey them; but, since individual interest, as well as the pleasure or allurement of resistance and opposition, is in itself frequently very strong, as selfishness is but too apt to grow up like a rank weed, we ought to imbue the young early with true loyalty, that is, a sincere desire to act as members of a society, according to rules not arbitrarily prescribed by themselves, and with a submission of individual will and desire to that of society. They ought to learn that it is a privilege of men to obey laws, and a delight to obey good ones. That these habits, early and deeply inculcated, may lead to submissiveness and want of independence, is only to be feared when education is imperfect or liberty at a low ebb. The greater the liberty enjoyed by a society, the more essential are these habits, especially in modern times, when various new and powerful agents of intercommunication and diffusion of knowledge have produced a movability and thirst for inquiry, which cannot leave in us any sincere fear on the ground of dull tameness in the adult wherever liberty is at all established. The ancients knew the value of these habits, and all their wise men

We also need to join with the spirit of enterprise, which is carrying forward all our people to an improved condition, a spirit of contentment with a life of labour, together with a just appreciation of its advantages and duties, and a cheerful acquiescence in the allotments of Providence.* And, finally, we need to cultivate, in the young, a settled detestation of all those incitements and indulgences, which are multiplied by a vulgar civilization, and which inflame their lower propensities, while they arm them against the holiest influences of truth and virtue—such as the intoxicating cup and the gaming-table.† And, while employing means for this purpose, "let us, with caution," to borrow again the words of the great and wise, "indulge the supposition, that

---

insisted upon them. Nations which lose the precious habit of obeying, that is, self-determined obedience to the laws, because laws, lose invariably, likewise, the precious art of ruling. Greece, Rome, and Spain, for the last centuries, as well as the worst times of the feudal ages, are examples."—*See Lieber on Political Ethics.*

* Idleness, as a political evil, reached its "classical age" in the worst periods of Grecian democracy and in Rome. In the former, attendance at the popular assembly came to be paid for, as in the worst times of the French Revolution. During the decline of Rome, the idling wretches sank so low, that, too cowardly to march against the conquering tribes, they nevertheless were delighted at seeing the agony of the dying gladiator. When Treves was devastated by German predatory tribes, the first thing which the inhabitants, deprived of house and property, asked for, was, Circensian games.—LIEBER's *Political Ethics*, vol. ii., p. 243.

† The contrast between the energy of barbarians, and the imbecility of a people rendered sensual and sordid by a vicious civilization, is forcibly exhibited, in the following passage from the late work of *Dumas on Democracy*. "He (Genseric) arrived before Carthage; and while his troops were mounting the ramparts, the people were descending to the circus. Without was the tumult of arms, and within, the resounding echoes of the games: at the foot of the walls were the shrieks and curses of those who slipped in gore and fell in the melée; on the steps of the Amphitheatre were the songs of musicians and the sounds of accompanying flutes."

morality can be maintained without religion. Whatever may be conceded to the influence of refined education on minds of peculiar structure, reason and experience both forbid us to expect, *that national morality can prevail in exclusion of religious principle.*"*

2. We need an *intellectual culture*, which will impart more knowledge and wisdom. Where laws are but emanations of public opinion, it is supremely important that that public opinion should be enlightened; and it can hardly become so, unless men acquire, in youth, a love for reading, and habits of patient thought. In proportion, as the people are called to act, through legislation and by voluntary association, on a greater number of important questions, in the same proportion is it necessary that their range of information be extended, and their judgments more thoroughly developed. Tempted as Americans are by bright promises in the future, and living, too, in the midst of intense activity and excitement, they need, more than any other nation, habits of careful and deliberate inquiry. They need, moreover, that enlightened estimate of the difficulties inherent in many subjects, which they can obtain only by candid study, and which would tend to make them at once more tolerant towards those who think differently, and less clamorous, in public affairs, after one exclusive line of policy. In theory, we are supposed to think each one for himself, and to carry, to the ballot-box, the unbiased result of our own convictions, and preferences. Is it not most desirable, that the education of the whole people should become so improved, that this theory can be reduced to practice, and that demagogues and all the leaders of faction shall see, in the growing intelligence of the people, warning signs of the decline of their own power and consequence?

Without enumerating, here, the various branches of study, which are called for by the state of the times, and of our

* Washington's Farewell Address.

own country, I may remark, *that more thorough instruction in the first principles of politics is all-important.* We all read enough about political affairs; but fundamental instruction in the elements of the science of government—in those great truths which guided our fathers through times of trial, and which can alone give strength, and enduring glory to our institutions and our freedom—this is greatly needed. Much time, which is now given to other studies, might be profitably devoted to the history and structure of our government, and to those noble examples of public virtue and achievements, which shine as lights along the tract of the past.* In holding up such examples, however, one caution ought to be observed. The noblest specimens of our fallen nature are marred by imperfection. Instead, then, of teaching our children to admire great men in the gross, we should rather teach them to discriminate between their acts of wisdom and their errors, as well as between their virtues and their vices. Otherwise the power of judgment is gradually obscured; distinctions the most sacred and important are confounded; and men are taught first to tolerate, and at length to admire and imitate, what they ought most anxiously to shun. In one of the numbers of the Spectator, the writer judiciously suggests, " whether, instead of a theme or copy of verses, which are the usual exercises, as they are called in the school phrase, it would not be more proper that a boy should be tasked once or twice a week to write

* To illustrate the disproportioned attention paid, even in elementary schools, to mathematics as compared with moral science, I may mention the following fact, with which I met recently on visiting the teachers' department in one of our largest and best-conducted academies. Out of seventy-five young persons in this department who were preparing to teach district and other elementary schools, but *five* were studying history of any kind; none were studying the history of the United States; while *thirty-four* were studying Algebra, and almost all, Geometry, Trigonometry, and Surveying.

down his opinion of such persons and things as occur to him in his reading; that he should descant upon the actions of Turnus or Æneas, show wherein they excelled or were defective, censure or approve any particular action, observe how it might have been carried to a greater degree of perfection, and how it exceeded or fell short of another. He might, at the same time, mark what was moral in any speech, and how far it agreed with the character of the person speaking. This exercise would soon strengthen his judgment in what is blamable or praiseworthy, and give him an early seasoning of morality."*

3. I have already insisted on the necessity of having some reference, even in the school-education of children, to their future pursuits. I now remark that, after leaving school, each child should be bred to some regular occupation. This *industrial* training is even more important than that given at school. Without a definite pursuit, a man is an excrescence on society. He has no regular place or part to fill, and is apt to feel little concern for the general welfare. In isolating himself from the cares and employments of other men, he forfeits much of their sympathy, and can neither give nor receive great benefit. If rich enough to live in idleness, he is, now, morbid through want of object or interest, and now, through profligacy, reckless of himself and a curse to others. If he is poor and yet idle, or, even though not idle, if he lives rather by shifts than by regular and systematic industry, he rarely becomes useful or respectable, and, in a vast proportion of cases, sinks to infamy or crime. This is apparent from the statistics of our prisons; and it would be equally obvious if we could analyze

---

* The teacher and parent may derive useful hints and assistance in prescribing such exercises, from that part of Rollin's Belles Lettres which is devoted to the study of History. The author dwells at length, and with many interesting examples, on the moral lessons to be gathered from the leading events and characters of history.

the composition of most mobs, or the character and history of those who lead a life of vice. Dr. Lieber states, that of three hundred and fifty-eight criminals whose cases he had examined, *two hundred and twenty-seven had never been bound out to any trade or regular occupation*, seventy-nine were bound out, but ran away before they had stayed out their time, *and only fifty-two were bound out and remained* with their respective masters until the completion of their proper time; while the average term for which they were imprisoned was, in case of those who had served out their time, not quite *four* years, whereas, in case of those who ran away, it was more than *five* years.* Similar facts might be multiplied to almost any extent, and they show that this kind of education is truly of the last importance. Among the ancients, the parent who neglected to give his son a trade was deemed to have forfeited, in his old age, a claim upon that son for support; and by the law of Solon, which enforced it most strenuously in ordinary cases, this claim was expressly dispensed with, when the parent had been delinquent in this matter.†

* Political Ethics, ii., 242.

† One of the most striking features, in the improved system of German education, is the great attention paid to order, economy, and neatness. "One of the circumstances," says Professor Stowe, "that interested me most, was the excellent order and rigid economy with which all the Prussian institutions are conducted. Particularly in large boarding-schools, where hundreds, and sometimes thousands of youth are collected together, the benefits of the system are strikingly manifest. Every boy is taught to wait upon himself; to keep his person, clothing, furniture, and books in perfect order and neatness; and no extravagance in dress, and no waste of fuel, or food, or property of any kind, is permitted. Each student has his own single bed, which is generally a light mattress laid upon a frame of slender bars of iron, because such beds are not likely to be infested with insects, and each one makes his own bed and keeps it in order. In the house there is a place for everything, and everything must be in its place. In one closet are the shoe-brushes and

4. The state of our country, and the character of the age, call loudly *for a more elegant and humanizing culture.* In the habits of a people, few things have a more important influence, for good or evil, than the use they make of leisure. Some relief from labour men must have; something to vary the monotony of life, and restore the mind to a sense of its elasticity. If this relief be not afforded by innocent and improving recreations, it will be sought for in sensual indulgence.* In our country it is peculiarly so. The ardour

blacking, in another the lamps and oil, in another the fuel. At the doors are good mats and scrapers, and everything of the kind necessary for neatness and comfort, and every student is taught, as carefully as he is taught any other lesson, to make a proper use of all these articles at the right time, and then to leave them in good order at their proper places. Every instance of neglect is sure to receive its appropriate reprimand, and, if necessary, severe punishment. I know of nothing that can benefit us more than the introduction of such oft-repeated lessons on carefulness and frugality into all our educational establishments; for the contrary habits of carelessness and wastefulness, notwithstanding all the advantages which we enjoy, have already done us immense mischief. Very many of our families waste and throw away nearly as much as they use; and one third of the expenses of housekeeping might be saved by a system of frugality. It is true, that we have such an abundance of everything, that this enormous waste is not sensibly felt, as it would be in a more densely populated region; but it is not *always* to be so with us."—Stowe's *Report on Elementary Public Instruction in Europe.*

* This want of resource and recreation is not to be supplied in all cases by mere intellectual pursuits. There are many whose minds are not sufficiently cultivated to avail themselves of these; they have little or no taste for them, and yet are quite capable of being made very worthy, sensible, respectable, and happy men. Resources must be provided of sufficient variety to supply the different tastes and capacities we have to deal with; and we must not shut our gates against any, merely because they feel no ambition to become philosophers. By gently leading them, or rather, perhaps, by letting them find their own way, from one step to another, you may at length succeed in making them what you wish them to be.

"It is with these views that I have endeavoured to provide objects

with which men engage here in business, they carry to their pleasures; and, in the absence of higher sources of exhilaration, they rush to the gaming-table, and, above all, to the intoxicating cup. The contrast, in this respect, between our people, and those of countries in which the fine arts are generally cultivated, is most striking and instructive. Take Germany, for example. There, the people have access to ardent spirits as well as wine; moral restraints are not more powerful than with us; and yet, in many provinces, drunkenness is almost unknown. It will not be easy to find an explanation for this fact, except in the prevalence, throughout the same provinces, of a taste for music and other arts; a taste which has been developed by culture, and in which all the people, from the highest to the lowest, find an inexhaustible resource. Efforts to avert the progress of intemperance are doubtless most necessary and important, and they are eminently worthy of encouragement; but, to be permanently useful, they should be coupled with

of interesting pursuit or innocent amusement for our colony. The gardens and the cultivation of flowers, which is encouraged by exhibitions and prizes, occupy the summer evenings of many of the men or elder boys. Our music and singing engage many of both sexes—young and old, learned and unlearned. We have a small glee class, that meets once a week round a cottage fire. There is another, more numerous, for sacred music, that meets every Wednesday and Saturday during the winter, and really performs very well; at least, I seldom hear music that pleases me more. There is also a band, &c., &c.; and when you remember how few families we muster, not more than seventy or eighty, you will think, with me, that we are quite a musical society, and that any trouble I took at first to introduce this pursuit has been amply repaid. You must observe that all these instruments are entirely their own, and of their own purchasing. I have nothing to do with them farther than now and then helping them to remunerate their teachers."

"We find drawing almost as useful a resource as music, except that a much smaller number engage in it."—*Letter of an English Manufacturer on the Elevation of the Labouring Classes*

measures to supply, from higher and purer sources, the exhilaration which men, when at leisure, always require. If the mind of the reclaimed drunkard be left to brood over vacancy, we must not be surprised that he returns to his cups; nor must we wonder that so many, who are now forming habits of indulgence, decline surrendering their pleasures when they are offered no substitute. In order to effect a lasting change in the habits of the people, we must raise and purify their tastes. Hence the importance of libraries, of associations for mutual improvement, and of every institution which proposes the diffusion of knowledge.*

The fine arts, however, have one advantage which can hardly be claimed for books. As things now stand, each

---

* "Let no superficial judgment regard as illusory the beneficent moral effect here imputed to general diffusive education."

"The most prevalent vice of the United States is intoxication. How many youth of bright promise, how many really amiable men of advanced age, annually fall victims to this destructive habit! Would this occur if the head of each family found in its bosom the soothing enjoyment of intellectual converse in his hours of domestic retirement and leisure? if among his domestic circle each member could contribute something to enliven his hours of rest in the sultry midday heat of summer, or the long nights of winter? or, when conversation had exhausted its stores, could cheer him with agreeable narratives of biography and history, of voyages and travels, or the lessons of more profitable knowledge extracted from the neighbouring newspaper and village library?"

"Would well-educated youth, brought up to respect labour, after seeking in vain for lucrative employment in the crowded professions of law and physic, abandon themselves to this suicidal vice, rather than seek an honourable subsistence in rural and mechanical pursuits?"

"Would old men of amiable, and even polished manners, after a life of generous hospitality, or a manhood devoted to the public service, but uninspired by that religious hope that brightens at approaching dissolution, sink into this Lethean gulf, because they could find nothing to interest them longer in this world, and time had become an insupportable burden?"—C. F. MERCER.

one reads such book as gratifies his own taste, or as may be thrown in his way by chance, or by the design of others. The consequence is, that the reading of many men only contributes to strengthen their lower propensities. This can hardly be the case with the fine arts. Their productions are more limited in their range, and are exposed to more general scrutiny. Among a people, too, who have such notions of decorum as prevail with us, these arts can hardly venture to appeal, openly and directly, to our worst passions.

There is another benefit, to be anticipated in our country, from the cultivation of a taste for the arts, to which I will advert in this connexion. Foreign travellers have complained of the American people, that they rarely have leisure, and that, when they have, they know not how to enjoy it. There is some truth in the remark. We are eminently a working people. Part of this industry results, no doubt, from our condition, and from the powerful incitements to enterprise, afforded by a young and prosperous country. Part of it, however, seems to result from impatience of rest. Not a few of the rash adventures and ruinous speculations, by which we have distinguished ourselves of late, had their origin in a love of excitement, and in our aversion to being without employment. A partial remedy for this evil, might be found by diffusing a taste for the elegant and ornamental arts. These arts would furnish that moderate and agreeable excitement which is so desirable in the intervals of labour. They would tranquillize, in some degree, the minds which have been agitated by business, and would dispose them to seek more frequent relief from its cares, and to plunge with less haste into new, hazardous, and anxious undertakings. They would teach us all, that there is a time for rest and refreshment as well as for exertion ; and that the one may conduce as well as the other, not only to our enjoyment and dignity, but also to our permanent prosperity in business.

It may be alleged, by way of objection, that the arts are liable to abuse, and that they have, sometimes, been enlisted, in the service of vice and licentiousness. This is doubtless true of art, as it is of literature. But in regard to the latter, we encourage men to cultivate it, and we give them access to books of all kinds, because we are confident that, with a fair field, truth and right must ultimately triumph. So we would encourage the arts, because we believe that the natural affinities of the human mind will in the end secure a preference for works conceived in a pure taste; and that in our country, this would at once be the case, so far as moral considerations are involved. It must be remembered, that the noblest efforts of art have been made in the service of virtue and religion. History shows that the wing of Fancy has always drooped when she attempted to soar in a sensual or misanthropic mood. At such seasons she cannot gaze upon the unveiled sun; her visions are dim and earthly; they do violence to truth and nature, and are soon consigned to merited obscurity.

Among a volatile and dissipated people, the arts would doubtless be rendered subservient to amusement and licentious indulgence. It would be at the expense, however, of their highest excellence. On the other hand, among a grave people, charged with serious cares, they would be likely to take a different type, and contribute, as music has always done in Germany since the days of Luther, to the refinement of taste and the strengthening of moral feeling. The greatest composers of that land have consecrated their genius to the service of religion. Haydn, whose memory is so honoured, was deeply religious. His Oratorio of the Creation was produced, as he himself tells us, at a time when he was much in prayer. In writing musical scores, he was accustomed to place, both at the beginning and at the close of each one, a Latin motto, expressive of his profound feeling, that he was dependant on God in all his efforts, and that to His glory should be consecrated every offspring of his genius.

The mention of music leads me to notice the special claims which that art has upon us. All men have been endowed with susceptibility to its influence. The child is no sooner born, than the nurse begins to sooth it to repose by music. Through life, music is employed to animate the depressed, to inspire the timid with courage, to lend new wings to devotion, and to give utterance to joy or sorrow. It is pre-eminently the language of the heart. The understanding gains knowledge, through the eye. The heart is excited to emotion, through tones falling on the ear. And so universal, is the disposition to resort to music, for the purpose of either expressing or awakening emotion, that the great dramatist, that master in the science of the heart, declares that

> " The man that hath no music in himself,
> Nor is not moved with concord of sweet sounds,
> Is fit for treason, stratagems, and spoils;
> The motions of his spirit are dull as night,
> And his affections dark as Erebus:
> Let no such man be trusted."

Well may this be said of an art which has power to raise the coarsest veteran to noble sentiments and deeds, and to inspire the rawest and most timorous recruit with a contempt of death.

It is worthy of remark, too, that, as the susceptibility to no other art is so universal, so none seems to have so strong an affinity for virtue, and for the purer and gentler affections. It is affirmed as a curious fact, that the natural scale of musical sounds can only produce good and kindly feelings, and that this scale must be reversed, if you would call forth sentiments of a degraded or vicious character. It is certain that, from the fabled days of Orpheus and Apollo, music has always been regarded as the handmaid of civilization and moral refinement. Wherever we would awake the better affections, whether in the sanctuary or the closet, in the school for infants or in the House of Refuge for juvenile delinquents, we employ its aid.

The Germans have a proverb, which has come down from Luther, that, where music is not, the devil enters. As David took his harp, when he would cause the evil spirit to depart from Saul, so the Germans employ it to expel obduracy from the hearts of the depraved. In their schools for the reformation of youthful offenders, (and the same remark might be applied to those of our own country), music has been found one of the most effectual means of inducing docility among the stubborn and vicious.* It would seem that so long as any remains of humanity linger in the heart, it

---

* "At Berlin I visited an establishment for the reformation of youthful offenders. Here boys are placed, who have committed offences that bring them under the supervision of the police, to be instructed and rescued from vice, instead of being hardened in iniquity by living in the common prison with old offenders. It is under the care of Dr. Kopf, a most simple-hearted, excellent old gentleman; just such a one as reminded us of the ancient Christians, who lived in the times of the persecution, simplicity, and purity of the Christian Church. He has been very successful in reclaiming the young offender; and many a one, who would otherwise have been forever lost, has, by the influence of this institution, been saved to himself, to his country, and to God. As I was passing with Dr. K. from room to room, I heard some beautiful voices singing in an adjoining apartment, and, on entering, I found about twenty of the boys sitting at a long table, making clothes for the establishment, and singing at their work. The doctor enjoyed my surprise, and, on going out, remarked, 'I always keep these little rogues singing at their work; for while the children sing the devil cannot come among them at all; he can only sit out doors there and growl; but if they stop singing, in the devil comes.' The Bible and the singing of religious hymns are among the most efficient instruments which he employs for softening the hardened heart, and bringing the vicious and stubborn will to docility."—*Report of Professor Stowe on Elementary Public Instruction in Europe.*

retains its susceptibility to music. And as proof that this music is more powerful for good than for evil, is it not worthy of profound consideration that, in all the intimations which the Bible gives us of a future world, music is associated only with the employments and happiness of Heaven?

We read of no strains of music coming up from the regions of the lost. To associate its melodies and harmonies with the wailings and convulsions of reprobate spirits would be doing violence, as all feel, to our conceptions of its true character.* Nothing could illustrate more impressively its natural connexion with our better nature. Abused it doubtless may be—for which of God's gifts is not abused?—but its value, when properly employed as a means of culture, as a source of refined pleasure, and as the proper aid and ally of our efforts and aspirations after good, is clear and unquestionable. "In music," says Hooker, "the very image of vice and virtue is perceived. It is a thing that delighteth all ages and beseemeth all states—a thing as seasonable in grief as joy, as decent being added to actions of greatest solemnity, as being used when men sequester themselves from actions."

So the pious Bishop Beveridge: "That which I have found the best recreation both to my mind and body, whensoever either of them stands in need of it, is music, which exercises at once both my body and soul, especially when I play myself; for then, methinks, the same motion that my hand makes upon the instrument, the instrument makes upon my heart. It calls in my spirits, composes my thoughts, delights my ear, recreates my mind, and so not only fits me for after business, but fills my heart at the present with pure and

---

* Has not Milton offered violence both to nature and revelation, in the picture which he draws towards the close of the first book of his Paradise Lost, where he represents the legions of Satan as moving " in perfect phalanx to the Dorian mood of flutes and soft recorders," " soft pipes that charmed their painful steps," &c., &c.

useful thoughts; so that, when the music sounds the sweetliest in my ears, truth commonly flows the clearest in my mind. And hence it is that I find my soul is become more harmonious by being accustomed so much to harmony, and adverse to all manners of discord, that the least jarring sounds, either in notes or words, seem very harsh and unpleasant to me."

I have spoken of the fact, that all men are more or less susceptible to the influence of music. It is also true that all can acquire the rudiments of the art. It has long been supposed that, in order to learn to sing, a child must be endowed with what is called a musical ear. That this, however, is an error, is evident from experiments which have been made on the most extensive scale in Germany, and which are now repeating in this country. In Germany, almost every child at school, is instructed in singing, as well as in reading. The result is, that though in this respect, as in many others, there is great difference in the natural aptitude of children, still all who can learn to read, can also learn to sing.* It is found, farther, that this knowledge can be ac-

* "The universal success, also, and very beneficial results, with which the arts of drawing and designing, vocal and instrumental music, moral instruction, and the Bible, have been introduced into schools, was another fact peculiarly interesting to me. I asked all the teachers with whom I conversed, whether they did not sometimes find children who were actually incapable of learning to draw and to sing. I have had but one reply, and that was, that they found the same diversity of natural talent in regard to these as in regard to reading, writing, and the other branches of education; but they had never seen a child who was capable of learning to read and write, who could not be taught to sing well and draw neatly, and that, too, without taking any time which would at all interfere with, indeed, which would not actually promote, his progress in other studies. In regard to the necessity of moral instruction, and the beneficial influence of the Bible in schools, the testimony was no less explicit and uniform. I inquired of all classes of teachers, and of men of every grade of religious faith; instructers in common schools, high

quired without interfering with the other branches of study, and with evident benefit both to the disposition of the scholars, and the discipline of the school. A gentleman who, in this country, has had more than 4000 pupils in music, affirms that his experience gives the same result. The number of schools among us, in which music is made one of the regular branches of elementary instruction, is already great, and is constantly increasing, and I have heard of no case in which, with proper training, every child has not been found capable of learning. Indeed, the fact, that among the ancients and in the schools of the Middle Ages, music was regarded as indispensable in a full course of education, might of itself teach us, that the prejudice in question is founded in error.

Another consideration which gives music special claims on our regard as a branch of culture, is, that the best specimens of the art are within our reach. It is rare, that the pupil can ever look, in this country, on the original works of a master, in painting or sculpture. We have engravings, casts,

schools, and schools of art; of professors in colleges, universities, and professional seminaries in cities and in the country; in places where there was a uniformity and in places where there was a diversity of creeds; of believers and unbelievers; of rationalists and enthusiasts; of Catholics and Protestants, and I never found but one reply; and that was, that to leave the moral faculty uninstructed was to leave the most important part of the human mind undeveloped, and to strip education of almost everything that can make it valuable; and that the Bible, independently of the interest attending it, as containing the most ancient and influential writings ever recorded by human hands, and comprising the religious system of almost the whole of the civilized world, is in itself the best book that can be put into the hands of children to interest, to exercise, and to unfold the intellectual and moral powers. Every teacher whom I consulted repelled with indignation the idea that moral instruction is not proper for schools, and that the Bible cannot be introduced into common schools without encouraging sectarian bias in the matter of teaching."—STOWE's *Report*, &c.

and other copies, but they can give us only faint conceptions of the artist's design, and of his execution hardly an idea. In written music, we have a transcript of the conceptions of the composer, almost as complete as in written poetry or eloquence, and as easy of access.

In all these arts, however, much may be done to call forth and improve the taste of our people. By multiplying exhibitions of art; by extending patronage to the native talent for painting and sculpture which abounds among us; by promoting efforts for the diffusion of a correct taste in music, and a love for that art, so essential in our devotions, and so useful everywhere; and, finally and especially, by introducing elementary instruction, both in music and drawing, into our schools, we can do much towards securing for our land the multiplied blessings which would result from the general love of art.

Says a late Report of the School Committee of the City of Boston, when speaking of Drawing, "Your committee cannot help remarking, as they pass, that, in their opinion, there is no good reason for excluding the art of linear drawing from any liberal scheme of popular instruction. It has a direct tendency to quicken that important faculty, the faculty of observation. It is a supplement to writing. It is in close alliance with geometry. It is conversant with form, and intimately connected with all the improvements in the mechanic arts. In all the mechanical, and many of the other employments of life, it is of high practical utility. Drawing, like music, is not an accomplishment only; it has important uses: and if music be successfully introduced into our public schools, your committee express the hope and the conviction that drawing, sooner or later, will follow."

In the same report the committee observe, "There are said to be at this time not far from eighty thousand common schools in this country, in which are to be found the people who, in coming years, will mould the character of this democracy. If vocal music were generally adopted as a branch of instruction in these schools, it might be reasonably expected, that in at least two generations, we should be changed into a musical people. The great point to be considered, in reference to the introduction of vocal music into popular elementary instruction, is, that thereby you set in motion a mighty power, which silently, but surely in the end, will humanize, refine, and elevate a whole community.* Music is one of the fine arts; it therefore deals with

* "We have listened," says a recent traveller in Switzerland, "to the peasant children's songs, as they went out to their morning occupations, and saw their hearts enkindled to the highest tones of music and poetry by the setting sun or the familiar objects of nature, each of which was made to echo some truth, or point to some duty, by an appropriate song. We have heard them sing 'the harvest hymn' as they went forth, before daylight, to gather in the grain. We have seen them assemble in groups at night, chanting a hymn of praise for the glories of the heavens, or joining in some patriotic chorus or some social melody, instead of the frivolous and corrupting conversation which so often renders such meetings the source of evil. In addition to this, we visited communities where the youth had been trained from their childhood to exercises in vocal music, of such a character as to elevate instead of debasing the mind, and have found that it served in the same manner to cheer their social assemblies, in place of the noise of folly or the poisoned cup of intoxication. We have seen the young men of such a community assembled to the number of several hundreds, from a circuit of twenty miles; and, instead of spending a day of festivity in rioting and drunkenness, pass the whole time, with the exception of that employed in a frugal repast and a social meeting, in a concert of social, moral, and religious hymns, and devote the proceeds of the exhibition to some object of benevolence. We could not but look at the contrast presented on similar occasions in our own country with a blush of shame. We have visited a village whose whole moral aspect was changed in a few years by the introduction of music of this character, even among adults, and where the aged were compelled to express their astonishment at seeing the young abandon their corrupting and riotous amusements for this delightful and improving exercise."

abstract beauty, and so lifts man to the source of all beauty —from finite to infinite, and from the world of matter to the world of spirits and to God. Music is the great handmaid of civilization. Whence come those traditions of a reverend antiquity—seditions quelled, cures wrought, fleets and armies governed by the force of song—whence that responding of rocks, woods, and trees to the harp of Orpheus—whence a city's walls uprising beneath the wonder-working touches of Apollo's lyre? These, it is true, are fables: yet they shadow forth, beneath the veil of allegory, a profound truth. They beautifully proclaim the mysterious union between music, as an instrument of man's civilization, and the soul of man. Prophets and wise men, large-minded lawgivers of an olden time, understood and acted on this truth. The ancient oracles were uttered in song. The laws of the Twelve Tables were put to music and got by heart at school. Minstrel and sage are, in some languages, convertible terms. Music is allied to the highest sentiments of man's moral nature: love of God, love of country, love of friends. Wo to the nation in which these sentiments are allowed to go to decay! What tongue can tell the unutterable energies that reside in these three engines — church music, national airs, and fireside melodies — as means of informing and enlarging the mighty heart of a free people!"

In thus describing the kind of education which is called for by the situation of our country and the spirit of the age, I have referred, not only to school education, but to all the agencies, which tend to form the minds, and characters of the rising generation. It is one thing to set forth what this education ought to be, and quite another to determine what it actually is. On this latter point, all who wish well to their country ought to speak plainly; their evidence should be given in without prejudice or passion; with no alloy of party feeling; and with a single desire to see the American people fulfilling the high destiny marked out for them by Providence. He is the best friend of his country who, on such subjects, utters the truth, and the whole truth. It is, unhappily, the interest of many in every party, who wish to use the people for the accomplishment of their own sordid purposes, to lavish upon them the most unbounded professions of confidence in their wisdom; and it is not easy, in such a state of things, for one, however loyal to the institutions of his country, or however devoted to the popular welfare, to hint at prevailing imperfections, without incurring reproach and exposing himself to misapprehension. And yet, if this is not done, if he who thinks he sees dangerous maxims pervading the popular mind, and radical defects in existing systems of education, may not proclaim them boldly, and with impunity, too, where is our boasted freedom, and where the hope that our future shall be better than our past? All advancement in a higher civilization must be the result of a clear perception of existing evils and dangers; and such perception can evidently never be attained unless individuals are free to discuss and expose them.

I ask, then, what is the aggregate intelligence and moral culture bestowed by education on the people of this country? I answer, in the words of one who has always been known as the advocate of the largest liberty, and whose firmness in the declaration of his opinions has only been equalled by the sincerity with which, in the estimation of all his fellow-citizens, he has held them.*

"Nothing is more common than for public journalists to extol in unmeasured terms ' the intelligence of the community.' On all occasions, according to them, *Vox populi est vox Dei.* We are pronounced to be a highly cultivated, intellectual, and civilized people. When we, the people,

* Lecture on Civilization, by Samuel Young.

called for the exclusion of small bills, we were right; when we called for the repeal of the exclusion, we were equally right. We are divided into political parties nearly equal, but we are both right. We disagree respecting the fundamental principles of government; we quarrel about the laws of a circulating medium; we are bank and anti-bank, tariff and anti-tariff, for a national bankrupt law and against a national bankrupt law, for including corporations and for excluding corporations, for unlimited internal improvement, judicious internal improvement, and for no internal improvement. We have creeds, sects, denominations, and faiths of all varieties, each insisting that it is right, and that all the others are wrong. We have cold water societies, but many more that habitually deal in hot water. We are anti-masonic and masonic, 'pro-slavery and anti-slavery;' and are spiced and seasoned with *abolitionism*, *immediateism*, *gradualism*, mysticism, materialism, agrarianism, sensualism, egotism, skepticism, idealism, transcendentalism, Van Burenism, Harrisonism, Mormonism, and animal magnetism. Every public and private topic has its furious partisans, struggling with antagonists equally positive and unyielding, and yet we are told that we are a well-informed, a highly civilized people.

"If we look to our legislative halls, to the lawgivers of the land, to the men who have been selected for the greatest wisdom and experience, we shall see the same disagreement and collision on every subject.

"He who would play the politician must shut his eyes to all this, and talk incessantly of the intelligence of the people. Instead of attempting to lead the community in the right way, he must go with them in the wrong.

"It is true, he may preach sound doctrine in reference to the education of youth. He may state the vast influence it has upon the whole life of man. He may freely point out the imperfections in the moral, intellectual, and physical instruction of the children of the present day. He may urge the absolute necessity of good teachers, of the multiplication of libraries, and every other means for the diffusion of useful knowledge. He may expatiate upon the superstitious fears, the tormenting fancies, the erroneous notions, the wrong prepossessions, and the laxity of morals which most children are allowed to imbibe for want of early and correct instruction, and which, in the majority of cases, last through life. He may, with truth and freedom, declare, that the mental impress, at twenty, gives the colouring to the remainder of life; and that most young men of our country, of that age, have not half the correct information and sound principles which might, with proper care, have been instilled into their minds before they were ten years old.

"But here the politician must stop his censures and close his advice. At twentyone, the ignorant, uneducated, and wayward youth is entitled to the right of suffrage, and mingles with a community composed of materials like himself. He bursts the shell which had enveloped him; he emerges from the chrysalis state of darkness and ignorance, and at once becomes a component part of 'a highly intelligent, enlightened, and civilized community.'

"If we honestly desire to know society as it is, we must subject it to a rigorous analysis. We must divest ourselves of all partiality, and not lay the 'flattering unction' of vanity to our souls. The clear perception of our deficiencies, of the feeble advances already made in knowledge and civilization, is the best stimulus to united, energetic, and useful exertion. Bitter truth is much more wholesome than sweet delusion.

"The gross flattery which is weekly and daily poured out in legislative speeches and by a time-serving press, has a most pernicious influence upon the public mind and morals. The greater the ignorance of the mass, the more readily the flattery is swallowed. He who is the most circumscribed in knowledge, perceives not a single cloud in his mental horizon. Attila and his Huns doubtless believed themselves to be the most civilized people on earth; and if they had possessed our editorial corps, they would have proved it to be so.

"Weak and vain females, in the days of their youth, have been charged by the other sex with an extraordinary fondness for flattery. But, judging by the constant specimens which are lavishly administered and voraciously swallowed, the male appetite for hyperboles of praise is altogether superior.

"The vainglorious boastings of the American press excite the risibility of all intelligent foreigners. According to the learned and philosophic De Tocqueville, this is the country, of all others, where public opinion is the most dictatorial and despotic. Like a spoiled child, it has been indulged, flattered, and caressed by interested sycophants until its capriciousness and tyranny are boundless.

"When Americans boast of their cultivated minds and humane feelings, foreigners point them to the existence of negro slavery. When they claim the civic merit of unqualified submission to the rules of social order, they are referred to the frequent exhibition of duels and of Lynch law. When they insist upon the prevalence among us of strict integrity, sound morals, and extensive piety, they are shown an American newspaper, which probably contains the annunciation of half a dozen thefts, robberies, embezzlements, horrid murders, and appalling suicides.

"Burns, the eminent Scotch poet, seems to have believed that good would result

"'If Providence the gift would gie us,
To see ourselves as others see us.'

If we had this gift, much of our overweening vanity would

doubtless be repressed, and many would seriously ponder on the means of reformation and improvement.

"But that any great improvement can be made upon the moral propensities of the adults of the present day is not to be expected. The raw material of humanity, after being even partially neglected for twenty years, generally bids defiance to every manufacturing process.

"The moral education—that is, the proper discipline of the dispositions and affections of the mind, by which a reverence for the Supreme Being, a love of justice, of benevolence, and of truth are expanded, strengthened, and directed, and the conscience enlightened and invigorated, must have its basis deeply and surely laid in childhood. Truth, in the important parts of moral science, is most easily taught, and makes the most indelible impressions in early life; before the infusion of the poison of bad example; before false notions and pernicious opinions have taken root; before the understanding is blunted and distorted by habit, or the mind clouded by prejudice."

The length to which this quotation has extended will hardly be regretted by our readers; and it prepares us to enter at once on the last topic which remains to be discussed in this chapter, viz., THE IMPORTANCE OF EDUCATION.

SECTION VI.

THE IMPORTANCE OF EDUCATION.

I. TO THE INDIVIDUAL.

" What is a man
If his chief good and market of his time
Be but to sleep and feed?—a beast, no more.
Sure, He that made us with such large discourse,
Looking before and after, gave us not
That capability and godlike reason
To rust in us unused."—SHAKSPEARE.

" Men generally need knowledge to overpower their passions and master their prejudices ; and, therefore, to see your brother in ignorance is to see him unfurnished to all good works ; and every master is to cause his family to be instructed, every governor is to instruct his charge, every man his brother, by all possible and just provisions. For if the people die for want of knowledge, they who are set over them shall also die for want of charity."—JEREMY TAYLOR.

IT may be proper to remind the reader, that by education, we understand a system of training and instruction, which aims at the due culture of all the powers of the soul, both intellectual and moral. We shall be the better prepared, to appreciate the necessity and importance of such culture, if we consider that, in its absence, the individual will be educated by circumstances. Even when he is most neglected, there will still be companions, parents, or masters, daily occurrences, and other causes, both physical and moral, which will act forcibly upon some of his powers to develop and excite them. But which of his powers will these be? When parents do not take the trouble to provide for the proper education of their children, it must be obvious that neither their example, nor the associations with which they will surround those children, whether in high or low life, will be likely to foster their better and purer sentiments. Add to the force of natural propensity, the sensualizing influences which in such cases will inevitably be applied from without to the young and plastic mind, and what can be expected?

Beyond a doubt, whatever this little being has in common with animals will be cherished and strengthened; whatever he has in common with angels of light and purity will be repressed and stifled. The gratification of his lower appetites will be predominant among the objects of his desire; and as these appetites are essentially selfish, he will become less and less regardful of the claims of justice and of charity. He may improve in cunning, in the readiness with which he invents and the pertinacity with which he employs expedients to compass his base ends; but he will have less and less of true wisdom. When sorely pressed by danger or difficulty, he will show that he is not unacquainted with moral distinctions; but then the dexterity with which he tries to make the worse appear the better reason, and the facility with which he invents specious apologies for the worst acts, these will show, too, that in his mind the light has emphatically become darkness, and that even his highest faculties are little better than panders to his lowest appetites.

An ignorant, uncultivated mind, then, is the native soil of sensuality and cruelty, and the whole history of the world proves, that in a large proportion of instances, it does not fail to bring forth its appropriate fruit. In what countries, are the people most given to the lowest forms of animal gratification, and also most regardless of the lives and happiness of others? Is it not in pagan lands, over which moral and intellectual darkness broods, and where men are vile without shame, and cruel without remorse? If from pagan we pass to Christian countries, we shall find that those in which education is least prevalent are precisely those in which there is the most immorality, and the greatest indifference to the sufferings of sentient and animated beings. Spain, in which, until recently, there was but one newspaper, and in which not more than one in twenty of the people are instructed in schools, has a population about equal to that of England and Wales. What is the relative state of morals? In England and Wales the whole number of convictions for murder in one year (1826) was thirteen, and the number convicted of wounding, &c., with intent to kill, was fourteen, while in Spain the number convicted during the same year was, for murder, *twelve hundred and thirty-three!* and for maiming with intent to kill, *seventeen hundred and seventy-three.**

* I add an extract from a late traveller (Inglis) on the state of manners and morals. "If vice degrade the manners of the upper and middle classes in Seville, crime of a darker turpitude disfigures the character and conduct of the lower orders. Scarcely a night passes without the commission of a murder. But these crimes are not perpetrated in cold blood from malevolent passions, still less from love of gain; they generally spring from the slightest possible causes. The Andalusian is not so abstemious as the Castilian, and the wine he drinks is stronger; he has also a great propensity for gambling, the fruitful engenderer of strife; and the climate has, doubtless, its influence upon his passions. 'Will you taste with me?' an Andalusian will say to some associate with whom he has had some slight difference, offering him his glass. 'No gracias,' the other will reply. The former, already touched with wine, will half drain his glass, and present it again, saying, 'Do you not wish to drink with me?' and if the other still refuses the proffered civility, it is the work of a moment to drain the glass to the dregs, to say, 'How! not taste with me?' and to thrust the knife an Andalusian always carries with him into the abdomen of the comrade who refuses to drink with him. It is thus, and in other ways equally simple, that quarrel and murder disfigure the nightly annals of every town in Andalusia, and of the other provinces of the south of Spain. There is an hospital in Seville dedicated to the sole purpose of receiving wounded persons. I had the curiosity to visit it, and ascertained that, during the past fourteen days, twenty-one persons had been received into the hospital wounded from stabs; they would not inform me how many of these had died."—*Spain in* 1830, vol. ii.. p. 56.

We cannot be surprised that, in such a land, scenes of cruelty and blood should constitute the favourite amusement of the people. Their greatest delight is in bullfights; "and how," says an eyewitness, "do the Spaniards conduct themselves during these scenes? The intense interest which they feel in this game is visible throughout, and often loudly expressed; an astounding shout always accompanies a critical moment: whether it be the bull or man who is in danger, their joy is excessive; but their greatest sympathy is given to the feats of the bull. If the picador receives the bull gallantly, and forces him to retreat, or if the matador courageously faces and wounds the bull, they applaud these acts of science and valour; but if the bull overthrow the horse and his rider, or if the matador miss his aim and the bull seems ready to gore him, their delight knows no bounds. And it is certainly a fine spectacle to see the thousands of spectators rise simultaneously, as they always do when the interest is intense; the greatest and most crowded theatre in Europe presents nothing half so imposing as this. But how barbarous, how brutal is the whole exhibition! Could an English audience witness the scenes that are repeated every week in Madrid? A universal burst of 'shame!' would follow the spectacle of a horse gored and bleeding, and actually treading upon his own entrails while he gallops round the arena: even the appearance of the goaded bull could not be borne; panting, covered with wounds and blood, lacerated by darts, and yet brave and resolute to the end.

"The spectacle continued two hours and a half, and during that time there were seven bulls killed and six horses. When the last bull was despatched, the people immediately rushed into the arena, and the carcass was dragged out amid the most deafening shouts."—*Spain in 1830*, vol. i., p. 191.

In another passage, the same writer, after describing a

fight, in which one bull had killed three horses and one man, and remained master of the arena, adds, "This was a time to observe the character of the people. When the unfortunate picador was killed, in place of a general exclamation of horror and loud expressions of pity, the universal cry was 'Que es bravo ese toro!' ('Ah! the admirable bull!'). The whole scene produced the most unbounded delight; and I did not perceive a single female avert her head, or betray the slightest symptom of wounded feeling."

How different is the spirit and character developed by a proper system of education. Discipline gives its subjects command over their passions, and instead of a love for vicious excitement, cultivates the taste for simple and innocent pleasures. Objects higher than any gratification merely animal awaken desire; objects in the pursuit of which the faculties find a healthful and agreeable employment, and the individual, though intent on his own advantage, still serves the community. His charities, too, are enlarged and strengthened. From a mere child of impulse, he is transformed into a reflective being, looking before and after with large discourse of reason. He forms plans for a distant future, and thus rises nearer and nearer to a spiritual existence; while, divested of no sentiments or principles which the Creator has bestowed upon him, all are still made to occupy their proper places, and to move together in subordination to the great ends of his being.

It is to be observed here, again, that we mean by education a large and generous culture, which comprehends the whole man, and which assigns, therefore, the first place to the immortal nature. We would never forget, that there may be much knowledge and much discipline of the intellectual powers, which leaves, in darkness and sin, the moral and spiritual man. Such education we repudiate. Instead of a narrow and partial training, which would make its subject a monster rather than a man; we go for one which would build up that subject to the perfection which corresponds to his nature and position.

And let us add, if mere knowledge cannot make men wise, much less can ignorance. Her appropriate office is not to improve, but to deteriorate and degrade. It has been said that "ignorance is the mother of devotion." It would have been much nearer truth, to represent her as the parent of a dark idolatry, which bows the spirit to an abject but unholy service, and robs it of its noblest instincts. This has been well put in an old allegory of the days of Bunyan. Apollyon invades the country of Nonage, and, in order to accomplish more fully his designs, resolves "that a great part of the weak and feeble inhabitants should be tutored by Mrs. *Ignorance*." Accordingly, accosting that personage, he says, "My dear cousin and friend, I have a great number of pretty boys and girls for you to tutor and bring up for me: will you undertake the charge?" "Most dread and mighty Apollyon," she replies, "you know I never yet declined any drudgery for you which lay in my power." Apollyon then, after complimenting her upon what she had already done for the advancement of his kingdom and greatening of his power in the world, turns to his associate and says, "Noble Peccatum (Sin), this gentlewoman, Madam Ignorance, is your child, your natural offspring, your own flesh and blood; therefore I charge you to help and assist her in this great work; for I should be glad if she had the education of all the children in the whole world."

The influence of education, on *happiness*, is also worthy of deep consideration. Man has been supplied with various desires, sensual, intellectual, and moral; some prompting him to serve others, and some to benefit himself, but all intended to yield him happiness. Education enlarges the capacity for enjoyment, of each of these desires. Even his sensual appetites need the guidance of knowledge to keep them from excess, while they are refined and elevated by the culture of his other powers. And then that brood of hopes and fears which must always cluster round man's heart — taking him out of the present, and in some sort compelling him to live and labour for an unseen future — how these are all rectified and enlightened by knowledge and culture. Imagination, chastened and regulated, no longer fills the view with lying spectres of horror or delusive anticipations of bliss. She becomes the handmaid of the understanding and the heart. The mind is steadied; its vision purged and enlarged. It sees objects as they are, neither magnifying our blessings nor multiplying our sorrows.* Hopes are built on a solid and rational foundation, and fear, which to so many is the disease of the soul,† making more

* "Wisdom makes all the troubles, griefs, and pains incident to life, whether casual adversities or natural afflictions, easy and supportable, by rightly valuing the importance and moderating the influence of them. It suffers not busy fancy to alter the nature, amplify the degree, or extend the duration of them, by representing them more sad, heavy, and remediless than they truly are. It allows them no force beyond what naturally and necessarily they have, nor contributes nourishment to their increase. It keeps them at due distance, not permitting them to encroach upon the soul, or to propagate their influence beyond their proper sphere.—DR. BARROW."

† "Ignorance," says a writer, "can shake strong sinews with idle thoughts, and sink brave hearts with light sorrows, and doth lead innocent feet to impure dens, and haunts the simple rustic with credulous fears, and the swart Indian with that more potent magic, under which spell he pines and dies. And by ignorance is a man fast bound from childhood to the grave, till knowledge, which is the revelation of good and evil, doth set him free."

Among the numberless superstitions which have been dissipated by science, may be instanced the Spectre of the Brocken, which had appeared from time to time, near the Hartz Mountains in Germany This was a gigantic figure, seen indistinctly in the heavens, in form always resembling a human being, and the appearance of which was regarded, for ages, as a certain indication of approaching misfortune. At length a celebrated philosopher (Abbé Haüy) determined to investigate this apparition. After ascending the mountain thirty

danger than it avoids, becomes, to a well-trained and enlightened mind, the instrument of caution rather than anxiety—" a guard, not a torment, to the breast." It is sufficiently vigilant in anticipating and guarding against earthly evils, but the loss of immortality is the object of its supreme dread. "It is fixed," to use the language of South, "on Him who is only to be feared, God; and yet with a filial fear, which at the same time both fears and loves. It is awe without amazement—dread without distraction. There is a beauty in its very paleness, giving a lustre to reverence and a gloss to humility."

In estimating the happiness to be derived from education, let us not overlook the vast addition which may thus be made to domestic and social enjoyments. Without the facts and ideas which are supplied by reading, how meager and spiritless would conversation prove! In rearing children, and in the difficult task of making home pleasant and attractive, books form an unfailing resource, and many who now waste life and talent in a round of harassing dissipations or in low vice, might have been both happy and useful, if they had early imbibed a taste for good books.

It is worthy of consideration, too, that the highest and purest pleasures to be derived from gratifying curiosity, are confined to cultivated minds, which are intent on truth rather than novelty, and which look beyond mere facts and events, to their causes and reasons.* The vague interest

---

times, he at last saw it, and soon discovered that it was nothing but his own shadow cast upon clouds. "When the rising sun," says he, "throws his rays over the Brocken upon the body of a man standing opposite to fleecy clouds, let him fix his eye steadfastly upon them, and in all probability he will see his own shadow extending the length of five or six hundred feet, at the distance of about two miles from him."

    * " How charming is divine philosophy!
      Not harsh and crabbed, as dull fools suppose,
      But musical as is Apollo's lute,

with which the ignorant look on the beauties and sublimities of nature—how much inferior is this, to that intelligent and ever-new delight, with which the well-informed and curious mind traces these same objects as parts of a great system of law and order, resplendent as well with moral as with material charms. A poet has asked,

> And a perpetual feast of nectar'd sweets,
> Where no crude surfeit reigns."
> MILTON's *Comus*.

"It is not the eye that sees the beauties of heaven, nor the ear that hears the sweetness of music, or the glad tidings of a prosperous accident, but the soul that perceives all relishes of sensual and intellectual perfections; and the more noble and excellent the soul is, the greater and more savoury are its perceptions."—BISHOP TAYLOR.

"The pleasure and delight of knowledge and learning far surpasseth all other in nature; for shall the pleasures of the affections so exceed the pleasures of the senses, as much as the obtaining of desire or victory exceedeth a song or a dinner? and must not, of consequence, the pleasures of the intellect or understanding exceed the pleasures of the affections? We see in all other pleasures there is a satiety, and after they be used their verdure departeth; which showeth well they be but deceits of pleasure, and not pleasure, and that it was the novelty which pleased, and not the quality; and therefore we see that voluptuous men turn friars, and ambitious princes turn melancholy; but of knowledge there is no satiety, but satisfaction and appetite are ever interchangeable, and therefore appeareth to be good in itself simply, without fallacy or accident. Neither is that pleasure of small efficacy and contentment to the mind of man, which the poet Lucretius describeth elegantly:

> "'Suave mari magno, turbantibus æquora ventis,' &c.

"'It is a view of delight,' saith he, 'to stand or walk upon the shore side, and to see a ship tossed with tempest upon the sea, or to be in a fortified tower, and to see two battles join upon a plain. But it is a pleasure incomparable for the mind of man to be settled, landed, and fortified in the certainty of truth, and from thence to descry and behold the errors, perturbations, labours, wanderings up and down of other men'—so always that this prospect be with pity, and not with swelling or pride."—LORD BACON.

> "Do not all charms fly
> At the mere touch of cold philosophy?
> There was an awful rainbow once in heaven:
> We know her woof and texture; she is given
> In the dull catalogue of common things.
> Philosophy will clip an angel's wings,
> Conquer all mysteries by rule and line,
> Empty the haunted air and gnomed mine,
> Unweave a rainbow:"

Let another poet (Akenside) answer:

> "Nor ever yet
> The melting rainbow's vernal tinctured hues
> To me have shone so pleasing, as when first
> The hand of science pointed out the path
> In which the sunbeams, gleaming from the west,
> Fall on the watery cloud:"

So Wordsworth:

> "My heart leaps up when I behold
> A rainbow in the sky:
> So was it when my life began,
> So is it now I am a man,
> So be it when I shall grow old," &c.

To those who imagine that the progress of knowledge may be unfavourable to enjoyment, by dispelling illusions and mysteries, it may be sufficient to remark, that science dispels one mystery only to encounter another and a higher one. Whatever pleasure, therefore, can be derived from obscurity, is enjoyed in common by the educated and uneducated; while the former has the additional satisfaction of discovering some of the links in the long chain of causes, and of combining an admiration which reasons and understands, with one which can only wonder and adore.

I cannot close this branch of the subject without adverting to the influence which education has on our *usefulness and success in life*. The practice of holding up, before the young, the prospect of a vulgar, worldly success as the great motive to study, I have already condemned; and I want words to express my deep conviction of its danger and folly. But it would be a grievous omission, to overlook, on the other hand, the intimate connexion which does subsist, between knowledge and culture, as cause, and the capacity to act wisely and successfully, as effect. We all know, how perfectly fettered and helpless a man is, in the present state of the world, who cannot read and write; and yet these mechanical accomplishments are but the *means* to education, rather than education itself. Education, properly understood, aims not merely to qualify a man to read and write letters, to look over newspapers, and to keep accounts; it aims to make him a thoughtful and reflecting being; to habituate him* to the systematic applica-

---

* The effects of a deficiency of education on success in mechanical pursuits is strikingly illustrated in the evidence recently given by an intelligent engineer, accustomed to employ many hundred workmen of different nations (Mr. A. G. Escher, of Zurich), before the British Poor-Law Commissioners. He says, these "effects are most strongly marked in the Italians, who, though with the advantage of greater natural capacity than the English, Swiss, Dutch, or Germans, are still of the lowest class of workmen. Though they comprehend clearly and quickly, as I have stated, any simple proposition made or explanation given to them, and are enabled quickly to execute any kind of work when they have seen it performed once, yet their minds, as I imagine, *from want of development by training or school education, seem to have no kind of logic, no power of systematic arrangement, no capacity for collecting any series of observations, and making sound inductions from the whole of them.* This want of capacity of mental arrangement is shown in their manual operations. An Italian will execute a simple operation with great dexterity; but when a number of them are put together, all is confusion. For instance: within a short time after the introduction of cotton-spinning into Naples in 1830, a native spinner would produce as much as the best English workman; and yet, up to this time, not one of the Neapolitan operatives is advanced far enough to take the superintendence of a single room, the superintendents being all Northerns, who, though less gifted by nature, have had a higher degree of order or arrangement imparted to their minds by a superior education."—*See last Report of Poor-Law Commissioners.*

tion of his powers to the production of useful results; to render his mind active and enterprising, by storing it with ideas; and to give him power over the world of mind and matter, by teaching him the laws to which they are subjected. In bestowing on all men *mind*, and then allotting to most of them a life of labour and care, God has plainly taught us, that even the handicraftsman is to work with his intellect and his heart, rather than with his muscles. Every occupation, even the humblest and simplest, requires *skill*, and skill requires some training and instruction. Every occupation may be made more easy, as well as more productive, if the labourer understands his own powers, and the properties of the objects with which he deals; and it will be certain to be more pleasant, too, if his mind is cheered while he is at work with pleasant and profitable thoughts, and with the consciousness that he lives as becomes an intelligent being. And while education thus tends to make the labourer a more happy as well as a more efficient producer; to add to his own enjoyments while he is himself adding to the sum of purchaseable enjoyments in the world; it tends, also, to make him more provident. The ignorant are usually wasteful;* and when not so, they

---

* Those who have conversed familiarly with the very poor, and especially with the inmates of poorhouses and workhouses, must have discovered the entire absence among them of that *prudential* wisdom which is the result of education. "Out of sixteen paupers," says a late writer, "examined at the Workhouse of the Union in Faversham (Eng.), only two had ever saved up so much as *ten pounds*, notwithstanding that several of them had been in the receipt, for some time, of from twenty to forty shillings a week! and not one had ever kept any account of receipt and expenditure! The being merely able to read makes little difference in this respect, for, in the number examined, there were several who could do so. Indeed, the most prudent of the two who had saved had received no education. He had been a workman in the powder-mills at Faversham, and out of his wages of thirty shillings a week, had amassed a sum of 200*l.*, which

rarely form those plans of a snug and far-reaching economy, which combine present comfort and liberality, with a steady increase of wealth.

The Chinese have a saying, that "by learning, the sons of the common people become great; without learning, the sons of the great become mingled with the mass of the people." This remark is particularly applicable among that people, because, with them, all offices are bestowed according to talent and literary acquirement; and there seems to be a settled design, to maintain an aristocracy of learning, instead of one founded on wealth. But in every civilized country, and especially where there is any great degree of liberty, knowledge and mental cultivation form the most certain means of success.* Capital invested in the heart and

he afterward lost by the failure of a bank. He bitterly regretted his want of education, which, he said, had prevented his embracing many opportunities that offered of bettering his condition, and compelled him to finish a life of industry in the workhouse, instead of occupying a respectable situation in society. Several others complained that they had never been taught to look forward to the consequences of their own acts. One man, a shoemaker, about twenty-eight years of age, who was in the house with his wife and five children, attributed his poverty and pitiable condition entirely to this cause. When asked if he did not calculate, before marrying so early, his means to support a wife and family, his answer was, 'No, sir—never gave it a thought—never thought of anything. You see, sir, we ain't used to look forward.' "—*See A Paper, by F. Liardet, Esq., on the State of the Peasantry in the County of Kent (Eng.), in the third volume of the Publications of the Central Society of Education.*

* On this point I quote again from Mr. Escher. Having been asked whether education would not tend to render workmen discontented and disorderly, and thus impair their value as operatives, he answers: "My own experience, and my conversation with eminent mechanics in different parts of Europe, lead me to an entirely different conclusion. In the present state of manufactures, where so much is done by machinery and tools, and so little done by mere brute labour (and that little diminishing), mental superiority, system, order, punctuality, and good conduct, qualities all developed

head is better than a mere money capital, not simply because it is inalienable, but because it enables its possessor to avail

and promoted by education, are becoming of the highest consequence. There are now, I consider, few enlightened manufacturers who will dissent from the opinion, that the workshops peopled with the greatest number of educated and well-informed workmen, will turn out the greatest quantity of the best work in the best manner."

In another place he states that, " as workmen *only*, the preference is undoubtedly due to the English; because, as we find them, they are all trained to special branches, on which they have had comparatively superior training, and have concentred all their thoughts. As men of business or of general usefulness, and as men with whom an employer would best like to be surrounded, I should, however, decidedly prefer the Saxons and the Swiss, but more especially the Saxons, because they have had a very careful general education, which has extended their capacities beyond any special employment, and rendered them fit to take up, after a short preparation, any employment to which they may be called. If I have an English workman engaged in the erection of a steam-engine, he will understand that, and nothing else."

In regard to the *moral* effect of education, his testimony is explicit and worthy of deep consideration : " The better educated workmen, we find, are distinguished by superior moral habits in every respect. They are discreet in their enjoyments, which are more of a rational and refined kind ; they have a taste for much better society, which they approach respectfully, and, consequently, find much readier admittance to it ; they cultivate music, they read, they enjoy the pleasures of scenery, and, consequently, make parties for excursions in the country ; they are, consequently, honest and trustworthy." " The Scotch workmen get on much better on the Continent than the English, which I ascribe chiefly to their better education, which renders it easier for them to adapt themselves to circumstances, and especially in getting on better with their fellow-workmen, and with all the people with whom they come in contact." " The English workmen are in conduct the most disorderly, debauched, and unruly, and least respectful and trustworthy of any nation whatsoever which we have employed (and in saying this, I express the experience of every manufacturer on the Continent to whom I have spoken, and especially of the English manufacturers, who make the loudest complaints). These characters of depravity do not apply to

himself of the advantages of any position in which he may happen to be placed. The activity of his mind, the enterprise and forecast with which he forms plans, the readiness with which he avails himself of every opportunity—all will be proportioned, to the degree in which his mind has been developed by culture.

I have before me the history of two families—children of brothers, who occupied adjoining farms, and started in life with the same advantages. The one was blessed with an intelligent, high-principled wife, who was fond of books, and was always giving impulse and enlargement to the minds of her children. The wife of the other, though a worthy person, was ignorant and without cultivation. The result has been, that the sons of the latter are ordinary men, with torpid minds, and coarse tastes, though free from vice. The children of the other are full of a generous and useful activity, and are all rising to stations of great respectability and influence. Some part of this difference may doubtless be ascribed, to differences in the organization and natural endowments of these children. But it is believed that, had the same difference obtained in the education of children *of the*

the English workmen who have received an education, but attach to the others in degree in which they are in want of it. When the uneducated English workmen are released from the bonds of iron discipline in which they have been restrained by their employers in England, and are treated with the urbanity and friendly feeling which the more educated workmen on the Continent expect and receive from their employers, they (the English workmen) completely lose their balance; they do not understand their position, and, after a certain time, become totally unmanageable and useless. *The educated English workmen in a short time comprehend their position, and adopt an appropriate behaviour.*" The reader will find much similar testimony on these points, from various sources, in the same report. He is referred especially to the examination of William Fairbarn, Esq., a manufacturer of Manchester.—*See Report to the Secretary of State for the Home Department, on the Training of Pauper Children, London,* 1841.

same parents, the result would have presented a **contrast** hardly less striking.

Apprehension is often expressed, and no doubt felt, lest education should inspire a restless and discontented spirit—lest it should make men unhappy, under the toils and obscurity which always await the majority in every land. If, in educating people, we teach them, directly or indirectly, that the only use of knowledge is to enable them " to get along," or " to get up in the world," as it is termed; if, in other words, every appeal is addressed to a sordid ambition, then, doubtless, such result will not be unlikely to follow. But let it be observed here, that there neither is nor can be, in this country, any such prevailing ignorance and mental torpor as will keep the masses perfectly at rest, after the manner of older countries, or as will prevent them from struggling to better their condition. Such multifarious and multitudinous incitements to activity surround them on every hand—so many examples of individuals rising rapidly from the humblest circumstances to wealth or influence, that they who are looking on, must be agitated with some desire to share in the same success. But whose minds are most likely to be unsettled by these desires? Are they those of the educated, or those of the ignorant and unreflecting? Who are most likely to forget, that happiness is to be found, not in any measure of outward success or distinction, but in ruling our own spirits, and in cultivating a proper sense of our duties and privileges? Who is most likely to find, in his regular pursuits, however humble, as well as in his hours of leisure, that full and pleasant occupation for his thoughts and faculties, which will render a feverish excitement from without, unnecessary and undesirable? It seems to me, that these questions carry with them their own answer. It can hardly be doubted that, the more fully the mind is stored with knowledge, and with resources of an intellectual and moral nature, the less is it likely to become restless or discontented; that, while education imparts higher and more refined tastes, it imparts, at the same time, the means of satisfying those tastes, without struggling perpetually against the allotments of life, and the claims of our station.

But two causes can interfere with this, the natural order of things. The one may be found in the practice, so monstrously absurd—would we could add, so rare—of teaching that education is useful only so far as it enables its possessor to *rise* in the world—as if position were everything, and the soul nothing. The other is, that we restrict the blessings of knowledge, and of a taste for reading, to a small portion of those who spend their lives in labour; and by that means leave them without sympathy among their companions, while we at the same time invest them with a distinction which will not be unlikely to inflame their vanity, and which may thus render them objects of envy and dislike. We occasionally meet those, whom education does seem to have made unhappy; because it has brought with it, to their minds, the mistaken notion that knowledge and talent are out of place in an humble sphere or in a life of labour; but we must remember, that they owe such unhappiness, not to education, but to an entire misconception of the end and use of education.* Those who suffer through education, or higher

* " Already," says Howitt, in his Rural Life of England, " I know some who, through books, have reaped those blessings of an awakened heart and intellect, too long denied to the hard path of poverty, and which render them not the less sedate, industrious, and provident, but, on the contrary, more so. They have made them, in the humblest stations, the happiest of men; quickened their sensibilities towards their wives and children; converted the fields, the places of their daily toil, into places of earnest meditative delight—schools of perpetual observation of God's creative energy and wisdom.

" It was but the other day that the farming man of a neighbouring lady having been pointed out to me as at once remarkably fond of reading and attached to his profession, I entered into conversation with him, and it is long since I experienced such a cordial pleasure as in the contemplation of the character that opened upon me. He

intellectual tastes, merely because they are deprived thereby of the sympathy of their associates, are more rare; and they

was a strong man, not to be distinguished by his dress and appearance from those of his class, but having a very intelligent countenance; and the vigorous, healthful feelings and right views that seemed to fill not only his mind, but his whole frame, spoke volumes for that vast enjoyment and elevation of character which a rightly-directed taste for reading would diffuse among our peasantry. His sound appreciation of those authors he had read—some of our best poets, historians, essayists, and travellers—was truly cheering, when contrasted with the miserable and frippery taste which distinguishes a large class of readers."

"I found this countryman was a member of our Artisans' Library, and every Saturday evening he walked over to the town to exchange his books. I asked him whether reading did not make him less satisfied with his daily work; his answer deserves universal attention. 'Before he read, his work was weary to him; for in the solitary fields, an empty head measured the time out tediously to double its length; but now, no place was so sweet as the solitary fields; he had always something pleasant floating across his mind, and the labour was delightful, and the day only too short.' Seeing his ardent attachment to the country, I sent him the last edition of the 'Book of the Seasons;' and I must here give a *verbatim et literatim* extract from the note in which he acknowledged its receipt, because it not only contains an experimental proof of the falsity of a common alarm on the subject of popular education, but shows at what a little cost much happiness may be conveyed to a poor man. 'Believe me, dear sir, this kind act has made an impression on my heart which time will not easily erase. There are none of your works, in my opinion, more valuable than this. The study of nature is not only the most delightful, but the most elevating. This will be true in *every station* of life. But how much more ought the *poor man* to prize this study! which, if prized and pursued as it ought, will enable him to bear, with patient resignation and cheerfulness, the *lot* by Providence assigned him. Oh, sir, I pity the working man who possesses not a *taste* for reading. 'Tis true, it may sometimes lead him to neglect the other more important duties of his station; but his better and more enlightened judgment will soon correct itself in this particular, and will enable him, while he steadily and diligently pursues his private studies, and participates in intellectual enjoy-

all admit that, while this inconvenience may be charged in part to their own indiscretion, in not sufficiently cultivating those associates, it is overbalanced, on the other hand, a thousand times, by the inexhaustible fund of pleasure, which they find in books, and in the exercise of their reflective faculties.

The remedy for these evils is obvious. In the first place, let *all* be so far educated, as to awaken a taste for reading and a desire for improvement, and knowledge will then cease to be a distinction, and can no longer make its possessor an object of envy. In the second place, let all be taught that education is given, not that we may buy a short-lived and doubtful success, but that we may have enlightened minds and improved hearts, and be better able to fill with dignity and pleasure the claims of any station, however lowly, and then contentment will prevail just in proportion as instruction becomes more general and more thorough. How much wisdom is there in the following lines of Wordsworth—the most philanthropic as well as the most philosophical poet of our age—whose heart and fancy have always been among the poor, and who, at the same time, has looked with more than doubt, on many modern schemes for social improvement. He is speaking of the early years of his Wanderer:

> " Early had he learned
> To reverence the volume that displays
> The mystery, the life which cannot die :
> What wonder if his being thus became
> Sublime and comprehensive ! Low desires,
> Low thoughts, there had no place ; yet was his heart
> Lowly ; for he was meek in gratitude,
> Oft as he called those ecstasies to mind,
> And whence they flowed ; and from them he acquired
> Wisdom, which works through patience : hence he learned,
> In oft-recurring hours of sober thought,
> To look on nature with an humble heart,

---

ment, to prize as he ought his *character as a man,* in every relative duty of life.' "

Self-questioned where it did not understand,
And with a superstitious eye of love.
   So passed the time; yet to the nearest town
He duly went, with what small overplus
His earnings might supply, and brought away
The book that most had tempted his desires,
While at the stall he read. Among the hills,
He gazed upon that mighty orb of song,
The divine Milton. Lore of different kind,
The annual savings of a toilsome life,
His schoolmaster supplied; books that explain
The purer elements of truth, involved
In lines and numbers, and, by charm severe
(Especially perceived where nature droops
And feeling is suppressed), preserve the mind
Busy in solitude and poverty.

In dreams, in study, and in ardent thought,
Thus was he reared; much wanting to assist
The growth of intellect, yet gaining more,
And every moral feeling of his soul
Strengthened and braced, by breathing in content
The keen, the wholesome air of poverty,
And drinking from the well of homely life."
The Excursion, **b. l**

SECTION VII.

THE IMPORTANCE OF EDUCATION (CONTINUED).

II. TO SOCIETY.

"Whether a wise state hath any interest nearer heart than the education of youth."—BERKELEY's *Querist*.

"When the clouds of ignorance are dispelled by the radiance of knowledge, power trembles, but the authority of law remains immovable."—BECCARIA.

"Almost all the calamities of man, except the physical evils which are inherent in his nature, are in a great measure to be imputed to erroneous views of religion or bad systems of government, and these cannot be coexistent for any considerable time with an extensive diffusion of knowledge. Either the freedom of intelligence will destroy the government, or the government will destroy it. Either it will extirpate superstition and enthusiasm, or they will contaminate its purity and prostrate its usefulness. Knowledge is the cause as well as the effect of good government."—DE WITT CLINTON.

SOCIETY may be regarded as a *partnership*. It is an extended system of co-operation, in which every individual has a part to perform, and from which, in return for his efforts, each individual receives a greater amount of benefit than he could have attained, had he relied only on his own unaided and solitary exertions. It is the object of civilization or social progress, to increase these advantages, or, in other words, to enable individuals to obtain from society, with a given amount of effort, a greater and greater amount of resulting benefit. Now, in regard to limited partnerships, which include but a small number of persons, nothing is more evident than that their success, and the success, of course, of each individual member, will be in exact proportion to the sagacity, integrity, and diligence with which each applies himself to his proper duties. If all the partners are ignorant, idle, and unprincipled, bankruptcy and ruin must be the speedy result. If this be the character of some only of the firm, even then, hardly any amount of effort and skill on the part of the remainder will prevent great losses; whereas, should all devote themselves to business with singleness of purpose, and with intelligence and activity, the result must be great prosperity. The application of these principles to the subject under consideration is obvious.

Let us consider society, in the *first* place, as a *material* partnership, or, in other words, as an association established merely for *the production and accumulation of wealth*. It is a truth often overlooked, but yet most unquestionable as well as most important, that the richest capitalist and the poorest labourer are joint proprietors in that great co-operative firm, through which, God ordains that man shall procure most of his blessings. A poor emigrant, who has just reached our shores, with no other means than his health and strong sinews, and who has skill but just sufficient to enable him to handle a pickaxe and shovel, is set at work in excavating a canal or grading a railroad. He knows nothing of the wealthy proprietor in New-York, who lives in luxury, and who wields his tens and hundreds of thousands in daily operations on 'change, and that proprietor knows still less of him. Yet it is no less true that they are *partners*—joint owners and managers of stock, in the same great company. Every dollar that the capitalist acquires by fair and legitimate business, goes to swell the facilities of the labourer, in getting employment, and in getting liberal remuneration for his services. It is by him, and others like him, that capital is furnished, not only to construct public improvements, but to carry forward private undertakings of a useful and productive character. On the other hand, every blow which the labourer strikes, tends to enrich the capitalist. As he deepens and widens the canal, or grades the railroad, he contributes to cheapen and to accelerate the transit of those commodities, in which the capitalist deals, thus enabling him to extend his operations, and to increase his profits. And these are but examples. Take any two men, however remote from each other, within the limits of the state or of the Union, and no matter how dissimilar their pursuits, nor how unequal their apparent positions, they are still, if engaged in lawful callings, partners,—co-operating for their mutual benefit, and for the common benefit of all their associates, or, in other words, of all their fellow-citizens. Is it not, then, a matter of unspeakable importance, that each one should be qualified to perform his part, in the most efficient and useful manner?

After what we have advanced in previous sections, and especially in the last, it can hardly be necessary to insist that *education* does contribute most powerfully to render men more efficient both as *producers* and *preservers* of property. If properly conducted, it renders them, in the first place, more *trustworthy*, and thus multiplies the ways, in which they can be employed with profit to themselves, and with advantage to the community. In the *second* place, a labourer, whose mind has been disciplined by culture, works more steadily and cheerfully, and, therefore, more productively, than one who, when a child, was left to grovel in ignorance and idleness. In the *third* place, such a labourer, having both knowledge and habitual activity of mind, is fruitful in expedients to render his exertions more diversified and profitable* And while, in these several ways, education contributes to swell the aggregate of values, pro-

---

* Since I wrote this chapter, I have read, with great interest, the last report of the Hon. Mr. Mann, as secretary of the Massachusetts Board of Education. During the last year he directed his attention to the relative productiveness of the labour of the uneducated, and of those who have had the advantages of a good commonschool education; and he gives the following as the substance of

duced in a community in any given time; it also secures, in the *fourth* place,* that these values, instead of being

the answers which he has obtained from a number of the most intelligent manufacturers and business men of New-England. "The result of the investigation is a most astonishing superiority in productive power on the part of the educated over the uneducated labourer. *The hand is found to be another hand when guided by an intelligent mind.* Processes are performed, not only more rapidly, but better, when faculties which have been cultivated in early life furnish their assistance. Individuals who, without the aid of knowledge, would have been condemned to perpetual inferiority of condition, and subjected to all the evils of want and poverty, rise to competence and independence by the uplifting power of education. In great establishments, and among large bodies of labouring men, where all services are rated according to their pecuniary value; where there are no extrinsic circumstances to bind a man down to a fixed condition, after he has shown a capacity to rise above it; where, indeed, men pass by each other, ascending or descending, in their grades of labour, just as easily and certainly as particles of water of different degrees of temperature glide by each other, there is it found as an almost invariable fact, other things being equal, that those who have been blessed with a good common-school education rise to a higher and higher point in the kinds of labour performed, and also in the rate of wages paid, while the ignorant sink, like dregs, and are always found at the bottom."

*" From the accounts which pass through my hands," says M. Escher, " I invariably find that the best educated of our work-people manage to live in the most respectable manner at the least expense, or make their money go the farthest in obtaining comforts. This applies equally to the work-people of all nations that have come under my observations; the Saxons, and the Dutch, and the Swiss, being, however, decidedly the most saving, without stinting themselves in their comforts or failing in general respectability. With regard to the English, I may say, that the educated workmen are the only ones who save money out of their very large wages. By education, I may say, that I, throughout, mean not merely instruction in the art of reading, writing, and arithmetic, but better general mental development; the acquisition of better tastes, of mental amusements and enjoyments, which are cheaper, while they are more refined. The most educated of our British workmen is a

wasted through improvidence and vice, shall be employed as instruments of reproduction, and thus become permanent sources of welfare and happiness. Nor ought we to omit, in this brief enumeration of the *material* advantages of education to society, that it tends both to *multiply* and to *refine* our artificial wants; thus stimulating us, on one hand, to greater exertion in order to satisfy these wants, and shielding us, on the other, from those coarse temptations which tend to make men idlers and sots.

Here is a truth which seems all but self-evident, and yet it is one, grievously neglected in the speculations of political economists, and in the measures of practical statesmen. Writers on Political Economy dwell much, on the importance of enlisting science in the service of industry; but it is science confined for the most part to physics, and to be studied by the proprietor or superintendent, rather than by the operative. So statesmen, especially in older countries, bestow much time, and invent many fruitless expedients, in order to improve the condition of the working classes, at the very time that the intellectual and moral condition of those classes renders improvement next to impossible.

Scotch engineer, a single man, who has a salary of 3*l.* a week, or 150*l.* a year, of which he spends about the half; he lives in very respectable lodgings; he is always well-dressed; he frequents reading-rooms; he subscribes to a circulating library; purchases mathematical instruments, studies German, and has every rational enjoyment. We have an English workman, a single man, of the same standing, and who has the same wages, also a very orderly and sober person; but, *as his education does not open to him the resources of mental enjoyment, he spends his evenings and Sundays in wine-houses,* because he cannot find other sources of amusement which presuppose a better education, and *he spends his whole pay, or one half more than the other. The extra expenditure of the workman of lower condition, of 75l. a year, arises entirely, as far as I can judge, from the inferior arrangement, and the comparatively higher cost of the more sensual enjoyment in the wine-house."* — *Report of Poor-Law Commissioners.*

In all these matters we must begin at the **beginning.** We must remember, that *mind* forms the chief prerogative of man, and that he can never exercise his proper or most useful agency in any capacity, however humble, unless that mind be cultivated by discipline and enlightened by knowledge. England has neglected the education of her labouring population, and the consequence is, that the land swarms with paupers and vagabonds; New-England, on the contrary, from the first, made the intellectual and moral instruction of every child a sacred duty, incumbent both on his parents and on the commonwealth; and what was the result? "The first years of the residence of the Puritans in America," says Bancroft, "were years of great hardship and affliction; yet it is an error to suppose that this short season of distress was not promptly followed by abundance and happiness. The people were, from the first, industrious, enterprising, and frugal, and affluence followed, of course. When persecution ceased in England, there were already in New-England 'thousands who would not change their place for any other in the world,' and they were tempted in vain with invitations to the Bahama Isles, to Ireland, to Jamaica, to Trinidad." "One might dwell there from year to year, and not see a drunkard, or hear an oath, or meet a beggar.* The consequence was universal health, one of the chief elements of public happiness. The average duration of life in New-England, compared with Europe, was nearly doubled; and the human race was so vigorous, that of all who were born into the world, more than two in ten, full four in nineteen, attained the age of seventy; of those who lived beyond ninety, the proportion, as compared with European tables of longevity, was still more remarkable."—*See* BANCROFT, vol. i., p. 467.

In order to appreciate these *material* and *economical* advantages, which education confers on society, we may insti-

---

* New-England's First Fruits, printed 1643.

tute various other comparisons. We may, for instance, compare New-England, with her free-schools and her universal education, moving steadily and rapidly forward in wealth and population, in spite of a steril soil and an ungenial climate, and while destitute of all natural channels for inland commerce—we may compare her, thus physically crippled, with other portions of our Republic to which nature has been more bountiful, but on which the light of general education has not shined,—and we shall at once perceive that such education is unspeakably more important than a luxuriant soil, fine climate, or noble rivers.

So, if we compare the largest manufacturing town of England (Manchester) with that which holds a corresponding place in our own country (Lowell): in Manchester, full *one third* of all the children between the ages of five and fifteen receive no instruction at all in schools, while a large portion of the remaining two thirds attend schools of the most wretched description.* In Lowell, schools of a high char-

---

* See Reports of the Statistical Society of Manchester on the State of Education. Also vol. i. of the Publications of the Central Society of Education, p. 292, &c.

The following extracts will show the condition of many of them. "Under the head of dame-schools are included all those in which reading and a little sewing are taught. This is the most numerous class of schools, and they are generally in a most deplorable condition. The greater part of them are kept by females, but some by old men, whose only qualification for this employment seems to be their unfitness for any other. Neither parents nor teachers seem to consider instruction as the principal object in sending the children to these schools; they seem to regard them as asylums for mischievous and troublesome children."—" These schools are generally found in very dirty, unwholesome rooms, frequently in close, damp cellars, or old, dilapidated garrets."—" More than one half of them are used as dwelling, dormitory, and schoolroom, accommodating, in many cases, families of seven or eight persons. Above forty of them are in cellars."—" Very few of the teachers of dame-schools allow the duties which they owe to their scholars to interacter, supported at the public expense, and under the supervision of gentlemen of the first respectability, are open to all. Not only are parents anxious to send their children to these schools, but they are constantly urged to do it by the proprietors themselves, who are convinced that they gain more by having their operatives educated than they can lose by having them absent from the mills, when children, during a portion of each year.

The results of these opposite systems are such as we might anticipate. The operatives of Manchester are improvident and immoral; they are at war with their employers;* and multitudes of them are on the verge of beggary. The consequence is, that they consume almost as rapidly as they produce. In Lowell, on the other hand, "The factory operatives," to use the language of a late English traveller,† " form a community that commands the respect of the neighbourhood, and of all under whose observation they come. A

---

fere with their household occupations." Very few of these schools were found to possess more than fragments of books; and, in many cases, *no books were to be seen, the children depending for their instruction on the chance of some one of them bringing a book, or a part of one, from home.*

* " I have uniformly found," says H. Bartlett, Esq., of Lowell, " the better educated, as a class, possessing a higher and better state of morals, more orderly and respectful in their deportment, and more ready to comply with the wholesome and necessary regulations of an establishment. And in times of agitation, on account of some change in regulations or wages, I have always looked to the most intelligent, best educated, and the most moral for support, and have seldom been disappointed. For, while they are the last to submit to imposition, they *reason*, and if your requirements are reasonable, they will generally acquiesce, and exert a salutary influence upon their associates. But the ignorant and uneducated I have generally found the most turbulent and troublesome, acting under the impulse of excited passion and jealousy."—*See Report of the Secretary of the Massachusetts Board of Education for* 1841.

† A Visit to the United States in 1841, by Joseph Sturge.

considerable number of the girls are farmers' daughters, and come hither from the distant states of Vermont and New-Hampshire, &c., to work for two, three, or four years, when they return to their native hills, dowered with a little capital of their own earnings. No female of an immoral character could remain a week in any of the mills. The superintendent of the Boott Corporation told me that, during the five and a half years of his superintendence of that factory, employing about nine hundred and fifty young women, he had known of but one case of an illegitimate birth—and the mother was an Irish 'immigrant.' Any male or female employed, who was known to be in a state of inebriety, would be at once dismissed."

We cannot be surprised to hear that such a community is eminently prosperous. " The average wages, clear of board, amount to about two dollars a week.* Many an aged father or mother, in the country, is made happy and comfortable by the self-sacrificing contributions from their affectionate and dutiful daughter here. Many an old homestead has been cleared of its encumbrances, and thus saved to the

* The average of women's wages in the departments requiring the most skill is $2 50 per week, exclusive of board. The average of wages in the lowest department is $1 25. To show the influence which education has on the earnings of the female operative, one of the directors of the largest establishment at Springfield (J. K. Mills, Esq., of Boston) states that two thirds of those who are unable to write are employed *in the lowest department*, and that their wages are lower by 66 per cent. than the wages of an equal number of the better educated class. He also states it " as his belief, that the best cotton-mill in New-England, with such operatives as these, who are unable to write their names, would never yield the proprietor a profit; that the machinery would soon be worn out, and he would be left in a short time" with a population no better than one of sixty-three persons which they had imported from England, and which, being destitute of education, proved to be unable to earn sufficient to pay for their subsistence.—*See Report for* 1841 *of the Secretary of the Massachusetts Board of Education.*

family, by these liberal and honest earnings. Of the depositors in the Lowell Institution for Savings, nine hundred and seventy-eight (being about one half of the whole number of depositors) are factory girls, and the amount of their funds now in the bank is estimated, in round numbers, at one hundred thousand dollars, which is about one third of the whole amount on deposite. It is a common thing for one of these girls to have five hundred dollars in deposite, and the only reason why she does not exceed this sum is the fact that the institution pays no interest on any larger sum than this. After reaching this amount, she invests her remaining funds elsewhere."

I might easily multiply proofs of this kind; but I proceed to two most important *conclusions* which they seem to suggest, and which are worthy of deep consideration in this country. The *first* is, that *education affords the most certain and effectual means of developing the industrial resources of a country, and promoting its growth and prosperity*. Freedom is doubtless indispensable to the largest development even of wealth; but, unless it be combined with the diffusion of knowledge among the whole people, and with the refined tastes and orderly habits induced by education, it will often degenerate into vice and idleness, and will employ itself, now in wasting property, and now in obstructing the best means for increasing it. So, again, much may be accomplished by associations for the encouragement of manufactures and agriculture, and much, too, by legislation so directed as to foster native enterprise, and protect the labour of our own citizens against the overwhelming competition of foreigners. But these expedients are often transient and irregular in their action; and they also promote, too frequently, a spurious and premature growth in some branches of industry, to the neglect of others equally important. Render the people intelligent, frugal, and industrious, by means of education, and there need, then, be no fear. They will find means to protect themselves. They will be equally ready to apply individual effort, the power of associated action, and the influence of wise and well-digested laws. In order to encourage native talent and enterprise, and promote the amplest development of their resources, they will maintain all necessary restraints on freedom, but they will submit to none that are not necessary. What is yet more important, the inhabitants of each section of the country will be able to comprehend the capabilities of their own position, and will be impelled to make the most of them.*

* "It is a fact of universal notoriety, that the manufacturing population of England, as a class, work for half, or less than half, the wages of our own. The cost of machinery there, also, is but about half as much as the cost of the same articles with us; while our capital, when loaned, produces nearly double the rate of English interest. Yet, against these grand adverse circumstances, our manufacturers, with a small per centage of tariff, successfully compete with English capitalists in many branches of manufacturing business. No explanation can be given of this extraordinary fact, which does not take into account the difference of education between the operatives of the two countries." It follows, too, "as a most important and legitimate inference, that it is our wisest policy, as citizens—if, indeed, it be not a duty of self-preservation as men—to improve the education of our whole people, both in its quantity and quality. I have been told by one of our most careful and successful manufacturers, that *on substituting, in one of his cotton-mills, a better for a poorer class of operatives, he was enabled to add twelve per cent. to the speed of his machinery, without any increase of damage or danger from the acceleration.*"—*Report of H. Mann for* 1841.

To the same effect is the opinion of Mr. Bartlett, of Lowell, from whom I have already quoted. " From my own observation and experience," says he, " I am perfectly satisfied that the owners of manufacturing property have a deep pecuniary interest in the education and morals of their help; and I believe the time is not distant when the truth of this will appear more and more clear. And, as compe-

I would suggest here, whether, in addition to a good general education, it is not important, at this time, that our youth should receive some *special* instruction, in the theory and processes of the various useful arts. In other countries, great pains have been taken, for the last twenty years, to instruct young persons, intended for trades, in a knowledge of such branches of science and art, as are most nearly related to those trades; and also, to give them some acquaintance with general technology. Schools of arts and manufactures, agricultural seminaries, and institutions in which the children of the poor may be early trained to habits of industry, and to some skill in the rudiments of art, are now rapidly multiplying over Europe. On the Continent, in particular, they are much relied on, as among the most efficient means of developing and perfecting the arts of industry, and of thus enabling the several governments to compete successfully with the immense skill and capital which England has invested in these arts, and by means of which, in connexion with her restrictive policy in trade, she has made herself, until recently, the workshop of the world. The states of Europe are now fast emancipating themselves

tition becomes more close, and small circumstances of more importance in turning the scale in favour of one establishment over another, I believe it will be seen that the establishment, other things being equal, which has the best educated and the most moral help, will give the greatest production at the least cost per pound. So confident am I that production is affected by the intellectual and moral character of help, that, whenever a mill or a room should fail to give the proper amount of work, my first inquiry, after that respecting the condition of the machinery, would be, as to the *character of the help*; and if the deficiency remained any great length of time, I am sure I should find *many who had made their marks* on the pay-roll, being unable to write their names; and I should be greatly disappointed if I did not, upon inquiry, find a portion of them of irregular habits and suspicious character."

from this state of dependance, by cultivating their own resources; and in doing this, they place great reliance on the improved education of their people, and especially on such education as will develop the industrial skill and talent which are now required. Is it not of the utmost importance, that a similar policy should be pursued in our own country?

A *second* conclusion, forced upon us by the views which we have now taken, is, that *general education among a people forms the best preventive of pauperism.* This is a disease which, once ingrafted on the state, seems hardly to admit of remedy. It is the very cancer of the body politic, and tends to reproduce and perpetuate itself, in the most insidious and inveterate manner. The only wise or effectual expedient, then, is to anticipate, and prevent it. To ward off such indigence as results from mental imbecility, and from those sudden and fearful reverses which Providence sometimes sends to teach us our frailty, is, of course, impossible; but nearly nine tenths of all pauperism actually existing in any country may be traced directly to *moral* causes, such as *improvidence, idleness, intemperance,* and a *want of moderate energy and enterprise.* Now it is hardly necessary to add, that education, if it be imparted to all the rising generation, and be pervaded, also, by the right spirit, will remove these fruitful sources of indigence. It will make the young provident, industrious, temperate, and frugal; and with such virtues, aided by intelligence, they can hardly fail, in after life, to gain a comfortable support for themselves and their families. I have already (p. 102, *note*) quoted one fact which confirms this position, and others, not less impressive and convincing, would be found in every almshouse in the world. Could the paupers of our own state be collected into one group, it would be found, I doubt not, that *three* out of every *four,* if not *five* out of every *six,* owe their present humiliating position, to some defect or omission in their early training. I annex, in a note, one statement, which will show, how closely, pauperism and a defective education are related in England.*

* The committee of the Central Society has been favoured by a gentleman connected with the Poor-Law Commission, with returns exhibiting the state of education among paupers above the age of sixteen, the inmates of workhouses in the two incorporated hundreds and ten unions in the county of Suffolk; in the three incorporated hundreds and twelve unions in the county of Norfolk, and the twelve unions in the eastern division of Kent. The number of paupers included in these returns is 2725, viz., 1323 men and 1412 women, and the time when the information was collected was June, 1837.

Besides the distinction of sexes, the paupers are divided into three classes, viz., able-bodied, temporarily disabled, and old and infirm; and it is stated, with reference to each class, how many can read in a superior manner, how many can read decently, and how many imperfectly; their acquirements in regard to writing are also given with the same gradations; the number of paupers who can neither read nor write is next stated, and, lastly, the number of each class who had been the inmates of workhouses before the formation of the respective unions.

The difference observable in these various respects between the paupers of the different counties is not so great as to require their being separately noticed; and it will, therefore, be sufficient for the present purpose to present the result of the inquiry as though the whole were belonging to the same community.

	Men.			Women.			Total
	Able-bodied.	Temporarily disabled.	Old and Infirm.	Able-bodied.	Temporarily disabled.	Old and Infirm.	
Number of each class in workhouses	161	147	1015	508	196	698	2725
Number who can read superiorly	6	7	22	26	13	14	88
Number who can read decently	49	46	292	149	50	174	760
Number who can read imperfectly	14	21	125	106	33	99	398
Number who can write superiorly	1	2	4	4	2	1	14
Number who can write decently	21	39	167	43	13	44	327
Number who can write imperfectly	12	23	113	40	30	33	251
Number who can neither read nor write	86	62	544	211	95	404	1402
Number of inmates of workhouses before union	84	90	710	235	129	513	1761

It cannot fail to strike every one who sees these figures, how exceedingly small is the proportion of those persons who, having been so far instructed as to be able to read and write in a superior manner, are found to be inmates of the workhouse. Fluency in the art

II. If, again, we consider society as a *political* and *moral* partnership, intended to protect its members in the enjoyment of their rights, and to enlarge their means of happiness and improvement we shall find education equally useful. Though its ostensible object should only be to improve the intellect, it will still be apt to operate benignly on the moral sentiments and habits, and will tend to make its subjects better men and better citizens. By its lessons and tasks it tends to substitute reflection and deliberative effort in place of mere impulse. By its discipline it contributes, insensibly, to generate a spirit of subordination to lawful authority, a power of self-control, and a habit of postponing present indulgence to a greater future good; and, finally, by the knowledge which it communicates, it enlarges a child's conceptions of his true interests, and teaches him that forecast, self-restraint, and a correct moral deportment are indispensable prerequisites to success in life. The same effects must follow, in a much higher degree, when intellectual instruction has been combined with proper moral culture. We never expect, in such cases, that men will employ the power which education has given them, in injuring their country by violence or by more insidious means; we expect to find them obedient to the laws, careful of the public welfare, judicious and exemplary in the management of their families, and upright and respectable in all their deportment. If they live under a popular form of government, where they choose their own magistrates, and have a controlling voice in legislation, we expect to find

---

of reading, unaccompanied by proficiency in writing, affords no proof of adequate instruction. It would be more correct to say, that the absence of the latter acquirement is in itself evidence of the uncultivated condition of the mind. It will be seen that among the 2725 paupers, included in the foregoing statement, only fourteen, or one in 195, could write well; and that if we add to the 1402 persons who can neither read nor write those who can read only imperfectly, they make up just two thirds.

them distinguished for enlightened attachment to their country, and for the sagacity and honesty with which they exercise their political powers.

"It has been observed," says a judicious writer,* " that if the French had been an educated people, many of the atrocities of their revolution would never have happened; and I believe it. Furious mobs are composed, not of enlightened, but of unenlightened men; of men in whom the passions are dominant over the judgment, because the judgment has not been exercised, and informed, and habituated to direct the conduct. A factious declaimer can much less easily influence a number of men who acquire at schools the rudiments of knowledge, and who have subsequently devoted their leisure to a Mechanics' Institute, than a multitude who cannot read or write, and who have never practised reasoning and considerate thought. And as the education of a people prevents political evils, it effects political good. Domestic rulers well know, that knowledge is inimical to their power. This simple fact is a sufficient reason to a good and wise man to approve knowledge and extend it. The attention to public institutions and public measures which is inseparable from an educated population, is a great good. We well know, that the human heart is such, that the possession of power is commonly attended with a desire to increase it, even in opposition to the general weal. It is acknowledged that a check is needed, and no check is either so efficient or so safe, as that of a watchful and intelligent public mind: so watchful that it is prompt to discover and expose what is amiss; so intelligent that it is able to form rational judgments respecting the nature and the means of amendment.† In all public institutions there exists, and it is happy

---

* Dymond: see Essays on the Principles of Morals, Ess. ii., chap. xiii.

† A striking example of this powerful and salutary restraint on arbitrary power is thus noticed by a late traveller: "The victory of

that there does exist, a sort of vis inertiæ which habitually resists change. This, which is beneficial as a general tendency, is often injurious from its excess. The state of public institutions, almost throughout the world, bears sufficient testimony to the truth, that they need alteration and amendment faster than they receive it; that the internal resistance to change is greater than is good for man. Unhappily, the ordinary way in which a people have endeavoured to amend their institutions, has been by some mode of violence. If you ask when a nation acquired a greater degree of freedom, you are referred to some era of revolution, and probably of blood. These are not proper—certainly they are not Christian remedies for the disease. It is becoming an undisputed proposition, that no bad institution can permanently stand

intellect over the trammels of aristocracy has been powerfully exemplified within the space of sixty years, in the Protestant states of Germany. Constitutional governments they may not have secured; forms of liberty they still want; but the lethargy and servitude of mind which the olden dynasties had so rigorously cherished, have passed away through the one opening left to the freedom of the German people. They were permitted to read, and they had men to write. Imposts, oppressions, and the whole train of feudal bequests have fled, one by one, before the minds emancipated and moulded by the newborn literature of the present century. The people have possessed themselves of the records of their ancient glory and independence. Müller, Goëthe, and Schiller revived and immortalized the faded memory of foregone greatness, and gave imperishable impulse to worthier and yet more fruitful influences. The press of Germany has achieved the freedom of more than was ever enslaved. The Prussian government, a nominal oligarchy, is among the most essentially popular of all the governments of Europe. The people do not elect their representatives, but the government, nevertheless, faithfully represents the people. They have, therefore, the substance without the outward form of freedom. This must not be attributed to any virtue inherent in irresponsible power. It is because the power of the Prussian government is responsible to an educated opinion, an opinion of which it too thoroughly partakes not to regard."—*London Athenæum*, No. 746, p. 148.

against the distinct opinion of a people. This opinion is likely to be universal, and to be intelligent only among an enlightened community."

If this is everywhere true, it must be pre-eminently so, in a republic. In this country it has become almost a truism, that general education is indispensable, in order to qualify our people, for the discharge of their political and social duties. The vast responsibilities with which they are charged, are not to be duly met by means of any *instincts*, however powerful or generous. God has not given to man, as to the beasts of the field, blind but unerring impulses, which supersede all vigilance and painful effort, and which conduct him by a path, never to be mistaken, to his true destiny. The people of this great Republic, have no more a native and inherent ability to exercise wisely the privilege of voting, than they have to predict without instruction, and yet with unfailing precision, the return of a comet, or the occultation of some bright star in the heavens. All these are powers to be unfolded and enlightened by culture; and the culture which qualifies a free people for their political duties must be generous and comprehensive, including the moral as well as the intellectual faculties, and aiming to make *good citizens* by first making *good and enlightened men*. It must be a culture which, though commenced at school and under the guidance of others, shall be subsequently prosecuted by the individual himself, and carried forward amid the cares of active life; and which, if it would fulfil completely its high purposes, must never count itself to have apprehended. Wo to the people with democratic institutions who shall forget or underrate this momentous truth.*

---

* A late eloquent writer on Education in France (Girardin) has touched upon this truth with force: "The best institutions," says he, "where the education of the people is not sufficiently profound and general to develop their principles, are only elements of disturbance cast into the bosom of society; for they create wants which

Already, to the provident and reflecting mind, does Ichabod seem inscribed on that land which forgets its own weakness, and which does not, with prayer to the God of nations, couple general and generous efforts to cultivate mind, and to uphold in its midst the interests of truth and virtue. When such a land allows itself to be lulled to sleep by the siren song that the people cannot err, and that they have only to be left without restraint or guidance, in order to develop the greatest perfection of the social state—when this, the cant of demagogues, becomes the real creed of the people themselves, in their homes and their hearts, is it presumptuous to say that such a nation, so deceived and betrayed, must soon, however bright with promise now, be numbered among the *republics that have been;* that its name, at no distant day will be quoted only as a beacon, by the prejudiced to warn against all free institutions, and by the wise to prove the folly and peril of such institutions —when not based on intelligence and virtue.*

they cannot satisfy they are lavish of rights and duties; they weaken governments, which, by the multiplication of laws, render their execution impossible; they concentre to excess in a few ardent minds those ideas which ought to be imperceptibly absorbed by the whole population. These ideas ferment and explode for want of vent. It is thus that institutions which produce more *power* than they can usually employ, perish by the excess of that which it becomes necessary to compress.—The instruction of the people endangers absolute governments; their ignorance, on the contrary, imperils representative governments; for the parliamentary debates, while they reveal to the masses the extent of their rights, do not wait till they can exercise them with discernment; and when a people knows its rights, there is but one way to govern—to educate them."

* One of the most striking proofs of the aid and support afforded to republican institutions by a good system of popular education, is presented by the democratic cantons of Switzerland. The condition of the people is described by tourists as one of great social comfort, great equality of condition, and, under all their peculiarities of

The power of education is never displayed more strikingly, than when it enters some community which has been hitherto deprived of it. Dr. Johnson has somewhere no-

soil and climate, as one of singular prosperity. They seem to live like one great family rather than in the distinct relations of classes, demarcated and distanced by degrees of wealth and rank. "This intermixture of classes, however," says a traveller, "is wonderfully divested of the offensive familiarities *which would infallibly arise from it in less educated countries.* Deferential respect is paid, perhaps, rather to age and moral station than to mere affluence; but I have seldom witnessed any departure, from a tone and manner of affectionate courtesy, on the part of the poorer towards the higher classes. This may, however, be mainly attributable to the habitual and kindly consideration, shown to the working classes, by their superiors. Whether this results from a higher religious sense of the duty of doing to others as we would be done by; whether from natural kind-heartedness, or whether from a knowledge of the power possessed by each man, merely as a man, in a country where they assemble round the fountain in the market-place, and select their law-makers after their own free choice and judgment, I know not; but, be it from love or be it from fear, certain is it that a kindly feeling is evinced by employers to the employed in Northern Switzerland, of which few other countries afford an example."

After referring to the rapidity with which, owing to their general intelligence, this people overcame their deep repugnance to the introduction of cotton-mills and machine power, the same writer proceeds to account for their happy social condition. "Switzerland is clearly indebted to the highly-educated, or, to speak more correctly, to the extensively-educated mind of her people, for her singular prosperity and advancement. Brilliant talents, or any eminent powers of intellect, are very rarely found among the Swiss; but for sound good sense, and general proficiency in the commoner branches of education, I do not think that there is a people equal to them. A family in one of the villages I visited in the canton of Zurich was pointed out to me as unusually disreputable, and I was cautioned not to take anything I saw there as a sample of the rest. One of the heaviest charges made against the conduct of the master was, that he had been repeatedly warned by the gemeindamman to send two of his children to school, who were turned of eight years old; that he had proved so refractory that at length the stadtholder had been

ticed the reformation of a parish in a very savage state, by the civilizing influence of a decayed gentlewoman, who informed of his conduct, and it was only when he found he was about to be fined that he complied with the law."

The effect of an improved and extended education on the inhabitants of Prussia is thus stated by Mr. Wyse, after a tour of personal inspection in that country: "What is the real social result of all this? How has it affected the population for good or ill? How is it likely to affect them in future? The narratives given by Pestalozzi, De Fellenberg, Oberlin, and the Père Girard, of the singular revolution, mental and moral, I may also add, physical, effected by the application of their system of teaching on a hitherto ignorant and vicious population, though admitted to be isolated experiments, ought not the less to be considered evidences of the intrinsic force of the instrument itself, and of its power to produce similar results, wherever and whenever fairly tried, without reference to country or numbers; that is, whenever applied with the same earnestness, honesty, and skill in other instances as in theirs. And of this portion of Prussia—of the Rhenish provinces—it may be surely averred, that it has now been for some time under the influence of this system, and that during that period, whether resulting from such influence or not, its progress in intelligence, industry, and morality, in the chief elements of virtue and happiness, has been steadily and strikingly progressive. In few parts of the civilized world is there more marked exemption from all crimes of violence." "The same abstinence from offences against property is conspicuous." "Doubtless much of this most gratifying result may be ascribed to comfort and employment. But this, again, must be ascribed to some still higher cause. There is comfort, because there is frugality; there is employment, because there is the desire, and search, and love of it. There is industry, incessant, universal, in every class, from high to low, because there are the early habits of useful occupation, and there are these habits because there is sound and general education." "The clergyman admitted that his flock had not become worse Christians for becoming more intelligent men; the officer, that his men had grown more obedient as they had grown more instructed: a word now led where a cane formerly was insufficient; the farmer for the increased profits of his farm, as the manufacturer for those of his factory, thanked the school. Skill had increased, and conduct had improved with knowledge—profits with

came among them to teach school. It was a subject worthy of his pen. The world has recently witnessed a similar transformation, effected, in part, through the same means, by the Pastor Oberlin, on the Mountains of Alsace. Nothing could exceed the poverty, ignorance, and wretchedness which prevailed among the peasants who composed his parish. The state of education in the principal village may be inferred from the character of their only schoolmaster. Oberlin's predecessor (M. Stouber), a man of like spirit, began his efforts to improve the parish by inquiring into the state of instruction. Asking for the school, he was conducted to a miserable hovel, where there were a number of children crowded together, without occupation, and in so wild and noisy a state, that it was with some difficulty he could gain a reply to his inquiries for the master. "There he is," said one of them, as soon as silence could be obtained, pointing to a withered old man, who lay on a little bed in one corner of the apartment. "Are you the schoolmaster, my good friend?" inquired Stouber. "Yes, sir." "And what do you teach the children?" "Nothing, sir." "Nothing! How is that?" "Because," replied the old man, with characteristic simplicity, "I know nothing myself." "Why, then, were you instituted schoolmaster?" "Why, sir, I had been taking care of the Waldbach pigs for a great

both. Even household management had reaped its advantage when the first vanity and presumption arising out of the partial nature of instruction had worn off—when it had become general, sound, and appropriate; the servant, especially the female servant, was not less faithful, and had become far more useful than before." It may not be improper to add, that the education of Prussia fits its subjects for the government under which they live, but wants that spirit of freedom and self-reliance which would qualify them for a government like ours. The depreciating accounts which some recent travellers, such as Laing, have given of the state of morals in Prussia, is declared, by those who have had the best opportunities and the strongest disposition to judge impartially, to be without foundation.

number of years, and when I got too old and infirm for that employment, they sent me here to take care of the children!"

Under the superintendence of these wise and faithful men, good schools were established; a liberal course of instruction was instituted; religious influence was carefully and constantly applied; and the industry and enterprise of the inhabitants fostered by the presence, counsel, and example of their pastor. The results were delightful, and, to most persons, amazing. In spite of all the physical disadvantages of their position, they became prosperous. Their manners were refined, their tastes elevated, population rapidly increased, concord reigned among them, and they were alike intelligent and contented. Now the results produced in this humble district, by a wise system of education, have always followed, in other places, just in proportion as such a system has been introduced. Take the countries, in which the instruction of the people has made most progress during the last century, and it will be found that they are the very countries, in which the social and political condition of the inhabitants has most improved. The average length of human life has materially increased; there has been a great advance in the wealth and comfort of all classes; while, at the same time, crime, mendicity, riots, and political tumults have greatly diminished. Indeed, so powerful is education, as a means of national improvement, that, to borrow the language of a late writer, who has made an extended survey, of the relative state of instruction and social welfare, in the leading nations of the world, "*if the different countries of the world be arranged according to the state of education, they will also be found to be arranged, with few exceptions, according to wealth, morals, and general happiness:* and not only does this rule hold good, as respects a country taken as a whole, but it will generally apply to the different parts of the same country. Thus, in England, education is in the best state in the northern agricultural district, and in the worst state in the southern agricultural district, and the agricultural parts of the midland district; while in the great towns and other manufacturing places, education is in an intermediate state; *at the same time, the condition of the people, and the extent of crime and violence among them, follow a like order.*"*

I cannot refrain from placing on record one fact, as a farther confirmation of the latter part of this statement. It is derived from a chart, published a few years since in England, by Joseph Bentley, which professes to exhibit the moral condition, of the different counties of England, as compared with their means of education. In parallel columns, are placed the population, number of schools, number of libraries, number of literary and scientific institutions, number of places for the sale of intoxicating liquors, and, lastly, the number of criminal convictions within the year. I am well aware that the number of schools in a country is not a certain criterion of the proportion of the children under instruction, nor of the degree and quality of such instruction. Still, it affords an approximation to the real state of education, and the best returns on this subject, considered as tests, are but approximations. The result to which I have referred, as gathered from these returns, is most striking; it is this: *If you take the four best instructed counties of England, as exhibited on this chart, and also the four worst instructed, it will be found that the average amount of crime is almost exactly in the* INVERSE *ratio of the average amount of instruction.*†

* See National Education, its Present State and Prospects, by Fred. Hill, in 2 vols., London, 1836.

† The *four best instructed counties in England*, according to this table, are:

	Inhabitants.		Inhabitants.
Rutland, having 1 school to every	625,	and 1 crim'l. conviction per ann. to every	718
Westminster, " "	696,	" " "	2201
Cumberland, " "	736,	" " "	1101
Middlesex, " "	747,	" " "	415

But, it may be asked, what charm is there about reading and writing, that these should forthwith banish the propensities to crime and vice? "I am simple enough," says a late writer, "to believe that a man may be utterly ignorant of A B C, and yet be not given to cutting throats; and wholly unskilled in the art of penmanship, and still have no bias in favour of burglary. Nay, it is my deliberate opinion—mad as it may appear in these days of societies for the diffusion of horn-books and propagation of primers—that Mavor is no preventive to murder, nor Vyse any corrective of vice. And I cannot, by any course of reasoning, bring myself to perceive that an inability to read must be generally accompanied with a like inability to distinguish between right and wrong, as if the question of *meum* and *tuum* had more to do with Lindley Murray than morals."*

Or an average of

One school to every 701 inhabitants, and one criminal conviction to 1108 inhabitants.

The four *worst instructed* counties are:

			Inhabitants.				Inhabitants.
Northampton,	1 school	to every	1757,	and 1 crim'l. conviction per ann.	to every	601
Dorset,	"	"	1435,	"	"	"	610
Somerset,	"	"	1427,	"	"	"	393
Hereford,	"	"	1386,	"	"	"	596

Or an average of

One school to every 1501 inhabitants, and one criminal conviction to 550 inhabitants.

* This passage is extracted from a work recently published in England, entitled, *What to Teach, and how to Teach it so that the Child may become a wise and good Man.* By HENRY MAYHEW. Part I.—THE CULTIVATION OF THE INTELLECT. It contains many valuable suggestions in regard to the nature and end of education, stated, however, with somewhat too much of flippancy, and with an unnecessary parade of metaphysical learning. In his zeal to correct the prevalent error of putting reading and writing in place of real education, the author gravely proposes that we should first teach the pupil science, and then, as the last step, "add a *knowledge of reading*, so that he may be able to trace the history and progress of it, which is extremely curious and interesting; and *of writing*, so that he may be able (should he have it in his power, by any new discovery, to increase the general knowledge) to give that discovery to the world. We must recollect that, educationally, writing is the means of educating those who are absent and future; reading, the

It seems hardly necessary to say, that these remarks are entirely irrelevant to the point now under discussion. We have insisted, throughout this volume, that we mean by education much more than the ability to read and write. We mean something, by which the pupil shall be taught to respect both himself and others; to find pleasure in the cultivation of his intellectual powers, and to act habitually upon the impulse of his higher sentiments. Why, then, it may be urged, do you insist so much, in your reasoning and statistical surveys, upon the proportion of criminals, &c., who are unable to read and write? I answer, because, in treating of the state of education in a country, we must fix upon some index or exponent. Nothing is more indefinite than the term education, nor than the thing signified by that term. It is to be presumed, however, in the present state of the world, when the means of education are so abundant, and when they are so easy of access even to the very poor, that children who have not been taught so much as to read and write, have been neglected in other respects. Such children will be found, in a large proportion of instances, to have been trained to no regular occupation nor to any habits of industry, and to have grown up, in truth, without instruction of any kind. In referring, then, so constantly to reading and writing, we use them merely as *signs*, not as causes, and as negative rather than as positive signs. In other words, while we regard ignorance, of these simplest elements of knowledge, as proof that the education of the child has been greatly neglected, we do not regard a knowledge of them, as proof that that education has been properly cared for.* In the ab-

means of being educated by those who are absent and past; *and speaking, the means of educating those who are present!!"*

* It is evident, however, that comparisons made on this principle bear unjustly against education, or, rather, do not bear with sufficient force in its favour; since they rank, as educated, many, who, though they can read and write, are yet destitute of the appropriate fruits of a sound and thorough education.

sence of any other criterion, more definite and tangible, we take the best which offers itself; but we would always insist, most strenuously, upon the necessity of aiming, in education, at something vastly higher. It is of education, in this higher and more real sense, that we always speak throughout this work; we maintain that it is a controlling power in society; and we appeal to the fact that, in improving and extending the education of a people, we invariably improve their social condition, as proof that this power is benignant, as well as great.*

* "It is with grief," says M. Cousin, in his Report on the State of Education in Holland, "that I contemplate the mistaken zeal, the illogical reasoning of certain philanthropists, and even of certain governments, who bestow so much pains upon prisons, and neglect schools: they allow crime to spring up, and vicious habits to take root, by the utter neglect of all moral training, and of all education in children; and when crime is grown, and is strong and full of life, they attempt to cope with it; they try to subdue it with the terror of punishment, or to mitigate it, in some degree, by gentleness and kindness. After having exhausted all their resources both of thought and of money, they are astonished to find that their efforts are vain; and why? because all they do is in direct opposition to common sense. To correct is very important, but to prevent is far more so. The seeds of morality and piety must be early sown in the heart of the child, in order that they may be found again, and be made to shoot forth in the breast of the man whom adverse circumstances may have brought under the avenging hand of the law. To educate the people, is the necessary foundation of all good prison discipline. It is not the purpose of a penitentiary to change monsters into men, but to revive, in the breasts of those who have gone astray, the principles which were taught and inculcated to them in their youth, and which they acknowledged and carried into practice in former days, in schools of their infancy, before passion, and wretchedness, and bad example, and the evil chances of life, had hurried them away from the paths of rectitude. To correct, we must excite remorse and awaken the voice of conscience; but how can we recall a sound that has never been heard? How are we to revive a language that had never been taught? I approve of, nay, I bless with my whole heart, every kind of penitentiary; but I consider

It is alleged, however, that, notwithstanding the progress of education, crime and immorality increase. If the present be compared with any distant era of history, even the most brilliant, it will be found that the very reverse is true. In the reign of Elizabeth, for instance, of which Hume boasts that "learning had not then prostituted itself by becoming too common," England was covered with gipsies and banditti, and every year, there were from three to four hundred executions for capital crimes. In Scotland, before the parochial schools were established, and education made universal, two hundred thousand vagrants, according to Fletcher of Saltoun, roamed over the land, living by pillage and beggary, and having "no regard or subjection either to the laws of the land, or even to those of God and Nature." What a change has since been wrought! and who can doubt that, in producing it, education has been a most powerful, though certainly not the only cause? It is not to be forgotten, that the causes which affect social welfare are various, and hence crime may for awhile increase, and civilization decline, even though education does advance; not, however, because education is powerless, but because its influence is, for the time, overborne or counteracted by other agencies.

Is it a truth, however, that crime and immorality do increase? Let us consider this question for a moment with regard to our own state; and that we may limit the inquiry, let us speak only of crime in the technical or judicial sense. I remark, then,

First, That, so far as our own state is concerned, the returns of criminal convictions, annually made to the office of the secretary of state, show that the increase of crimes of

---

that they must forever remain almost fruitless, unless their power to reclaim is made to rest upon the effect of schools for the people universally established, attendance upon which is obligatory, and where instruction is considered as only one of the means of education."

every description, within the last ten years, is not greater than the increase of population, even on the supposition, by no means probable, that the returns were as full and complete, when first required, ten years since, as they are at present.*

Secondly, This increase of crime would have been much less, but for the unusual influx of foreigners within the last few years. Dr. Julius states, as the result of a laborious examination of all the principal prisons of the United States, that about *one third* of the convicts are foreigners. The returns of this state show that, with us, the proportion is even larger, being in some years nearly *one half*.

Thirdly, Before this increase of crime could, under any circumstances, be ascribed with plausibility to an increase of education, for this is gravely maintained by some persons, it would be necessary to show that those offences have multiplied fastest which, in their conception and preparation, require the greatest knowledge and forethought. The facts, however, are remarkably the reverse. In this state, as appears by a late annual report (for 1840) of the secretary of state on criminal convictions, the crimes of forgery, perjury, burglary, &c., which imply skill and knowledge, have been diminishing, while those which are the usual concomitants of ignorance and mental debasement have increased. To the same effect is the experience of other states. Says the chaplain of the Connecticut State Prison, in a late report, " that knowledge is not very frequently used as an instrument in the commission of crime, may be presumed from the fact that, of the 66 committed to this prison last year, the crimes of only four were of such

---

* It ought to be considered, also, that in proportion as the detection and punishment of offences is facilitated by an improved police, and by a better state of public morals, in that proportion criminal arrests and convictions may become more numerous, though crime itself is decreasing.

a nature as to require for their commission ability either to read or write." The directors of the Ohio Penitentiary state that " it is an erroneous impression that the convicts are intelligent, shrewd men, whose minds have been perverted to vice, rather than blunderers into low and vicious habits, and ultimately into the commission of crime, from idleness, ignorance, and opacity of mental vision. It will be seen that nearly the whole number of convicts are below mediocrity in point of information; and, indeed, our inquiries and observations have long since fully satisfied us that, not only in our own prison, but in others which we have visited or inquired after, depraved appetites and corrupt habits, which have led to the commission of crime, are usually found with the ignorant, uninformed, and duller part of mankind. Of the 276, nearly all below mediocritry, 175 are grossly ignorant, and in point of education scarcely capable of transacting the ordinary business of life." Is it not a question for grave reflection, how far society, after thus suffering individuals to grow up in ignorance and incapacity, retains, in respect to them, the right of inflicting punishment?*

Fourthly, To show, however, still more clearly that education, instead of being responsible for any portion of this increase of crime, is directly and greatly calculated to ar-

---

* It has been said, that, though ignorance and want of education are *concomitants* of crime, they are not the causes of it, but are only effects, conjointly with crime, of some other cause or causes, such as poverty. I reply that, though the proximate cause of some crimes is poverty, the ultimate cause, even in such cases, is generally the want of a good education. Poverty itself, as we have already shown, may, in most instances, be attributed, in this country, to a neglected or erroneous education; and, moreover, it is not true, that our criminals are generally from among the suffering poor. Their crimes have, in most cases, resulted from idleness and vice; and these, as all know, are the effect usually of bad training in childhood and youth.

rest it, I would place in juxtaposition, and ask attention to two facts, which seem to me alike conclusive and striking.

I. It appears by the late census, that there are but 43,000 white adults in this state, who are unable to read and write. If to this number, we add one half of the whole coloured population of the state as suffering from a like inability, and make a large allowance for children old enough to commit crime, yet without education, we shall get a total of about 83,000; i. e., about $\frac{1}{29}$th of the whole population of the state, who cannot read and write. If, then, education has no tendency to diminish crime, so that a person, after having enjoyed its advantages, is as likely to commit crime as the ignorant, we should expect, on examining the records of our courts and prisons, to find the same proportion between the instructed and uninstructed among the convicts, as among the whole population. In other words, we should expect to find 28 convicts able to read and write to every *one* unable to do so. Now what is the fact?

II. If we take the whole number of convictions in this state for the last two years, in courts of record and at special sessions, we find not 1 in 29 who is unable to read, but 1 in 2; showing that the tendency to crime among the ignorant is fourteen and a half times greater than it ought to be, on the supposition that education has no tendency to diminish crime. An examination of the Auburn prison, made something more than a year ago, gave, out of 244 prisoners, but 59 who could read well, and but 39 who could read and write.

In the New Penitentiary of Philadelphia, out of 217 prisoners received during the year 1835, but 85 could read and write, and most of these could do either the one or the other in but a very imperfect manner. Facts of this kind might be adduced to almost any extent. By showing that the proportion of uneducated convicts is much greater than that of uneducated inhabitants, they seem to me to *demonstrate* that ignorance is one of the great highways to crime, and that, in proportion as men are left without instruction, in that proportion they are likely to become convicts.

In dismissing this subject, I ought, perhaps, to refer to a statement, made a few years since by a distinguished French writer (M. Guerry), which seems to militate seriously against the views here taken, and which is frequently adduced, as proof that education is powerless in preventing, if it be not efficient in producing crime. It was alleged by M. Guerry, after an elaborate survey of the " moral statistics" of France, that there was more crime in the best instructed than in the worst instructed provinces of the kingdom. Admitting the fact to be as stated, and admitting, also, that education was the cause of this increase of crime, it must be obvious to every one bestowing a moment's reflection on the subject, that the true explanation is to be found in the absence, until recently, from French systems of instruction, of a moral and religious spirit.

It has been ascertained, however, on a more thorough examination, that it did not hold, as a general fact, that crime was more prevalent in the better instructed provinces; and, moreover, that, if such were the fact, it was susceptible of demonstration that education was not to be held responsible for it. From a paper read a few years since before the Statistical Society of London, by G. R. Porter, Esq., it appears that the conclusions of M. Guerry were based upon *the returns of a single year*, whereas five years taken in succession would furnish a result entirely different. The returns for the five years ending 1833 show, that the annual average number of criminals was nearly ten per cent. greater in the least instructed, than it was in the most instructed departments; and it so happens that the year (1831) taken by M. Guerry for examination, was the only one of the five, in which the excess of criminals was not arranged on the side of the least instructed departments. It is farther to be considered—and this, indeed, is the all-essential point—that an excess of crime, in the best instructed provinces in 1831, proves nothing against education, unless it can be shown, that the criminals themselves were educated. But it turns out, on examination, that $\frac{7}{8}$ths of the whole number were unable to read and write well, and that the *proportion of ignorant criminals, as compared with the whole number of uninstructed inhabitants*, was even greater in the more enlightened provinces than elsewhere. The reason for the latter fact probably is, that where education is pretty generally imparted, the wholly ignorant find themselves more embarrassed in obtaining employment, and hence are more likely to betake themselves to lawless courses.*

* It is usual now, in the criminal statistics of France and England, to divide the persons accused or convicted into four classes, as it respects their education. The 1st class is composed of those who are unable to read and write. 2. Able to read and write imperfectly. 3. Able to read and write well. 4. Superiorly instructed. In France, during seven years, the proportion borne by the well educated to the other three classes of the accused was, on an average, 227 to 9773. In Scotland and England, where the proportionate number of well-educated persons must be much greater than it is in France, the proportion of the accused of that character was (in 1836) considerably less. In Scotland it was but 188 to 9812, while in England it was no more than 91 to 9909. The following table is worthy of inspection:

	England and Wales.		Scotland.	
	No. accused.	Centesimal proportion.	No. accused.	Centesimal proportion.
Unable to read and write	7,033	33.52	539	18.45
Able to read and write imperfectly	10,983	52.33	1427	48.84
Able to read and write well	2,215	10.56	489	16.73
Superiorly instructed	191	0.91	55	1.88
Degree of instruction not ascertained	562	2.68	412	14.10
	20,984	100.00	2922	100.00

Of the 55 educated persons, accused in Scotland, 41 were convicted, viz.: 15 for common assaults, 15 for simple thefts, 2 for frauds, 3 for forgery, 1 for subornation of perjury, 2 for house breaking, 1 for a nameless offence, 2 for other slight offences. It is obvious that intemperance must have occasioned a large proportion of these

We have thus shown that education, even in its present state, though so imperfect, so wanting in a lofty moral aim, and so destitute of a truly intellectual spirit, still does much to diminish crime, and to promote the social well-being of communities and nations. How much more would this be the case, if all young persons enjoyed such training and instruction as might be bestowed, and such as we are bound to claim and struggle after in their behalf.

Throughout this and the preceding section, I have assumed that the education of a whole people is *practicable*. It would be worse than mockery, to unfold and dwell on the vast importance of the education of the masses, if it be a blessing beyond their reach, or beyond the reach of most of them. That a good *moral* and *industrial* training might be enjoyed by all, in a well-ordered state of society, will probably be admitted; but it is not so generally conceded, that we can bestow on all, *knowledge*, and the blessings of an active, cultivated mind. It must not be forgotten, says De Tocqueville, that a great majority, in every civilized country, must spend their lives in manual labour; and that, in their case, no high degree of culture can be expected. It seems to me, however, that this remark is founded on a great, though very prevalent misconception in regard to the nature and effects of manual labour. It was for ages supposed that its tendencrimes; for example, the assaults. The punishments awarded were as follows:

Tried and discharged	11
Imprisoned one month and under . . .	8
" above 1 and not exceeding 2 months	8
" " 3 " " 6 " .	5
" " 6 " " 12 " .	3
Outlawed	2
Transported for 7 years	1
" 14 years	1
" life	2
Total	41

cy and effect must be, to deaden and debase the powers of the soul. The rudeness and ignorance which abounded among the working-classes, and which ought to have been ascribed to the neglect or oppression of their superiors, were, by a strange perversion, attributed to their occupations; and this, too, in the face of the undeniable fact, that those classes were, over all Europe, forcing their way upward in the scale of intelligence and political power, in spite of the most strenuous and formidable opposition; and in face, too, of the fact, now so obvious, that they owed their increasing intelligence and consideration, in a great measure, to their industry. It has been assumed, also, that a labouring man has no time for mental culture, and that it is preposterous to expect, that reading and thinking beings can be made out of those whose lives are doomed to unceasing toil.

The answer to these objections is, *first*, that labour has no tendency, to debase and deaden the intellect. To think so, is to impeach the wisdom and goodness of that Being who has made labour our great duty. It is to overlook the fact, that no labour is so humble or so circumscribed, but that knowledge and mental culture will assist the workman to perform it cheerfully, and will also enable him to make it more productive to himself, and more useful to others. It is to forget, too, that no one is condemned by Providence to one dull round of toil; that it is the right and duty of every one to seek, if he be duly qualified, a less laborious or a more intellectual employment, and that it is education alone which can thus prepare him, to vary his condition. If the labouring population were educated, as thoroughly as their situation admits, and were made provident, we should no longer hear of multitudes being obliged to spend their whole lives in heading nails, or pointing pins. It is also worthy of consideration, that most kinds of manual labour require some degree of thought and intelligence, thus contributing to improve the mind; and that there are many moments, even when most busy, that the workman can devote his mind to reflection on the contents of the books he has read, or to those excursions of a healthy and well-regulated imagination, which tend to strengthen the understanding and to improve the heart.

But, *secondly*, is it true that a life of labour affords no *time* for reading and self-culture? I can hardly conceive of any occupation so incessant or toilsome that it would not afford two or three hours in a week, besides many " odd ends of time," to be appropriated to books and lectures. Add to these, the time which God has especially consecrated to the improvement of the mind in knowledge as well as virtue—*the Christian Sabbath*. Add, also, the opportunities for improving thought, and for instructive conversation, which the labourer has when at work,* and it becomes evident, that no inconsiderable part of the time of the most industrious may be spent in gaining knowledge and wisdom. It can be deemed no exaggeration, if we maintain that, in addition to days of sacred rest, which form one seventh part of life, there are other seasons of leisure which may be given to mental culture, sufficient to form,

---

* " Where workmen are employed in the same apartment, and there is nothing noisy in the work, one may always read while the others are employed. If there are twenty-four men together, this arrangement would only require each man to make one extra day in four weeks, supposing the reading to go on the whole day, which it would not; but a boy or a girl might be engaged to perform the task at an expense so trifling as not to be felt. This expedient, too, it may be observed, would save money as well as time; one copy of a book, and that borrowed for the purpose, or obtained from a reading society or circulating library, would suffice for a number of persons. I may add, that great help would be given by the better-informed and more apt learners to such as are slower of apprehension and more ignorant; and discussion (under proper regulations) would be of singular use to all, even the most forward proficients."
—LORD BROUGHAM.

with those days, a portion of life not less than one sixth, and in many cases, not less than one fourth of the whole. "I begin," says Lord Brougham, at the opening of a pamphlet, published several years since, on Popular Education, "by assuming that there is no class of the community so entirely occupied with labour as not to have an hour or two, every other day at least, to bestow upon the pleasure and improvement to be derived from reading, or so poor as not to have the means of contributing something towards purchasing this gratification; the enjoyment of which, besides the present amusement, is the surest way both to raise our character and better our condition."

CONCLUSION.

I have thus dwelt at great length upon the *nature*, *objects*, and *uses* of Education. It may be thought, that on these subjects, so protracted a discussion was unnecessary, since they are already well understood, and thoroughly appreciated, in this country. But is it so? Our people have absolute control over the whole subject of education, not only as it respects their own families, but, to a great extent, in schools and seminaries of learning. If, then, the people were fully awake, to its importance and true nature, we should soon have a perfect system, and we should witness results from it, for which we now look in vain.

Here, in truth, is the great desideratum. We all complain that our schools are defective, our teachers imperfectly qualified, and the training which our children receive, both at home and at school, wanting, in some of the first elements of a good education. Why is this? Why do not the people demand, and compel an immediate change? Why are so many instructers allowed to occupy places for which they are incompetent, and to return our children to us, after months, or even years, of attendance at school, without any generous improvement in mind or manners?

Why is it so difficult to gain a liberal and prompt support for efforts that are made to extend, and, above all, to perfect education? And why are these efforts, when they are sustained, so often leavened by a sordid spirit, or by a total misconception of what education ought to do for youth? Is it not because, as a people, we do not, after all, appreciate as we ought the inestimable importance of " a right virtuous and noble education?" Is it not because, we misapprehend the ends to be answered by it, as well as the best means for attaining those ends? How few of us look upon education, as that which is to rear our children to high mental and moral excellence, and inspire them with an ambition above this world; an ambition to perform, with unfailing and unfaltering fidelity, the humblest as well as the most exalted duties! How few of us rank such an education, higher in our esteem, than all worldly wealth or distinction, and feel that, in bestowing it, we give to our children the richest inheritance, the noblest and most enviable patrimony! How few apprehend, clearly, the uses to which a good education ought to be applied, or entertain views, sufficiently large and liberal, of the spirit of self-culture which it ought to inspire and cherish!

I cannot, in closing this chapter, do better, perhaps, than recapitulate the leading principles which I have developed, and ask the reader, as he reviews them, to inquire how far they have hitherto been appreciated, and acted upon by himself. Let him consider, that our efforts to train up our children in the way that they should go must be misdirected, and, therefore, be in part or wholly fruitless, unless we understand well the end and object of education. Let him consider, too, that errors on this subject are exceedingly prevalent, and that, even when they do not infect our own minds, they are very apt to reach and taint our children, and that special efforts are needed, not only to guard those children, but also to enlighten and correct public opinion, and thus to secure, in behalf of the real welfare of the rising generation, the talent and strength which are now wasted in efforts that are either idle or pernicious. Let him consider, finally, whether he is fully sensible, to what a vast and immeasurable extent, his own welfare, the happiness of his children, and the honour and interests of his country, are identified with the success of judicious efforts to improve our systems of training and instruction, and to make their influence coextensive with our land. If he cannot but feel, that on some of these subjects, his convictions have hitherto wanted clearness and force, he will then perceive the need there is, for a renewed and thorough discussion of those subjects, from time to time. I will not conceal my own settled conviction, that we shall never have the education we need in this country, till the people are roused to a more adequate sense of its importance, and have a clearer perception of its true nature, objects, and uses.

SUMMARY OF PRINCIPLES IN CHAP. I.

SEC. I. WHAT IS EDUCATION?

Education is the due development, of all the primitive powers, and susceptibilities of our nature.

It is peculiarly necessary in youth, because then this nature is most plastic, and impressions made upon it are most lasting.

It does not obliterate all original differences in character or inequalities in talent, but aims to modify and improve.

Its object, is rather to form a perfect character, than to qualify for any particular station or office.

Man needs it the more, because he has few instincts, and because he is endowed with unbounded capabilities of improvement.

Intellectual Education should aim, to make its **subject, a successful** learner, and teacher of truth.

Moral Education, to harmonize the contending **impulses** of our nature, and subject all to conscience and the **moral** law.

Æsthetical Education, to refine the taste, regulate and exalt the imagination, and render both subservient, to energy of action, and purity of purpose.

Physical Education, to perfect the delicacy of the senses, establish vigorous health, and form habits and impart knowledge calculated to preserve that health.

SEC IV.—IV. PREVAILING ERRORS IN REGARD TO EDUCATION.

To correct these, and form clear notions of the nature and end of education, is the first and most essential step towards improvement.

These errors are:

1. The notion, that education is comprehended in certain scholastic acquirements.

2. That it consists in knowledge.

3. Cultivating the intellect to the neglect of the heart, or the heart to the neglect of the intellect.

4. Overlooking the necessity of good example, and the power of bad.

5. Overlooking the proper culture of taste and imagination.

6. Disregarding the danger of a premature development of intellect, at the expense of health.

7. Forgetting, how manifold are the causes, which tend to form character, or give " heart to a nation."

8. Not adapting itself, sufficiently, to the different characters and circumstances of children, nor to peculiarities of age and sex.

9. Making a too free use of stimulants.

10. Not attaching sufficient importance, to **intellectual** and moral *character*, and too much to *success*.

11. In not having sufficient reference to the future pursuits and condition of children.

SEC. V. THE EDUCATION NEEDED BY THE AMERICAN PEOPLE.

1. *Moral* and *religious*, as a means of cultivating habits of self-control, and of obedience to lawful authority.

2. *Thorough intellectual culture*, in order to promote habits of inquiry, and of deliberating before we act; and also to render us more tolerant of opinions differing from our own.

3. *Industrial training*, as a security against the temptations of idleness, as affording useful discipline to the mind and feelings, as promoting habits of order and regularity, as favourable to health, and as a pledge of interest in the common welfare.

4. A *more elegant and humanizing culture*, as, 1. A security against sensual indulgence. 2. A resource in leisure. 3. An innocent and healthy source of enjoyment. 4. Improving manners. 5. Strengthening virtuous principles and feelings.

The education now bestowed on the mass of the American people does not answer this description.

SEC. VI. IMPORTANCE OF EDUCATION.

I. *To the Individual.*

Education of some kind is unavoidable. We must choose, therefore, between the casual education of circumstances, which is bad, and the formal tuition of teachers and parents, which may, and should be, good.

1. The uneducated are sensual, and, therefore, selfish and cruel.

2. They are the victims of groundless hopes and fears; therefore credulous, superstitious, and unhappy.

3. They are prejudiced; therefore averse to new truths, and unable to appreciate them.

4. They are deprived of the personal and domestic resources enjoyed by all who love books.

5. They do not enjoy the emotions even of surprise, wonder, or adoration, as highly as those, who inquire and reason.

6. They are unfitted for the more profitable and honourable employments of life.

7. They are less likely to be satisfied with their station in life, and with the labours and cares to which they are subjected.

SEC. VII. IMPORTANCE OF EDUCATION.

II. *To Society.*

Society is a partnership, and may be considered, first, as a *material* partnership; second, as a *political* and social one.

1. As a *material partnership*, engaged in producing and distributing wealth, it is benefited by education, because,

(*a*) Education makes men more industrious; (*b*) more trustworthy; (*c*) more active and systematic; (*d*) more cheerful; (*e*) more far-sighted; (*f*) more economical, as producers and preservers of property.

By neglecting these truths, England has suffered. By observing them, *New-England* has greatly prospered.

Cor. It follows: 1. That education affords the most certain means of developing the industrial resources of a country, and promoting its growth and prosperity. 2. That general education is the best preventive of pauperism.

2. As a *political and moral partnership*, society is benefited by education, because,

(*a*) It tends to make a people more orderly, and to substitute reflection for passion; (*b*) to predispose them to respect lawful authority; (*c*) to indispose them to submit to oppression; (*d*) to render political revolutions gradual and bloodless; (*e*) to qualify men for the exercise of more and more political power; (*f*) to make refinement and civilization universal.

Examples of the benignant social effects of general education are afforded, 1. By small communities, like the parish of Oberlin or the manufacturing town of Lowell (Mass.). 2. By states or nations, such as the states of New-England, the democratic cantons of Switzerland; Holland, Prussia, &c.

The influence of education in diminishing crime, is proved by many particular facts, and by the general result, that crimes decrease, usually, in proportion, as a good system of popular instruction becomes more prevalent.

This education, so important to individuals and to states, may be made attainable to *all*, even the most indigent and laborious; for,

1. Labour does not deaden the intellect, but tends rather to quicken and invigorate it.

2. The claims of labour are not inconsistent with leisure sufficient for mental culture.

There must be a deeper conviction, among the people, of the necessity and value of education, and a clearer perception of its nature and objects, before we can expect any great improvement.

CHAPTER II.

COMMON SCHOOLS.

SECTION I.

RELATION OF COMMON SCHOOLS TO OTHER MEANS OF EDUCATION.

"Mothers and schoolmasters plant the seeds of nearly all the good and evil which exist in our world. Its reformation must therefore be begun in nurseries and in schools."—Dr. Rush.

"At home, a boy can learn only what is taught him; but in school he can learn what is taught to others."—Quintilian.

"That education which will secure to the future, the civilization of the past and present, is what the country really requires."—Whewell.

I have hitherto spoken of the education of the people, without referring to the sources, from which they derive it. I now come to consider *Common Schools*, as forming one of the most important of these sources, and the one with which we are especially called to deal, in this work. In order to understand, more clearly, the precise agency which these schools exert, it will be proper, however, to notice some of the other causes, which contribute to form the mind of a people, and the relations, which these sustain to Common Schools.

Among these causes, some are *physical*, such as climate, soil, and geographical position; and these, while they exert great power over the character and history of nations, are not liable to be modified materially by education. On the other hand, *moral* causes, such as those of a political, religious, and literary nature, are subject to human control; and there is, between them and prevailing systems of education, action and reaction, of the most intimate and powerful kind.

The agencies, however, which share most immediately with Common Schools, in the office of moulding a nation's spirit and character are, 1. the family; 2. higher seminaries of learning; 3. the means of self-culture, provided in books, lyceums, &c. I propose, in this section, to confine my in quiries to the precise place which the Common School oc cupies in respect to each of these; and I shall endeavour to show that, while all of them are necessary in a complete system of national education, each one derives from the Common School essential aid and support, and, in its turn, affords corresponding aid and support to it.

I. What relation, then, in the first place, does *the Common School bear to the family*, as an instrument of education? It is, evidently, the intention of the Creator, that the first years of a child's life should be passed under the immediate eye of its parents, and especially under that of an affectionate and judicious mother. It needs, then, a tenderness and watchful care, which can be expected from no other source, and in the retirement of home it drinks in, from the lips and deportment of those so much loved and revered, the most precious lessons of wisdom and virtue. There are cases, however, in which parents are so occupied that they are obliged to neglect their children, even during their infant years; and other cases, in which they are disqualified, by their character and habits, from applying any salutary influence. In these cases, it may be necessary to place even very young children in infant schools, where they can be treated with proper tenderness, and can have the benefit of good moral, and intellectual training. At a later period, when a child attains, for example, the age of seven or eight, and requires more formal and thorough instruction; it is expedient, in most instances, that he should be separated, for a part of each day, from his parents (whatever may be their character and circumstances), and enjoy the peculiar advantages of a good school. In thus preferring a mixed education—partly scholastic and partly domestic—to one purely domestic, I am influenced by the following considerations:

1. If a child, at this period, is educated entirely at home, and by his own parents, he will, in many cases, have ignorant or vicious instructers, who have no proper sense of the value, of knowledge or of virtue. In such cases, of course, he can never advance beyond them in intelligence or character, and the effect of making home-education universal, would be, to fix society in a stagnant condition, without progress or change.

2. If, on the other hand, parents are qualified, by knowledge and disposition, to give a good education to their children, they rarely have sufficient leisure for the purpose, in this country; and when they have, they rarely employ it, in such a manner, as to give the child the full benefit of a *systematic* and *thorough* training.

3. Even allowing to parents the highest qualifications and the utmost fidelity and perseverance, they are still, in most instances, too blind to their children's character and capacity, or too impatient for their improvement, to make wise and judicious teachers. "The intense interest," says Godwin, "which a parent feels in the improvement of his offspring, frequently renders him totally unfit for the office of a teacher." Add to this, that a parent who spends some hours each day amid the vexations of the schoolroom, is not likely to carry the requisite equanimity to other household cares, and rarely exercises authority, in other matters, with the same comfort or effect, as if the children were separated from home, for a part of the time.

If, instead of superintending the education of our children personally, we employ a private or family instructer, we subject our children, by such an arrangement, to the following disadvantages, even though our instructer be, in the highest degree, capable and faithful:

1. It is physically impossible that a teacher can throw as much spirit and energy into his instructions, when they are given in the presence of but one, or of a very small number, as when they are communicated before a large school. The efficacy of teaching, depends, very much, on its vivacity.

2. The pupil of a private instructer depends too much on him, and too little on himself.

3. Such a pupil is deprived of a great amount of oblique or indirect instruction, both mental and moral, which a scholar at a public school derives from what he hears addressed to others, and from what he sees of the discipline of the school, and of the results which follow different courses of conduct.

4. The pupil of a private instructer is too constantly an object of attention, the effect of which is, *first*, that he is very apt to overrate his own consequence, and, *secondly*, he is liable to be too much hurried in his studies, and too frequently interrupted, by unnecessary aid and interference.

5. Such a student needs the inspiring influence of others who are engaged in the same pursuits, and who, while they quickened his efforts, would also teach him the true measure of his own abilities, and the proper standard by which to estimate his personal importance.

6. He is deprived of the advantage of living under a government of fixed rules, which are framed for the common benefit and government of several persons of different conditions and character in life, and of thus being gradually prepared to become the subject of civil government. The regulations of a family are less like those of civil society, than the regulations of a school.

7. As a child must ultimately separate from his family, and adapt himself to the ever-varying emergencies of life, and struggle with its difficulties and temptations, he should be early prepared for all this by a training which he can

hardly get, in the sheltered and uniform experience of domestic life.

But if children ought to be sent to school, the question may arise, Why not prefer a *select* school, where they will mingle only with those of the more respectable and opulent class, and enjoy more thorough instruction and discipline? I answer,

1. That, in most cases, a select school can be made superior to the common school, only, by absorbing the patronage of those who are best able to support education, and who appreciate most deeply its importance; and that, in absorbing that patronage, it condemns the common school to inefficiency, and thus deprives the bulk of the community of the advantages of thorough instruction.

2. Select schools serve to create and perpetuate prejudices against the common school system, as though it were necessarily inferior or unimportant, when the general welfare requires, that it should be an object of universal regard and solicitude.

3. Such schools encourage invidious distinctions between the rich and poor, which are misplaced everywhere, and especially in our country; and they also separate those who, in after-life, will have to meet, on the broad ground of free and equal competition.

4. They have also the effect, of making the position of a common school teacher less pleasant and respectable, thereby repelling, from the pursuit, those who are best qualified for it.

In cities, and wherever population is dense and property abundant, it may be well to have some select schools of the highest excellence, in order to stimulate the teachers and patrons of common schools. But in the present condition of our country, and especially of the agricultural districts, it is a matter of the last importance that all efforts for the support and encouragement of primary education should be combined in behalf of the district school.*

* The able superintendent of common schools in Connecticut (H. Barnard, Esq.), thus sums up a review of the effect of select schools in that state: "During the past year (1839-40), I have given particular attention to this subject, and without going any farther into detail, I am constrained to say that, in most instances, this class of private schools have their origin in the defective organization and administration of the common schools, and that they are now exerting a most unhappy influence on their prosperity, and the efforts to improve them. I know of no other way to restore the common school to its true position in our system of education, as the broad platform for all the children of a district, be they rich or poor, than by making it the best school; and I know of no other way of making it such, than a resolute determination to remove the defects which now make it inferior to the private school."

"As far as an estimate can be formed, from the returns of this and the previous year, there are more than two hundred thousand dollars expended yearly on private schools, of a grade no higher than a class of our common schools should constitute. A large portion of this sum can be directed into the broad and thirsty channel of the common schools so soon as the people make them not only cheap, but good, and not till then."—*See Second Annual Report of the Board of Commissioners of Common Schools in Connecticut*, together with *Second Annual Report of the Secretary of the Board, May*, 1840. I cannot omit this opportunity of recommending the reports which have emanated from this source as rich in important suggestions, and full of the most sound and practical views in regard to the whole subject of common school education.

If private schools are as extensively supported in New-York as in Connecticut, it would follow, from the above statement, that they divert annually one million five hundred thousand dollars, which ought to be applied in sustaining and improving our common schools, and which would be thus applied, were common schools good and efficient.

A late writer on Education in Europe gives a somewhat different view of the policy of sustaining select schools. "Let public schools," says he, "be rendered really efficient, and private schools would become still more efficient, or they would soon cease to be encouraged. The best system appears to be that of promoting a spirit

But if parents need the aid of good common schools, it is obvious, on the other hand, that these schools require the aid and countenance of parents. They will, in most cases, benefit children, only, in proportion as the precepts and instructions of the teacher are enforced by the parent. If he shows, by his deportment, that he values the school, and is anxious to increase its efficiency and usefulness; if, instead of obstructing the teacher in his plans or disputing his authority, he assiduously furthers both; if he manifests a lively interest in the progress of his children, and takes pains to ascertain, personally, how far they discharge their duty and how far the instructions they receive are adapted to their wants—in such case both teacher and taught will have the strongest inducements to exertion, and the school will prove most fruitful of good. Such attentions, however, cannot be expected from all parents, and are therefore the more incumbent on those, who are competent to bestow them, and who know the value of a good education. If *they* discharge their duty in this respect, the result will be, that all the children of the vicinity, even those of the most vicious and ignorant parents, will be brought under the benign influence of a good school. On the other hand, when this great duty is neglected, and no cheering influence is extended from the family to the school, the teacher must be more than man if his

of honourable rivalry between the conductors of public schools and those of private establishments. Let the government do well, and individual professors, if they can, do better. This rivalry, in Scotland, has worked very beneficially. The parochial schools are indifferent, but they have stimulated into existence a multitude of private schools, supported entirely upon the condition of giving better instruction than can be obtained in the public schools. Had the public schools not been established, the private schools of Scotland would have been far less efficient than they are." These observations are applicable to cities and large villages, but not to the rural districts of our own country, where population is sparse, and where select schools usually prove fatal to the district school.

heart does not fail him in the midst of his unrequited, unaided labours. How can he keep alive his zeal, or how shall he rekindle the waning fires of his enthusiasm, when he meets around him nothing but cold indifference and neglect? No agent can be expected to be permanently vigilant and faithful without supervision from his employers; and even were it otherwise, a teacher's lessons can make but little impression on children, who feel that their parents, who ought to be most deeply interested in their improvement, are, in fact, indifferent to it.

II. We proceed now to consider the *relations between common schools, and higher seminaries of learning.* All these institutions are necessary, in a complete system of public instruction. In order to supply a city with water, it is requisite, in the first place, to construct a reservoir on an elevated site, and of sufficient capacity, to answer all demands that may be made upon it. From this reservoir, a main trunk or aqueduct is carried to the borders of the city; and from it, again, numberless branches diverge, which divide and subdivide, till the pure element is brought to every door, and enjoyed by every inhabitant. It is the same with knowledge, and with the other blessings of civilization. Books and other records form the principal reservoir, in which these are collected. Of these books, some are exceedingly rare, and are accessible only to a favoured few; others are written in foreign languages, or in those no longer spoken; some of them can be expounded only after years of arduous study, and some need to be illustrated, by experiments with expensive apparatus, or by costly specimens and graphical representations.

It must be apparent, that as the inhabitants of a city cannot all resort to the main reservoir, so neither can all students draw knowledge from the original sources. There must be various orders of teachers. Besides bold and gifted minds, who are not content unless they push their **way** unto undiscovered regions, and add something new to the great storehouse of truth, there must be others to reduce their researches to some definite form, and incorporate them with pre-existing systems. There must be others, again, to divest science and philosophy of their more recondite forms, and to present them, in such a way, as to meet the apprehension, and arrest the interest of the reading world.—In the education of the young, we need, *first*, those who can deal with minds that have been so far trained to the higher efforts of the reasoning faculty, and so far furnished with elementary knowledge, that they can comprehend, not, indeed, the highest truths of science, but yet such as are expressed in the most rigorous and logical manner. As, however, but a small proportion of the young can be thus trained, we need a still larger class of teachers, who, through oral instruction and by books, shall expound the results of scientific discovery in a less exact and rigorous form, and thus render some of its great principles, intelligible to those who have been but partially educated. And since there are vast multitudes, especially among the young, whose minds have either not been developed at all, or in only a slight degree, it is evidently necessary, that a still larger class of teachers should be occupied, in conveying the first elements of knowledge to the uninstructed, and in doing it, in that form, which shall most perfectly combine simplicity with attractiveness.

Thus we see the necessity, of three grades of seminaries, in order to a complete system of national education—colleges, academies, and common schools. Colleges, communicate more immediately with the great reservoirs of science and literature, and dispense their treasures to a limited number of minds. These last, as teachers, authors, and professional men, serve as conductors to carry knowledge over a wider surface, and to impart it to a greater number of minds in academies and elsewhere. Common schools are the last ramifications of the great system, and serve to convey the rudiments of learning and civilization to every hamlet and every inhabitant. It is hardly necessary to say, that if the main trunk or larger branches were stopped up, the lesser ones would soon cease to perform their office. Colleges and academies are necessary to common schools, as channels, through which the treasures of a civilization, always expanding and improving, may flow down to every teacher. They keep up an intercourse, between the highest science and the lowest scholarship, inciting the one to make itself useful and intelligible, and animating the other to more generous aspirations after knowledge. One effect of closing our academies and colleges, or of paralyzing their influence, would be, that the people would soon cease to value knowledge, or would be content with its humblest rudiments. Another effect would be, that the few who can afford it, would send their sons to foreign countries to gain an education, which, though not adapted to our state of society, would still be sure to invest its possessors with a commanding influence; and thus the governing power of society would be placed, forever, in the hands of the wealthy. Under our present system, the highest advantages of education that the country affords, are placed within the reach of those of humble means; and it is a cheering fact, that the majority of students, both in our colleges and academies, are not drawn from the circles of the affluent. They are the children of our farmers, mechanics, and tradesmen, and have, often, no other fortune than a stout heart and a burning desire for knowledge.

On the other hand, common schools are equally necessary to academies and colleges.* If there were no places of

---

* This remark needs some qualification. Colleges have subsisted where there were no common schools, because education, being regarded as the privilege of the few, was dispensed in such cases, not in seminaries open for the common benefit of all, but only in select places of instruction. It is evident, however, that, if colleges are

primary instruction, or if they performed their work in a slovenly and wretched manner, the result would be great, if not universal, indifference to all high science and fine literature. In improving common schools and extending their benefits, we, in effect, multiply the minds which will be awakened to the love and pursuit of knowledge; and in multiplying such minds, we multiply those who will seek admittance to higher seminaries of learning. Knowledge, like water, seeks its own level, and will therefore rise to the height from which it flowed. As it descends into the common school, it seizes upon many a generous spirit, and bears it back to its own native eminence. The youth, who has tasted the pleasures of a little knowledge, will be almost certain to thirst for more, and will thus be prompted to pass from the common school to an academy, and from the academy to a college. In proportion, too, as these common schools are improved, they will render it necessary for other institutions to offer instruction of a higher order, and to meet the wants of more enlarged and better disciplined minds. In short, a community could afford no more conclusive evidence, that it appreciates the value of the most thorough and liberal culture, than by being universally and ardently interested in common schools.

To show that this mutual dependance of common schools and colleges is not imaginary, I might adduce many facts. One will be sufficient. New-England, from the earliest period in its history, has been, as we all know, the land of common schools. Has it not been, also, the favourite soil of colleges and academies? The population of the six New-England States, is not so great, as that of Virginia and the two Carolinas, by some three hundred thousand; yet it

confined to their legitimate object, there must be primary schools, and in such a country as ours, the former will flourish and fulfil their appointed work, only in proportion as the latter multiply and become common.

has more than twice as many students in its colleges, and nine times as many scholars in its common schools.*

III. In regard to the mutual *relations between common schools on the one hand, and books, lyceums, &c., on the other*, but one or two remarks are necessary. It must be evident, that books are multiplied to no purpose, so far as they are concerned who cannot read, or who find no pleasure in that employment. So with lectures, and the various means of instruction afforded by lyceums, and young men's associations; these will have little attraction, for minds that have received no scholastic culture in childhood. Give a child the rudiments of a good English education, and imbue

---

* The population of the New-England States is 2,234,822; that of Virginia, North and South Carolina, is 2,587,614. According to the last census, the whole number of students in the colleges of New-England is 2857, and the whole number of common school scholars is about 574,000. In Virginia, North and South Carolina, the whole number of collegiate students is 1423, and the whole number in common schools is 63,000. In making this comparison, it should be remembered that in the Southern States a large proportion of the children (in Virginia about one third of the whole number) are slaves, and are, of course, denied access to schools. Of the remainder, but about one out of three seem to be at primary and common schools in Virginia; whereas, in New-England, seven out of eight enjoy that privilege. 2. It is also worthy of remark, that in the Southern States, of the whole number of scholars, those in attendance at the higher seminaries (academies and colleges) form a much greater proportion than at the north; the number being in the former case as one to three, whereas, in New-England, they are as one to twelve. This result might be anticipated. In proportion, as social arrangements depart from the democratic form and spirit, in the same proportion, will the higher classes be likely to appropriate to themselves the benefits of education; and in the same proportion, too, is interest in the whole subject likely to decline. Under a system purely republican, education becomes the common and equal interest of all; and institutions of every grade are likely to be supported, in the degree, in which they are useful.

his mind with a spirit of activity and of liberal inquiry, and he will gladly avail himself of every opportunity for self-cultivation. Hence we see the active interest, which ought to be taken in common schools by authors and publishers, and by every friend to the establishment of public libraries, and to the formation of associations for mutual improvement. It is through such schools, mainly, that we may hope to inspire our people with a taste for reading, and with a desire for all useful knowledge and liberal accomplishments.

And, on the other hand, common schools must fail to produce their legitimate effect, unless the people are liberally supplied with books, and with other means of self-culture. What boots it that a child has learned to read, if he never exercises the talent? Of what use can it be, that he has in his hand the key of all knowledge, when he is denied the privilege of applying it to the lock, or feels no desire to enjoy such privilege? Books, and lectures, awaken the torpid intellect. They afford it scope for the exercise of its powers, and teach it that there is pleasure and profit in the employment. The great object of school-training, as we have often remarked, is to implant in the youthful mind the germs of a liberal and active self-culture. If it fails in this, it fails wholly; and yet it will succeed in vain, unless the child, when he leaves school, has ready access to books, and to other sources of instruction. As friends, then, of common schools, and of universal education, we cannot but welcome, with inexpressible satisfaction, the generous efforts which are now making, to plant libraries in every neighbourhood, and to spread far and wide, associations for the diffusion of knowledge, by lectures, debates, &c.

In closing this section, I would remind the reader, how intimate and striking is the connexion, which subsists between common schools on the one hand, and the progress of civilization on the other. Why is it, that the blessings of civilization have failed for so many ages to reach the great mass of mankind? Is it not, simply, because that mass has been left to grovel in ignorance, and mental debasement? The result of knowledge and profound thought, civilization can neither be appreciated, nor enjoyed, by the rude and unlettered. Its progress, from age to age, has been the result of merely augmentiug and remoulding the treasures of intelligence and refinement already stored up; and hence, where there is no mental cultivation, there can be no progress. The wheels of the social system may roll on triumphantly, and new conquests may be made for humanity in the aggregate; while multitudes, unknown to history, may not only have no share in such conquests, but may actually form the blood-stained price, with which they are won. That *all* may have a part, in the blessings of civilization, *all must be educated*. The light of instruction must conspire, with the labours of industry, in lifting the masses out of the dust, and in admitting them to the sunshine of a higher and better life. Already, have these two causes worked wonders of deliverance for oppressed and neglected humanity; but miracles, yet greater and more wondrous, are still needed, and must still be wrought.

It must be evident that education, one of these great missionaries of civilization, can be made *universal*, only in common schools. To these humble seminaries, then, we must look, if we would see all mankind, and especially all our own countrymen, becoming civilized indeed. It is through them, and them only, that we can reach four fifths of our people, at that interesting period in life, when impressions are most deep and lasting; that we can open upon them the genial light of knowledge, religion, and law; and animate them with the all-comprehending spirit of wisdom and charity. A narrow and exclusive civilization, which is intended to shine only on the favoured few, may come forth, from the high places of science. The common school is the lens, which collects the scattered lights of a more comprehensive and democratic civilization, and brings them to bear on the opening minds of a whole people. Let the people see to it that that lens is made more and more transparent; that it collects from every quarter the rays of intellectual and moral light, and casts them with an intenser brightness, over all our land.

SECTION II.

PRESENT STATE OF COMMON SCHOOLS.

"I promised God that I would look upon every Prussian peasant child as a being who could complain of me before God, if I did not provide for him the best education, as a man and a Christian, which it was possible for me to provide."—*School-counsellor* DINTER.

In order to judge the better of the present condition of our common schools, it may be well to determine, in the first instance, what they ought to accomplish. It is by comparing them, as they are, and as they ought to be, that we shall most clearly ascertain, how far they answer their end, and in what respects, they ought to be improved. In attempting to make this comparison, we must remind the reader, that we shall be obliged to deal in general statements; and that, as such statements are always subject to exceptions, so, in the present instance, both important and numerous exceptions ought to be allowed for. Our task will require us to exhibit the dark side of the picture; but we would not forget ourselves, nor have others forget, that it is relieved, by many bright spots. We know well, that there are, in all parts of the state, faithful and able teachers, and well-conducted schools. We know, too, that our common school system, whatever may be its defects, is accomplishing vast good; and that on such a subject, " our business," to borrow the language of Guizot, " is rather to methodise and improve what exists, than to destroy, for the purpose of inventing and renewing, upon the faith of dangerous theories." To preserve what is good, and to repair or reconstruct what is defective, should be our single object.

It was once thought sufficient, if schools were provided in sufficient numbers for a whole population, and if all the children were brought to attend. It was not considered, that these schools might fail of their great design; owing either to the irregular attendance of the scholars, or to the incompetency of the teacher, or to the inadequate support or defective organization of the school. It is quite evident, that children cannot improve at school, who are one day present and the next day absent, and who, besides this irregularity in their ordinary attendance, are kept entirely from school during several months each year. It is equally clear, that the same evils may result, from a frequent change of teachers, or from having the school badly organized, and subjected to the control of parents and trustees who are insensible to its importance, and as ready to embarrass as to strengthen and sustain it. The greatest calamity, however, which can befall the education of a people, is to have teachers without competent knowledge; with no aptness to teach or govern; and who feel, at the same time, no strong desire to improve themselves, nor any deep sense of their responsibility to God, and to their youthful charge. " Like priest, like people," is an old proverb, full of wisdom. It holds as true of the district schoolmaster, as of the parish clergyman. It holds, indeed, of every one, who is to operate on the character of others, and especially of the young, by precept and example. In all other cases, we seem to appreciate its importance. If apprentices have an idle or bungling master, we expect them to be bad workmen. If a family has a drunken father or mother, we expect the children to be idle, vicious, and improvident. Is it not madness, then, to expect that the scholars, in a common school, can be trained to vir-

P

tue, and imbued with knowledge and good intellectual habits, by instructers, who themselves are destitute of these qualities?

We have said enough, in the last chapter, of the nature and ends of education, to authorize us in assuming, that the schools, in which nine tenths of our people are to acquire the rudiments of knowledge, and become qualified to act as men and citizens, ought to be,

1. Places of agreeable resort—connecting pleasant associations with study, and promoting health and vigour of body.

2. They should be so conducted, as to promote neatness and order, and cultivate good manners and refined feelings.

3. They should cherish the moral sentiments, and cultivate habits of purity, and truth.

4. They should lay the foundation of good intellectual habits, and awaken a spirit of liberal self-culture.

5. They should extend their benefits, to all the children in their vicinity, not otherwise well instructed.

In endeavouring to ascertain, how far these conditions are fulfilled, by the common schools of our country, and more especially of our own state, I shall confine myself to official returns. About three years since, special visiters were appointed by the State Superintendent in each of the counties, who were requested to visit and inspect the schools, and to report minutely in regard to their state and prospects. The most respectable citizens, without distinction of party, were selected to discharge this duty; and the result of their labours is contained in two reports, made, the one in April, 1840, the other in February, 1841. These documents are full of minute and detailed information, furnished by men interested in the great cause of popular instruction, and who were not likely to misapprehend, nor to misrepresent its condition. It is from this source, that I shall derive my statements.

SCHOOLHOUSES, GROUNDS, &c.

I. I ask, then, *first*, are our common schools places of agreeable resort, calculated to promote health, and to connect pleasant associations with study?

Ans. Say the visiters, in one of the oldest and most affluent towns, of the southeastern section of the state, "It may be remarked, generally, that the schoolhouses are built in the old style, are too small to be convenient, and, with one exception, too near the public roads, generally having no other playground." Twelve districts were visited in this town.—See *Report of Visiters* (1840), p. 47.

Say the visiters of another large and wealthy town in the central part of the state, "Out of the 20 schools they visited, 10 of the schoolhouses were in bad repair, and many of them not worth repairing. In none were any means provided for the ventilation of the room. In many of the districts, the schoolrooms are too small for the number of scholars. The location of the schoolhouses is generally pleasant. There are, however, but few instances where playgrounds are attached, and their condition as to privies is very bad. The arrangement of seats and desks is generally very bad, and inconvenient to both scholars and teachers. Most of them are without backs."—P. 28 (*Rep.*, 1840).

From another town, in the northwestern part of the state, containing a large population, and twenty-two school districts, the visiters report of district No. 1, that the schoolhouse is large and commodious, but scandalously cut and marked; the schoolroom but tolerably clean; the privies very filthy, and no means of ventilation but by opening the door or raising the window. No. 2 has an old schoolhouse; the room not clean; seats and desks well arranged, but cut and marked; no ventilation; the children healthy, but not clean. No. 3 has an old frame building, but warm and comfortable. No. 4 has a very poor, dilapidated old frame schoolhouse, though the inhabitants are generally wealthy for that country. No. 5 has a frame schoolhouse, old and in bad condition; schoolroom not clean; seats and desks not convenient. No. 6 has a frame schoolhouse, old and in bad condition; the schoolroom is not clean; no cup or pail for drinking water. No. 7 has a log schoolhouse, in a very bad condition; desks and seats are inconvenient. "Here, too," say the visiters, "society is good, and people mostly in easy circumstances, but the schoolhouse very unbecoming such inhabitants. It does not compare well with their dwellings." No. 8, say the visiters, is "a hard case." No. 9 has a frame house in good condition and in a pleasant location, but is "too small for the number of children." No. 10 has a log schoolhouse. No. 11 has a "log shanty for a schoolhouse, not fit for any school." No. 12 a log house. No. 13 has a log shanty, in bad condition, not pleasantly located, schoolroom not clean. "The schoolhouse or *hovel* in this district is so cold in winter, so small and inconvenient, that little can be done towards preserving order or advancing education among so many scholars; some poor inhabitants and some in good circumstances; might have a better schoolhouse." No. 14 has a good frame house, in good condition, pleasant location, with ample and beautiful playground; schoolroom in clean condition. The visiters add, "In this district the inhâbitants are poor, and the scholars attend irregularly; *the house was built by one man in low circumstances, who has a large family of boys to educate; a noble act.*" No. 15 has a frame house, in a good, warm, and comfortable condition, with a pleasant and retired location and a playground. No. 16 has a log shanty for a schoolhouse. No. 17, "no regular schoolhouse other than some old log house." No 18, no schoolhouse. No. 19, a log shanty. No. 20 and 21 are new districts. No. 22 has a frame schoolhouse, in good repair and pleasantly situated.

Thus, out of twenty-two schoolhouses, not more than *five* are reported as respectable or comfortable; none have any proper means of ventilation; eight are built of logs; and but one of them, according to the visiters, has a privy.— *Report* (1840), p. 142.

I will quote but one other example. It is from the report of the only town in the county of Oswego returned as visited in 1840–1. " The same fault," says the visiter, " exists in most of our schoolhouses that is common throughout this section: they are placed too near the road; no playground attached; no privy (in most cases); too much exposed to the noise of all passers-by; the windows are too low, so much so as to be very convenient for the scholars, on hearing a noise, to look out and see what is going on. There is, in general, too little attention to having good and dry wood provided, or a *good supply of any;* or to have a woodhouse or shelter to keep it from the storm;* though I would say that the districts, as a whole, have within a few years improved much."—*Report* (1841), p. 52.

It is also a subject of frequent complaint in these reports, that the seats are too high (too high, say the visiters in one case, for a man of six feet, and all alike), and are, therefore, uncomfortable for the children, as well as productive of much disorder. " We have found," says the report from one town, " except in one school, all the seats and desks much too high, and in that one they were recently cut down at our recommendation. In many of our schools, a considerable number of children are crowded into the same seat, and commonly those seated beyond the entering place have no means of getting at their seats but by climbing over those already seated, and to the ruin of all regard to cleanliness."

" We have witnessed much uneasiness, if not suffering,

---

* Another neglect, noticed by many of the visiters, is the cold and comfortless state, in which the children find the schoolroom; **owing to** the *late hour, at which the fire is first made in the morning.*

among the children, from the dangling of their legs from a high seat, and, with the one exception, have seen them attempting to write on desks so high that, instead of the elbow resting to assist the hand in guiding the pen, the whole arm has, of necessity, been stretched out; for, if they did not this, they must write rather by guess than sight, unless some one may have the fortune to be near-sighted, and, from this defect, succeed in seeing his work. This is a great evil, and ought to be remedied before we complain of the incompetency of teachers."—*Report* (1841), p. 38.

These specimens will serve to show, how far many of the schoolhouses, in this state, are pleasant places of resort, or study, and in what degree they are likely to inspire a respect for education, or a desire to enjoy and improve its advantages. We do not look for deep religious feeling, in a community, who occupy good dwelling-houses, but are content to worship in poor and neglected churches; nor do we expect, great reverence for Christianity, from children, if the sanctuary to which they are carried on Sunday is old and dilapidated—disfigured by abuse—without paint—its windows broken—and not a shrub, or tree, or square yard of verdure in its neighbourhood. The schoolhouse is dedicated to education, as the house of worship is to religion. In one case, as in the other, the state of the edifice indicates the regard, which its builders and guardians have, for the object to which they have devoted it. Nor this only The condition and aspect of the building, with its appendages and surrounding landscape, are inseparably associated, in a child's mind, with his first day at school, and his first thoughts about education. Is it well, then, that these earliest, most lasting, and most controlling associations, should be charged with so much that is offensive? Is it to be expected, that the youthful mind can regard that as the cause, next to religion, most important of all others, which is upheld and promoted, in such buildings, as the district schoolhouse usually is? Among the most comfortless and wretched tenements, which the pupil ever enters, he thinks of it with repugnance; the tasks which it imposes, he dreads; and he at length takes his leave of it, as of a prison, from which he is but too happy to escape.

This seems to me, to be the greatest evil, connected with our schoolhouses. But their deleterious effect, on health, is also to be considered. Air which has been once respired by the lungs, parts with its healthy properties, and is no longer fit for use. Hence a number of persons, breathing the air of the same apartment, soon contaminate it, unless the space is very large, or unless there is some provision for the introduction of fresh, as well as the exclusion of foul air. This ventilation is especially important for schoolhouses, since they are usually small in proportion to the number of scholars; the scholars remain together a long while at once, and are less cleanly in their personal habits than adults. Yet, important as it is, probably not one common school in fifty, in this state, will be found supplied with adequate means to effect it. The cracks and crevices, which abound in our schoolhouses, admit quite enough of cold air in winter, but not enough of fresh. What is wanted at that season, for both health and economy, is a constant supply of fresh warm air; and this is easily obtained by causing the air, as it enters from without, to pass through heated flues, or over heated surfaces. Another simple expedient for ventilating schoolhouses, is to adjust the upper sash of the windows, so that it can be lowered; instead of raising the lower sash and opening the door, a practice which, in cold weather, is always hazardous to those over whom the current of fresh cold air passes.

It is also important, to the health of scholars and teachers in common schools, that the rooms should be larger and have higher ceilings; and that much more scrupulous attention should be paid, to the cleanliness of both the room and its inmates. "An evil," say the visiters of one of the towns, "greater than the variety of schoolbooks or the want of necessary apparatus, is having schoolrooms so unskilfully made and arranged. Of our 13 schoolrooms, only 3 are ten feet high, and of the residue only one is over eight feet. The stupidity arising from foul, oft-breathed air, is set down as a grave charge against the capacity of the scholars or the energy of the teacher. A room for 30 children, allowing 12 square feet for each child, is low at 10 feet, and for every additional ten children an extra foot in elevation is absolutely necessary, to enable the occupants of the room to breathe freely."—*Report* (1841), p. 38.

II. Are common schools so conducted, as to *promote habits of neatness and order, and cultivate good manners and refined feelings?* These are important to all children, but all have not, at home, the same facilities for acquiring them. Hence, unless cultivated at school, they can never reach many children at all, especially at that period in life, when impressions are made most easily and deeply. Even where this is not the case, and home affords, in these respects, the most salutary influence, children still need attention, at school, to counteract the pernicious example of coarse companions, as well as their own strong propensity to carelessness and irregularity. What are our schools, then, in this respect?

From the quotations already made from the reports of visiters, it appears that the schoolrooms, in many cases, were not clean; and the same thing is often alleged of the children. I will add but one other passage, to which I happen to open on p. 39 of the Report (1840). It relates to a town containing 24 school districts, of which 16 were visited. Of these 16, one quarter are represented to have been almost entirely regardless of neatness and order, viz.: No. 4 "has a dirty schoolroom, and the appearance of the children was dirty and sickly." No. 2 " has a dirty schoolroom, inconveniently arranged, and *ventilated all over ;*" the children " rather dirty," and no means of supplying fresh water except from the neighbour's pails and cups. No. 3 has " an extremely dirty schoolroom, without ventilation, the children not clean, and no convenience for water." No. 24 " has a schoolhouse out of repair, dirty, and inconvenient in its arrangements."

It is also a subject of almost universal complaint, that the *schoolhouses are without privies.* On an average, probably not more than one in twenty, of the schoolhouses throughout the state, has this appendage ; and in these, it was almost invariably found, by the visiters, to be in a bad state. This fact speaks volumes, of the attention, which is paid at these schools, to delicacy of manners, and refinement of feeling. None but the very poorest families think of living without such a convenience at home ; and a man, who should build a good dwelling-house, but provide no place for retirement when performing the most private offices of nature, would be thought to give the clearest evidence, of a coarse and brutal mind. Yet respectable parents allow their children to go to a school where this is the case ; and where the evil is greatly aggravated by the fact, that numbers of both sexes are collected, and that, too, at an age of extreme levity, and when the youthful mind is prone to the indulgence of a prurient imagination. Says one of the visiters (*Report*, 1840, p. 77), " In most cases in this town, the scholars, male and female, are turned promiscuously and simultaneously into the public highway, without the shelter of so much (in the old districts) as a ' stump' for a covert to the calls of nature. The baneful tendency, on the young and pliant sensibilities, of this barbarous custom, are truly lamentable." So the visiters of one of the largest and oldest counties : " We regret to perceive that many of the districts have neglected to erect privies for the use of the children at school. This is a lamentable error. The injury to the taste and morals of the children which will naturally result from this neglect, is of a character much more serious than the discomfort which is obviously produced by it."—(*Report*, 1840, p. 131.)

III. We have said, that schools should be so conducted as to strengthen the moral sentiments of children, and rear them to habits of virtue and purity. There is probably no one respect, in which they so generally, or so grievously fail of their object. In the reports of visiters already often referred to, there is scarcely an allusion to the subject; and though this silence may have been owing, in part, to the hasty manner in which the inspection, in that instance, was necessarily conducted, it must have been owing, still more to the fact, that the importance of moral culture is not appreciated. Common schools have been regarded, as nurseries of the intellect only. Parents and teachers have seemed to think, that there would be opportunities enough, at home, for the cultivation of the heart and conscience. They have forgotten that, *while men sleep, the enemy comes and sows tares;* that if the all-important work of moral training be suspended each day, for some hours, while the child is removed beyond the parental eye, and is mingling promiscuously with his schoolmates, he can hardly escape injury. Vicious influences will rain down upon his mind from various sources; and hence one, who is improving fast in knowledge, may be ripening yet faster in wickedness; and though he bears to his home the highest character as a scholar, he may be losing, meanwhile, all that makes scholarship a blessing, either to himself or to the world.

When we urge the importance of moral culture in schools, we do not mean that the teacher should deal only, or often, in long moral lectures. We would remind him, that *example* is the most impressive of all teachers; and that he cannot live and move, so constantly, in the presence of susceptible and watchful minds, without making, by his deportment, a deep impression on their characters. We would remind him, too, that there are various sources of temptation at school; such as the influence of one or more corrupt companions; the rivalries and contentions to which the young as well as old are liable; the absence of restraint during play-hours, and while children are passing to and fro, between the schoolhouse, and the home. All these are points, about which teachers, and all who take an interest in schools, or who feel for the safety and welfare of their own offspring, can hardly be too solicitous, or too vigilant.

There is one kind of moral training and instruction, little known in our schools, and too much neglected even in our families, which appears, to me, pre-eminently important. It is based on the principle, that the virtues are habits, and are to be acquired thoroughly, only by acting repeatedly, in the right manner, from the right motive. To cultivate virtue in this way requires, not so much formal precepts or lectures, as incidental but constant inculcation. Whenever a child does wrong, he should, in the kindest and most private manner, be taught to feel and own it; and opportunity should be given him, to act on the opposite principle. In all his relations, whether with teachers, parents, schoolfellows, or others, he should be accustomed to inquire, always, after the right, and to observe it. There should be a code of *school-morals*, to embrace thoughts and feelings as well as overt acts, and to be administered, under the jurisdiction of the child's own conscience, and sense of honour. With injunctions to virtuous effort, should be joined frequent mementoes of his own frailty and insufficiency, and of the necessity of Divine aid and illumination. In administering the discipline of the school, the teacher should be careful to carry with him the moral sense of his pupils, and to have it felt, that he will punish whenever the sanctity of law and the welfare of the school demand it, but never otherwise.

It is much to be deplored, that principles, so **obvious and important** as these, should have come to be so generally disregarded. No one imagines, that a young man can be trained to make a good shoe or a good coat, except by repeated trials, and persevering effort. Yet we do seem to expect, that he will be a calm and placable man who has been only irascible and vindictive as a boy. We do forget, that in one most important sense, the "boy is father of the man." We seem to think that, though his youthful mind has been allowed to revel without check amid images of shame, he may still be chaste at last; that a long series of evasive, or self-indulgent or criminal acts, may only end in honesty, temperance, and patience; and that, *though he sow*, through all his childhood and youth, *to the flesh*, still it need not follow that *he must of the flesh reap corruption*.

SECTION III.

PRESENT STATE OF COMMON SCHOOLS.

"In proportion as the discoveries in arts multiply, and as we make progress in improvement, in like proportion ought the moral and intellectual condition of the species to rise; the progress of civilization does not depend alone on the increase of wealth; it chiefly depends on the improved moral and intellectual condition of the population."—DE GERANDO.

IV. WE have to inquire, in the next place, whether our schools tend *to cultivate good intellectual habits*, among the rising generation; and to *inspire them with a liberal taste for knowledge?* If they fail, in too many cases, to inculcate high moral principles, and to cherish refinement of thought, feeling, and manner, they ought, at least, to fulfil the one end to which most of them profess to be devoted: this is the development, and cultivation, of intellect. During a period of ten or more years, most of our children are nominally at school. Does their proficiency correspond with the opportunities, which they seem to enjoy?

It is now many years since Dr. Dwight, speaking of the common schools of Connecticut, declared that they consumed ten years in teaching badly what ought, in two, or, at most, three years, to be learned well. More recently, the late De Witt Clinton thus expressed himself in one of his messages: " Our system of instruction, with all its numerous benefits, is still susceptible of great improvements. Ten years, of the life of a child, may now be spent in a common school. In *two years* the elements of instruction may be acquired; and the remaining eight years must be spent either in repetition or in idleness, unless the teachers of common schools are competent to instruct in the higher branches of knowledge. The outlines of Geography, Mineralogy, Agricultural Chemistry, Mechanical Philosophy, Surveying, Geometry, Astronomy, Political Economy, and Ethics, might be communicated in that period of time by able preceptors, without essential interference with the calls of domestic industry."

More than fifteen years have elapsed since this passage was written, and it may be well to inquire, how far the improvements, it suggests, have been introduced. I would remark, however, that no child should be advanced to higher branches of study, until he has been made perfectly familiar with those, which form the indispensable groundwork of all knowledge. The least that can be demanded of any common school is, that it make all its pupils thoroughly proficient in reading, writing, arithmetic, and the use of the English language. How is this *minimum* requirement fulfilled, by the common schools of this state?

The reader is qualified to answer this question for himself. He is surrounded, by the young of both sexes, who are leaving these schools, and who are never more to enjoy their advantages. In the daily business of life, he meets those who have had no other scholastic culture. If, then, he would know what our common schools are doing for the intellectual education of our people, let him endeavour to collect, from his own neighbourhood, correct replies to the following interrogatories.

What proportion, of those who leave these schools, or are known to have been educated at them, can read aloud from any book, which may chance to fall into their hands; and can do it so fluently, intelligently, and forcibly, as to afford both instruction and pleasure, to those who listen?

What proportion of them have acquired the power of writing legibly and neatly, and are able to express themselves with perspicuity, propriety, and ease, in letters of business or friendship, and in other documents?

What proportion understand thoroughly the most important operations of arithmetic, and are able to apply the rules, promptly and correctly, to any questions that may arise in the course of business?

What proportion can point out, readily, the location of the important places, of which they are likely to read in the newspapers of the day, or in books of voyages, travels, history, &c.?

What proportion are even moderately versed, in the history of their own country, in the fundamental principles of its government and legislation, and in a knowledge of such laws, as bear most directly on their own and the common welfare?

Until this elementary knowledge is thoroughly mastered, it would be absurd to proceed to higher branches. The latter are desirable; the former indispensable. Reading, writing, and arithmetic are implements, without which, in the present state of society, a man can neither do business, nor make progress in self-education. In the process of acquiring them, his mind, if properly treated, will be materially strengthened and enlarged; and when once acquired, they render it both possible and easy, for him to advance indefinitely in knowledge. One prevailing defect, of the education of the present day, consists in the neglect of these rudiments. Teachers and parents are, both, too apt to forget, that facts or principles can do little for the pupil's mind, if they are only deposited in his memory, without awakening his imagination or exercising his understanding. Hence, without waiting to ground him thoroughly in the most essential elements, he is hurried forward to studies for which he is wholly unprepared, and which often require the exercise of our higher faculties. From these, again, so soon as he can repeat the prescribed portions of a text-book, he is hurried to others, equally remote from his tastes or preliminary studies; and thus his whole education is made to consist, of a hasty and superficial survey of many subjects, which are no sooner dismissed, than they are forgotten.

Sometimes, this prevailing and injurious practice is to be ascribed to the teacher alone, who does not seem to know that such attainments are worthless; or who, if he does know it, is careless of his pupil's welfare, and only intent on the honour, which he hopes to gain, from having accomplished so much, with his classes, in so brief a space of time. Happy will it be, when the intelligence of the community enables them to discern the dishonesty, and quackery of such a system. It is but just, however, to add, that in many cases the fault is in parents, and their children. Say the visiters of one of the counties (1840), " Our common schools are not advancing in proportion to their cost. One reason is, that the children do not fully understand what they profess to learn. The system is too superficial. Pupils are eager to have it said, ' We have been through the book.' This expression has been made use of to us in several instances, when, at the same time, the scholars could not answer questions in the most fundamental rules. If scholars make a favourable report of progress, parents are very apt to receive it as correct without examination, *and the teacher who wishes to check this disposition to advance without knowledge, is very liable to incur the displeasure of both pupil and parent.*"

But, in whatever way this abuse originates, it is deeply to be deplored, and it ought to be strenuously resisted. Nothing can well be more unfavourable, to all true and high culture of the intellect. In so far as it leaves its victims ignorant, or unaccomplished, in regard to the very first rudiments of knowledge, it disqualifies them, by necessity, for all thorough and rapid progress, in more advanced studies. It also induces loose and inaccurate habits of investigation; and these habits, being acquired early, are in most cases invincible; proving fatal to thorough scholarship, and to intellectual efforts of the most useful and commanding character. It tends, moreover, to engender a spirit of self-sufficiency in the young, and a feeling of satiety in regard to books and mental cultivation, which are wholly incompatible with self-culture. "There is nothing," says Erasmus, in one of his Colloquies, "more pernicious than to be glutted with anything; and so likewise with knowledge." "I hate," says Dr. Johnson, "by-roads in education. Endeavouring to make children prematurely wise is useless labour. Suppose they have more knowledge at five or six years old than other children, what use can be made of it? It will be lost before it is wanted, and the waste of so much time and labour of the teacher can never be repaid. Too much is expected from precocity, and too little performed."

It is difficult to say, whether the evil, here referred to, be more inveterate, or prevalent. A wordy, superficial rote-method of teaching and learning, may be regarded as, at this time, the great and special bane of our common schools. That there are many honourable exceptions, I know well. But in too many cases, text-books are relied on to do the work of the teacher; and hence these books have been simplified, and furnished with questions, and encumbered with commentaries, as if the great object, were, to supersede all effort, on the part both of instructer and learner. In this way, too, that active and ardent collision of mind between the two, which forms the secret of all good intellectual instruction, comes to be hardly known. The pupil studies words, not principles; tasks his memory much, his judgment little; and a foolish ambition to have it said, that much ground has been passed over, or many branches pursued, usurps the place of that true ambition, which aims at a radical and thorough culture; one that draws out, disciplines, vivifies, and strengthens, all the faculties of the soul. Such a culture may impart less knowledge, but it will be found to make that which it imparts, the pupil's own forever; and it will, at the same time, give such a spring to the intellectual powers, as to ensure future advancement.

I ought, perhaps, in closing this subject, to add, that, so soon as a child has mastered the common branches, so that he reads, both aloud and mentally, with ease and understanding, writes a good hand, and is familiar with the most important processes in arithmetic, he ought to be advanced to other studies. The great fault, at present, is, that he is advanced too soon; takes up many branches before he is prepared for them; and pursues too great a number, at the same time. The result is, that his mind is distracted; no one of them is studied thoroughly; one text-book having been despatched, another, perhaps on the same subject, is introduced; and the child is, in effect, occupied during most of his school life, in retracing ground over which he has already travelled—doing it, however, in such a manner, that his interest is deadened, his powers of discrimination impaired, and his mind fixed, and almost petrified, in habits of torpid and vacant listlessness. The concurrent testimony of those who have examined common schools most exten sively and thoroughly, both in our own and other states, represents that, in very many cases,

1. They fail to teach even the common branches thoroughly.

2. They engender, or encourage, loose and superficial habits of thought, and study.

3. They fail to inspire a love for the reading of good and useful books.

4. The pupils, in many instances, continue stationary, from year to year.

IRREGULARITY OF ATTENDANCE, ABSENCE, &c.

V. The last great requisite in our common school system, is, that its benefits should be enjoyed, by *all the children of the state*, not otherwise instructed. Though the best possible schools were opened, in every neighbourhood, they would be useless to those who never attend, and of but partial service, to those who attend irregularly. There are many children of both classes in this state.

Of those who never attend. This class includes children of both foreigners, and natives. The former, usually arrive in this country, poor. Many of them are unable to speak our language; some of them do not appreciate the necessity and importance of education; others lead a vagrant life, as labourers on canals and railroads, or as hired workmen.*

---

* The children of persons employed upon our public works, says the secretary of the Massachusetts Board of Education, in a late report, heretofore have not shared in the provisions for education made by our laws, and have rarely been embraced in any of the numerous plans for moral improvement devised and sustained by private charity; and hence they have been growing up in the midst of our institutions, uninstructed even in those rudiments of knowledge without which self-education is hardly practicable. During the last year, a few of the inhabitants of the town of Middlefield (which is situated in the western part of Hampshire county), commiserating the destitute condition of the children along the line of

In some of these cases it is impossible to make an English common school available. More frequently, however, the

the railroad in their vicinity, took active measures to supply them with the means of instruction. A gentleman of that town, Mr. Alexander Ingham, was the first to engage in, and has been most active in carrying on this Samaritan enterprise. The good example extended, and a considerable number of children along the line of work were soon gathered, either into the public schools, or, where that was impracticable, into schools established expressly for them at private expense. At the Common School Convention in the county of Hampden, held in the month of August last, the condition of these children, and the necessity of some farther measures in their behalf, constituted one of the topics of inquiry and discussion. A committee was appointed, of which Mr. Ingham was chairman, to collect the facts of the case. From this committee I have learned that there were, in the month of September last, more than three hundred children, between the ages of four and sixteen, belonging to the labourers on the railroad west of Connecticut River, who were not considered as entitled to the privileges of the public schools, or were in such a local situation as not to be able to attend them. A pregnant fact, also, in relation to the subject is, that, in the enumeration of all the children of all ages belonging to that class of people, " a large proportion of them are under the age of four years." Owing to efforts since made by private individuals, a very large majority of all these children who are of a suitable age are now enjoying the benefits of common school education.

There is still another class, says the late secretary of the Connecticut Board of Education, who are among the absentees from schools: I refer to coloured children. There is no reluctance to include them in the enumeration return. Why, then, should not the district, or society, or city authorities, see to their education? Their education would be cheaper to the community than their crimes and vices, which are the offspring of neglect and ignorance. While the blacks constitute but one twentieth of our population, they furnish about one eighth of all the crime of the state. It costs the state annually, to prosecute and convict the coloured inmates of the prison alone, a sum sufficient to educate nearly all the coloured children of the state between the ages of four and sixteen. Separate schools for this class of children exist in Hartford, and perhaps elsewhere. They should be opened in all our large cities.

difficulty results from the inability, or indifference of parents, and the culpable negligence of the community. It ought to be considered the duty of some one, to search out such forlorn and unhappy children, and bring them to the notice, as well of the trustees of the school districts in which they respectively reside, as to that of benevolent individuals. The children of temporary or transient residents *are entitled, by law, to attend the school in their respective districts;* and it is even made the duty of trustees, whenever it shall be necessary for their accommodation, to hire temporarily, an additional room or rooms for that purpose. This duty is imposed on the trustees, because they are authorized, by the same law, to include all such transient children in their returns; and to draw money from the treasury of the state, for their instruction. It is superfluous to add, that this money ought to be regarded as a sacred trust, held for their exclusive benefit, and to be diverted to no other object. Too often, however, the poor foreigner, or labourer on the canal, remains ignorant of this benevolent provision of the state in his behalf; and when, in other cases, he would avail himself of it, obstructions are sometimes placed in his way, lest, in consequence of the presence of his poor children in the school, the expenses of the wealthy inhabitants should be slightly increased. When we exclude them under such circumstances, is it considered that we, in effect, appropriate to our own use what is not ours, having been given simply as a deposite for the stranger and the destitute?

The children of many native, and other citizens, are also to be found among those, who never attend school.* In too

---

There is, I should think, power enough already in the school societies to do this. If not, for these and other purposes, cities should be clothed with the power of school societies.

* "Next to our cities, the largest number of children not in attendance on any school, public or private, is found in the districts in which are located factories and manufacturing establishments.

many instances, this results from the profligate habits of the parents, who are wholly regardless of the welfare of their offspring; in other cases, it should be charged to an ignorance which cannot comprehend the advantages of education; and in others, again, to extreme indigence, which disables a parent from providing proper clothes, or renders the presence and assistance of the child necessary to the support of the family. *In ordinary cases of indigence, it ought to be understood, that the law, as it now stands, recognises the* RIGHT *of every poor child, to share in the instruction imparted by common schools.* Of this right, every parent should feel,

The comparative cheapness of the labour of females and of children, where it can be resorted to at all, has led to its extensive introduction into factories, to the exclusion, as far as possible, of the more costly labour of men. From a statement in a report to the Legislature of Massachusetts a few years since, it appeared that more than 200,000 females are employed in the various manufacturing establishments of the United States. Most of this number are young; many are still of the proper school age. In this single fact are involved considerations of the most weighty character as to the influence of such establishments, which have grown up all about us, and, from the peculiar advantages of Connecticut, are likely to increase still farther, upon the future destinies of the state and the country. One thing is clear, from the experience of the past, both at home and abroad, that about such establishments will always be gathered a large number of parents who, either from defective education in themselves, or from the pressure of immediate want, or from the selfishness which is fostered by finding profitable employ for their children, do not avail themselves of the means offered by the state, and not unfrequently increased by the liberality of the proprietors, to secure an education for their children. In addition to these influences, the self-interest of proprietors is a temptation constantly operating to withdraw children of both sexes at too early an age from the schoolroom to the employment of the factories, which, if always healthful, are not the proper training-ground for the moral and mental habits of the future men and women of the state."—*Report of the Secretary of the Board of Education in Connecticut.*

himself bound, as well as entitled, to take advantage. If *he can* pay, wholly or in part, his spirit as a free and a Christian man should constrain him to do it; but if he cannot, let him know, that the *trustees of the district are obliged, by law to exempt him, and to levy the necessary amount, as a tax on the property of that district.* And it ought to be considered a sacred duty of trustees, to administer this law in its true spirit, and to use their influence to bring every child within their bounds, to share its blessings. These children will presently be men and women; their influence will be felt in families—in the operations of industry—at the polls. Let all, then, who are charged by the state with the care of common schools, and all who feel that, as individuals, they owe something to their country and the world, see to it, that these children are trained up in the way that they should go, that when they are old they may not depart from it.

These various causes cannot but exclude vast numbers of children from our schools. It was recently estimated, by the Superintendent of Common Schools of this State, that in the city of New-York alone, there are more than *thirty thousand* children, who go to no school at all. Similar estimates have been made in regard to other cities, and villages throughout the state, and it has been found, that a proportion of the children of these places, varying from one third to one tenth, seem destitute of all visible means of education. It is not supposed, that such calculations can be received with implicit confidence. In some instances the evil has doubtless been exaggerated; in others, the important fact has been overlooked, that children kept from school at one season, or in one year, may attend in another, and that, in the present state of public opinion, few children are likely to grow up, in our country, without some scholastic instruction. Still it must be admitted, that the records of our jails and prisons do show a fearful proportion, who are unable to read and write. The late census, likewise, disclosed the astounding fact, that *in some counties of this state*, as many as one out of every ten adult inhabitants (in one county it was one out of every five) could neither read nor write. It is computed, that five thousand boys, of a proper age to attend school, are employed, on the Erie and Hudson Canal, as drivers during eight months of the year, and it is supposed that few of them attend school at all.* If to these, we add the children who are employed in manufactories, and the offspring of foreigners recently arrived in the country, or speaking a different language, or engaged on public works; and if to these, we add, again, those whose parents are too depraved, or too indifferent, or too poor to send them to school, we shall have a vast and fearful aggregate, who are growing up without any proper culture. Ability to read, some of them may acquire, by attending a Sunday School occasionally; but how meager is such instruction, when compared with the wants of the citizen, the Christian, and the man.

2. *Those who attend irregularly.* It must be apparent, on slight reflection, that the best schools can do little for those who are frequently absent. By such absences, a child forfeits his standing in his class, and is disqualified from advancing with the requisite speed and accuracy. He forms habits of irregularity, and soon becomes listless or discouraged. His absences tend, also, to disorganize the school, and to add, grievously, to the labours and vexations of the teacher. One needs not be surprised, then, if, where the attendance of scholars at school is not only suspended, for some months each year, but is extremely irregular at other times, that in such cases, the proficiency is very slight.

It is worthy of remark, that, until lately, the great importance of this subject, seems to have been overlooked. In the returns of school officers, no distinction was made between the *total*, and the average, attendance; the whole

* It is said that *three thousand* of these boys are *orphans!*

number registered, throughout the year, being reported as attendants. Some of these might have been present but a few days; others but a few weeks; and others, again—having entered, withdrawn, and entered a second, or even a third time within the same year—might be returned twice or thrice over. In this way, the returns have been swelled, until the number reported as at school has, in several instances, been greater than the whole number of children between the ages of 5 and 16 in the state, and this, though many thousands were known to be in select schools and academies; and though thousands, besides, entered no schoolhouse at all. By the same means, the average nominal period, during which common schools have been kept open, was extended to *eight* months, though it is not believed, that the average attendance of the scholars exceeded half that time. Within the last few years, a corrective has been applied, in some of the states, by adopting a new form of making re ports, and in all, public attention has been directed to the necessity of producing greater regularity.*

I quote from the last school returns of Massachusetts, to show the magnitude of the evil, in that state. Say the school committee of a large and populous town, "Although able teachers have been employed, the school registers, accurately kept through the summer and winter terms, show an average daily attendance which is less than one half of the whole number of scholars." Say the committee of another town, "*The school registers* have brought to light one of the *most prominent evils* which exist in our schools,

---

* In the State of New-York, trustees of school districts will be required to report, hereafter, "the number of pupils who have attended for a term less than two months in each year; the number attending two and less than four months; the number attending four and less than six months; the number attending six and less than eight months; the number attending eight and less than ten months; and the number attending twelve months."—See *Statutes relating to Common Schools, &c.*, p. 148.

and which *has existed* from time immemorial, and which *would have remained undiscovered, or been but partially revealed, probably, for years,* if not centuries, but for the aid of that or of some similar contrivance. They have disclosed the astounding fact that, even in this town, a little more than one fourth part of the money raised for the support of schools is annually *lost, actually thrown away*, and has been so for years. It is found, by consulting these registers, that the average attendance of the scholars, in all the schools, is a fraction less than three fourths of the whole number of scholars belonging to the schools, which shows that a fraction more than one fourth part of the time allowed for the cultivation of the minds of our children, and, consequently, the same proportional part of the school money, is squandered away by the irregular attendance of the scholars. If we extend these inquiries to other towns, through the state, we find that the proportion materially increases, and, *in the whole, taken collectively, it exceeds one third.* For out of a little more than 477,000 dollars, raised for the support of schools in the state, more than 200,000 dollars are annually directly thrown away by this voluntary abandonment of privileges. But this *enormous waste of money* is but an *atom* in the scale when weighed against the *opportunities neglected which can never be recalled.* Nor is this the extent of the evil: whenever any scholar unnecessarily *absents himself* from the school, or is unnecessarily *detained by his parents*, not only is so much of his time lost, and (as it regards him) so much of the school money is lost, but the *whole school suffers*, by the interruption, in the arrangement and progress of the class."

It appears, then, that in the State of Massachusetts, more than one third of the whole number of scholars are absent, on an average, each day. If such is the fact, and it seems verified by precise and authentic returns, the absences in the State of New-York must form a still greater proportion. All the causes which can operate in Massachusetts to produce irregular attendance, exist here, and, in addition to them, there is another and powerful cause, which operates, probably, in no other state. There, the parent pays alike, whether his child be present or absent; here, he pays only when he is present. The teacher is required, by law, to keep an exact record of the number of days and half days that each child attends, not for the purpose of enabling the inspectors, superintendent, and public to know how far parents and children avail themselves of the advantages of school, but that the teacher may know how much shall be *deducted* from each employer's rate-bill on account of absences. In this way a *premium* is, by law, actually offered to the parent to *induce him to detain his children from school, or to gratify them when they wish to stay away.* Nor this alone. As though it were not enough, to subject a teacher to the inconvenience and pecuniary loss, which he incurs by this arrangement, he is himself compelled to keep a record of it, *for the benefit of the parent.* It is difficult to conceive a more preposterous law. As a rule, no private school would tolerate it; and if, in Massachusetts, where it is happily unknown, the average absentees of each day form more than one third of the whole number of scholars on record, there can be little doubt that, in this state, under the fostering hand of such a law, they must have swelled to at least one half.

We have thus reviewed the condition, and character of our common schools. We have endeavoured, to ascertain the influence which they are likely to exert on health, manners, and morals, as well as on intellectual improvement. It has been our anxious desire, neither to exaggerate, nor to extenuate, the evils which prevail. As we remarked at the outset, such general statements must be qualified in favour of many instances, in which, teachers are capable and faithful, school-officers are vigilant, and parents both liberal and attentive. It must be admitted, too, that, with all their imperfections, these schools still do render unspeakable service, by affording, to our entire population, some opportunities for instruction. It is to be considered, farther, that our institutions, and the state and prospects of our country, exert an animating influence on the minds of our people, which is felt powerfully everywhere, and which renders the most imperfect instruments more efficient and useful with us, than they could be under older or less popular governments. If tried by a strict scholastic test, it may be doubted, whether our common schools are greatly in advance of those which were spread over the states of Germany when Frederic the Great first undertook the work of their regeneration; a work which has been advancing ever since, with the highest success. There can be no question, however, that their usefulness is immeasurably greater.

Our present common school system was established, something more than twenty-five years since. The effect of it has been, to add immensely to the number of schools, as well as to diminish the expense of the people in supporting them. It is sometimes suggested, however, that this system has not contributed, in the same proportion, to improve the *character* and *efficiency* of our schools, and that in these respects they have, in fact, deteriorated. On this point, various opinions are advanced by the special visiters before referred to. In the estimation of some of them, the schools are decidedly less thorough in their methods of teaching, and secure less actual proficiency, than they did twenty years ago. In the opinion of others, they are more advanced, and have been improving rapidly, especially, for the last four or five years.

It is believed that both of these opinions are in a degree correct, and that they will be found less discordant than they appear to be at first sight. The immediate effect of the establishment of common schools *by law*, in 1815, was a great and sudden increase in their number, requiring an increase equally sudden and great, in the number of teachers. This sudden demand was of course supplied, in the first instance, by persons but poorly qualified; and the evil was afterward perpetuated, by the unnecessary multiplication of school districts, which had the twofold effect of extending the demand for teachers too rapidly, and of so depressing the rate of wages, that none but persons of inferior qualifications could be obtained. Another serious evil, which at first resulted from the interposition of the state, was a great diminution of interest on the part of parents, and other citizens. So long as the support and supervision of the schools was left entirely to them, they felt the necessity of care, in selecting teachers, and in overlooking their proceedings. When the law, however, provided for the appointment of inspectors, and for the partial support of schools, employers naturally concluded, that less vigilance on their part would be sufficient. It ought, therefore, to have been expected, that the introduction of this system would tend, in the first instance, to depress the standard of teaching, though it might secure the extension of its blessings to all the inhabitants.

Had this result been foreseen, it might have been provided for. As this, however, was not the case, it is apprehended that most persons who have had occasion to compare the state of common schools in 1822-6, with what they were previous to 1814, must have observed some degree of deterioration. When this deterioration became apparent, it led, in the first instance, to the establishment of select schools, which, though they gave relief to a few of the more wealthy inhabitants, tended still farther to depress common schools, and thus to fasten the evils of a bad system on the community, in a manner which seemed at one time to defy remedy. Within the last few years, however, the necessity, and practicability of some reform, has been growing more and more apparent. Enlightened citizens have discovered, that good schools are important, not only to their own families, but to all; that common schools will always be preferred by most of the inhabitants; that it is therefore of the utmost consequence that *they* should be good schools; and that this can be the case, only when they unite in their support the wealth, respectability, and intelligence of the whole district. Hence select schools are decreasing; parents and employers bestow more care in the choice of a common school teacher; more liberality is evinced in constructing schoolhouses, and defraying the expenses of instruction; and much more personal attention is given to the character and operations of the school, and to its influence on the young. It must be admitted, however, that the progress of this auspicious change has hitherto been slow, and that its influence now is lamentably circumscribed.

I proceed to inquire how it can be made general.

SECTION IV.

HOW CAN COMMON SCHOOLS BE IMPROVED?

" When, therefore, we attempt to construct institutions of education for the countless youth of centuries still to come, we enter on a task full of solicitude and responsibility, but full, also, of hope and promise."—WHEWELL.

To be able to answer this question fully, we ought to ascertain the precise *causes* of the evils which we seek to remedy. It is believed that they may be included under the following heads: I. *Want of interest on the part of parents and others.* II. *Frequent change of teachers.* III. *Excessive multiplication of school districts.* IV. *Diversity of class-books.* V. *Teachers not qualified.* VI. *Defective supervision.* We propose to examine each of these in their order, and to endeavour to point out the appropriate correctives.

I. *Want of interest on the part of parents,* &c.—This is doubtless the sorest evil, with which we are called to contend. Indifference and neglect, on the part of those who ought to feel the most lively concern for the welfare of our schools, cannot fail to chill the zeal of all other persons. Neither teacher, nor scholar, nor trustees can be expected to labour with ardour and perseverance, when they find no sympathy where they have the best right to expect it. This apathy manifests itself in many ways: in the preference which is so frequently given to the poorest teachers, provided only that they are the cheapest; in permitting children to be irregular in their attendance; in the neglect of parents to visit the school, that they may know whether the teacher understands his duty and discharges it; in omitting such examination of the children at home as will animate them to greater diligence, and, at the same time, reveal the true degree of their proficiency; in allowing the schools to be closed for a large part of each year; in opposing every plan which involves an increase of expense or efficiency; and, finally, in encouraging a contentious spirit among the employers, and a want of respect towards the teacher.

It would seem, at first, as if no man could have the least sense of the importance of schools, or of his duty towards them, who gives his countenance to any one of these practices. Charity, however, requires us to admit, that in some cases, this may be owing to ignorance, or inconsideration. All persons do not know that schools may, in some cases, be useless—in others, a positive nuisance. They usually feel that education is very desirable, and, in the present state of the world, even necessary. They have built a schoolhouse, provided it with a teacher, supplied their children with books, and enjoined their attendance; and it never occurs to many of them, that more can be necessary. When they propose to raise a crop of good marketable wheat, they are very careful to get the best seed, to see that the ground is carefully prepared to receive it, to have it deposited after the most approved manner, and to guard the young plant, at every stage of its growth, against noxious animals and every hostile influence. They trust no workman, who is unacquainted with his business, and omit no precaution which can secure them against loss or injury. It is not possible that these men would refuse to apply the same care to the training of their children, if they felt it to be necessary. They do not feel this. They say that their children are at school, and that they intend to keep them there. They have yet to learn that all this may be without benefit; that morally they may become worse at school; that even their intellectual tastes and habits may degenerate, and their prospects in life only be shrouded in deeper gloom.

What, then, is the *remedy for this evil?* It must be found, *in a full and free discussion, before the people, of the claims of common schools.* Every means must be invoked by which, on other subjects, men are enlightened and aroused. The *press* must be made to speak; not that portion of it only which is especially devoted to schools,* but the daily and weekly press; also the magazine and the review. *Meetings* must be convened in every town and neighbourhood, at which those who have hearts to feel, and minds to comprehend the vastness of this theme, may give utterance to their convictions. Arrangements must be made, to have these meetings recur frequently, and to secure the presence of those, whose opinions command respect and attention.†

---

* The District School Journal, edited by Francis Dwight, Esq., and published at Albany, under the supervision of the Superintendent of Common Schools, should be read and circulated.

† The following remarks (from the last report of the secretary of the Massachusetts Board of Education) on the influence of these

Every individual who appreciates at all the magnitude of the subject, must endeavour to fill his mind with impressive meetings, and on the relative advantages of town and county conventions, are worthy of consideration: "These annual county meetings, which have now been held for five successive years in the counties of the state, have been eminently useful in diffusing information as to a better system of school district organization, better modes of instruction, and so forth. Especially, by bringing the sympathy of numbers to bear upon individuals, they have diffused a spirit, and created an energy, more worthy of a cause which carries so much of the happiness of the community in its bosom. But it seems to me that the mode of operation heretofore pursued may now be modified with evident advantage.

"To explain my views in regard to the most eligible course for the future, it will be necessary to recur for a moment to the practice of the past. At the county conventions, a considerable portion of the day has usually been spent in discussing such topics as were deemed most intimately connected with the welfare of the schools in the section of country where the meetings were respectively held. All persons present have been invited to participate in the proceedings. Questions have been freely put, and replies given. On these occasions I have always been requested to deliver an address in the course of the day, and have never felt at liberty to decline the invitation. I have also invariably held myself ready to answer such inquiries, and to meet such suggestions as might be proposed; but the friends of education assembled from the vicinity have always been consulted as to the topics for discussion, and, through the medium of a committee, have generally proposed them. Out of a general similarity of circumstances and of objects has naturally arisen a considerable degree of uniformity in the modes of proceeding; and it is with the sincerest pleasure that I bear witness, that at all times, and in all places, the greatest harmony has prevailed. I do not mean that opinions have always coincided, but that different views have been presented in an amicable spirit; and it has oftentimes happened that some modified course, some third measure, has been elicited, better than either of those originally suggested.

"Such has been the common mode of proceeding, the advantages of which have been clearly discovered in regard to those towns and districts which have been most regularly and fully represented at the meetings. In regard to a considerable number of towns, an

facts and arguments, and, as he goes abroad, scatter the good seed by the wayside, in the field, at the market-place,

entire reform in their schools has been distinctly traceable to the fact that a few of their most worthy and influential inhabitants had been present at one of these conventions; and, having listened to the counsels, or been inspired by the zeal of their fellow-citizens from other towns, have returned home to diffuse the information they have obtained, and to animate others with the spirit they have caught.

"But the benefits of this course are too limited. It has served the purpose of exciting an interest, but it will not consummate the work of reform. Except in some half dozen or dozen cases, the conventions have lasted but a single day. Persons coming from any considerable distance desire to leave at an early hour, that they may return home; and, as some time is necessarily spent in organization and in preliminary arrangements, the day is shortened at both ends. Unlike most other conventions, too, these are attended by ladies, whose paramount influence in the cause of education renders their presence exceedingly desirable; and this is another reason for dissolving the meetings at an early hour. In addition to this, most of the counties are too large, in point of territory, to allow persons whose residence is remote from the respective places of meeting, to go and return on the same day, although, in some of the counties whose territory is greatest, there are individuals who have never failed of being present at them. It may be said, indeed, that other conventions, abolition or political, are attended by persons who traverse half the length of the state for the purpose; that they are continued for two or more days; or, if held but for one, that the meeting is prolonged by borrowing many hours from the night. But, as an answer to this, it must be remembered that the cause of education—the cause of ransoming our own children from the bondage of ignorance and vice—the cause which is not merely to affect, but to control their destiny, and that of the Republic, through all future time—has not yet aroused that degree of enthusiasm which will gather crowds of people from distant places, and hold them together for days in succession, while they descant upon their own virtues and denounce the wickedness of their opponents

"But the best minds in our community have been reached. What is now wanting is to reach another class of persons, numerically greater, but having less appreciation of the value of education,

and in the shop. Each one must remember that **he *can do*** something for this good work, and that what he *can do, he is bound to do.* Especially, in his own district or town, ought each one to give his whole influence towards the diffusion of sound views, and the introduction of a wiser and more liberal policy.

II. *Frequent change of teachers.*—This is a subject of almost universal complaint. The evil arose, at first, from the fact that schools were kept open but a part of each year; and more recently, it has resulted from the prevailing practice of hiring male teachers in winter, and females in summer. Another cause, which has contributed to this pernicious practice, is *the change which is annually made in the government of the school.* By law, new trustees are required to be elected once in twelve months, and these, being often chosen on the principle of rotation, are either wholly inexperienced in the duties of the office, or ignorant, at least, of the policy of their predecessors, and of the reasons which induced them to adopt particular measures. In many cases, too, they are anxious to propitiate persons who have been disaffected, or to secure some sinister object, and hence the system is changed and teachers are dismissed.

It is impossible to overrate the evils of such a course. The business of education is essentially *progressive.* It

and less knowledge of the means by which it should be conducted. This class of persons do not attend the county conventions, either from a lack of interest in the general subject, or because the distance is too great, or because the conventions are held in the daytime, which they appropriate to labour. But many of this class would attend such a meeting in their own town, especially if held in the evening. *What seems to be desirable now is frequent meetings in smaller sections of territory, that sounder views and a livelier interest may be carried to the doors of those who will not go abroad to obtain them.* Such has been the course pursued from the beginning in Connecticut, whose laws on the subject have been, in many respects, very similar to our own."

consists of a series of processes, the later always depending upon the earlier, and requiring, therefore, to be conducted, within certain limits, on the same principles, and by the same methods. But, in the present state of our schools, hardly any two teachers have the same methods. No opportunity is afforded the one who succeeds to become acquainted with the state of the school, and with the methods of his predecessor, by actual observation. The one has gone, before the other arrives. He enters the school, a stranger to the children and to their parents, unacquainted with the relative propensity and aptitude of the different scholars, ignorant of the course which was pursued by former teachers, and with the prospect, probably, of retiring himself, at the end of three or four months. Is it not evident, that the progress of the school must be arrested, until he can learn his position? As each teacher is apt to be tenacious of his own system, is it not also evident that, after having arrested the work which his predecessor began, he will, in many cases, proceed to undo it? Thus the children will often spend the whole period of his stay, in retracing their studies in a new book, or according to a new method. There will be movement, but no progress.

The effect, on the teacher, must be equally bad. This practice makes him, in truth, little better than a vagrant. He can have no fixed residence, since the period for which he engages is never over a year, and rarely over four months; and even, in these cases, it is liable to be curtailed by the caprice of his employers or the arbitrary interference of the trustees. He of course cannot marry. He has little ambition to form a character; his employment occupies without improving him; and, in most cases, he either hastens to leave it, or becomes a contented but useless drone. Can we wonder that there are few good teachers under such a system?

Is there any remedy for such an evil? We believe there

is. The apology for this constant change is, that the district cannot support a good male teacher, throughout the year. They must either close the school during summer, or have it taught by a female. Then, we say, *let it be taught by a female, throughout the year.* The sum which is now divided between the two teachers would pay a female handsomely for the whole year, and would thus supersede the necessity of closing the school at all, except for a vacation of three or four weeks.*

The advantages of this course would be various. 1st. It would give to the scholars the advantage of having the same instructress throughout one entire year at least; and, if she proved worthy of the charge, she could hardly fail, during that time, so to enlist the affections of the children, the good-will of the parents, and the confidence of the trustees, as to be secure of a renewed engagement. Thus we should gradually return to the good old practice of *permanent schools under permanent instructers.*

2d. It would be a *cheap* system. The best-qualified female teachers, in common schools, would be glad to accept what is now paid to men of the poorest capacity.

3d. It would secure teachers of higher intellectual capacity and qualification. Women have a native *tact* in the management of very young minds, which is rarely possessed by

---

* Suppose a male teacher is employed four months at $25 per month, including board, a female for four months at $12 50 per month. The whole expense for teachers' wages would be $150, and the school would be kept open but eight months out of twelve. Apply the same sum to a female teacher at $12 50 per month, and it would keep the school open during every day of the year. Pay her $15 per month, which is the least that a good female teacher ought to receive, and this sum would sustain the school for ten months, which is probably sufficient, since children ought to have occasional vacations of considerable length. Employ her but eight months and pay her but $12 50 per month, and there would be a saving to the district of $50 annually.

men. The prospect, also, of permanent employment, at a fair rate of compensation, would induce many young women of narrow means to prepare themselves for teaching; and it will hardly be disputed, that, with limited opportunities as to time and money, they would make greater proficiency in knowledge and in the art of teaching, than young men having only the same opportunities. It should be considered, also, that the prospect of profitable employment would awaken competition, and in this way higher qualifications would be secured.

4th. It would furnish a desirable resource, and a useful as well as respectable mode of life, to many females, who are cast upon the world without property.

5th. It would conduce to the improvement of manners and morals in schools, since females attach more importance to these than men; and they have a peculiar power of awakening the sympathies of children, and inspiring them with a desire to excel.

6th. It would diminish the number of select schools, since many of these are taught by women, whose services would then be required in common schools; and these schools would also be less necessary, than at present, for very young children.

But can you propose, seriously (some one will say), that timid and delicate women should retain charge, through the winter, of country schools, in which large and rude boys are congregated? This forms the only objection, which can be plausibly urged against this plan, and it is one which deserves full and respectful consideration. I would remark in regard to it,

1. That it is by no means so formidable, as it might appear at first thought. It is now admitted, that in the government of schools, moral influence should be substituted, as far as possible, in place of mere coercion, and that corporal punishment should be reserved for young children,

and be applied but very rarely even to them. It is admitted, too, that the teacher ought to aim, first of all, to cultivate the higher sentiments of our nature, to awaken self-respect, and to induce the child to become a law to himself. If this be true (and few will be disposed to question it), then it must follow that women are, in most respects, pre-eminently qualified to administer such a discipline. Their very delicacy and helplessness give them a peculiar claim to deference and respectful consideration; and this claim large boys, who are aspiring to be men, can hardly fail to recognise. I need not add, that they are honourably distinguished from the other sex by warm affections, by greater faith in human nature, and in its capacity for good, and by disinterested and untiring zeal in behalf of objects that they love. Says the present chief magistrate of this state, " He, it seems to me, is a dull observer, who has not learned that it was the intention of the Creator to commit to them a higher and greater portion of responsibility in the education of youth of both sexes. They are the natural guardians of the young. Their abstraction from the engrossing cares of life affords them leisure both to acquire and communicate knowledge. From them the young more willingly receive it, because the severity of discipline is relieved with greater tenderness and affection, while their more quick apprehension, enduring patience, expansive benevolence, higher purity, more delicate taste, and elevated moral feeling, qualify them for excellence in all departments of learning, except, perhaps, the exact sciences. If this be true, how many a repulsive, bigoted, and indolent professor will, in the general improvement of education, be compelled to resign his claim to modest, assiduous, and affectionate woman. And how many conceited pretenders, who may wield the rod in our common schools, without the knowledge of human nature requisite for its discreet exercise, too indolent to improve, and too proud to discharge their responsible duties, will be driven to seek subsistence elsewhere."*

This, however, is no longer a subject, for speculation and conjecture. The experiment has been tried. It was commenced, some four years since, in the State of Massachusetts, and has been continued, with constantly increasing success, down to this time. The annual reports of the Board of Education during that period have exhibited a rapid increase in the proportion of female teachers; and the last report shows, that the increase of female teachers, during the preceding year, had been more than four times greater than that of males. Of the whole number of teachers (6600) employed in the common schools of Massachusetts during the year 1841, nearly two thirds were females; and with what success many of them conducted winter schools will appear from the following extracts from the returns: "In two of our schools," say the school committee of the town of Boylston, "the West and the Centre, *we have tried the experiment, this year, of employing females to teach our winter schools;* and we feel confident in saying that it is no disparagement to those who have had the charge of these schools in winters past, to say that we have never known them to be more ably managed, more successfully governed, or more faithfully instructed. The scholars have made all the proficiency that we could have expected under teachers of the other sex. The large scholars have uniformly in the West school, and generally in the Centre, been more cheerfully submissive to the rules and regulations of the school than in former winters, when these schools have been under the instruction of male teachers."

"We are not prepared to say that it would be advisable to dispense with male teachers altogether in our winter schools, but we are satisfied that female teachers might be

* Discourse on Education, delivered at Westfield, July 26, 1837, by Wm. H. Seward.

employed to a far greater extent than they have hitherto been, without any detriment to our schools. And, by adopting this course, our schools might be lengthened one fourth or one half."

Say the school committee of the town of Petersham, "Four of our winter schools were taught by females, and without any disparagement to the young gentlemen teachers, some of whom did very well, yet justice compels us to say, that the schools taught by females during the past winter have made as good progress as those taught by males. And it is not too much to say, that the school which made decidedly the best appearance at the close, was taught by a young lady."—" It is frequently the case, that large and turbulent boys, whom it was quite difficult for men to govern by severe means, have been won into good behaviour by the gentle treatment of a female teacher."

Say the school committee of the town of Brimfield: " The winter schools, eleven in number, were taught by five males and six females. To say nothing in disparagement of those under the care of males, we hazard the opinion that those taught by females will suffer nothing in comparison. Indeed, to some of these we are constrained, in justice, to give the preference before any and all others."

" Some have objected to female teachers for the winter schools on the ground that the large scholars would not be willing to submit to female authority and dictation, and hence that, on the score of government, we might expect trouble. But, so far as the experience of the last winter goes, this objection is removed. It has been just as we always supposed, from the very nature of the case, would be the fact, viz., that the older scholars, and especially the young men, would have too much self-respect and regard for the feelings of a kind, amiable female teacher, to allow them unnecessarily to wound her tender sensibilities. Now it is a fact, *that in four schools taught by females, we have found older scholars than in any taught by males.* In three of these schools we found young men from eighteen to twenty-one or two, and in every instance in the most perfect state of subordination, treating their teacher with great deference and respect, and yielding with perfect good feeling to all her wishes. We have heard not a breath of complaint, as it regards the conduct of the older scholars in particular, except in one instance, and that was the case of a very ignorant, and, one should say, a very foolish boy, who, though nineteen or twenty, could scarcely read, and who, it was said, went to school, not to learn, but to make disturbance. We cannot forbear, in general, to bestow the highest encomiums on the conduct of the older scholars, especially of the young men, who have attended the several schools taught by females." The committee proceed to state, that they found the female teachers quite as well versed as the males in the higher branches of mathematics; that they used the black-board more, and with greater success, in the exercises of the school; that they were more ingenious in "introducing little devices calculated to animate and encourage children," and to relieve the monotony of school exercises; and that they were more attentive to *cleanliness* and good manners, and more successful in making good readers.

2. Wherever the winter school is too large, or it is thought inexpedient, on some other account, to intrust it altogether to females, a male teacher might be employed, for the express purpose of taking charge of the larger and more advanced scholars, who attend only at that season; the female being retained as an associate or assistant teacher. In this way, unnecessary changes would be avoided, and the benign influence of the gentler sex in schools would become permanent, and be secured to that class of children, especially, who most need it.

3. There is another expedient, now frequently adopted

in Massachusetts and Connecticut, which seems to meet completely, though in a somewhat different way, the objection to female teachers, founded on their supposed inability to manage large boys. It consists, in establishing, at some point which will be convenient and central for three or four districts, a *Union* or *High School*, to be open, in most cases, only in winter, and to be frequented only by scholars so advanced in age that they can go a considerable distance from home, and so far versed in the rudiments of learning that they need instruction in higher branches. These schools might be taught by males; the common district schools being left to females, and being frequented only by young children. The advantages of this plan will be more obvious, when we come to the discussion of the next topic.

III. *Unnecessary multiplication of school districts.*—This has become a sore evil. In 1815, when the system was organized, the whole state contained but *two thousand seven hundred and fifty-six* districts. These have since been divided and subdivided, till they number, now, *ten thousand seven hundred and sixty-nine*. As population became more dense, there was some reason for reducing the larger districts, in which the schoolhouse was too remote to be frequented, by the smaller children of those inhabitants who lived on the outskirts. It may be doubted, however, whether even this consideration is entitled to all the weight which is usually conceded to it; since, in the country, where children have ample space to play in, and various resources and occupations of a domestic character, much is often lost to health, and nothing gained to character or intellect, by sending them prematurely to school. Admitting, however, the utmost that can be claimed for this argument, it will only follow, that school districts should be multiplied as population increases, in the *more sparsely settled parts of the state*. Where the territorial extent of a district is not unreasonably large, a mere increase of population would form no sufficient ground for dividing it. In point of fact, however, the process of subdivision has gone on over the whole state; and this, too, not only as fast as the increase of population, but much faster; the number of school districts having increased, since 1815, in *a nearly fivefold ratio, while the population has not trebled*. The consequence is, that the number of inhabitants, in each district, is, on an average, materially less, than it was when the system was established.

The average population in each district is about 230; the average number of children between 5 and 16, 55; and the average extent of territory, four square miles, or two miles square. If the schoolhouse occupies a central position, the greatest distance which any child has to travel will be less than one mile and a half, and the greatest number of scholars who can be expected to attend, on an average (after deducting those who go to select and other schools), will not be over thirty-five. The present average rate of attendance appears, from the reports of the visiters in 1840 and 1841, to be *less than thirty-five*. It must be evident, that such a school is not sufficiently large to fully occupy, or remunerate the services of a first-rate teacher; and hence, instead of multiplying districts still farther, as is often the disposition at present, it is very important to diminish their number. It is justly observed by the secretary of the Massachusetts Board of Education, in his last report, that "there is but one class of persons in the whole community, and that class not only small in number, but the least entitled to favour, who are beneficially interested in the establishment of small and feeble districts. This class consists of the very poorest teachers in the state, or of those who emigrate here from other states or countries in quest of employment as teachers, who are willing to teach for the lowest compensation, and for whose services even the lowest is too high. These teachers may safely look upon the small and feeble districts as estates in expectancy.

Such districts, having destroyed their resources by dividing them, must remain stationary, from year to year, amid surrounding improvement; and hence, being unable to command more valuable services, they will be compelled to grant a small annual pension to ignorance and imbecility, and this class of teachers stands ready to be their pensioners."

This subdivision of districts not only deteriorates the standard of instruction, it adds also to its expensiveness. If two districts are established, where one would be sufficient, two buildings must be erected and kept in repair, and two fires supplied with fuel, and two teachers maintained, where, one of each would answer the same ends. Suppose that a space of four square miles, the average size of our school districts at present, contains a population of 450 souls, of whom from 90 to 100 are children, between the ages of five and sixteen. The average number attending school would, in summer, be about fifty, and about sixty-five in winter. If, now, instead of having two feeble districts, two poor schoolhouses, and two indifferent teachers, there were to be but one district, with a good and commodious edifice, and an efficient teacher, no child would be required to travel farther than would conduce to good health, and there can be no doubt that the instruction and influence would be much more salutary. How would it be with the relative expense of the two systems?

I. With two districts, under the present system, there would be a female teacher for four months in summer, and a male for the same period in winter.

The annual expense would be, say,

Interest on cost of two schoolhouses ($400 each) at 7 per cent.	$56 00
Wear and tear, and repairs of two houses	20 00
Fuel, &c., for two houses	20 00
Wages of two female teachers, four months, at $12	96 00
" male teachers, four months, at $24	192 00
Incidentals	10 00
	$394 00

II. With one district, there might be a female teacher throughout the year or for ten months, with the addition of a good male instructer, for three or four months in winter. The annual expense on a *liberal* plan would be, say,

Interest on cost of one good schoolhouse ($600)	$42 00
Wear and tear, &c.	15 00
Fuel, &c.	15 00
Wages of female teacher, ten months, at $15	150 00
" male teacher, four months, at $30	120 00
Incidentals	10 00
	$352 00

If the male teacher were dispensed with, the whole annual expense would be but $232. If a male were employed for ten months without a female, at $30, even then the expense would be but $382, so that the present system is not only the least efficient and useful, but also the least economical.

The process of uniting two or more adjacent districts, or of forming two out of three, ought to be commenced at once, and it might be carried on, through our smaller villages, and the more thickly-settled rural districts, with the greatest advantage. A law, authorizing it, has recently passed the legislatures of this and adjoining states, and it is believed that, in New-York, the whole number of districts might be reduced one third without material inconvenience to any, and with the greatest benefit to all. The number of teachers in demand would thus be reduced, while the rate of compensation might be increased without adding to the burdens of the people; and thus the facilities for obtaining good instructers would be multiplied, in a twofold ratio. The schools, being larger, would admit of a more thorough classification of the scholars; being kept throughout the year, the organization would be more permanent and effective, and the manifold evils, growing out of the constant change of teachers, might be obviated. The present is an auspicious time for this work. In many towns or counties, the schoolhouses are old and inconvenient, and must soon be renewed. Would it not be wise, in such cases, to induce the trustees and inhabitants of neighbouring districts to assemble, and to consider the expediency of so combining their energies, as at once to increase the value, and diminish the expense, of an education for their children.

Where it is not found practicable or expedient, to reorganize the school-districts on this principle, another plan may be adopted, which has found great favour in Massachusetts and Connecticut, and which is thus described by the enlightened gentleman who presides over the interests of primary instruction in the former of those states: " The population of many towns is so situated as conveniently to allow a *gradation of the schools*. For children under the age of eight or ten years, about a mile seems a proper limit, beyond which they should not be required to travel to school. On this supposition, one house, as centrally situated as circumstances will admit, would accommodate the population upon a territory of four square miles, or, which is the same thing, two miles square. But a child above that age can go two miles to school, or even rather more, without serious inconvenience. There are many persons whose experience attests that they never enjoyed better health, or made greater progress, than when they went two miles and a half or three miles daily to school. Supposing, however, the most remote scholars to live only at about the distance of two miles from the school, one house will then accommodate all the older children upon a territory of about sixteen square miles, or four miles square. Under such an arrangement, while there were four schools in a territory of four miles square, *i. e.*, sixteen square miles, for the younger children, there would be one central school for the older. Suppose there is $600 to be divided among the inhabitants of this territory of sixteen square miles, or $150 for each of the four districts. Suppose, farther, that the average wages for male teachers is $25, and for female $12 50 per month. If, according to the present system, four male teachers are employed for the winter term, and four female for the summer, each of the summer and winter schools may be kept four months. The money would then be exhausted; *i. e.*, four months summer, at $12 50=$50, and four months winter, at $25=$100; both =$150. But, according to the plan suggested, the same sum would pay for six months' summer school instead of four in each of the four districts, and for a male teacher's school eight months at $35 a month, instead of four months at $25 a month, and would then leave $20 in the treasury.

2 m.	2 m.
a	a
a	a

"By this plan, the great superiority of female over male training for children under eight, ten, or twelve years of age would be secured; the larger scholars would be separated from the smaller, and thus the great diversity of studies and of classes in the same school, which now crumbles the teacher's time into dust, would be avoided; the female schools would be lengthened one half; the length of the male schools would be doubled, and for the increased compensation, a teacher of fourfold qualifications could be employed."—"If four districts cannot be united, three may. If the central point of the territory happen to be populous, a schoolhouse may be built consisting of two rooms, one for the large, the other for the small scholars; both upon the same floor, or one above another."

The principal objection to this plan, is, that it suspends

the schools for children under ten years of age, during **half** of each year, and keeps open the union or high school but eight months. Thus both schools would, in effect, be broken up each year, and that class of children who can be best spared to attend throughout the year would, many of them, be deprived of access to school for six months out of every twelve. Would it not be better to require the female schools to be kept open ten months each year, and to receive all children under twelve years of age, and girls even later, the central or union school being kept four months? Four female teachers at $12 50 would be $50 a month; this for ten months =$500, leaving $100 to be paid to the male teacher.

That some arrangement, by which the evils of feeble districts can be avoided, is absolutely necessary, will be more obvious, if we consider the peculiar distribution of population, over the face of our country. Prussia, with whose school system we are most accustomed to compare our own, has, on an average, *one hundred and thirty inhabitants* to every square mile, while in this state we have but about *fifty-five*. In another respect the difference is still greater. In Prussia, the inhabitants, even of rural districts, instead of living, as with us, in isolated dwellings, a quarter of a mile apart, are grouped together in hamlets or villages, almost any one of which is sufficiently large to furnish a school with sixty-five or seventy children. It must be evident that, in such a country, there is little occasion for that subdivision of districts, which here, though carried much too far, is still, in some degree, unavoidable. When, in addition to this facility which exists in Prussia for forming large schools, we consider that, there, every profession or calling is already crowded, and that multitudes of men have no higher ambition than to be schoolmasters for life in some village or primary school; and when we consider, farther, that a sum, which, in Prussia or

France, would be adequate to remunerate a master, would not, in this country, pay the wages of a day-labourer, we shall perceive how visionary it must be, to hope that a class of *men* can be trained up here, willing to teach common schools for life, at the rates which feeble and thinly-peopled districts can pay. The necessity, therefore, for employing females, seems, here, to be clear and irresistible. Even in Prussia, it is thought, by many judicious friends of popular education, that they might be employed, in many instances, with much benefit. Says a late writer,

"There is this peculiarity in Dutch and German schools, that women are rarely employed in them except to teach sewing and knitting, or as mistresses of infant schools. In large rooms, filled entirely with girls, we rarely found a schoolmistress or a female teacher, unless the children belonged to the lowest class in the school, and were merely learning the alphabet, or unless the hour for needlework had arrived. The Germans greatly underrate the physical strength and intellectual power of women, as adapted for the work of instruction. They affect a great contempt for female authorship, arising partly, perhaps, from the fact that they have but few writers of that sex, or but few to be compared with the best of those of England and France. We believe this prejudice against female talent to be unfortunate and mischievous. There is nothing that a girl can learn that a woman is incapable of teaching when properly trained; and, in many cases—as every one knows who has frequented Sunday-schools—women make better instructers than those of the other sex. Women have often more talent for conversational teaching (the best of all forms of instruction), more quickness of perception in seizing difficulties by which the mind of a child is embarrassed, and more mildness of manner than a master commonly possesses; and when these important qualities are combined with the proper degree of firmness (and that, too, may be acquired), they cannot be excelled. For teaching singing they are especially qualified, as the pitch of their voices enables them to sing in unison with children, instead of an octave below; and for the physical strength said to be wanting, no instruction can be fit for a child that is given in a form that would exhaust any frame but one of iron or brass. But we need not dwell upon this part of our subject, for English notions of delicacy would not permit schools to exist, in which girls of 13 or 14 should be left, for hours together, without any person to consult belonging to their own sex Normal schools, therefore, if ever established in this country, must be established for women as well as for men."*

Having discussed, so much in detail, the best methods of organizing schools in the country, where population is sparse, it may be well, before dismissing this branch of our subject, to consider the various plans which have been proposed for the improvement of schools in cities.

SECTION V.

THE IMPROVEMENT OF COMMON SCHOOLS.

"A school ought to be a noble asylum, to which children will come, and in which they will remain with pleasure; to which their parents will send them with good-will."—Cousin.

SCHOOLS IN CITIES AND VILLAGES.

CHILDREN residing in large towns, and, indeed, in all compact places, are exposed to peculiar dangers and temptations, and they need, therefore, more than others, the benignant influence of good schools. It is an influence, however, which very many of them are not likely to enjoy. They are, in many instances, afflicted with improvident or immoral parents; and being generally doomed, in

* Westminster Review.

such cases, to poverty, they are crowded together in dark and neglected districts, where their condition escapes observation, and where they rapidly corrupt one another. It is not strange, therefore, that a larger proportion of children grow up with idle and profligate habits, in towns, than in the country; and it is plain, that to prevent this mournful result calls for special care and attention, on the part of the friends of education. To determine, then, on the best system of public instruction for a city; to bring its advantages to every one's door, and especially to the doors of the poor; and to provide that all shall avail themselves of those advantages, is an object of the very highest interest and importance. It touches intimately the general welfare, which is always endangered by the presence of the ignorant and unprincipled; especially in large cities, where such persons have peculiar incitements, and enjoy signal opportunities for confederation and outrage.

I. DISTRICT SYSTEM.—The methods which have been proposed for school organization, in cities, are various. By one, which is considerably prevalent, the territory of a city is divided, as in the country, into small districts, and in each, a school is kept, sufficiently large for the accommodation of all the children in said district. Where the districts contain, each, but a small number of children, this system appears to be obnoxious to the most serious objections. It collects together in one apartment, and under the supervision of but one teacher, children of every age and grade of attainment; and these so divide the labours and distract the attention of their instructer, that a large portion of his energies are wasted. In a school composed of none but small children, many exercises might be introduced, admirably adapted to interest and improve them, which, in a school composed in part of larger scholars, would be quite out of place. So with discipline: if it has to be accommodated to the mixed and heterogeneous character of a school composed of children of all ages, it must fail in adapting itself with skill and precision to the wants and capacities of those of any particular age. *Division of labour* seems to be quite as important in education as in the production of wealth; and we might with as much wisdom require that cotton should be picked, and carded, and spun, and woven, and bleached, and dressed, by one machine or by one person, as that children of different ages and attainments, as well as dispositions, should be successfully governed and instructed by one teacher. In the country, where schools can be maintained only by means of local districts, such an evil is, in a degree, unavoidable; but in cities and villages it is gratuitous, and ought, therefore, to be avoided.

A modification of the district system has been recently introduced in Buffalo, and a few other cities of this state, which seems to obviate some of the most material of these objections. The population is divided into larger districts, varying from one thousand to fifteen hundred, so that each district will contain nearly three hundred children. In each a schoolhouse is erected, containing two apartments, in one of which a female teacher is employed to superintend the instruction of the younger pupils, and in the other a male teacher, at a fixed and competent salary, to give instruction in the higher branches. In Buffalo, a city superintendent has been appointed, who reports that " the system has thus far succeeded beyond the most sanguine hope of its projectors and friends. Its good effects are already apparent from the anxiety to obtain admission into the schools, the prompt and constant attendance of the children, and their correct and orderly deportment while under the authority of their teachers." The estimation in which the public hold it, may be inferred from the fact that, in 1837, the whole number of children taught in all the public schools was but 679, whereas, in 1839, when the system had become fully established, it had swelled to 2450; and in

1840, to 4068. It ought to be added, that nearly four fifths of the expense of maintaining this system is defrayed voluntarily by the citizens, that it has materially reduced the expense of educating children, and has greatly increased the attendance.* Prior to its adoption it was found that a very large proportion of all the children of Buffalo were at no school, public or private, and that the average annual expense of instructing those who did attend, was two thirds greater than at present.

* Among the most efficient systems of Municipal Education in this country, may be instanced the one organized in the city of New-York under the auspices of the *Public School Society*. With a wisdom as enlarged as it is uncommon, the more affluent, and therefore the largest tax-payers in that city, made application several years since to the Legislature that the amount levied on its inhabitants for the support of education might be increased fourfold. They clearly saw that good schools form the cheapest system of police for a city, as well as the best guarantee for its improvement and prosperity. The large amount of funds thus raised has been applied hitherto, for the most part, to the support of schools organized and superintended by an association of enlightened and philanthropic individuals, known as the *Public School Society*. Composed of all persons who have, at any time, paid the sum of ten dollars into its treasury, the association confides its duties to a Board of fifty trustees, chosen annually from among those members who have been most distinguished for zeal and efficiency in the cause of primary education. During the recess of the Board, which meets quarterly, the superintendence of the schools, and its other duties, devolve on an executive committee, and on *sections*, into which the Board divides itself; each section being charged with the oversight of one public school building, and the primary schools attached to it.

The schools are called *Primary* and *Public*. The primary schools, of which all the teachers are females, are open to all girls over four years of age, and to boys between four and ten. When a pupil has learned in one of these schools to *spell* correctly, *read* audibly and distinctly, and *write* pretty well on slates, he is recommended for admission to the *public*, or higher schools, and if he can pass a satisfactory examination, is received. In the *public* schools, which receive all boys over ten years, even though they have not been instructed in the primary schools, the instruction of the boys and girls is conducted in separate rooms under teachers of their own sex. It includes spelling, reading with definitions and explanations, making and mending of pens, arithmetic, geography, use of the globes and drawing of maps, English grammar, composition and declamation, bookkeeping, and the elements of history and astronomy, with the addition of needlework

II. The MONITORIAL PLAN, or, as it is sometimes called, the system of *Mutual Instruction.*—This method seems to have been borrowed from the Hindu schools at Madras, and was introduced into England by Bell and Lancaster. Its

when the pupils are girls, and of declamation, algebra, geometry, and trigonometry when they are boys.

The mode of instruction in the *public* schools is a modification of that which is usually known as the Monitorial or Lancasterian system, and is said to be distinguished for its vivacity and thoroughness, as well as for cheapness.

To the children, the instruction, including text-books and necessary materials, is given *in all cases gratuitously.* To the city, the annual expense for teachers' wages is about $2 75 per child, which is about one half that usually paid for the same service in the district schools throughout the state. No trustee receives any compensation.

The number of children instructed in these schools in 1840 was about forty thousand, who were distributed through something more than one hundred schools, so located as most effectually to promote the convenience of parents and secure the largest attendance of scholars. To further the latter object, it is made the duty of teachers to visit the inhabitants in their vicinity, especially those of the poorer and more improvident classes, and to urge the attendance of their children. Agents are also employed for the same purpose. The system of teaching throughout the schools is uniform, so that a child removing from one neighbourhood to another is not interrupted in his course by the change of his school. In order to secure, at the same time, any advantages that may accrue from the experience of the teachers, or the suggestions of others, stated meetings are held by the teachers for the purpose of comparing the progress of their respective schools, and considering the best means of improving them.

The whole amount of duty performed by each trustee in the way of visitation and superintendence is matter of record, and is exhibited publicly at the recurrence of each annual election. The fidelity of the teachers is secured by frequent and careful visitations of the trustees as individuals, as committees, and in their collective capacity as a board. The system seems to have been organized with great care, and it has been administered with eminent zeal and disinterestedness. The services which it has rendered to the city during the last twenty years must have been incalculable. As suggesting a method by which the voluntary and unpaid efforts of enlightened private citizens can be made to co-operate with public functionaries in the supervision of schools, it seems worthy of special attention. All experience shows that supervision, in order to be most effective, should be the joint work of parents, public officers, and benevolent individuals.

essential feature consists in employing scholars as assistant teachers, or monitors; the office of the master being confined, for the most part, to a superintendence of the school, and to the instruction of the monitors. It was originally intended only for large schools, containing children of all ages, and, in such cases, is, of course, the cheapest of all systems, since but one master or mistress suffices for the instruction of several hundred children. Its immediate results, too, in imparting a certain mechanical skill in reading and writing, as well as its effect in maintaining order and precision in the operations of a great school, were calculated to strike and dazzle spectators, and hence the system, when first introduced, was unboundedly popular. Experience, however, soon revealed capital defects, which might have been anticipated from the very nature of the method, as compared with the true principles of education; and these have led to its entire abandonment, in some countries, and to its essential modification, in all. In Prussia and Holland, it is wholly repudiated, on the ground that it does not tend to *develop* and *discipline* the faculties of the mind, but only to give a limited amount of information. In countries like England, where there are hordes of poor children growing up in ignorance, and for whose education the government does nothing, this system may be profitably retained, since it enables the benevolent, with limited funds, to accomplish something in behalf of a most important object, which would otherwise be neglected. There can, moreover, be no doubt that some of its expedients might be adopted with advantage in all schools; and that even young children may sometimes be profitably employed, in hearing each other *repeat* lessons, while older ones may *assist*, in the vastly higher and more difficult work, of *teaching*. But it is believed that the Lancasterian method can be well administered, in a large school, only by masters eminently well qualified, and that even then, they will find the **task too arduous**.

In most cases, it degenerates into a lifeless mechanism, which deadens the faculties of a child, and which is apt, also, to be unfriendly to his morals. I cannot but regard it as a subject for congratulation, that the system is going into disuse in our own country; and the extent to which it has been retained in the new public schools of Buffalo and of other cities of this state, seems to me to constitute one of the most serious defects, with which those schools are chargeable.

III. Another plan of school organization, now popular in Germany, is termed by them the Fächer system. It consists *in employing separate masters for separate studies*. It assumes that a teacher who has nothing to do but teach writing, will teach it better than any one else; so with reading, geography, history, mathematics, music, and every other branch of instruction. The head master is looked to for nothing but the moral and general superintendence. This system applies the principle of dividing labour, to the greatest possible extent, in education, and has, therefore, its peculiar advantages. It can be employed, however, only in large schools and in very large towns. Even there it is liable to the objections, that the instruction, by being too much subdivided, will be given in a narrow and exclusive spirit; that the sub-masters will feel too little responsibility for the moral culture of their pupils; and that the number of children congregated in the same school will multiply dangerously the temptations to which they are exposed. As compared with the plan of dividing a city into small districts, with a small school in each, to be composed of children of all ages between five and sixteen, and to be taught by one instructer only, this system has great and unquestionable merits. It is believed, however, that its benefits can be retained, and its inconveniences excluded, under a system better adapted to the condition and wants of our own country, and which may be called, therefore,

IV. The AMERICAN SYSTEM.—By this system, small primary schools, for both sexes, are established in every part of the city, to receive none but small children (say) under eight or ten years of age, to be kept open throughout the year, and to be taught by well-qualified females. In these schools, children of both sexes are taught to read and write, and to understand the simplest elements of arithmetic, while girls are instructed in sewing, knitting, &c.; and all receive assiduous moral culture. If found necessary, in order to save the expense of separate lots and buildings, such schools might each be held in a single apartment of edifices devoted to other purposes, ample provision, however, being made for play-ground, ventilation, &c.

Having acquired, in these schools, a knowledge of the simpler rudiments, and having also reached the prescribed age, children should then be advanced to schools of a higher character, which might, for convenience, be termed High Schools. In these, a much larger number of scholars might be collected, and it would probably be found expedient, also, to have separate establishments for boys and girls. These schools should be sufficiently large, to authorize the employment of the best masters in the various branches, on the principles referred to in the last article, and also to favour the use of simultaneous instruction, and such other improvements as have been well tested by experiment.

The advantages of this system may be briefly summed up under the following heads :

1. It will classify scholars according to age and attainment, and thus enable us to procure teachers exactly adapted to their respective capacities and wants.

2. It will prevent the necessity of sending very small children far from home, and of exposing them to the contaminations inseparable from large assemblages.

3. It will secure to young children, when most they need it, the genial influence of female care and culture.

4. It will, by providing good public schools in every neighbourhood for small children, supersede private schools, and thus bring together the children of all ranks and classes of our people. Destined, as all are, to meet hereafter on the broad field of competition, and, at the same time, to labour together for the common weal, it is unwise to separate them early in life, and to make schools which ought to be so many bonds of union, the occasions for jealousy and misunderstanding.

5. It will contribute to enlarge the circle of juvenile studies, by relieving the high schools from attention to the mere rudiments, and by securing that children are taught thoroughly at every step of their progress.*

---

* This is substantially the plan adopted in the city of Boston. In Philadelphia, one somewhat different, but well calculated to secure the same ends, is in operation. "The existing system of public schools," says the last report, "founded on the will of the people, owes its present organization to an act of Assembly, passed on the 3d of March, 1818. By this act, the city and county of Philadelphia form the first school district of Pennsylvania, and the law which regulates its schools is separate and distinct from the general school law. *Practical wisdom is thus manifested in not applying the same rules to this densely-populated portion of the state as to those more extended and sparsely-peopled districts in the country parts.* The first district is subdivided into sections, numbered from one to eleven. The organization and direction of the schools, the election of teachers, and, in general, the local concerns of public education in the several sections, are confided to directors, whose number is regulated by the amount of duties to be performed. The directors of each section constitute a board, with a distinct organization. They are elected in the city and incorporated districts by the councils or commissioners of the districts, and in the townships and boroughs by the people at the spring elections. By a recent law, the term of service of one third of each board is to expire annually.

"The general control and regulation of the school district is vested in a higher board, composed of representatives from the board of directors of the several sections, and called the 'Controllers of the Public Schools.'

I would add here, that, owing to the cupidity or the necessities of parents, and also to other causes, many children

"The powers of this board are large, and their duties laborious. The board determines the amount of money to be raised annually by taxation for the schools, and which, by law, the county commissioners are required to place in the county treasurer's hands, subject to its orders; the tax-fund being made up, in addition to the state appropriation, of one dollar for each taxable inhabitant in the district. This board purchases sites for schoolhouses, erects the buildings, furnishes them, determines the number of teachers to be employed, and the salaries to be paid, and prescribes and furnishes the books to be used, and other supplies. It makes the appropriations required by the different sections, reviews their expenses, and draws the orders upon the county treasurer for their payment. The Model School and Central High School are under its immediate direction. Occasional visits of inspection are made to the schools of all the sections by its members."

"The act of the Legislature of the 13th of June, 1836, directing the education of all children over four years of age, annulling the obligation to use the Lancasterian system in the schools, and authorizing the establishment of a central high school, gave a new impulse to the school system. In execution of its provisions, the board has provided schoolrooms or erected schoolhouses wherever the wants of the community required them, and as rapidly as the resources of the county appeared to warrant. No effort has been spared in extending the number of primary schools, and in providing them with convenient and comfortable rooms, in adding to the number of grammar schools, erecting suitable and commodious buildings for them, and procuring instructers of acknowledged ability and qualifications, in introducing useful improvements into the methods of teaching, and in adding to the facilities of instruction. Sound education has thus been diffused through the district, while by close attention to the expenses of the system, they have been kept within limits proportioned to the increased wants of the public. Under the present organization of the system, a boy may receive an entire and thorough education in the public schools. Beginning in the primary schools, where the rudiments are taught, he is advanced in turn, when duly prepared, to the secondary and grammar schools, where, receiving the advantages of a good English education, he is prepared for the high school, and may thus enter, with a thorough training, any busi-

are removed from school, and placed at trades before they are properly instructed. Hence no system of public instruction for cities should be regarded as complete, which does not provide *evening* schools for boys under sixteen years of age, and young men's associations, or lyceums, with their lectures and libraries, for those who have passed that age. "We shall never," says an able writer already referred to, "live in the midst of an educated community, until the machinery is provided for carrying on, at suitable opportunities, the instruction commenced in childhood, to the years of manhood, and even throughout life. Beyond the age of ten, or, at most, of twelve, the children of the poor, without a compulsory law, or without presents of clothes and money, will not be retained in day schools." On the other hand, "a boy who, from the age of fourteen to twenty-one, has no means of obtaining books, and none of hearing lectures upon scientific subjects, will never make an intelligent, well-informed man."

V. DIVERSITY OF CLASS-BOOKS.—No evil connected with the present condition of our schools calls more loudly for immediate correction than this. It is a subject of earnest and continual complaint on the part both of teachers and parents, and it seems to prevail throughout the whole country. In Massachusetts it has been remedied in part, but is represented, in the last report of the secretary of the Board of Education, as still prevalent, and as most mischievous in its effects. In Connecticut, according to the report of the secretary, made in 1839, the returns, although incomplete, showed that there were *more than two hundred different schoolbooks* used in the several studies pursued in the common schools, viz.: 12 in spelling, 60 in reading, 34 in arith-

ness, profession, or occupation to which his inclination and talent may direct him. In all the schools the pupils are upon a footing of perfectly republican equality: the system, while it ensures the acquisition of knowledge to all, ensures also the ultimate general elevation and refinement of society."

metic, 21 in geography, 14 in history, 19 in grammar, 4 in natural philosophy, 40 in other branches. I have not the means of stating the whole number to be found in the common schools of New-York, but there is no reason for supposing it to be less than in other states.

This subject occupies a prominent place, in the reports of the special visiters appointed in 1839. Hardly a return is made, in which the multiplicity of schoolbooks is not presented as an intolerable grievance, which must be removed, before teachers can do their duty, or scholars make proper proficiency. For example: "The first complaint and the last complaint which greets a visiter in every district is, 'My time and the time of my scholars is half wasted; my patience is put to the severest trials; my scholars are not advancing, from the simple want of uniform class-books.' Your committee are not aware of a single instance, where the town boards of inspectors have acted on this subject, or of a single common school in the county where the books are uniform." So from the town of Avon: "Our schools suffer much, also, from the want of uniformity in books. In all our visits, we seldom found more than three scholars to read in a class, for the want of corresponding books. The same difficulties exist relative to grammar, geography, arithmetic, &c." From the town of Peru: "We find a great deficiency in the kind of books, and the number of them; generally from five to ten different kinds of reading-books in one school—no two schools using the same books." From the town of Fishkill: "The scholars are usually not properly classed—*i. e.*, according to ability and progress; each division having the same studies and using the same books. Such a classification seems very desirable for obvious reasons." "In each case coming under the observation of the visiters, it has been pronounced impracticable; and in proof of the declaration, it has been said that the following difficulties exist:

"1st. *As to studies.* Parents object, one to this, another to that. 'My child,' says one, 'must learn nothing but ciphering and writing.' 'Mine,' says another, 'must not learn grammar.'

"2d. *As to books.* 'Parents will not get them,' say the teachers. 'Every teacher must have new books,' say the parents. In some cases, two or three different systems are taught in the same school, for one or both of these reasons."

The evils of such a system are obvious. It tends, in the first place, to multiply classes to such an extent, that the whole time of the teacher is frittered away in listening to hurried recitations. No opportunity is allowed for explanations and illustrations, nor any for awakening and disciplining the mind of the pupil, by a searching and skilful examination, which will reveal the true amount of his knowledge, and the process by which he acquires it. The pupil's efforts are soon reduced to the mere act of remembering, and the teacher's to that of hearing him repeat by rote. 2d. It operates oppressively on the teacher if he purchases all the different text-books which he may be called to teach in different schools; and if he does not purchase them, he is unable to prepare himself on the different lessons, before he hears them recited. 3d. It prevents the introduction of the system of *simultaneous* recitation, which has been found so beneficial in other countries, and in some parts of our own. 4th. The stimulating effect which a large class exerts upon each member of it, not only when reciting, but also when studying, by reminding him constantly that many besides himself are engaged, at the same time, on the same lesson, and that he will soon be required to appear in their presence, and to be measured by as well as with them; all this is lost where classes are so subdivided. 5th. It adds seriously to the cost of education; not only as it protracts the period required to make a child master of a study, but also as it increases the expense for text-books. Instead of being worn out, they are soon cast aside to make way for new ones. If the additional expense imposed on each district annually, in this way, be but $5, the annual cost to the whole state would be nearly $55,000. 6th. This system, also, holds out a continual and direct invitation to book-makers, publishers, agents, &c., &c., to multiply text-books, and thus to perpetuate and extend these various mischiefs.

This diversity of text-books, though the source, at present, of unmixed evil, has grown up naturally and insensibly, and is not, therefore, to be charged, as a crime, on any party. Some books, in use twenty years since, were very defective, and called for change; and, in the absence of central authority to regulate these changes, and of proper skill and experience on the part of teachers, it is not surprising, that they have often been determined, by the caprice of parents, or the enterprise of booksellers. It is also to be considered, that the constant change of teachers has added much to this evil; it being the interest of a new teacher, on the one hand, to introduce such books as he has been used to, and of parents, on the other, to prevent an unnecessary sacrifice of their property. Hence has come the practice, whenever a book wears out, of replacing it by one, which may happen to be acceptable to the teacher temporarily employed; and, as hardly any two in succession have the same preferences, we need not wonder, that the aggregate number has become immense.

It is a subject for hearty congratulation, that the people are beginning to awake to a proper sense of this evil, and that they are demanding a reform. On this account, as well as on several others, the present seems a most auspicious time, for devising some plan, which may prove reasonably permanent, and which will gradually displace the almost endless variety of schoolbooks, by as much uniformity as can be expected in our country, and by all, perhaps, that is consistent with the highest improvement. It is not to be supposed that we have yet reached perfection in making text-books; and it would be injustice, therefore, to authors, as well as to children, to close the door against all future changes. But it may be assumed, that the experience of the last twenty years has thoroughly tested the relative merits of the different works now in market, and that judicious and enlightened men might make such a selection from them, as would answer well the present wants of our schools. This selection, too, might be so arranged, that, while the books harmonize* with each other on the one hand, they should, on the other, be furnished by different authors and publishers, thus preserving proper regard for the rights and interests of those who have devoted themselves to the work of supplying this species of commodity. A selection, made with some reference to this end, would have two special advantages. It would, in the *first* place, make it the interest of publishers, to issue some one or two works at the least possible cost, and in the most perfect form, that thus they might secure a great and permanent sale, instead of multiplying, as they now do, works of many different kinds, of which a large portion prove to be without value, and a source only of loss. In the *second* place, authors would be induced, by such a course, to limit their ambition to the composition of one book of the highest excellence, instead of aspiring, as so many now do, to the composition of a whole series, embracing all the different branches of knowledge.

* In regard to the selection of books by committees, I have had occasion, during the last year, to notice a mistake or oversight which deserves to be mentioned. It consists in the selection of books which, on important points, conflict with each other, and therefore leave teacher and pupil in doubt what course to pursue; as, for instance, the selection of Webster's Dictionary, with Worcester's or Pierpoint's Reading-books, where the rules for pronunciation contained in the former are so different from those of the latter.—*Horace Mann—Report* (1842) *to the Massachusetts Board of Education.*

But by what means can this selection be made, and be commended to general favour? This problem is, doubtless, a difficult and delicate one; and it ought to be approached with caution, and in the spirit of true conciliation. Teachers and school officers must remember, that the schools are in the hands of the people, and that no plan can permanently prosper, that does not secure their confidence and cordial co-operation. On the other hand, parents and employers must remember, that to decide on the relative claims of different text-books is no easy task; that nothing but experience and special preparation can qualify any one to perform it as it should be performed; and that no portion of the community are so deeply interested as themselves, in having the work done well and wisely. They should also consider that, in sending their children to common schools, supported in part by the public, they have virtually consented that the state shall share in the work of regulating and superintending those schools, and that they are bound, therefore, to yield their own judgment to that of the proper functionary, and to the will of the majority. The state has created a general superintendent, with deputies in each county, and has also provided for the appointment, in each town, of inspectors, commissioners, &c., who are to exercise, severally and in due subordination, all powers necessary for the general welfare of the schools. Is it not through these officers, aided by an enlightened and patriotic public sentiment, that the reform so much desired must be accomplished?

I would suggest that, in undertaking it, the following principles ought to be kept in view:

1. It should commence in the several towns, and should be the result of a cordial understanding between the deputy superintendent, the inspectors and trustees, and the most judicious and active friends of education, whether teachers or otherwise. Town conventions for the promotion of ed-

ucation would afford a most favourable opportunity for bringing about a good understanding on this subject.

2. It should aim at *preserving* the most valuable text-books now in use, excluding the worthless, and reducing the number to that point necessary for uniformity within each school.

3. It should contemplate *gradual* rather than sudden changes. Parents should not be required, in all cases, to purchase new books immediately, but only so fast as old ones are worn out. A list of books selected should be kept posted up in the schoolhouses, and when new books are wanted, it should be understood, that none can be used but such as are on this list. To accelerate the progress of the reform, the late and present superintendents have suggested the expediency of *exchanges*. An extract, to be given presently, will explain this plan.

4. The body which selects books should take pains to set forth the urgent necessity for some reform in this matter, and should *recommend* rather than *enjoin*.

5. In adopting a series of books, regard should be had to the practice of neighbouring towns or counties. The most important thing is to have uniformity in each district; the next most important is to have it in towns; then in counties, &c.

6. Changes should be subject to the supervision of the state and deputy superintendents; and when a uniform series of books has once been introduced into any school, it should not be altered without their consent.

7. A uniform system for the whole state, if desirable, can only be reached after a term of years, and ought to be adopted on the recommendation of the state superintendent, by and with the advice of the deputy superintendents.

I close this subject with an extract from the *instructions* lately issued from the office of the state superintendent, and which are intended as a guide to the deputy superintendents.—(*Instructions*, p. 195.)

"*The books of elementary instruction.*—It is believed that there are none now in use in our schools that are very defective; and the difference between them is so slight, that the gain to the scholar will not compensate for the heavy expense to the parent, caused by the substitution of new books with every new teacher; and the capriciousness of change which some are apt to indulge on this subject, cannot be too strongly or decidedly resisted. Trustees of districts should look to this matter when they engage teachers."

"One consequence of this practice is the great variety of text-books on the same subject, acknowledged by all to be one of the greatest evils which afflict our schools. It compels the teacher to divide the pupils into as many classes as there are kinds of books, so that the time which might have been devoted to a careful and deliberate hearing of a class of ten or twelve, where all could have improved by the corrections and observations of the instructer, is almost wasted in the hurried recitations of ten or a dozen pupils in separate classes, while, in large schools, some must be wholly neglected. Wherever the (deputy) superintendents find this difficulty existing, they should not fail to point out its injurious consequences, and to urge a remedy by the adoption of uniform text-books as speedily as possible. To accomplish this, let the trustees, under the advice of the teacher, inspectors, and superintendent, determine what text-books shall be used in each study, and require every child thereafter coming to the school to be provided with the designated books. This very desirable uniformity may, perhaps, be facilitated by exchanges between different districts, of the books that do not correspond with those in general use, for such as do. For instance, in one school the great majority of spelling-books may be those of Webster, with some of Marshall's, while the latter may predominate in another district, in which there are also several of

Webster's. In such cases, an exchange of the differing books between the two would obviously be mutually beneficial. The superintendents might assist in the execution of such an arrangement, by noting the proportions of the various books in the different schools."

SECTION VI.

IMPROVEMENT OF COMMON SCHOOLS.

"All the provisions hitherto described would be of none effect, if we took no pains to procure for the public school thus constituted an able master, and worthy of the high vocation of instructing the people. It cannot be too often repeated, that it is the master that makes the school."—GUIZOT.

VI. INCOMPETENCY OF TEACHERS.—That a large proportion of common school teachers are not well qualified for their duties, is so generally admitted, that proof of it would be superfluous. I proceed, therefore, to inquire how the evil can be corrected.

It is quite evident, that such an evil can be thoroughly cured only by removing its cause. What, then, is the cause of this prevailing incompetency of teachers? It will be found, if I mistake not, in the single fact, that the public, including more especially parents and employers, have had no proper notion of the nature, difficulty, and importance of the office which the teacher discharges. The state of public opinion on this subject, in our country, has not been greatly in advance of that which prevailed in Prussia sixty years since. " Public instruction," says a late Prussian writer (Wittich[*]),

---

[*] See a paper on the Former and Present Condition of Elementary Schools in Prussia, by N. Wittich, native of Tilsit, Prussia, in the first volume of the publications of the Central Education Society.

referring to the state of common schools in his country at that period, " public instruction was then a mechanic art, not unlike that of a cobbler; for teaching was synonymous with filling the memory of a child; reading was imparted by the most simple method of syllabication, and arithmetic without the least indication of the natural relations existing between numbers. At this time any man was deemed fit to hold the office of schoolmaster in an elementary school. If he was uninstructed in some branch of the requisite knowledge, the study of a few days or weeks was considered sufficient to supply the deficiency. Hence it happened that most of these teachers were persons who had previously tried their fortune in some other business, and had not succeeded. They commonly continued to practise their art, as mending old clothes, &c., either after schooltime, or even, sometimes, during the attendance of the children. The discipline was as simple and as ineffective as the method of teaching, consisting of a continual use of the stick."

With this portrait, which would serve to represent the character of primary instruction throughout Europe at the time referred to, and which, in its essential features, is but too much like the teaching now prevalent in our own common schools, contrast the following description of a good schoolmaster, by one of the first statesmen and philosophers of the age. Says Guizot, in the speech with which he introduced " the law of primary instruction" to the French Chamber of Deputies: " What a well-assorted union of qualities is required to constitute a good schoolmaster? A good schoolmaster ought to be a man who knows much more than he is called upon to teach, that he may teach with intelligence and with taste; who is to live in an humble sphere, and yet have a noble and elevated mind, that he may preserve that dignity of mind and of deportment, without which he will never obtain the respect and confidence of families; who possesses a rare mixture of gentleness and firmness; for, inferior though he be, in station, to many individuals in the *commune*, he ought to be the obsequious servant of none; a man not ignorant of his rights, but thinking much more of his duties; showing to all a good example, and serving to all as a counsellor; not given to change his condition, but satisfied with his situation, because it gives him the power of doing good; and who has made up his mind to live and to die in the service of primary instruction, which to him is the service of God and his fellow-creatures. To rear masters approaching to such a model is a difficult task, and yet we must succeed in it, or we have done nothing for elementary instruction. A bad schoolmaster, like a bad parish priest, is a scourge to a *commune*; and though we are often obliged to be contented with indifferent ones, we must do our best to improve the average quality."*

The first step towards rearing teachers of this lofty spirit

---

* In the same spirit he addresses teachers in a circular: "No sectarian or party spirit," he exclaims, "in your schools; the teacher must rise above the fleeting quarrels which agitate society. Faith in Providence, the sanctity of duty, submission to parental authority, respect for the laws, the prince, the rights of all, such are the sentiments he must seek to develop." So in the following picture of the painful duties of the teacher, and of the consolations which he must find within himself. "There is no fortune to be made; there is little renown to be gained in the obligations which the teacher fulfils. Destined to see his life pass away in a monotonous occupation, sometimes even to experience the injustice or ingratitude of ignorance, he would often be saddened, and perhaps would succumb, if he did not derive courage and strength from other sources than the prospect of immediate or personal reward. He must be sustained and animated by a profound sense of the moral importance of his labours; the austere pleasure of having served his fellow-creatures, and secretly contributed to the public welfare, must be his compensation, and that his conscience alone can give. It is his glory not to aspire to aught beyond his obscure and laborious condition; to exhaust himself in sacrifices scarcely noticed by those whom they benefit; to toil, in short, for man, and to expect his recompense only from God."

in our own country, is to satisfy the people of its necessity. In France and Prussia, it was sufficient if the *government* appreciated this necessity. But with us, where schools are placed under the immediate control of the inhabitants, nothing will answer but a profound conviction, on their part, that a reform is needed, and that that reform must be their own work. To desire better teachers is but the first step. With that desire, must be combined a readiness to provide the means for supporting them, and a disposition to assign them the rank, and consideration, to which they are entitled by their services. It is idle to talk of there being a real and *general* demand for the best teachers, so long as employers expect to procure an instructer for their children, at the same price, that they pay to labourers on the farm, or in the kitchen. When properly-qualified teachers are called for, in a distinct and emphatic manner, and when the people show that they are capable of distinguishing between real merit and noisy pretension, then, and not till then, there will be a demand indeed, and that demand will be supplied. The conscientious will feel urged to qualify themselves for a duty so high and important, and the enterprising will be incited, by the hope of a return, proportioned to the magnitude and responsibility of their labours.

It must not be forgotten, that in this country, broad avenues to success seem to open before every young man as he enters life, and that but few, who are properly qualified to teach, will consent to confine themselves, for life, to common schools. It is partly on this account, that I have already urged, so strenuously, the permanent employment of female teachers. But I would still more strenuously urge that, whether we employ males or females, we can never hope, in such a country, to have good permanent teachers, unless the prevailing method of hiring and treating them is changed. We not only offer them a pitifully small remuneration; **we also** engage them but for short periods of time; **we subject** them to no effective supervision; we provide them with but a small number of scholars, and those of all ages and degrees of attainment; and we finally dismiss them at the expiration of a few months—perhaps after subjecting them to studied indignities—without an expression of gratitude or interest. Is it in man, to labour perseveringly and faithfully under such a system, except it be on the single ground of benevolence? and to the benevolent, be it remembered, there are more inviting fields, since there are those, which promise an ampler and a quicker return.

We are told, that we must regenerate our schools by training up teachers specially qualified, and we are pointed to Prussia and Holland, where this measure has been the great instrument of reform. We forget, however, that to train up teachers is useless, unless they can be induced to devote themselves to their profession, and that, in this country, such will not be the case, unless schools are so organized and conducted, as to present the prospect of fixed and agreeable employment. Suppose a Prussian or Dutch teacher, after having been trained to his duties, were to be placed in a schoolhouse by the roadside, unpainted, and perhaps half unglazed; standing directly on the highway; without play-ground, or shade, or retreat for the performance of nature's most private and necessary offices; where he can collect but about thirty scholars, comprising those of both sexes and all ages; pursuing their studies in text-books whose name is legion; giving, perhaps, but half the days of each week to the school, and showing, too many of them, by their manners, that they are unaccustomed to restraint at home, and impatient of it when applied abroad. Then proclaim to him, as he enters on his duties, that his compensation shall, at the most, not exceed *one dollar* for every working-day, and, in many cases, be less than half that sum; that even this pittance can be extended to him only for three or four months at a time, when he must give place to a *cheaper* successor; that for one half of each year, at least, he must seek a precarious subsistence in another locality, and, perchance, in another pursuit; and that, while employed in his temporary school, instead of having a fixed and comfortable home, he must *wander* throughout his district, fixing his home successively in different families! I ask, how many of the twenty thousand teachers, who are now patiently pursuing their untiring and unostentatious, but not unhonoured labours in the common schools of Prussia, could be induced, on such terms, to plant themselves in the schoolhouses of free America, or who of them would not prefer the plough, or the mechanic's toil, before the thankless and unrequited office of a schoolmaster?

The Prussian schoolmaster devotes himself to teaching for life, because he knows that, for life, it will yield him an adequate support. The government assigns him a post, and this post it guaranties to him, during good behaviour. It supplies him with a house and garden, and encourages him to collect around him all the comforts of life. It secures, also, that his salary shall be punctually paid; prescribes a course of study to which every child is obliged to conform; enforces a regular and universal attendance of all children of the proper age, and provides a system of rigid inspection and supervision. The school is so connected with the Church, and so honoured by law as well as by usage, that the teacher is considered inferior only to the pastor. His employers dwell in the same hamlet, so that children can be always at school; and if eminent for his zeal and fidelity, his fame is certain to reach his superiors, and to command applause not only, but substantial reward or promotion. And, finally, he has the cheering assurance that when, in the discharge of his high, but toilsome and anxious duties, he has worn out his best days, he will not at last be dismissed and forgotten, but will be held in honoured remembrance by those whom he has instructed, and will be permitted to retire on a pension from his government.

It will be found that in Prussia, and the other countries of Europe most distinguished for improved systems of public instruction, the training of teachers has gone hand in hand with a reorganization of the schools, and with stringent regulations in regard to the attendance of scholars, the choice of schoolbooks, the construction of schoolhouses, and the rate of teachers' wages. It must be so here. What was accomplished in those cases, promptly and effectively, by the centralized and almost unlimited power of the government, must be accomplished, here, by the slow progress of public opinion. While discussion and agitation contribute to develop, on the one hand, the necessity there is for a better class of teachers, the example of even a small number, who may be trained up and stationed in different parts of the state, will soon serve to strengthen this feeling. Everything depends, in this country, on having the people thoroughly penetrated with the conviction that our common schools must be *good* schools; and that, in order to make them so, they must receive the united support of all citizens, and must be rendered attractive to a superior class of teachers. It must be felt, that not only better teachers are wanted, but better employers also. A spirit of co-operation and liberality must be awakened. The position of instructers must be made permanent, and they must receive that consideration, to which they are so well entitled by the intrinsic dignity of their office, and which will tend so much to lighten their labours. Every individual can do something, towards a consummation so desirable. By reading journals and books devoted to the subject of education, and, above all, by visiting schools, and reflecting on what he sees, each one can rouse in his own mind a clearer perception, and a deeper feeling of what is needed, and of what he himself should do. Teachers, however well qualified, need aid and encouragement, and it should never be forgotten that the regeneration of our schools must be the *joint work* of the people who employ, the instructers who teach, and the government which superintends.

While I thus insist upon the necessity of something besides new methods of training teachers, I would also remind teachers themselves, that they may do great things towards improving our schools, if they have but the will, and employ the right means. If their only object is, to teach for a few months for the sake of money, and if it is apparent that their thoughts and interests are away from their school, they will deserve little respect, and need expect none. So, if they betake themselves to this employment merely to escape hard work, and are satisfied, if they can, from year to year, wring a license to teach from careless or ignorant inspectors, they should, in such case, remember, that their labours are an injury rather than a blessing, and that they merit neither pay, nor consideration. If, on the other hand, they have a proper sense of their duties, and strive to qualify themselves for their due performance; if they are diligent, in acquiring more knowledge of the various branches of elementary learning, and more skill in imparting that knowledge to others; if they have a generous ambition to send back their pupils improved in wisdom and virtue, that thus they may be known as real benefactors of the world, let them be assured that such teachers will be honoured and rewarded. Their example will prove contagious. Not only will other teachers emulate their efforts, but parents will imbibe the same spirit, and the work of improving our schools will quickly become popular and general. " We have seldom known teachers," say the visiters (1840) of one of our largest counties, " who understand their business; who take a pride and satisfaction in devoting all their energies to the good of their school and of the district; who have made themselves acquainted with all the families in the district, with their weaknesses, prejudices, and wishes; and, in short, acted the part of the good Samaritan to all, without regard to compensation for the first quarter *only*—we say we have seldom known such a teacher under the necessity of leaving a district for want of the highest wages. Therefore, let those who wish good wages and a permanent situation be impressed with this fact, and act in view of it."

TEACHERS' SEMINARIES OR NORMAL SCHOOLS.

We have already intimated, that better means for educating teachers, and qualifying them for their peculiar duties ought to be provided; but we have been anxious, at the same time, to enforce the too-much-neglected truth, that in conjunction with such means, improvements should be made in the existing methods of organizing and conducting schools. Where population is crowded and employment scarce, young persons educated to a particular calling are not likely to quit it. But in a country like ours, where there are so many broad and open fields for enterprise, and where knowledge and talent bestow such influence, we may establish normal schools and educate young persons to become teachers at great expense, and yet fail to secure their services. We are not, therefore, to infer that such schools, when established here, will prove as efficient as they have been found to be in Europe, nor that they can supersede the call, for strenuous and judicious measures to reorganize our whole system of primary instruction.

There is another circumstance which deserves consideration, as distinguishing our system from that which prevails in Prussia, and Holland. In those countries, especially in Prussia, there is no connexion between common schools, and the higher seminaries of learning. The former are intended exclusively for the education of the working class; the latter for those who intend to devote themselves to the liberal professions. Very rarely does a child pass from a

Prussian common school into a gymnasium, and from thence to the University; as, here, he passes from the district school to an academy, and from thence, again, to college. With us, who know no distinction of *caste*, all are parts of one system for the education of the people. With them, primary schools, and normal institutions for preparing the teachers of primary schools, form one system—the seminaries for the education of the upper classes, as they are termed, form another. A young man, in Prussia, who enters the gymnasium,* expects to pass through the University; nor does he ever expect, during his own course of education or afterward, to become a teacher in a primary school. In this country, nothing is more common, than for a youth who has passed his earlier years in a common school, to go to an academy for a few months to *complete* his education, as he terms it, and often he does it for the special purpose of preparing himself to teach. Here, all profess to aspire to the best education they can possibly obtain; and hence, when a child enters a common school at the age of five, though his parents may be ever so humble in rank, and his own means ever so limited, it is still uncertain at what point his elementary instruction may stop, whether in the common school, in the academy, in the college, or in the professional school of law, medicine, or theology. Many, again, after leaving the common school in early life, and engaging for some years in active or laborious pursuits, return to study; and, without waiting to perfect their English education, proceed at once to Latin and Greek, or such other branches as will facilitate an immediate entrance on a profession. It is also to be remembered, that in this country, a considerable proportion of those who teach winter schools are actually

* If it be asked where a German youth, intended for the University, is placed until he becomes qualified by age and attainments to enter the gymnasium, we answer—under private tutors, or in schools specially intended for the higher classes of society.

students in colleges and academies, who take up the employment for a time; and who, though deficient in some important respects, are still useful, as they carry down to the district school, the spirit and views, which they have acquired in higher seminaries.

It will be evident, from this statement, that in Prussia, normal schools were indispensable. The primary schools had hitherto supplied their own teachers. They were furnished, in hardly any instance, from the higher institutions. When, then, the government came to infuse life and energy into the hitherto dormant system of primary education, it must needs have had recourse to some new expedient, for supplying competent teachers. As it would be idle to attempt to reanimate a lifeless body through means furnished only by itself; so it would be equally idle to think, that minds already deadened by studying in a primary school could be the means of awakening that school to a new life. Whenever schools supply their own teachers for a long period of time, there is a strong tendency towards mechanical and monotonous modes of instruction; and nothing can well arrest this tendency, but the stimulus of an active competition on the one hand; or the circumstance that the school favours so free and thorough a development, that both teachers and taught are fired with the spirit of self-improvement, on the other.

Hence new measures, for the supply of common school teachers, became necessary; and in Europe, it was natural that this want should be met, by the establishment of new seminaries. In this country, and especially in this state, it seems to have been equally natural to look, in the first instance, to academies. These institutions were already established in nearly every county; and they had long been regarded, as an important source for the supply of good teachers. They formed, too, an essential part of that system of public instruction which the state had matured; and the several parts of which, it was deemed most desirable to bind together, in close connexion. Departments in such academies for training teachers would, at the same time, be much less expensive than independent normal schools, and if sufficiently effective, they might be attended by some peculiar advantages. These considerations led, about seven years since, to their establishment, and it cannot be denied that some of them have rendered essential service. This they have done, as much, perhaps, by exciting other academies to supply similar facilities to those who may be preparing to teach, as by any aid which they have extended directly to common schools. The general effect of the measure has been, to render the public more sensible of the claims of common schools, and of the want of good teachers. It has contributed, also, to establish more intimate and kindly relations between our higher and lower schools; to awaken in the former more attention to the true principles of teaching; and to secure that every improvement, which is made in regard either to discipline or instruction, shall become the common property, of all our institutions of learning.

In one respect, however, these departments are seriously deficient. They make no adequate provision, for exercising the pupil in the *practice* of teaching. In most cases, too, the students in these departments are employed, too exclusively, in studies other than those which are pursued in primary schools,* while in these last they are often unskilled. It is also to be regretted, that the annual allowance

---

* The effect is, that such students, being overtaught in some respects, soon become dissatisfied with their duties, and are anxious to push themselves forward in a different career. Experience has shown that, even in the older countries of Europe, it is dangerous to push the instruction of those who are intended to act as teachers of primary schools, beyond that which is essential to a complete fulfilment of their duties. In this country the danger is evidently **much greater.**

which they receive from the state, is not large enough to give them precedence of the classical departments in the same academies; thus rendering them objects of paramount interest to the trustees and teachers, instead of their being regarded, as now, in the light of unimportant appendages. It is, moreover, a fair ground of exception, that the theory of teaching, instead of being kept constantly before the pupils, is only a subject for occasional discussion; and that, by mixing with other students, the ambition, which these pupils once had to become good teachers, is apt to be exchanged for a desire to enter some other profession. It is a fact now well ascertained, that but a small proportion of the members in these departments expect to become permanent teachers in common schools, and that a still smaller proportion ever fulfil such expectations.

These considerations render it evident, that something is needed, in addition to these departments. An institution is needed, in which the students shall be dealt with, simply as teachers preparing for their work, and in which the lessons they daily receive, in the theory of teaching, can at once be reduced to practice,* under the eye of an accomplished superintendent. It should be composed of those

---

* Mere lessons and lectures on the science and art of teaching are not sufficient. They may form good theoretical teachers, but practical skill can be gained only by experience; and, unless opportunities for acquiring it be afforded before they enter on their profession, it must be gained afterward at the expense of their pupils. Hence primary schools should be attached to every seminary for teachers, in which theoretical lessons can be exemplified before the eye of the scholar, and he can himself be fitted, by repeated trials, to take part in the regular business of instruction. Such schools are now universal in Europe, where normal seminaries are established. They are the more necessary, to prevent the teachers who are found in such seminaries from becoming mere theorists. On the other hand, care should be used lest these seminaries be imbued with a bigoted attachment to particular methods of teaching, or with a spirit of blind routine and imitation.

who are already well-grounded in the rudiments of an English education; it should propose, as its main object, to awaken inquiry among its pupils, and to train them to habits of intellectual activity; to show them at one and the same time how they can instruct others, and how improve and cultivate themselves. It should be an institution pervaded by the free spirit of learners; not one that proposes to lay down stereotyped processes of teaching, but one that will excite its members to propose to themselves high objects, and to prosecute those objects in a generous and ever-progressive spirit. It should aim to bring out the whole character and disposition of its pupils; and where it finds them disqualified, intellectually or morally, for the all-important work of teaching, it should require them to embrace some other pursuit. A few months, passed in such a seminary, would raise and enlarge a teacher's views, and give him an impulse, which he must feel through all his future life, and in which his pupils would ever have reason to rejoice.

Is it not the duty of the State of New-York to supply itself with at least *one* such institution? It has lately enacted a law giving new symmetry and efficiency to its common school system; a law which embraces several new and important features, and which promises to be rich in blessing. The effect of this and other causes will be seen, in an unusually great demand for *good* teachers within the next two years, and this demand will rapidly increase. Is it not incumbent on us, to take more effectual measures to supply it? Why not plant a teacher's seminary or normal school, sufficient to accommodate one or two hundred pupils, at the Capital, where it can be overlooked by the officer who has been charged by law with the superintendence of primary instruction; and where it can be visited by members of the Legislature, strangers, and others, thus sending its influence to the remotest extremities of the state, and even of the nation.*

Scholars instructed in such a seminary, in the various methods of teaching, and in the most effectual plans for organizing and conducting schools, would carry a benignant influence, not only to their own schools, but to all neighbouring districts. They would serve as missionaries, not only of better methods, but also of a higher spirit of instruction, and would operate to quicken and rouse many a fellow-teacher, now torpid and inefficient, but whose energies, once awakened and directed aright, would enable

---

* "*When education is to be rapidly advanced,*" says Mr. Bache, in his able Report on Education in Europe, "seminaries for teachers afford the means of securing this result. An eminent teacher is selected as director of the seminary; and by the aid of competent assistants, and while benefiting the community by the instruction given in the schools attached to the seminary, trains, yearly, from thirty to forty youths in the enlightened practice of his methods; these, in their turn, become teachers of schools, which they are fit at once to conduct, without the failures and mistakes usual with novices; for, though beginners in name, they have acquired, in the course of the two or three years spent at the seminary, an experience equivalent to many years of unguided effort. This result has been fully realized in the success of the attempts to spread the methods of Pestalozzi and others through Prussia. The plan has been adopted, and is yielding its appropriate fruits in Holland, Switzerland, France, and Saxony, while in Austria, where the method of preparing teachers by their attendance on the primary schools is still adhered to, the schools are stationary, and behind those of Northern and Middle Germany.

"These seminaries produce a strong *esprit de corps* among teachers, which tends powerfully to interest them in their profession, to attach them to it, to elevate it in their eyes, and to stimulate them to improve constantly upon the attainments with which they may have commenced its exercise. By their aid a standard of examination in the theory and practice of instruction is furnished, which may be fairly exacted of candidates who have chosen a different way to obtain access to the profession."—See *Report*, p. 325.

him to outstrip the most favoured competitors. To show how much can be done by such a school in a very short time, I add the following testimony, taken a few years since before a committee of the House of Lords (England). It relates to the effect of the instruction given in the training and model schools, which had been established for teachers, at Dublin, by the Irish Board of National Education. The witness is the Rev. Eugene Congdon:

What kind of schoolmaster have you? I have one schoolmaster who has been instructed under the board, and that schoolmaster has been of such use to me that I find the greatest possible advantage, satisfaction, and comfort with his services. I have put other teachers, male and female, under his tuition for some time, and he has prepared them in the same manner that he has been himself prepared, and thereby I find the business of the schools carried on very well.

Was he educated at the Model School of the National Board in Dublin? He was there for three months.

Do you think he was much improved by that education? He has been improved so far that it is a matter of astonishment to me how children, from the lowest ignorance of nature almost, are, in three quarters of a year under his tuition, not only able to spell and to write, but absolutely able to calculate with as much precision and accuracy as persons that have been for years at school before.

Where was he brought up? When I got permission from the board to send a person forward for tuition, I advertised for persons that would be fit and proper. A number presented themselves. I selected this man of the name of Casey. I sent him to Dublin, and he returned to me afterward with the approbation of the board, and with a token of their kindness in giving him some books.

Is Ballyduff school in your district? It is.

Is that a good school? He is the master of it, and I do not think there is in Ireland a better working school. I suppose he has at this moment above 300 boys in his school."

With a central normal school, such as we have proposed, aided by the departments now established in academies, and by the peculiar facilities which are afforded in all our higher seminaries to those who propose to teach, the work of raising the standard of teaching might be greatly accelerated.

This would be especially the case, if the institution received, at first, none but female teachers, who might be prepared more rapidly for the work, and who are likely to continue in it for a longer term of years. A central school would operate, not only on its own pupils, but also on those in academies, and would serve, particularly, to recall attention to the necessity of teaching the elementary branches more thoroughly. In the course of a few years, a number of teachers of the highest class, might be placed in every town; and these would rear, in their schools, or through the stimulus of their example, a multitude more, who would soon be sufficient to supply all the wants of the state. If, on the other hand, no such measure is adopted—if our sole reliance, for training teachers, is on academies, which regard the object as a subordinate one, which afford no proper facilities for practice, and which inspire, in too many cases, a distaste for the office of teaching, rather than a desire to excel in it—in such case, it is greatly to be feared, that our common schools must continue to languish.*

* I add here an extract from the report (1836) of M. Cousin on the State of Education in Holland, as regards schools for the working classes and the poor. Speaking of the education of teachers, he says, " In 1811 schoolmasters were trained in the same way as they now are generally; in all the public schools, those children are selected who show the most intelligence; they are kept somewhat longer, and are trained for their future destination by special instruction in the evening, and particularly by employing them in the different classes in succession; at first as assistants, with a very small remuneration, and then as undermasters, with a better allowance, until they are placed at the head of a school when a vacancy occurs. That method of educating teachers for the primary schools is still practised, and it is, in some respects, an excellent one. They are trained at a very moderate expense, and, farther, they are not made more than schoolmasters; they are not taught more than is necessary for their profession. Brought up in school, they acquire the habits of the place, they become attached to it, and cheerfully pass their whole life in it; while masters who are reared at

In connexion with the measure, which I have thus ventured to suggest, there are two others, to which I will refer briefly. Teaching is a duty, which God devolves, more or less, on all. Whenever a mind is visited by the light of truth, it ought to hold that truth, as a trust, for the benefit of others, as well as for its own good. As parents, we are not only called to teach, but also to govern and influence; and in many relations of life, we have occasion to employ a skill, nearly allied to that, which a teacher needs in the management of a school. It would seem, then, that more regard ought to be paid to this fact, in our systems of education. Every child should be taught, not only how to acquire, but also how to communicate knowledge; not only how to subject his own will to the regulations of a school, but how to proceed when he himself would acquire influence over the

greater expense and with more refined cultivation, run the risk of becoming less suited to the hard life that awaits them, take to it only when they can do no better, and quit it for something else as soon as they possibly can. These are the advantages of the system; but it has also great disadvantages. *It is very apt to engender habits of routine; every defect which has got into the school takes root;* the scholar and future teacher adopts, blindly at first, and afterward follows with interested minuteness, the whole manner of the master on whom all his hopes depend, and thus generation after generation of teachers may succeed, without one step in the way of improvement being made.

"*I attach the greatest importance to normal primary schools*, and consider that all future success in the education of the people depends upon them. In perfecting her system of primary schools, normal schools were introduced for the better training of masters. The government was cautious not to lay aside the old method, which was very good, but, at the same time that they continued it, they established in 1816 two normal schools. All the school inspectors whom I met with in the course of my journey assured me that they had brought about an entire change in the condition of the schoolmaster, and that they had given the young teachers a feeling of dignity in their profession, and had thereby introduced an improved tone and style of manners."

minds of others. Is not the true theory of teaching and discipline, as proper a subject of study in a college, as the true theory of metaphysics or electricity?

The German universities appreciate this consideration. A chair of Catechetics, or Pedagogy, is established in every University, as regularly as one of Philosophy, or Mathematics. Besides lectures on the theory of the art, students, who contemplate teaching as their profession, are actually exercised, in the presence of the professor, in making practical trial of various methods, and all possible pains are taken, to inspire them with high and enthusiastic notions of the dignity and importance of their office. It is from this source, that the German normal schools derive their best teachers. Were these schools superintended, only by those who have been trained within their own walls, who have enjoyed no higher or more comprehensive culture than they give even to their own pupils, the result would be seen in the want of progress, and in the absence of an active and catholic spirit. The higher seminaries of a country are most likely to introduce improvements in teaching, because they are able to command the highest and most cultivated talent; and it ought to be considered as their duty, to propagate a knowledge of these improvements, and to send forth, in the persons of their pupils, men who, even though they never become teachers, will still feel, that they owe something to the cause of popular education, and will be found among the active and enlightened friends of every effort, which is made to improve common schools.

The other measure, which I would suggest, is this. An argument, strongly urged in favour of the present departments for teachers, is, that the academies in which they are established are already in possession of buildings, apparatus, &c., and thus a great amount of money has been saved. On the other hand, it is objected, that by associating two objects so dissimilar as general education and normal instruction, we provide that both shall be inadequately cared for, or that one shall be cherished at the expense of the other; and it is added, that the normal branch is the one, which usually suffers from neglect. There is doubtless force, in both of these considerations, and they show the importance of endeavouring to find some intermediate line of policy.

Now it may well be doubted, whether the present number of our academies be not somewhat greater than is needed, since some of them seem to flourish at the expense of common schools. On the other hand, the grants of money, which are now made annually from the Literature Fund, to assist in the preparation of teachers, are distributed among so many academies that they do little good to any one of them, and create no sufficient inducement, on their part, to do justice to this branch of their labours. Would it not be better, to reduce materially the number of these departments; making the allowance to each one so great, that trustees and instructers would feel that they owed, to the teachers' department, their first and chief attention? And would it not be well, also, that the *classical departments* in the same academies *should be gradually merged in the teachers' departments;* that thus a small number of these institutions might be converted, in the course of a few years, into District Normal Schools? In this way, four or more of these district normal schools might be created in different parts of the state, without incurring any outlay for buildings or apparatus; and (if a judicious selection of the academies were made) without even any essential change of teachers. A sufficient number of academies would remain; and the *Central* and *District* normal schools, acting and reacting on each other, would operate with increased efficiency, and would rapidly revolutionize the teaching of our common schools.

DEFECTIVE SUPERVISION.

I come now to speak of the last great defect in the working of our common school system. This is *the want of proper care in licensing teachers and in inspecting schools.*

Common school teachers are confidential agents; employed, by parents, to discharge a duty, for which they are themselves disqualified, by the want either of the necessary leisure, or of the requisite ability. Now it is a settled principle, in regard to all agencies, that the zeal and fidelity of the agent will be proportioned, to the care and enlightened interest, with which his proceedings are superintended and encouraged by the principal. If an employer manifests little solicitude about his business, he can hardly expect great diligence or concern, on the part of those to whom he intrusts it. This is so universally acknowledged, that a government, which should neglect to act upon it, would be regarded as most unwise and unfaithful. In every department of the public service, a rigid system of accountability is looked upon as the main secret for securing efficiency and fidelity; and in order to maintain such a system, principals are held responsible for the proceedings of their subordinates.

The reasons for all this are obvious. In the *first* place, few men are sufficiently upright and disinterested, to be intrusted for a long time with irresponsible power, or with an agency which no human eye supervises.

In the *second* place, if such were not the case, the agent, however faithful and devoted, still needs the animating assurance, that his labours are known and appreciated by his employer, and that he is not left to pursue his solitary and exhausting toils, without sympathy or approbation.

In the *third* place, the principal should overlook the operations of his agent, for his own sake; since it is the only way, in which he can maintain a proper interest in, or a proper knowledge of, affairs which pertain to him, much more intimately than to any one else. I ought, perhaps, to add here, that the supervision, for which I contend, is a friendly, or, at least, an impartial, no less than a watchful one. Principals sometimes exhibit a restless and suspicious spirit, and a disposition to interfere with the proceedings of their agent, which is productive of no benefit; while it is often fraught with infinite vexation to the parties, and with nothing but mischief to the service.

Is there any reason, why teachers should be exempted from the operation of these principles? We employ them in one of the most delicate and important offices, which can be intrusted to man. On their fidelity and competency, depend alike our own happiness, and the dearest interests of our children. They are charged with duties, which can be properly fulfilled, only by those who have a rare combination of intellectual and moral qualities; and, however highly endowed, they still need, if they are to labour with pleasure to themselves, or profit to their pupils, the countenance and active co-operation of their employers. Whatever reasons, then, require that a wise and vigilant supervision should be applied to other agencies, hold, in their case, with tenfold force. Yet in this country, the schoolmaster, who most needs supervision, is almost the only agent, to whom no supervision is extended. He enters upon his duties, in many cases, without affording any adequate evidence* that he is qualified for them; and he discharges or

* "The most imperfect arrangement for providing teachers is that which requires an examination *into merely the knowledge* of the candidate in the *branches to be taught*. This is specially imperfect in the case of elementary instruction, where the knowledge required is small in amount, and where the art of teaching finds its most difficult exercise. The erroneous notion, that an individual can teach whatever he knows, is now generally abandoned; and in those countries which still adhere to the old method, of depending solely upon examinations for securing competent teachers, examination is made, not only of the acquirements of the candidate, but of his

neglects them, often from quarter to quarter, without notice or animadversion.

Whose is the fault? The law has provided four classes of officers, who are charged with the duty, of examining teachers or superintending their operations. 1. The trustees of *each district*, who are clothed with all requisite powers, for the immediate government of the school and teacher. 2. The inspectors and commissioners, who are elected *in each town*, and whose business it is to examine teachers, and to make a tour of personal inspection through all the districts, in the town, in each year. 3. The deputy superintendent, who is elected *in each county*, and who is clothed with most important advisory powers in regard to schools, teachers, &c. 4. The *state* superintendent, who, besides a general supervision, exercises an *appellate* jurisdiction over all cases, previously decided by trustees, inspectors, and other local officers. Of these four classes, the first two are chosen directly by the people; the third is chosen by the board of supervisors in each county; and the fourth by the members of the Senate and Assembly of the state, voting in joint ballot. They are all, therefore, *popular* officers.

These offices have been created, not to relieve parents from the necessity of bestowing their personal attention on schools, but to aid them in performing that duty more effectually, and also to subserve other important purposes. There are certain duties connected with supervision, such as the examining and licensing of teachers, which could not be properly discharged by the inhabitants, collectively or separately, even though all were competent to the task. There are others, again, which call for peculiar qualifications; and others which are essentially official, since the object is, to keep up a connexion between the schools and the state authorities, and to impart unity and harmony to the whole sys-

ability to give instruction."—BACHE's *Report on Education in Europe*, p. 323.

tem of primary instruction. But, inasmuch as this system was instituted for the sole benefit of the people, and must depend for its efficiency on their support and co-operation, the law has devolved on them, the duty of choosing those officers who have more immediate charge of the schools, and has also made it their right, to visit the schools personally. It must be obvious, then, that it rests with the people themselves, and with them only, to decide, how far there shall be thorough and searching supervision. If they are careful to elect competent trustees and inspectors, and to encourage them to perform their important duties, faithfully and fearlessly; and if, in addition to this, they give such personal attention to the teacher, and to his course of procedure, as is plainly due to one, who is moulding the character and destiny of their own children, then all will be well—otherwise, all will be ill.

What, then, has hitherto been the fact? I answer by a few extracts from the reports, already so often referred to, of the special visiters. I give but specimens, the returns being filled with passages of the same import.

And, first, in regard to the *licensing of teachers*. "Unqualified and unworthy teachers very often receive certificates of qualification and character. This is universally acknowledged to be the greatest evil our schools have to contend with. Trustees frequently interfere with inspectors when prejudiced in favour of the applicant; and inspectors being chosen at political meetings, little regard is had to their qualifications. Again, if they once disregard the views and wishes of one set of trustees, they are sure to be put out of office at the next election. Consequently, thorough and independent men, if they ever get the office, do not hold it long enough to work anything like a reformation. Under these circumstances, few men try to do anything while they are in office more than merely to avoid the penalty of the law." Thus write the visiters of one large county.

"It has come to the knowledge of the board, that the law in regard to qualified teachers is evaded in its spirit, and that schools are, in consequence, actually instructed by persons having no certificate of qualification, and really unable to obtain one from incompetency. The way in which it is done is to employ, for four months in the summer, when the school is small, a female teacher having a certificate, generally at a very low rate, say eight dollars per month. This fulfils the letter of the law, and enables them to draw the public money. For the residue of the year a male teacher is employed, without a certificate, and unqualified for the station. The low rate of wages he is willing to take is the inducement." Thus write the visiters of another large county.

"Ten years' experience in common school teaching," says another visiter, "has suggested to my mind many improvements. If much more were required of the districts to entitle them to the 'public money,' much good would be the result. I also think our system of inspecting teachers sadly deficient. Our commissioners and inspectors are elected so much in view of the *party*, that many can be found among them who know not the first rudiments of an English education."

"There is not," says another, "sufficient attention paid by the inspectors when examining teachers. Generally there is too great laxness in not refusing those who are poorly qualified. Again, if a teacher gets rejected in one town, he has but to go to the adjoining one, and there he gets a certificate with as much pomp and eclat as a lord. What he should be examined in should be specified by law, and not left for the inspectors to use their judgment upon. While young men who are too lazy to work can find a schoolhouse to while away three or four months of the winter in, and who care not whether they do well or ill, as at most they only intend to teach *one*, *two*, or *three* seasons, and, consequently, are not anxious about establishing a reputation as good teachers, enterprising, intelligent men, capable of teaching well, will not engage in teaching, for the very reason that they cannot command a compensation commensurate with the expenses of qualifying themselves. They can find much better business after advancing thus far." It is a fact worthy of much consideration, that, in order to procure a *supply* of good teachers, we must begin by excluding bad ones.

2d. In regard to *visitation* of *schools by inspectors, trustees, and parents*.

"The lamentable condition of our schools," says one of the visiters, " may be, in a great measure, imputed to the fact that they have not been heretofore visited by the inspectors. Indeed, the public schools have been much neglected by all concerned. So far as we have been able to learn, not one in five of the schools in this town have, in any year, been visited *by trustees or parents*, for the purpose of examining their condition or encouraging their progress."

Say the visiters of another town, " In connexion with the above report we will remark, that, among the evils pervading our district schools, *the general apathy of the people on the subject is the most prominent*, being, in our opinion, the one from which most of the others arise. *Parents, trustees*, and *instructers* are extremely *remiss in visiting schools*, and manifest little or no interest in the condition of the school or in the progress of their children."

Of another : " *The schools in this town have not been blessed by the watchful care of the intelligent and the educated, nor by the supervision of the parents themselves.*"

Of another : " It appears to be the great object of the districts to get rid of the public money in such a manner as to get more, the inhabitants paying little or no attention to the schools after they hire the teacher."

Of another : " It is painful to see parents so inattentive

as they are here. It would seem almost right to *compel* men to do their duty."

Of the 10,769 common schools in this state, *more than one third* were not visited by the inspectors, at all, during the last year; and but one quarter were visited more than once. These visits, too, were often useless. "The inspectors often sit as idle spectators instead of interested persons, on whom, in a great measure, hangs the destiny of the young. The schoolroom is frequently left with only this dry expression, 'We are pleased with the school.'"

The law requires that each inspector shall visit all the schools in the town once in each year, and oftener, if in his estimation it be necessary. That more frequent visits *are* necessary, to secure anything like thorough supervision, must be evident; yet they do not seem to be encouraged by the people. We have known instances in which inspectors and commissioners *have been refused re-election on the express ground that, being interested in the welfare of the schools, they had thought it their duty to visit more than once annually.*

The law providing for the remuneration of inspectors seems to be defective. It derives this remuneration from a tax on the inhabitants of the town; and thus makes it their pecuniary interest, to discourage the frequent and faithful performance of a duty so important to their children, and to the common welfare. It would contribute much to a reform of this evil, if the expense were defrayed by the county, or by the state.

It was to supply this lamentable deficiency on the part of trustees, town inspectors, and parents, that the office of *deputy superintendent* was created. It is the business of this officer "to visit the schools personally, give counsel and instruction as to their management, discover errors and suggest the proper remedy, animate the exertions of teachers, trustees, and parents, and impart vigour to the whole system." Having no authority except to grant and revoke li censes to teachers, it is their main duty to awaken interest, diffuse correct notions in regard to education, and ascertain the precise condition of the several schools, and the general state and prospects of primary instruction, in their respective counties. As the efficiency of the schools must depend chiefly on *local* efforts, and especially on the efforts of trustees, teachers, and employers, it is to encourage and sustain these, that the deputy superintendents should feel themselves especially called.

It is a subject for deep regret, that the law establishing this office, imposes one half of the annual expense of maintaining it, on the county in which the deputy labours; and thus predisposes the inhabitants, to regard it as a burden rather than a blessing. In this case, as in that of the town inspectors, it is much to be desired, that the law should be so framed, that the public will feel interested in promoting, rather than in obstructing, a thorough supervision. That such is really their interest, no reflecting person can doubt; and it is believed that no county can make the experiment, of employing an able and judicious superintendent for a few years, without feeling, that his services are worth tenfold all that they cost. Indeed, these services tend directly to diminish expense. In whatever degree, they contribute to raise the standard of teaching, or to improve school discipline, or to stimulate parents, trustees, and town inspectors to a more punctual and earnest discharge of their duties, in the same degree will they abridge the time, and, of course, the expense, necessary in order to impart a given amount of instruction to a child. The creation of this office seemed to be loudly called for, from all parts of the state. The law is framed, nearly on the model of that which is considered the best law for securing school inspection, that the world has yet seen;[*] and it is regarded now, by the

---

[*] Reference is here made to the system of school inspection in

most enlightened friends of popular instruction throughout the country, and, I may add, throughout the world, as *the one measure*, without which, our system must have remained comparatively inert; but with which, it must, if properly sustained, rise to excellence, and cover itself with honour. May the people be too wise, to brook the idea of its repeal, until its merits have been fairly tested by trial!

Holland. Each province is divided into a number of districts; a district being about equal in population, to one of our counties. An inspector is appointed for each district, whose duty it is to superintend the schools, attend examinations, preside at periodical assemblies of the schoolmasters, &c. To use the language of Cousin, they are " the officers in whose hands the whole system of primary instruction is virtually placed." Hence the care with which they are always selected. "Take care," said Mr. Van den Ende, chief commissioner for the primary schools of Holland, " take care whom you choose for inspectors; they are a class of men who ought to be searched for, with a lantern in one's hand."

There is one provision of the Dutch law, which might be ingrafted with much advantage upon our own. It is the plan of having *provincial boards of education*, composed of the inspectors of the several districts in each province, who meet three times a year in the chief town of the province. The same end would be attained, in our state, if the deputy superintendents, within each senatorial district, were to meet twice or thrice a year at some central point, and were there to constitute a board for mutual consultation, and were to be clothed with authority over certain matters.

It is the opinion of intelligent travellers, that education is, on the whole, more faithfully carried out in Holland than in most of the German states; and that, notwithstanding the numerous normal schools of Prussia (institutions in which Holland is deficient), the Dutch schoolmasters are decidedly superior to the Prussian, and the schools of primary instruction consequently in a more efficient state. *This superiority they attribute entirely to a better system of inspection.*

PART II.

THE SCHOOLMASTER.

THE

PROPER CHARACTER, STUDIES, AND DUTIES OF THE TEACHER

WITH THE

BEST METHODS FOR THE GOVERNMENT AND INSTRUCTION OF COMMON SCHOOLS,

AND THE

PRINCIPLES ON WHICH SCHOOLHOUSES SHOULD BE BUILT, ARRANGED, WARMED, AND VENTILATED.

BY

GEORGE B. EMERSON.

PREFACE.

In the following pages I have endeavoured to give an outline of what I consider most essential in the character, studies, habits, and duties of a teacher, and to present some of the most important methods and rules of teaching and governing. In doing this, I have made free use of what I found written upon the subject, my object being not so much to write an original treatise, as to collect what would be most valuable to the teacher of a common school. The writers to whom I am most indebted are J. Abbott, T. H. Palmer, and S. R. Hall, from "The Teacher," and "The Teacher's Manual," of the two former of whom I have, with their consent, made large quotations, and should have made still larger if I had not known that these works were in the hands of many persons interested in education, as they ought to be in all. Important suggestions have also been received from Lalor, Colburn, and others.

The great number of subjects of which it was necessary to treat, in a limited space, has prevented my going fully into any of them. This is particularly the case with the chapter on the Cultivation of the Faculties, which is little more than an indication of what should be done. General principles only are commonly given; and if repetition be sometimes observed, let it be understood that certain points seemed to be so essentially important as to deserve to be reiterated.

The chapter on the General Principles of Instruction I commend to the attention of practical educators, particularly to the superintendents of normal schools, not as being of great value in itself, for it may, perhaps, be considered more defective than any other chapter, but from the importance of a system of didactics, of which this is offered as a rude and imperfect sketch.

Whatever there is of original in the work, is the fruit of many years' experience in teaching, laborious but pleasant years, which have been cheered and rendered still more pleasant by the feeling that I was gradually finding my way to higher and more comprehensive modes of instruction, and more just and generous principles of influence and government.

Of the faults of the work—begun at the suggestion of another, for a particular object, to be completed at a specified time, composed amid numerous cares, and always with a mind and body sufficiently exhausted by daily toil—no one can be more sensible than the writer. With all its faults, I commit it to the generosity of my brother and sister teachers, for whose use it was written, assuring them that no one will rejoice more than myself to see the methods and principles it recommends giving place to better.

G. B. E

Boston, August 3, 1842.

CONTENTS.

INTRODUCTION 271

BOOK I.
QUALITIES.

CHAPTER I. Mental and Moral, important in a Teacher . . 277
II. Health. Exercise. Diet. Sleep. Recreation . 288

BOOK II.
STUDIES.

CHAPTER I. Laws of the Creation 300
II. Natural Laws 311
III. Independence of the Natural Laws . . . 315
IV. Higher Studies 320
V. Advantages of a Teacher's Life 329

BOOK III.
DUTIES.

CHAPTER I. To Himself. Self-Culture 337
II. To his Pupils, to give them means of Knowledge . 341
III. " " to form their Moral Character . 343
IV. " " Cultivation of their Powers . 359
V. " " Communication of Knowledge . 378
VI. To his Fellow-Teachers 385
VII. To Parents and the Community 390

BOOK IV.
THE SCHOOL.

CHAPTER I. Organization 394
II. Instruction. General Principles 405
III. Teaching: 1. Reading. 2. Spelling. 3. Gram-

mar. 4. Writing. 5. Drawing. 6. Arithmetic. 7. Accounts. 8. Geography. 9. History. 10. Physiology. 11. Composition 419

CHAPTER IV. Government 487

BOOK V.
THE SCHOOLHOUSE.

CHAPTER I. Situation 526
        II. Size 528
       III. Position and Arrangement 531
       IV. Light. Warming. Ventilation . . . 534

INTRODUCTION.

"Surely the great aim of an enlightened and benevolent philosophy is not to rear a small number of individuals, who may be regarded as prodigies in an ignorant and admiring age, but TO DIFFUSE, AS WIDELY AS POSSIBLE, that degree of cultivation which may enable the bulk of a people to possess all the intellectual and moral improvement of which their nature is susceptible."—STEWART.

THE wisest and best men that have appeared upon earth have come as teachers. In remote antiquity, Confucius came, a teacher of righteousness and wisdom among the Chinese. In refined and polished Greece, the wise Socrates was a teacher; and the most distinguished men of Athens walked with him about its streets, or in the groves in its neighbourhood, to listen to his instructions. His pupils, Plato and Aristotle, were teachers; and their teachings have enlightened and influenced the world down to the present time. Through all the history of the Jews, their most venerable men were teachers; to this day they are teachers by their writings. Our Saviour was first known as a teacher of righteousness. He is still our teacher. The office of teacher is in its nature the highest office. That it is not universally considered such, comes from the fact that so many have entered upon it without fitness of mind or character for its numerous duties, and that men are only beginning to estimate things according to their true value.

If a stranger should go into one of our cotton manufactories, and, seeing all the wheels and spindles moving on harmoniously and regularly, each performing its own part without interfering with the rest, and all doing their work well, should conceive that he could, without any knowledge of the principles on which the machinery is constructed, or of the kind of work that it ought to turn out, superintend and carry on the whole work, and should gravely propose to the directors to take charge of it, they might possibly consider the proposition as indicating something of self-sufficiency and presumption. And yet, if this same stranger, without experience, without special instruction, without acquired skill, but only with testimonials that he had a fair character, and could read and write, should apply, in the same town, to the same directors, acting as a school committee, or as supervisors, for the place of teacher in one of their schools, he would be considered as making a very modest request, and would probably consider himself hardly dealt with if he were not allowed to make a trial. And what is the difference? In the one case, every wheel and spindle, every cog, and cam, and spool, and thread, obeys perfectly the law to which it is subjected; a certain force gives a certain velocity, which keeps on undeviatingly until it is interrupted from without. In the other case, in the school, every wheel and spindle has a will of its own, and every one is constantly liable to be disordered by interruption, not only from without, but from within. Notwithstanding, you would hear the man who should undertake to manage this assemblage of dead matter, contrived by man, and easily comprehensible by man, following blindly the laws of gravity and of motion, without previously understanding the structure of each part, and all the nice and delicate adaptations by which they were suited to each other,—you would hear him called a foolhardy and conceited fellow; while the same individual, coming forward not only to manage and direct, but to improve that other infinitely more delicate machinery, every part of which is instinct with will and spirit, and every part made by an artificer, the simplest workmanship of whom the wisest man can but poorly comprehend, would be called a modest and humble man, who would doubtless succeed well enough if he would but condescend to undertake the task.

And is it, indeed, so small a matter to take charge of a school of thinking, immortal beings, to educate their faculties, and prepare them for all the business and duties of life, without some previous study of the nature of those beings, and some serious consideration of the manner in which they shall be best fitted for their future position and relations in life?

The importance and responsibility of the office of teacher are sadly undervalued. A very common impression is, that any person of tolerable character, who has been through a school, and acquired the elements of the branches taught, is qualified to teach; as if the art of teaching were nothing more than pouring into the mind of another what has been poured into ours; as if there were no such thing as mind to act upon, habits to form, or character to influence. The prevailing opinions in regard to the art are such as the common sense of mankind and the experience of centuries have shown to be absurd as to every other art and pursuit of civilized life. To be qualified to discourse upon our moral and religious duties, a man must be educated by years of study; to be able to administer to the body in disease, he must be educated by a careful examination of the body in health and in disease, and of the effects produced on it by external agents; to be able to make out a conveyance of property, or to draw a writ, he must be educated; to navigate a ship, he must be educated by years of service before the mast or on the quarter-deck; to transfer the products of the earth or of art from the producer to the consumer, he must be educated; to make a hat or a coat, he must be educated by years of apprenticeship; to make a plough, he must be educated; to make a nail, or a shoe for a horse or an ox, he must be educated; but to prepare a man to do all these things; to train the body, in its most tender years, according to the laws of health, so that it shall be strong to resist disease; to fill the mind with useful knowledge, to educate it to comprehend all the relations of society, to bring out all its powers into full and harmonious action; to educate the moral nature, in which the very sentiment of duty resides, that it may be fitted for an honourable and worthy fulfilment of the public and private offices of life; to do all this is supposed to require no study, no apprenticeship, no preparation!

Fortunately, this state of feeling and opinion is passing away. Men are beginning to see that, however valuable property may be to them, the happiness and character of their children are much more so: that it *is* of consequence who shall be their guides, the formers of their habits, and the instructers of their minds in the plastic period of their life; that it is quite as important to get suitable persons to take charge of their schools, as of their factories, workshops, or farms. Everything indicates this change: the acts of legislative bodies in reference to the common schools, the earnest inquiries of school committees and individuals for better teachers, and that not in one or two states only, but in the whole country,—everything shows that the value of good instruction is already felt, and that a higher tone on this subject is beginning to prevail.

It is with reference to this change, and in consequence of it, that this volume is prepared. It is an advantage possessed by the business of teaching over most others, that very much can be done towards preparing for it by self-cultivation. Its object is the culture of the faculties and the elevation of the character. How this is best to be done must be found out, in some measure, by the study of the faculties and of the elements of the character, as they exist within the mind of the student himself. To this end the experience of each individual, however humble, is valuable. He must be instructed by reflection on the operations of his own mind, on the action of his own affections and propensities. This is a most important part of the study; and if the faculties, affections, and propensities of all men were alike, it might almost take the place of all other modes of study. But the most cursory inspection of the children in any school, or even family, is sufficient to show that they differ extremely in the degree in which they are naturally endowed with the various powers of the mind and other elements of the character, and in the facility with which these are cultivated. This renders it necessary for us to profit by the experience of others. It is our own character only that we can know perfectly by looking into our own hearts. To know others, we must be able to look into theirs, or, since that cannot be done, we must take advantage of the conclusions to which they have come from the study of their own character, and their observation on the character and faculties of others.

Still more necessary is it to avail ourselves of the observation and experience of others in our attempts to teach, to call out and to discipline the powers of the mind, to communicate in the best manner the important arts of reading, writing, and calculating, and whatever else is or should be deemed essential in a good education, and to exert a wholesome and permanent influence over the future character. In regard to all or any of these things, each one of us can have made but few observations or experiments on himself, when he begins the work of instructing others. Each of us has been taught to read by some one particular method. If the method was a good one, we enjoy all its benefits our whole life long, but we can have no idea of the ill effects of bad methods that we have not tried. If, on the contrary, the method by which we have been taught is a bad one, we must daily feel its effects, in the little enjoyment we derive from reading, or in the difficulty we find in commanding our attention and fixing it on the book before us, or in the little pleasure we can communicate to others by reading aloud. But experience of the evil consequences of a bad method does not necessarily teach us anything in regard to a better, and we must learn from others that there are methods by means of which we might have acquired a distinctness of articulation, a command of our attention, and a love of reading, which would have made it a perennial source of enjoyment and improvement to ourselves and to others. Similar observations might be made upon other branches of study. The sad conviction that we have wasted our time upon a bad method, does not teach us that there is a better. To learn this, we must make inquiries; we must ask those who have tried experiments upon themselves or others. It is of vast importance to a teacher to have access to a large store of successful experiments.

The objects of the following work are,

1. To point out what qualities are important in a teacher.

2. To show by what course of study and thought he should discipline himself.

3. To point out particularly the duties of the teacher of a common school.

4. To recommend some modes of performing them; that is, to speak of the studies, modes of teaching, discipline, and government of such a school.

BOOK I.

QUALITIES.

CHAPTER I.

THE MORAL QUALITIES IMPORTANT IN A TEACHER.

"Every teacher who understands and who practices the genuine ethics of his profession, contributes more largely than any person except a teacher can do, to the elevation of the profession itself, and thereby to its elevation in the public esteem."—E. HIGGINSON.

THE teacher of the common school has, in so many instances, been appointed without choice; so often has he been an entire stranger to the work and to the district, or an applicant of whom it was only known that he needed the place, and would take it at a low rate of wages; and so often his only recommendation has been that he could find no other employment, that in many places the question of qualifications has become almost obsolete. A natural effect has been, that the office of teacher has come to be looked upon by many as a low and unimportant office, and the qualifications for it have been thought of little consequence. This view of the matter is totally wrong and false. Thousands are so situated that they must receive their whole preparation for future life at the district school. Here the bias which is to shape their course is given. The heart and the head, the health of the body and of the mind, will depend, in a great degree, upon what is done or what fails to be done here. Here the scroll of knowledge is to be unfolded to them; or, if it be not unfolded, their future path will lie in darkness. They are here at the period of life when their whole nature is in the highest degree susceptible of impressions, good or bad. They may be moulded almost like clay. They are impressible, impulsive, and full of sympathy. Everything noble and generous, as well as everything base and selfish, in the teacher, may waken an echo in the heart of a child. They are creatures of imitation. Every quality in the character of the teacher becomes an element in forming theirs. Who will dare to say that the character of a parent is of little consequence in forming the character of a child? Yet children often receive a far deeper impression from the teacher, who is with them several hours in the day, than from a father, who may not be with them so many hours in a week. Ought we not rather to say that every circumstance in the character of a teacher is of the highest importance, as it must produce an effect, not upon the five or six of a single family, but upon the fifty or hundred of a district?

What, then, are the qualities which should form the character of the teacher, for his own sake and for the sake of his pupils?

He should be patient; otherwise the anxieties and discouragements of his office will vex him, and soon wear him out. The words of instruction have been compared by the greatest of Teachers to seed sown in the earth. The growth of virtue, of truth, and of knowledge, cannot be seen. He who has sown the seed must wait days, and weeks, and months, and even years, before he can expect to see its fruits. Patience is one of the great virtues he must inculcate on his pupils. The art which it is an important business of an instructer of a common school to communicate, the art of reading, is perhaps the most difficult of all arts. Consider how many things it requires; how many varieties of sound,—how many letters, each representing, not one, but several sounds,—how many combinations of sounds,—how many thousands of words must be made familiar, not merely to the eye as representatives of sounds, but to the understanding as significant of ideas. Consider, too, how volatile and impatient of continued application the mind of the child is; how impatient of restraint is his body; how many times he must be recalled, and recalled kindly, to his task, before it can be accomplished. If there is any work assigned to man which requires untiring, inexhaustible patience, it is this. Let it not be said that this is a poor and humble virtue. Humble indeed it is, but not poor. Many of the greatest of men, Newton, Pascal, Buffon, and others, have declared it a principal element of their genius; and so it must be, for it is essential to the accomplishment of every great undertaking.

To be patient, the teacher must be hopeful. Let him not be discouraged that he accomplishes no more. All real progress is, by the law of nature, slow. The growth of the oak is imperceptible, and it requires a hundred years to come to maturity. He who has sown the acorn must remember that it is an oak which is to grow from it. All virtue is modest, silent, unobtrusive, hiding itself; and the highest virtues are most so. Of all things, the human character is most slowly brought to perfection. We must sow the seeds of good principles, and hope for the harvest. "In due time we shall reap, if we faint not."

While we hope, all labour is light. Hopefulness is contagious. The pupil catches ardour from our hope, and, thinking that he can accomplish all things, can. But despair deadens the energies. It is like the icy sarcar of Eastern fables. It blasts whatever it breathes upon. It passes over the valley, and the buds are nipped and the leaves blackened, and nothing remains but scathed trunks. Let him who is prone to despair go away and despair by himself, in the field or the workshop. Let him not blight youthful hopes, and chill the warm glow of confidence, by this death-wind.

The teacher should be cheerful. Cheerfulness in the face of a teacher is sunshine to the child; and while it gives play to all the faculties of its possessor, quickens into life and healthy action the powers of those around him. It diffuses happiness in the school; and if there were no other reason for its being a teacher's duty to be cheerful, this would be sufficient. For why should not the years of childhood be, what the benevolent Father willed them to be, happy? Is it not desirable that happiness should become habitual? The cheerful worker can do more and better than the sad one; and the dark cloud that comes over a school from the lowering of a gloomy brow, strikes a chill not only into the heart, but into the very power of action.

Cheerfulness should be natural to the teacher; and whoever has a morose, sullen, and gloomy temper, should seek some other employment. It may be answered, perhaps, that cheerfulness is not always constant, even to the naturally cheerful; that it depends on the health of the body. True; the teacher should therefore study and obey the laws of health, that he may not be a source of unhappiness to others by his neglect. But of this hereafter.

The teacher should be generous, unsuspicious, open, frank. These excellent and beautiful qualities should be cultivated in children. They cannot be well taught by precept; they must be communicated by the sympathy of example. There is a nobleness in the heart of a child which responds to the same quality in another. Approach him with kind and unsuspecting confidence, and you disarm his calculating selfishness. You place all that is generous and noble in him on your side. Your openness begets openness in his breast. I have seen this course tried with entire success in the management of a large school of boys, collected from all the quarters of a great city; from schools in which every variety of government had been exercised, from generous sentiment and sympathy to brutal violence, where a word was followed by a blow. To this motley collection a young teacher addressed himself. He told them that, though somewhat older than they, he was young enough to understand their feelings; that he should try the experiment of trusting to their honour, and should never strike a blow, or adopt other harsh measures, until they compelled him. In so large a number, of course, order must exist, and obedience was essential. He should endeavour to be reasonable, and should treat them as reasonable beings. If they would allow him, he would always conduct towards them as if they were his younger brothers. He believed there was a sentiment of honour and generosity among boys as much as among men, and on that he should rely. This experiment was continued for nearly two years, with a success which established, beyond a doubt, his confidence in the correctness of the theory on which it was attempted.

In a large school there will always be some boys in whom the feelings of honour are not high. The number is not great. It is smaller than is commonly thought; and by appealing to the sentiment of honour, such as it is, the almost latent principle will be kindled in many a breast in which it had been dormant, and the number of the obtuse become constantly smaller. A small minority may be safely left to the influence of the public opinion of the school.

The appeal to the generous qualities of children can be safely made only by one who has entire confidence in their existence and strength, and who has a sympathy and affection for children. A teacher, therefore, should be a *lover of children*. This is one of the most essential qualifications. He who has it will spontaneously feel such an interest in children as will enable him to bear with their faults, to encourage their efforts, to feel for their griefs, and do what he can to make plain their difficulties; to cheer the despondent, and lift up the heart of the timid; to check, without offending, the bold; to overcome the obstinate by gentleness; and to repress, without mortifying, the self-confident. This will make patience easy to him, and strip confinement of half its irksomeness.

There is a great difference in this respect among individuals otherwise equally amiable. One who is vexed by the noise of children, impatient of their slowness, and offended by their sportiveness, should never go inside of a schoolhouse. One who is indifferent to them, or feels little interest in them, may persuade himself, by a strong conviction of duty, to be faithful as a teacher, but he will do as a task what might otherwise be a pleasure. The lover of children will take delight in the employment.

The teacher should be kind and benevolent. The great lesson of the Gospel is love. How many there are who have not yet learned it. The power of kindness is but beginning to be fully known. No human heart is shut against it. The great improvements made in the treatment of prisoners, in recent times, come from the introduction of this principle, and are evidences of its power. The heart long hardened by severity and suffering, softens and yields when it feels itself addressed in the unaffected tones of real kindness. Can it be that the indurated tenant of a prison is more alive to the influence of this benignant principle than the innocent, unhardened child? When we see contrition and repentance for crime wrought in the heart of the old offender, through the instrumentality of love, shall we distrust its efficacy on the heart of the young, and delicate, and susceptible?

A still more remarkable evidence of the force of kindness is shown in the treatment of the insane. The truly kind man, whose kindness so pervades his character that it beams from the eye, irradiates the face, speaks in the voice, and controls the movements, has almost unbounded power over the will of the insane. Can it be that he should have less over the fresh and warm affections of children?

The broken current of thought, disturbed, perhaps, by the coldness of the world, or by bitter grief, or by passion, is brought back to its natural channel, and made to flow placidly, under the benign influence of truth and confidence, by the offices of religion and the irresistible power of kindness. Shall the effect of these motives be less in leading the streams of feeling and thought, near their fountain, to flow in their appointed courses?

A duty of the teacher is to inspire kindness—to form the habit of benevolence. Can he impart what he has not? Kindness must be his great instrument. By no other can he add so much to the happiness of his pupils, or so easily control them. Shall he not profit by the lesson which the Christian warden of the prison, and the Christian physician of the insane, afford?

A part of kindness is the forgiveness of injuries. A teacher should be of a forgiving spirit. Forgiveness wins more than punishment drives. The one appeals to the lofty qualities, the other to the grovelling. One forms the heart to nobleness, the other tends to harden it.

He should be just. A child is delicately sensitive to injustice. An instance of it offends him, and does much to shut his heart against the author of the injustice. He can hardly think him a good man, whatever else he may have to recommend him. The teacher should therefore have a strong sentiment and a quick perception of justice; and he should endeavour to be habitually and strictly just. This is, doubtless, the most difficult part of his duty. It is not easy to pronounce justly even in a difference between two; but when the rights of many become involved, the difficulty becomes proportionally greater. He should be severely true to his feeling of justice, while he should, at the same time, show his pupils how nearly impossible it is for him, without the power of looking into their motives, to do exact justice. There are some occasions on which it is quite impossible for him to do justice. When, for example, a single prize is offered, and there are, as there usually are, several candidates with apparently equal claims,—let him then beware of unperceived partialities. It is better to avoid such cases. Let him refuse to undertake to award a prize which it requires more than human penetration not to award unjustly.

The sentiment of justice is so important in the human character, its office is so high, and there are so frequent occasions for its exercise in human life, that a teacher's duty cannot be considered well performed unless he takes pains to form and cultivate it. Let the faithful teacher look to that. If all teachers could be roused to a sense of its importance, there would be less of injustice in the world.

In order to be just, the teacher should have equanimity: equally removed from indifference and passion. Here again comes in the importance of health; for ill health will disturb, almost inevitably, the even current of feeling on which equanimity depends.

He should be a lover of order; and, if possible, he should have the talent of establishing and preserving it. System is essential in a school. It helps all things. It renders government easy. It preserves quiet, and good feeling; it saves time. It prevents impatience; one waits patiently for the hour, when the hour is sure to come. It obviates confusion; it prevents injustice. Unless a system of just allotment of time, according to the claims of each and of all, be fixed and firmly adhered to, there must be some to suffer neglect. Once established, such a system has a tendency to preserve itself. It requires a talent of order, or some substitute for it, to establish such a system. Individuals differ very much in this talent. He who has little power to establish and preserve order, ought to cease to attempt to teach, unless he have extraordinary qualifications to compensate for its absence. If he have the talent in a moderate degree, he may adopt an order of proceeding settled by another, and by the help of a clock or watch, carefully observed, may keep it in operation.

His highest duty is to teach a reverence for God and for his laws. He should, therefore, himself be full of reverence. This cannot be taught by mere words, in abstract propositions; it must be communicated. Words must be used, but they must come from the heart, and they can come with effect only from a heart deeply imbued with the feeling. If he have not this feeling, the teacher ought not to attempt to excite it in his pupils; for it will sound like hypocrisy in himself, and there will be danger of his producing hypocrisy in them. Reverence is the foundation of the religious sentiment, and it will be better to leave it to the teacher of religion than to run the risk of making hypocrites of his pupils, or of debasing himself by the wretched cant of hypocrisy; for, while the genuine feeling is the highest and holiest of the human breast, the affectation of it is the basest.

He should be conscientious. A most important part of the duty of a moral teacher is to awaken the sense of duty. But it must exist in his own breast before he can arouse it in that of another. He must be conscientious for his own sake, for his own peace. Most of his exertions have not the visible external rewards which follow earnest and strenuous exertions in almost every other field of labour. Their immediate effects are secret, almost imperceptible changes in the feelings or habits of a child; and, however full of hope he may be, he will be liable to be discouraged if he have not the conscientious feeling whereby faithful exertion carries with it its own reward. The teacher is sometimes of no esteem with the world. He must be able to do good for its own sake, hoping for nothing in return; and his "great reward" must be in the consciousness of having done what he could.

He should be conscientious for the sake of his pupils.

A quick, clear sense of right and wrong, a resolute purpose to do right because it is right, and to avoid wrong because it is wrong, is the highest principle that can pervade the character of child or man. It is the deep foundation on which everything most excellent in the character must rest. The love of truth, that most beautiful trait in the human character, is but another name for it. We believe that it exists, faintly or manifestly, in the elements of every human character capable of free agency. But it must be educated. Like every other principle, it must be strengthened by exercise. It must be appealed to constantly, in every period of instruction, by those who have charge of it. The great neglect of moral education lies in this point more than in any other.*

Conscientiousness, then, is a great essential in a teacher. But it exists in different degrees. The sentiment of duty may be high, and yet the power of acting up to it may be deficient. A person so constituted may become a good teacher, for he will be likely to do his best to improve; and this master principle of our moral nature, if always respected, will at last obtain complete ascendency.

The teacher must be firm. This quality must come in to strengthen all the rest. Firmness saves time and prevents pain. Let it be once understood in a school: "This is fixed, after full deliberation, on just grounds; it cannot be yielded;" and every one submits as he does to necessity. The will of a man as unyielding as fate is submitted to as if it were another fate. But firmness never need be harsh. Gentleness and firmness should be united. The child should feel that the resistless hand of a strong man is upon

---

* It can hardly be essential to say, except to avoid being misunderstood, that I believe the religious sentiment closely connected with conscientiousness. That sentiment naturally expresses itself in worship. The conscience must be aided by Him who worketh in us to will and to do; and aid must be asked.

him, but that it is the hand of a father. This union the teacher should constantly endeavour to effect. Firmness is often natural. Where it is not so to any considerable degree, much may be done to gain or strengthen it. If we feel that it is kindness to be firm, that it is our interest and our duty to be firm, we may be so, though naturally wavering and irresolute.

He should have the talent for commanding, and he should be able to establish his authority. All the other influences he can exert are important,—some of them of the highest importance; but, after all, a school must be reduced to submission, and kept in subordination by authority.

Together with these natural qualifications, the teacher should have a strong predilection for the office. He should engage in it, not from compulsion and as a last resort, but as the most desirable and honourable of employments.

I have enumerated some of the moral qualities which seem to be most important to a teacher for his own sake and on account of his pupils. He should be patient, full of hope, of a cheerful spirit, generous, a lover of children, full of benevolence, just, a lover of order, a reverencer of God and his laws, conscientious, firm, with a talent to command. To one who is to be a teacher for life, all are essential. Yet all cannot often be united in an individual in the highest degree, and some may take the place of others. A lover of children will be patient, and kind, and full of hope towards them, though wanting in these qualities towards others; and a reverence for God's laws and the laws of conscience may make him firm, and just, and a lover of order.

CHAPTER II.

HEALTH—EXERCISE—DIET.

> "' Go to the hills,' said one; ' remit awhile
> This baneful diligence; at early morn
> Court the fresh air, explore the heaths and woods;
> . . . . . . construct
> A calendar of flowers, pluck'd as they blow
> Where health abides, and cheerfulness, and peace.'"
> WORDSWORTH.

> "A variety of exercises is necessary to preserve the animal frame in vigour and beauty; and a variety of those occupations which literature and science afford, added to a promiscuous intercourse with the world, in the habits of conversation and business, is no less necessary for the improvement of the understanding."—STEWART.

THE teacher should have perfect health. It may seem almost superfluous to dwell here upon what is admitted to be so essential to all persons; but it becomes necessary, from the fact that nearly all those who engage in teaching leave other and more active employments to enter upon their new calling. By this change, and by the substitution of a sedentary life within doors for a life of activity abroad, the whole habit of the body is changed, and the health will inevitably suffer, unless precautions be taken which have never before been necessary. To all such persons—to all, especially, who are entering upon the work of teaching with a view of making it their occupation for life, and to that other large and important class who are quitting the active life of a farmer or mechanic with the purpose of obtaining an education for themselves,—a knowledge of the laws of health is of the utmost importance, and to such this chapter is addressed. I shall speak of these laws briefly, under the heads of exercise, air, sleep, food, and dress.

So intimate is the connexion between the various parts of our compound nature, that the faculties of the mind cannot be naturally, fully, and effectually exercised without the health of the body. And the first law of health is that which imposes the necessity of exercise.

The teacher cannot be well without exercise, and, usually, a great deal of it. No other pursuit requires so much,—no other is so exhausting to the nerves; and exercise, air, cheerfulness, and sunshine, are necessary to keep them in health. Most other pursuits give exercise of body, sunshine, and air, in the very performance of the duties that belong to them. This shuts us up from all.

One of the best, as one of the most natural modes of exercise, is *walking*. To give all the good effects of which it is susceptible, a walk must be taken either in pleasant company, or, if alone, with pleasant thoughts; or, still better, with some agreeable end in view, such as gathering plants, or minerals, or observing other natural objects. Many a broken constitution has been built up, and many a valuable life saved or prolonged, by such a love of some branch of natural history as has led to snatch every opportunity for a walk, with the interest of a delightful study,

> "Where living things, and things inanimate,
> Do speak, at Heaven's command, to eye and ear."

The distinguished geologist of Massachusetts, Professor Hitchcock, was once, when teacher of a school, reduced to so low a state by a disease of the nerves, which took the ugly shape of dyspepsy, that he seemed to be hurrying rapidly towards the grave. Fortunately, he became interested in mineralogy, and this gave him a strong motive to spend all his leisure time in the open air, and to take long circuits in every direction. He forgot that he was pursuing health in the deeper interest of science; and thus, aided by some other changes in his habits, but not in his pursuits, he gradually recovered the perfect health which has enabled him to do so much for science and for the honour of his native state.

2. Riding on horseback is one of the best modes of exercise possible for a sedentary person. It leads to an erect posture, throws open the chest, gives a fuller breathing, and exercises the muscles of the arms and upper part of the frame. Though in many situations expensive in a pecuniary point of view, it is economical in time. I have often found it refreshing and invigorating when other kinds of exercise were ineffectual. In weakness of the digestive organs its efficacy is remarkable. It is essential to the beneficial effects of this exercise, that, if it be pursued in cold weather, the feet be kept perfectly warm.

3. A garden furnishes many excellent forms of exercise, and the numerous labours of a farm would give every variety, if the teacher could be in a situation to avail himself of them. This is not often the case. When accessible, the rake or the pitchfork, moderately used, cannot be too highly recommended. A garden is within the reach of most teachers in the country. It has the advantage of supplying exercise suited to every degree of strength, and of being filled with objects gratifying to the eye and the taste. The head of one of the first literary institutions in New-England secures to himself robust and manly health by two or three hours' labour every morning in his own garden; and he has the satisfaction, not a slight one, of eating vegetables raised by his own hands. The flower-garden and shrubbery commend themselves to the female teacher. To derive every advantage from them, she must be willing to imitate an example often set by the ladies of England, and use the hoe, the rake, the pruning-hook, and the grafting-knife with her own hands.

4. Rowing, when practicable, is a most healthful exercise. It gives play to every muscle and bone of the frame. For the manner in which it throws open and exercises the

chest, it has been recommended, with the best effect, in pulmonary cases. The story is told of two young men of Cambridge, England, being brought back to health, from a somewhat advanced stage of consumption, by the daily gradual use of the oar.

5. When the river is frozen, skating may take the place of rowing: and it is an excellent substitute. The teacher need never be ashamed of it. He should rather be ashamed of the ill health and low spirits it is so well adapted to dispel.

6. Driving a chaise or sleigh is a healthful exercise, if sufficient precaution be used to guard against the current which is always felt, as it is produced by the motion of the vehicle, even in the still air.

7. Sawing and splitting wood form a valuable exercise, particularly important for those who have left an active course of life for the occupation of teaching.

Exercise should be taken in the early part of the day. Warren Colburn, the author of the arithmetic, whose sagacity in regard to common things was as remarkable as his genius for numbers, used to say, that half an hour's walk before breakfast did him as much good as an hour's after. Be an early riser. The air of morning is more bracing and invigorating; the sights, and sounds, and odours of morning are more refreshing. A life's experience, spent in teaching, declares the morning best. There are doubtless those who cannot take exercise early in the morning—who are seriously injured by it. They are not many. But when any one finds that he is of the number, he must yield, and consent to take it at some other hour.

Exercise must always be taken, if possible, in the open air. Air is as essential as exercise, and often, in warm weather particularly, more so. They belong together. The blood flows not as it should; it fails to give fresh life to the brain, if we breathe not fresh air enough. The spirits cannot enjoy the serene cheerfulness which the teacher needs, if he breathe not fresh air enough. The brain cannot perform its functions; thought cannot be quick, vigorous, and healthy, without ample supplies of air. Much of the right moral tone, of habitual kindliness and thankful reverence, depends on the air of heaven.

Exercise must be taken in the light, and, if it may be, in the sunshine. Who has not felt the benignant influence of sunshine! The sun's light seems almost as essential to our well-being as his heat, or the air we breathe. It has a great effect on the nerves. A distinguished physician, of great experience, Dr. J. C. Warren, of Boston, tells me that he almost uniformly finds diseases that affect the nerves exasperated by the darkness of night, and mitigated by the coming on of day. All plants growing in the air lose their strength and colour when excluded from light. So, in a great degree, does man. They lose their fine and delicate qualities, and the preciousness of their juices. Man loses the glow of his spirits, and the warmth and natural play of his finer feelings. The sunshine of the breast is something more than a metaphor.

> "A little rule, a little sway,
> A sunbeam in a winter's day,
> Is all the proud and mighty have
> Between the cradle and the grave."

Let the teacher, who often has too much of the first, take care to get his portion of the last.

Next to air and light, water is the most abundant element in nature. It can hardly be requisite to enjoin upon the teacher the freest use of it. The most scrupulous cleanliness is necessary, not only on his own account, but that he may be able always to insist upon it, with authority, in his pupils. The healthy state of the nerves, and of the function of digestion, depends in so great a degree on the cleanliness of the skin, that its importance can hardly be overstated. Most diseases of the skin may be healed or avoided by the faithful application of soap and water, or of water alone, if enough be used, and often enough. Thence, probably, the wisdom of Oriental philosophers gave to the duty of frequent ablution the force of religious sanction.

Sleep. No more fatal mistake in regard to his constitution can be made by a young person given to study, than that of supposing that Nature can be cheated of the sleep necessary to restore its exhausted, or strengthen its weakened powers. From six to eight hours of sleep are indispensable; and, with young persons, oftener eight or more, than six. It is essential to the health of the body, and still more to that of the mind. It acts directly on the nervous system; and irritability, or what is called nervousness, is the consequence of its loss. This, bad in any person, is worse in the teacher than in any one else. It is an unfailing source of unhappiness to himself and to all his school. He would be unwise to subject himself to the consequences of loss of sleep; he *has no right* to subject others. The long-continued loss of sleep in early life inflicts a wound upon the constitution from which it never fully recovers. I knew two young men, who, in the early part of their college life, when they were about the age of seventeen, living together, agreed to restrict themselves to four hours' sleep each night. They were ardent in the pursuit of knowledge, and ambitious of being scholars, and had been persuaded, by reading Lord Teignmouth's Life of Sir Wm. Jones, that to sleep more than four hours was to be less than men. They resolutely tried the experiment for a term of thirteen weeks. Both had previously enjoyed excellent health, and been blessed with a strong constitution. Immediately after, one was obliged to leave college for nearly six months, to recover from an attack on his lungs, and, after he again resumed his studies, was afflicted for many years with weakness of the eyes. He often says that he feels, to this day, the effect of this violation of the laws of his constitution. The other was, for many years after, subject to a painful nervous complaint, and he has never enjoyed perfect health since. The offence was committed nearly thirty years ago.

Each person must determine for himself what number of hours of sleep is necessary to him. This varies not only with different individuals, but at different seasons of the year, and with different states of health. The rule given for the management of children, that they should go to bed early enough to wake of themselves at a suitable hour in the morning, may be taken as a useful one at any period of life. It is well to be an early sleeper as well as an early riser.

Diet. To no person is an attention to diet more important than to a teacher. For his own guidance, and that he may be able to give proper instruction in regard to this subject to his pupils, the conclusions of experience, or what we may consider the laws of diet, should be familiar to him. Some of these are the following:

1. Food should be simple; not of too little nor of too great variety. The structure of the teeth, resembling at once those of animals that naturally subsist on flesh, and of animals that take only vegetable food, and the character and length of the digestive organs, holding a medium between the average of these two classes, indicate that a variety of food, animal and vegetable, is natural to man, and in most cases, probably, necessary. The tendency in most parts of this country, from the great abundance of the necessaries of life, is to go to excess in the consumption of food, particularly of animal food. The striking evils of this course have led many to the opposite extreme—to renounce meats entirely. Experience of the evils of this course, also, has in most places brought men back to the wise and safe medium. No person needs to be more careful in regard to

the quality and nature of his food than the teacher, as his exclusion from air for a great part of the day leaves him in an unfit condition to digest unwholesome food; while the constant use of his lungs renders his appetite unnaturally great, or destroys it altogether. Animal food seems to be necessary, but not in great quantities, nor oftener, usually, than once a day. The natives of the highest northern latitudes subsist almost entirely on gross animal food, which they take in great quantities without injury. Those within the tropics may live exclusively on rice or other vegetable food. The truth seems to be, that a large amount of food, of the most nutritious kind, is required, in very cold regions, to keep up the supply of vital heat. In proportion as the climate is warmer, the demand for food, on this account, is less. This fact would suggest a difference of food at different seasons of the year. In winter it should be nourishing, and may be abundant; in summer, less nutritious, less of animal origin, and in more moderate quantity.

2. Food should be taken at sufficiently distant intervals. The excellent habits which prevail in most parts of the interior of the country, of breakfasting early, dining not far from noon, and supping in the beginning of the evening, make particular rules in relation to this point unnecessary. The operation of digestion is not completed, ordinarily, in less than four hours. Food should not be taken at shorter intervals than this, and intervals of five or six hours are better, as they leave the stomach some time to rest.

3. It should be taken in moderate quantity. In the activity of common life, excess is less to be dreaded than with the sedentary habits and wearying pursuits of a teacher. The body which has been tasked by many hours of severe labor at the anvil or the plough, needs to have its energies repaired by large supplies of nourishing food. The exhaustion of teaching is that of the nervous power, and would seem to call rather for hours of quiet, and freedom from

care, with cheerful conversation, and the refreshment of air and gentle exercise. Probably all the kinds of food in general use are wholesome when partaken of moderately. Those who, from choice or compulsion, pass from an active to a sedentary life, should, at the same time, restrict themselves to one half their accustomed quantity of food.

4. As a general rule, fat should be avoided. It is a gross custom of some parts of the country, the having food prepared by cooking with great quantities of fat. None but a person who uses a great deal of most active exercise, or is much exposed to cold, can long bear it with impunity. If taken, fat in a solid form is less injurious than liquid fat.

5. Fruit may be eaten with the recollection of the proverb of fruit-producing countries: " It is gold in the morning, silver at noon, lead at night." Ripe fruit, in its season, is wholesome, and preferable, for a person of sedentary habits, to more nourishing and exciting food. But it should be a substitute for other food, not an addition. A bad practice, common in some places, of eating fruit, especially the indigestible dried fruits, raisins, and nuts, in the evening, should be avoided by the teacher. He must have quiet and uninterrupted sleep, and early hours, to be patient, gentle, and cheerful in school.

6. The drink of a sedentary person should be chiefly water, and that in small quantities, and only at meals. The intelligent Arab of the desert drinks not during the heat of the day. He sees that watering a plant in the sunshine makes it wither; and he feels, in himself, an analogous effect from the use of water. There are few lessons in regard to diet so important to be inculcated as this: " Drink not between meals." The introduction of tea and coffee has justly been considered as one of the great advances in the art of living of modern times, and one cause, among others, of the increase in the duration of life. They cheer but not inebriate, and may be taken moderately as long as no ill effect

is perceived from their use. They are to be preferred to all other drinks except water, and especially to heavy and nourishing drinks.

7. The last rule to be observed is, that no unnecessary exertion of mind or body should be used immediately after a meal. If a walk must be taken, it should rather be a leisurely stroll than a hurried walk.

The teacher should be no sloven. He should dress well, not over nicely, not extravagantly; neatly, for neatness he must teach by example as well as by precept; and warmly, for so many hours of the day shut in a warm room will make him unusually sensitive to cold. The golden rule of health should never be forgotten: "Keep the head cool, the feet warm, the body free." The dress of the feet is particularly important. Coldness or dampness of the feet causes headache, weakness and inflammation of the eyes, coughs, consumptions, sometimes fevers. A headache is often cured by sitting with the feet long near a fire. Keeping the feet warm and dry alleviates the common affections of the eyes, repels a coming fever, prevents or quiets coughs, and serves as one of the surest safeguards against consumption. Many of our most sensible physicians trace the prevalence of consumption in the Northern States, not to our climate, but to the almost universal custom of wearing insufficient clothing, especially on the feet.

There is another subject intimately connected with health, which has been alluded to, but which ought, from its importance, to receive more than a passing remark. It is cheerfulness. This should be one of the ends and measures of health. It ought to be considered the natural condition of a healthy mind; he who is not cheerful is not in health. If he has not some manifest moral cause of melancholy, there must be something wrong in the body, or in the action of the powers of the mind.

A common cause of low spirits in a teacher is anxiety in

regard to the well-doing of his pupils. This he must feel, but he must endeavour, as far as possible, to banish it from his hours of relaxation. He must leave it behind him when he turns from the schoolhouse door. To prevent its haunting him, he must seek pleasant society. He must forget it among the endearments of home, the cheerful faces and kind voices of his friends. This is the best of all resources, and happy is the man who has a pleasant home, in the bosom of which he may rest from labour and from care. If he be among strangers, he must try to find or make friends to supply the place of home. He must seek the company of the parents and friends of his pupils, not only that he may not be oppressed by the loneliness of his situation, but that he may better understand the character of his pupils, and the influences to which they are subjected. The exercise of the social affections is essential to the healthy condition of a well-constituted mind. Often he will find good friends and pleasant companions among his pupils. Difference of years disappears before kindliness of feeling, and sympathy may exist between those most remote in age, and pursuit, and cultivation.

A less essential and genial, perhaps, but a surer, because a more independent resource, he will find in reading. He must be a reader. The constantly recurring lessons will exhaust his stock of ideas and illustrations, and he must renew his store by books. And in reading, if he have considerable freedom of selection, he must seek such books as at once instruct and give a cheerful flow to the thoughts. Poetry, wit, narrative, eloquence, biography, fiction, philosophy, devotion—let him choose whatever is suited to the mood of the hour. It may seem inconsistent to recommend so sedentary a recreation as reading with the sedentary labours of a school. But the powers of mind employed in reading are very different from those that are exercised in teaching. Much of the day may be spent in bodily exercise, and still leave many hours of daylight and night unoccupied; and the quiet enjoyment of reading refreshes the mind more than absolute rest. The whole mind of the teacher should be exercised, each faculty in its appropriate way; and after all the labours of a day, he may find that his imagination, his reasoning powers, or those of observation, have been but little employed.

I have already spoken of the study of Natural History. A delightful, but a somewhat dangerous recreation, is offered by Music; delightful, as always soothing to the wearied mind, but dangerous, because liable to take to itself too much time. It would be desirable if every instructer could himself sing or play. If he cannot, let him listen to songs or cheerful airs from voice or instrument, or to the notes of birds.

> "I'm sick of noise and care, and now mine ear
> Longs for some air of peace."

BOOK II.

STUDIES.

CHAPTER I.

THE LAWS OF THE CREATION.

" The object of the science of education is to render mind the fittest possible instrument for discovering, applying, or obeying the laws under which God has placed the universe."—WAYLAND.

THE social position of instructers is not yet everywhere what it should be. But already many of the best and wisest men see that a higher place should be given them, and the public are beginning to be prepared to render them due honour. Already thoughtful men see what vast influence is to be exercised, what vast good is to be done, by highly gifted, thoroughly qualified, well educated, and faithful teachers. It will depend on themselves to deserve and win the place they desire. The world will grant it when it is deserved. Every teacher may do something to remove prejudices, where they exist, against teachers, and to gain for them, as a body, a higher regard, and a nearer place in the affections of the community. Let him form for himself such a character as the guide of the young should have; let him make such acquisitions in science and letters as elevate the mind and polish the manners; let him gain the knowledge which is power, and he needs not claim, for he will receive unclaimed, honour from the rising and the risen generation.

Let him be just, generous, sincere, honourable, kind, charitable, modest, respecting himself and respecting others, fearing God and reverencing his laws, a model of the virtues that adorn a man, and he needs not fear that he shall fail of even the earthly reward of these virtues. They are of too high a character to be estimated by external measures, and their true reward is within. Still they meet a sympathy in the heart of others, and procure genuine respect for their possessor. But these qualities of the character, though the best and most indispensable, are not all that are required. The instructer must be intelligent, cultivated, well-informed.

The information he should possess must be, first, what will qualify him for his office of instructer, and, secondly, what he must have as a citizen and a man. If he attain all that belongs to the first, he will not have many deficiencies to make up in regard to the second.

The instructer should be the interpreter of the laws of the creation. The child is born into the world ignorant of them all; yet they are the laws by which every part of his own nature, and his use of all the powers of external nature, are controlled. He must know them,—the more perfectly and the earlier the better. The more fully qualified the teacher is to impart a knowledge of these laws, the better instructer he must be.

The first of these laws which attract the attention, inasmuch as they fall almost entirely within the dominion of the senses, are the properties of the objects about us. A great part of infancy is spent, very happily, in learning these properties, by the incessant experiments which all children delight to make. They thus discover the hardness, strength, shape, colour, size, weight, and other properties of all the common objects; their appearances at different distances; their relation to each other; and, what is still more important to them, their relation to themselves, and some of their uses. And in these observations and experiments, while learning to use their limbs, they exercise their senses, and those powers of the mind by which they observe and compare. Most, perhaps all of the happiness of infancy and early childhood,—and whoever looks upon children must see how much they enjoy, how happy they are,—is doubtless derived from this instinctive exercise of the infant faculties. If the art of instruction were what it might be, and teachers had the qualifications which they ought to have, this happy natural progress in knowledge and the development of the faculties would know no interruption.

This period in the education of a child, which we may call the period of nature's education, is managed so much better, usually, than any future part, that we might be tempted not to interfere with it, but to observe and admire, and to learn thence how to conduct in the periods that come after. But, even here, art and reason might step in, and improve upon those beautiful processes, not by changing them, but by carrying out more fully the principles indicated by nature. This I shall hereafter endeavour to show.

The next laws which draw the attention of the child are those of the elements, light, heat, air, water, and others. Many of these escape the immediate cognizance of his senses, and are those in regard to which he needs the aid of a well-informed instructer. Listen to a child's questions, and you find him very early inquisitive as to the causes acting upon him. The same curiosity which had been busy upon objects, extends itself to influences. Why is it so hot? Why do the buds begin to swell? Why do the birds come back, and begin to sing? What makes the rain? See the smoke, how it goes up into the sky; what makes it go up? These, and a thousand other questions, show that he is looking into causes. Now is the office of the teacher called in requisition; and to be able to answer these questions, he must possess himself of what is known of these elements. This kind of knowledge is contained in books upon Chemistry, Natural Philosophy, Natural History, and Meteorology; and with such must the individual, who aspires to be a useful and successful teacher of children in their early years, be familiar. The most important of these are certain parts of Chemistry and Natural History. That part of the former which relates to the nature and composition of the atmosphere is essential. How many children have suffered, and now suffer, from ignorance on the part of their teachers, of the simple truth, that air is gradually rendered poisonous by breathing, and that a supply of fresh air is constantly necessary in a room which many persons occupy. We every year read accounts of lives having been destroyed by the fumes of charcoal, which the knowledge of the fact that anything burning in the air rapidly consumes its vital portion, or that the gas formed by burning charcoal is destructive to life, would have saved. Many pupils will never have any means of learning these and similar facts but from the teacher of a public school. Such elementary truths should, therefore, be known to every teacher.

The teacher of the higher schools, or of the upper classes, ought to have a much fuller knowledge of Chemistry. He will then be able, in conversation with his pupils, to communicate innumerable facts of the highest practical value. To the future farmer he may give hints as to the part that clay, limestone, animal manure, peat, and even sand, act in the constitution of soils, which will lead him to investigate for himself, and thus to be able to render his farm more productive. To the future smith he may, by observations on the qualities of the different metals, impart a desire to inform himself, which will make him a better smith than he otherwise would have become. All the properties of acids and alkalies, of their action on each other and on metals, of the salts, harmless, useful, or poisonous, that are formed of them, have endless uses in the daily economy of common life, within doors and without, which every child, male and female, will be better for knowing, and will delight to learn. Only let the teacher be so familiar in his knowledge of these truths that he can introduce them **naturally** and intelligibly, and they will always interest.

So of the principles of Natural Philosophy. All men who are engaged in the active pursuits of labour or business, have occasion to use some forms of the mechanical powers. Thousands have no other opportunities of getting acquaintance with their principles than those furnished by the common schools. In most of these schools Natural Philosophy forms no part of the regular course of instruction. What incalculable good may an intelligent teacher be the means of doing, who shall communicate sufficient knowledge of the leading principles of Mechanics to make his pupil long for more, and induce him to get it when he can?

The economical use of materials in building, with the ability to select such forms as give the greatest strength in the least space and with the least weight, is an interesting application of Mechanics of great practical value. Many persons have occasion to build who have no means of studying books on the higher parts of carpentry. To such it will be an advantage even to know that there is such a thing as a science that treats of the form and strength of materials; and a few suggestions might set an ingenious person upon a course of thought which would lead him to many valuable practical conclusions.

Every traveller ought to know something of the construction of the steam-engine, which is doing such wonders for the world. Should not a teacher endeavour to know enough of the principles of Chemistry and of Pneumatics to give some idea of its structure and action? Enough, at least, to point out to an inquisitive pupil what studies he must pursue to find them out for himself?

There are no subjects of greater interest to children, of both sexes and of all ages, than the nature, habits, and uses of the animal creation. Humanity, as well as agriculture and the other arts, would be advanced by a general diffusion of knowledge upon these subjects. It will be sufficient to give a few instances. It is not uncommon to see pools or vessels of water allowed to remain stagnant in the vicinity of houses and of villages. These are usually full of animal and vegetable substances in a state of partial decay. Their offensiveness to the senses is borne with, because it is thought that this is the extent of the evil. Would they continue to deform the prospect if it were universally known that from the surface of stagnant water rise, in the warm season, miasmata that poison the air, and sometimes generate fever? and that these same pools give birth to innumerable insects, particularly moschetoes, greater pests to man than even disease? The same might be said of the low grounds on which, in the beginning of summer, water is allowed to stand, but which could be easily drained and made healthy.

Since the times of the ancients, or a few years in the early lives of our forefathers, insects are the only dangerous and really troublesome class of animals with which men have to contend. Most of the insect tribes are incredibly prolific, so that, if not checked, they would increase to such a degree that there would be no harvest for man to reap, no vegetables to gather, no trees to take shelter under. They are kept in check, not by man, for he could do comparatively nothing against them directly, but by the allies of man, the birds, and the reptiles, and some of the smaller quadrupeds. There are many species of birds whose aid is essential to our subsistence, against whom we, ignorantly or perversely, make war, as if they were our enemies. The robin, the blackbird, the numerous tribes of warblers which make the woods vocal with their songs, and multitudes of other birds, beautiful, melodious, innocent, spend their lives in our service, in doing what we, without their aid, can by no possibility do, and are, notwithstanding, but too often sacrificed in the cruel and thoughtless sports of boys, or the mistaken precautions of men. Wilson computes that a single pair of redwinged blackbirds consume, in a single season of four months, more than twelve thousand grubs.* Each of these grubs would have become a perfect insect, and each, on an average, would have produced hundreds of young. Let any one consider how much good is thus done by a single pair of harmless birds, and that there are perhaps a million of pairs in the State of New-York every summer, and as many more of each of several other kinds of birds, all equally devoted to the service of man, and he will form some conception of the extent of their services, and of the folly of exterminating them. In this instance, the humanity which would spare them is at the same time the wisest policy.

A great portion of the children at all the public schools of the interior are destined to spend their lives on farms. These schools are their only places of education. Should not the instructer be qualified to give them some intimation of the kind of knowledge which this mode of life requires; of the nature of soils; of the animals they are to employ; of the plants and trees by which they are surrounded? Should he not know something of the science which enters into every process that is carried on upon a farm, from the making of butter and cheese to the making of soap and the preparation of compost, and of that which explains the motion of the sap in the trees, and would teach to find medicines in the fields, and the material for the supply of many of the arts in the woods? The instructer should be an intelligent friend as well as a faithful teacher. How much might he add to his useful influence by being able to point out in the bark of the cherry-tree a substitute for the gum quinia of Peru, or in the bark of a sumach or oak a substitute for dyes imported from distant parts of the world.

The great study of the teacher must be Human Physiolo

* Peabody's Report on the Birds of Massachusetts, p. 278.

gy. This treats of the laws of the human body, and in some measure, consequently, of those of the mind; for so intimately are they connected, that the health and growth of the one depend, in a great degree, on the health of the other. There is no part of physiology of which a teacher should be entirely ignorant; but the portions with which he is more immediately concerned are those that treat of respiration, the circulation, digestion, the nervous system, and the functions of the skin.

Respiration is the process of breathing, by which air is alternately taken into and thrown out of the lungs. Without some knowledge of the extent of the cavity which is thus filled and emptied at every breath, and of the life-giving influence of pure air upon the blood, and thence upon the whole system, the teacher cannot be aware, as he ought, of the importance to his pupils of a position while at study, and of exercises in play, which shall expand and keep open the cavity of the chest, or of the vital necessity of a constant supply of fresh air. Neither can he, without this knowledge, be sufficiently awake to the danger of compression upon the chest, during the early years of each sex, from girdles, corsets, or any other unnatural articles of dress or fashion. This is one of the points at which the enemy consumption so often enters.

Not less important is some knowledge of the formation and circulation of the blood. This fluid, formed from the food taken into the stomach, and thus affected by the nature of the food, is carried into the heart, thence thrown into the lungs, where it is exposed to the action of air, thence carried back to the heart, which, like a central engine, throws it, through the blood-vessels, into every part of the body. Unless sufficiently supplied with air in the lungs, it does not carry an active and vital energy to the brain or to the limbs. A knowledge of this simple fact would have saved thousands of teachers from days of weariness and exhaustion, of low spirits and ill-temper: how many more than thousands of children from involuntary inattention, from stupidity, from habits of indifference and indolence, and from the punishments, immediate and remote, which all these bring down upon them. When a schoolroom is full of bad air, the lungs cannot perform their office. The brain, wanting the stimulus of healthy blood from the heart and lungs, becomes torpid. The child cannot command his attention; he cannot think; oftentimes he cannot avoid falling asleep. The master, himself oppressed by the same cause, and driven almost to distraction by what seems the hopeless stupidity or brutal obstinacy of his pupils, suffers bitterly himself, and visits heavily upon them the consequence of his own ignorance of this law of life. Imagine what sufferings generations of the occupants of schools have endured from its not being known that an abundant supply of pure air is necessary to the healthy action of the brain.

The nervous system consists of the brain, encased in the scull, and filling the head; the spinal marrow, occupying the cavity of the back bone or spine; and the nerves, which are delicate white threads proceeding from the brain or from the spinal marrow to every part of the body. It is by means of the nerves that sensations are conveyed from each of the organs of sense to the brain; and it is by their means that the will acts on the several limbs. If one of the nerves of the arm be cut through, all power over that arm is lost. If another be severed, sensation ceases to pass from the arm to the mind. The health of the nervous system depends upon the health of the brain, and indirectly upon whatever affects the general health of the body, particularly upon the supply of pure air. Thence it is that no class of persons are so liable to nervous diseases as those who, with sedentary habits, make great use of the brain in thought or study, and little use of the body, in active exercise, in the open air. It therefore behooves all sedentary, studious persons, and especially teachers, to make themselves familiar with what concerns the healthy condition of the organ of thought, the centre and source of the faculties which it is one important part of their office to educate. The brain is immediately connected, by nerves, with the stomach, and its healthy condition depends upon it in a very great degree. It is obvious, then, how important it is to be acquainted with the structure and character of the stomach and digestive apparatus. It is not my purpose to dwell upon this extensive subject. I wish only to say enough to show to such teachers as have not given it especial attention, how intimately it is connected with their calling, that they may be induced to look for full information to those authors who have treated upon it at large.

In regard to the office which the teeth perform in the preparation of food for digestion, by chewing or mastication, it is sufficient to say that it is essential to this process that it should be performed slowly enough to allow the food to be completely mingled with saliva. The too common practice of taking a large quantity of food into the mouth at once, and swallowing it after very slight and hurried mastication, is as injurious to health as it is offensive to good taste and good manners.

The principal offices performed by the skin, besides that of shielding and protecting every part of the surface, are, 1st, serving as a means of throwing off from the system that portion of its substance which has ceased to be of use, and, 2d, keeping a uniformity of temperature.

Every part of the body is in a state of constant renovation and decay. In every stage of life, and especially during the period of growth, the particles, of which every part is made up, are removed, and brought, by vessels designed for that purpose, to the surface of the skin, through the innumerable pores by which it is penetrated. From twenty to thirty, or even forty ounces of matter, are thus thrown out of the system in the course of every twenty-four hours. When the skin is clean and in a healthy state, these particles are thrown from its surface by what we call the *insensible perspiration*. They are thrown, mingled with an invisible vapour, into the air by which the body is surrounded, contaminating it, and thus giving an additional reason why there should be a constant supply of pure fresh air. A portion of them, however, is deposited on the surface, from which they must be daily removed by the application of water. If allowed to accumulate, they soon close the pores, stop or impede the perspiration, and cause various diseases of the skin. The eruptions so often seen on the skin of children allowed to be habitually dirty, may be usually traced to this source. This is a common, but it is not the worst effect. The waste and useless particles of old and dead matter, of which the body should be rid, being forced to remain within it, accumulate, and act upon it as foreign and poisonous substances, finally producing, when carried to excess, disorder and disease, in the various oppressive and horrid forms of headaches, consumption, dysentery, and fever. The simple and effectual preventive of these effects is cleanliness, co-operating with the *sensible* perspiration produced by active and continued exercise.

Another office of the skin is to regulate the temperature of the body. When the body is exposed to unusual heat, an oppressive, burning sensation is first experienced. This seems to excite to action vessels of the skin, which moisten the surface with the sensible perspiration or sweat, whose evaporation immediately produces an agreeable sensation of coolness. In health, this operation takes place whenever it is necessary. By cold the skin is contracted, perspiration checked, and a portion of the animal heat kept in. When excessive, cold must be guarded against by exercise, clothing, and artificial heat. These we have at our command; the remedy for the effects of extreme heat is provided by the beneficence of our constitution. A sudden check of the perspiration, sensible or insensible, by a current of cold air, by dampness, or by sudden cessation from exercise in a cold place, may be, and often is, productive of disease in a milder or more aggravated form.*

CHAPTER II.

THE NATURAL LAWS.

"All the happiness of man is derived from discovering, applying, or obeying the laws of his Creator, and all his misery is the result of ignorance or disobedience."—WAYLAND.

THE object of education, in its highest sense, is to draw out, naturally and fully, every faculty of the body, mind, and soul.† To be able to do this, or to do anything towards it, the teacher must know what are the faculties, and what are the laws of their action. A universal law, and one which applies equally to the physical, intellectual, and moral nature, is this: *Every power is improved by exercise.* This is the key to the teacher's duty.

Illustrations of the truth of this law are presented by the known effects of exercise on the limbs and muscles of the body. The bones and muscles in the arm of a blacksmith

---

* The whole object of these paragraphs is to show how indispensable to a teacher is some knowledge of the systems and functions to which I have adverted. For satisfactory information upon these subjects, I must refer to the excellent work of Andrew Combe on Health and Mental Education, which forms the 71st volume of the Family Library, and to the work of Dr. Hayward on Physiology. These two works should be studied in connexion, as they occupy different portions of the ground.

† It has been well described, "the harmonious development of every power for thought, action, duty, and happiness."

acquire strength and firmness which give to his grasp a force almost equal to that of his own vice. A similar effect is produced on the bones and muscles of the person who spends many hours every day in swift walking. So a weak voice may be gradually strengthened by moderate daily exercise in speaking. This is an important fact to the teacher. Though his voice may have little strength at first, daily practice, with a force constantly but very gradually increased, will at last enable him to fill without difficulty the largest schoolroom, and to continue talking for a long time at once. All the properties of the voice may be improved by cultivation. An indistinct utterance may be converted into the fullest and clearest articulation. A clownish and provincial accent may give place to beautiful and graceful pronunciation.

Delicacy and perfection, as well as strength, are also given by exercise. This is in no instance more remarkable than in that of the blind, who acquire, from necessity, a nicety of touch, inconceivable to one who has the use of his eyes. The effect of exercise upon the power of vision is exemplified in the case of the sailor, who, constantly exercising his eyes upon distant objects, reads the name of a ship at a distance at which a landsman can hardly see that there is a name to be read.

What is thus universally true of all the senses and faculties of the body, is no less so of the powers of the mind. This law, indeed, is the foundation of the theory of education. It is by exercise that all the faculties are improved. Address the love of knowledge,—that curiosity which is instinctive in every mind,—and you increase it. Tell an interesting story, or communicate facts which he can comprehend, to a child, every day for months, and you awaken and increase his desire for similar facts and his power of comprehending them. The perceptions are quickened, the power of observation is sharpened, the memory made ready and tenacious, the reason strengthened, the comprehension enlarged, the judgment matured, the taste corrected, by a process precisely similar to that by which the external senses are carried to their perfection. This is mental education. Must not the teacher know what these powers are, and what are the means by which they are to be trained? To dwell for a moment upon a single faculty. It becomes of the greatest importance to the teacher to cultivate the power of language. Much of his success must depend upon his skill in the use of words; not mere sounds, but words as the clothing of thought. If he exercise himself carefully in the use of language, in expressing himself upon all subjects and on all occasions, he will gradually, even if he have but moderate natural powers of expression, become fluent, clear, and impressive. It is a long process, but the object to be attained is worth all we can do to attain it.

The effects of use, of constant exercise, upon the development of the moral powers, are not less striking nor less certain than on those of the intellect or the body. This momentous part of a teacher's duty has been signally, sadly neglected.

Just as the memory is improved by cultivating it, so also are the animal propensities. So, for example, is the disposition to quarrel. If you excite this propensity often, you increase its violence. A violent child is not to be conquered and reformed by violence—that only makes him still more violent—but by gentleness and kindness. A propensity to hate is strengthened by exercise. Whatever is said or done to increase the feeling towards an individual, increases the power of the general habit. An object of affection must be substituted, in order to change the habit. Love must be introduced into its place. This shows what course is to be taken with a child of an unamiable character. Scolding should be entirely avoided; it only exasperates the unamiable feeling. We must not hate such a child.

If we do, the whole force of our example will be thrown on the side of his evil feelings. We must love him, and, following the golden rule, overcome his evil with our good. Really love him, and kindness will grow in his heart in answering sympathy to the kindness in ours.

Again, we must take care to exercise the principle which we wish to strengthen. The love of knowledge is not cherished by an appeal to the love of distinction, but only the love of distinction. Let a conscientious person daily and earnestly address the conscience of a child; he soon awakens it to action, and it becomes more and more active the more it is called to act. A duty is to be performed because it is right. Let that ground be taken and maintained, and the habit of acting from a sense of right will be constantly strengthened, till it is at last firmly established. But to prove that the performance of a duty will bring advantages, is to address a selfish principle. The habit of doing right may indeed thereby be formed, but, at the same time, the habit of doing it from an imperfect motive. To discourse upon morals is not necessarily to teach morality. The discourse may be addressed to the understanding, and not to the conscience; and if so, it will be the understanding, and not the conscience, which will be affected and exercised. Moral education consists in leading one to *act* from conscientious motives. So the truth should be told because it is the truth, and because its obligation is declared to be sacred by the conscience as well as by the Scriptures. It is, indeed, better to tell the truth for the reason that it is expedient and good policy to tell the truth, than not to tell it at all. But this is not making it a duty, but a part of worldly prudence. It is not exercising the conscience, but a far lower part of our nature. It is not enough to establish the habit of doing right; the essential thing is to establish the habit of acting only from the highest motives, of doing right from principle and conscience.

This most important part of a teacher's duty needs attention at every stage of the pupil's progress. Children are capable of acting from conscientious motives at a very early age. The sense of right begins to show itself as soon as language begins to be used. The best and most intelligible argument against falsehood, at any age, is, *It is wrong*. This a child can understand and feel, and no language or reasoning of a philosopher can add any force to it. So of all other vices and faults. The best argument against them is to show that they are wrong. The teacher should therefore study to acquire clear conceptions of right and wrong himself, and the power of expressing his conceptions in simple and forcible language.

CHAPTER III.

INDEPENDENCE OF THE NATURAL LAWS.

"Wherefore do the wicked live, become old, yea, are mighty in power?"—JOB.

> "Happy is he who lives to understand
> Not human nature only, but explores
> All natures, to the end that he may find
> The law that governs each."—WORDSWORTH.

EVER since the days of Job, the question has been constantly coming up, How happens it that the good are afflicted and the bad are prosperous? that "there is one event to the righteous and to the wicked?"* that the sinner often enjoys health, and fortune, and ease, while the good man is depressed by poverty and disease, and all the forms of trouble?

The instructions of Jesus Christ upon this subject, though not full, are, when we come to understand them, clear and

* Eccl., ix., 2.

satisfactory. But to understand them is not always easy, until we consider the truth of certain facts, and divest ourselves of the false views with which most of us are accustomed to consider them.

Upon this subject there are a few considerations with which the teacher should be familiar, of great importance, as they help him to reconcile the apparent contradictions in the beautiful system of God's providence.

One is, that the body is as really the workmanship of God as the mind, and the laws of its structure and health, though they may be of less extensive importance, are as really His laws as those of religion or morality. In regard to them, all men are treated with entire impartiality. He who makes his sun to rise on the evil and on the good, and sends his rain on the just and on the unjust, has made the laws of his material creation and of the body equally binding on all his creatures. The good man is just as liable to ill health, if he neglect the laws of health, as the bad man. The missionary, engaged in one of the holiest works that man can be engaged in, sickens and dies if he do not understand the climate in which he is living, or if, knowing its character, he neglect to take the necessary precautions against its malignancy. A congregation of worshippers, assembled in a house the supports of whose roof are insufficient or decayed, is overwhelmed by its fall no less certainly than a band of robbers would have been. A man of piety, embarked on board a leaky ship, sinks as surely as a profane man.* God interposes not to change his physical laws, but requires all, the good as well as the bad, to obey them. Does it seem unreasonable that he should expect his friends, as well as his enemies, to obey *all* his laws—those of the body and the material world as well as those of the soul and the spiritual world?

Another important general consideration is, that these laws

* This seems to be the doctrine of Christ in Luke, xiii., 1-5.

are independent of each other. The man who understands and obeys the laws of physical health, will probably enjoy it, though he may be unjust, unmerciful, and profane; while the good man, who wears out his constitution in exertions which are beyond his strength, though he do it in the service of God or his fellow men, brings upon himself disease and all its consequences. In this case the good man obeys the moral laws, but disobeys the laws of the body, and is punished in consequence of this disobedience.

A third consideration is, that the observance of each law is followed by its own reward. Labour and skill accomplish their purposes independently of the character of those who employ them. If the bad man cultivates his field diligently and skilfully, he will have a plentiful crop, while the field of the good man, neglected, or managed without regard to the nature of the soil or the seed sown in it, will be barren. It is the hand of the diligent that maketh rich. So it is with the mind. He who observes the laws of the intellect, and diligently employs all its faculties, will reap the fruits of his labour, whether he observe the higher moral laws or not. Let a man of natural talent apply himself to the acquisition of knowledge, and give his days and nights to study—he will gain knowledge, he will become learned, whether he be virtuous or vicious, a profane scorner or an humble worshipper.

If we observe all the laws, those of the material world, those of our own bodies, those of the intellect, and the revealed laws,—those of our moral nature, we shall do our whole duty, and our reward will be proportionally great. The true and appropriate reward of obedience to the moral laws, so far as this world is concerned, is peace of mind, the approbation of our own conscience, the satisfaction of doing good, and the favour of good men. All these we lose by violating these laws. Would it be just that we should also lose health, property, and reason?

Another important law in regard to each of the faculties is, that while its due and natural exercise develops, strengthens, and improves it, undue or untimely exercise, overexertion, strains, weakens, and tends to destroy it. It is therefore of the highest importance to know, not only what kind of discipline each faculty requires for its growth and healthy development, but also what are the times at which it should be given, and what are the limits within which it should be confined. The happiness of life may be destroyed, and life itself shortened, by excess in the use of the powers of the body, mind, or moral nature.

First, of the powers of the body. Each one of these acquires its full strength very slowly. The body itself comes to maturity at different ages in different individuals, but not usually in man before twenty-five or thirty years, and in woman not before twenty or twenty-five. To subject any one part to great and continued exertion before the period of its full strength, is to endanger its health ever after. To require of the whole body, before maturity, the constant and severe exercise to which the mature body only is fitted, is to ensure ill health and to invite premature death.

It is found in the French and English armies, that young recruits, such as enter the army before the age of 23, are poorly able to bear the labours and exposures of a military life, even in time of peace. A writer referred to in Dr. Andrew Combe's work on Health,* states that "volunteers received into the French army at the age of 18 or 20, pass two, three, or four years of their period of service (eight years) in hospital, solely from inability to bear up under difficulties which scarcely affect those who are a few years older." The same author states, that in the English army in Spain, "sickness and inefficiency prevailed almost in proportion to the youth and recent arrival of the soldiers." In a single regiment, the number of young recruits was 353, of

* Health and Mental Education, p. 287.

whom "more than one half died within the first eleven months;" while the number of old soldiers was 1143, of whom only 77 perished in the same time. The same principle would probably be found to hold true wherever very young men are subjected to the labours of the full-grown man. It is, however, not easy to get statements except from the army, as there only is an exact record kept of the ages of all persons employed.

Indeed, it seems to be a universal truth, that during those years in which the body is acquiring its growth and strength, it should not only be supplied with abundance of nourishing food, and be allowed a great deal of sleep, but neither body nor mind should be exposed to severe or long-continued, much less sudden labour, or that which is not prepared for by gradual exercise.

The pernicious effects of premature or excessive application of the mind are exemplified by the cases of precocious children. They are usually very short lived, and, if they live to maturity, are very ordinary men. Also, by the numerous instances of sedentary men, especially religious teachers, who, by extreme devotion to their duties, those particularly which require great action and produce great excitement of mind, as the preparation of sermons, often bring on a nervous or consumptive habit, which obliges them afterward to lead useless and miserable lives.

Instances of excess in the use of the moral powers are easily found in the records of asylums for the insane, which present the cases of many who have had the equilibrium of their minds disturbed by anxiety in regard to religious duties, while they neglected those other laws of their nature which an enlightened view of their whole system, body as well as soul, as the workmanship of God, would have shown them to be laws to be observed as really, if not as sacredly, as the laws of the moral code.*

* See Combe on the Constitution of Man.

CHAPTER IV.

HIGHER STUDIES.

"To ask or search, I blame thee not, for heav'n
Is as the book of GOD before thee set,
Wherein to read his wond'rous works, and learn
His seasons, hours, or days, or months, or years."
MILTON.

"Truth has her pleasure-grounds, her haunts of ease
And easy contemplation;
These may he range, if willing to partake
Their soft indulgences, and in due time
May issue thence, recruited for the tasks
And course of service Truth requires from those
Who tend her altars, wait upon her throne,
And guard her fortresses."—WORDSWORTH.

ANOTHER study, with the great truths of which the teachers of the highest schools should be acquainted, is Astronomy. Nothing else gives us so exalted ideas of the vastness of the Creator's dominions, and the infinity of the power and goodness which he is constantly exerting. Nothing, therefore, so elevates and expands the mind. If we would fill our minds with high thoughts of the greatness of our Father, and of the unlimited expansion of that benevolence which is extended to the inhabitants of thousands of worlds—of the comprehensiveness of those laws of beauty and order which embrace countless systems of worlds, we must study Astronomy. But, independently of the dignity of the science as an occupation for the intellect, and as a preparation for higher conceptions of that love which, while it has an infinite universe to act in, and countless intelligences to bless, takes care even of the sparrows, and hears the cry of the young raven, Astronomy has claims upon us on account of its numerous daily applications. The seasons of the year, the recurrence of light and darkness, the lengthening and shortening of the days, the beautiful changes of the moon, the wonderful eclipses, are subjects about which we should be familiar, for they are the theme of the watchful and insatiable curiosity of children, and in regard to them every tolerably educated individual should have his questionings answered. To do this in some degree not entirely unsatisfactory, requires no profound knowledge, but such only as may be obtained from some of the common treatises upon the subject.* The size, shape, and motions of the earth, the distances, magnitudes, and motions of the sun and moon, the difference between the fixed stars and the planets, the extent of the atmosphere, the tides of the ocean,—these are nearly all the essential points, though more would be useful. In connexion with Astronomy, something of the nature and laws of light may be explained. A few articles of optical and astronomical apparatus will be of great use; but, when they are not to be had, substitutes can be found for all except a prism. There are thousands of districts in which children will be able to obtain information on these interesting subjects from no one except the teacher of the district school. Shall they look to him in vain?

Another subject is the arts, especially the common and useful arts. Children are curious as to the manner in which the things about them are made. What is glass made of? How are books made? and tables, chairs, knives, earthenware? Such questions they ask in regard to all objects that meet their sight. The more satisfactorily we can answer them, the more pleasure shall we give, the greater interest shall we excite in the minds of children, the more fully shall we answer the demand upon us

* For example, Celestial Scenery, by Dick, the 83d number of the Family Library.

to furnish them with knowledge of practical use, and the more effectually shall we excite that curiosity which is only another name for the activity of certain powers of the mind, the energies of whose action is one of the important circumstances that make a difference between man and man. A study of the arts is among the preparations we are to make to teach Geography satisfactorily and profitably. Oblige a child to commit to memory the boundaries, cities, and rivers of Poland, and he will be likely to forget all; but if you give him a description of the salt-mines of Cracow, and the mode of preparing the salt there, he will remember it, and the other facts associated with it. Some such fact in regard to the arts may be a part of each day's preparation for the lesson. What can be more interesting than the coal-mines, and the preparation of iron, gold, and the other metals?*

In teaching Geography, you will find constant need of a knowledge of History, and there is no way in which both can be made so interesting as by teaching them in connexion. A place which would soon be forgotten if nothing but its name and situation were mentioned, becomes engraven on the mind, by being associated with some remarkable event in history, some curious phenomenon in nature, or some interesting operation in art. History, therefore, should be one of your studies. The most important portions of history are that of our own country, and of England, as thence are derived our government, laws, institutions, language, and literature; and the history of the modern Western nations of Europe, of Greece and Rome, and of the Jews and other nations in the west of Asia, as contained in the scriptures of the Old Testament.

An ancient philosopher, being asked what a child should *learn*, answered, what will be of use to him when he be-

---

* Hazen's Technology contains a great deal of valuable information on the useful and fine arts.

comes a man. It is our happiness to live in a country where all men have equal rights; where each individual man has a voice in the government, by helping, through his vote, to elect those who carry on the government; where every man may be called to take a part in the government by being elected to office; and where he is almost sure to take a part in the administration of justice, by being called to serve on a jury. These rights give birth to corresponding duties. Every man ought to understand the frame of the government under which he lives; to know something of the constitution on which that government is based; of the laws which he is bound to obey, and of his rights and duties as a citizen. This knowledge comes not by intuition, nor is it the dictate of mere unassisted common sense. It ought to be communicated in the course of his education. The masters of the highest class of common schools,—those masters from whose hands a large part of the population pass directly to the business and duties of life, should therefore be able to communicate something of this kind of knowledge. A study of the Constitution of the State and of the Union, of the general frame of our government, and of the character of our institutions and laws, must therefore be a part of the duty of those teachers. Instruction in this department may not be a part of the course prescribed, but it may, and, if possible, should, be given in the indirect conversational mode of which I have so often spoken. One or two volumes will be sufficient for the purpose of giving the teacher what he will wish to communicate. Several such exist; Story's Constitutional Class Book, Sullivan's Political Class Book, and others of a similar class.

A distinguishing attribute of man,—that which, more than any other, raised him to his high place in the creation,—is the faculty of language, by means of which he holds communion with his Maker, matures his own thoughts and avails himself of the thoughts of others, makes himself master of the accumulated wisdom of time, and imparts to him who comes after whatever he has gleaned. It behooves the teacher to perfect himself in the use of this faculty. It is his instrument. Very much of his success, of the influence he is to exert on his pupils, will depend upon his skill in the use of it.

If he is not by nature highly gifted in the power of expression, he may, by proper self-discipline, improve the power almost indefinitely. To this end he must give his attention to three points: 1. Utterance. 2. Pronunciation. 3. Command of language, or fluency. Of the two former I shall speak hereafter.

Command of language is to be gained by much reading of good books. This is the first requisite. He who would use language freely and well must be a great reader. But this is not enough. He must also write. Dr. Franklin recommends an excellent method, upon which he successfully practised himself, to form a good style and obtain command of language. He took some essay from the Spectator, made short hints of the sense of each sentence, and laid them aside until he had forgotten the language in which they were written. Then, without looking at the book, he tried to complete the paper again, by writing out each hinted sentence at length in the best words that occurred to him. He then improved his own writing by comparing it with the original and correcting the faults Another method, which he thought still more effectual, as giving a greater choice of words, was turning some tales of the Spectator into verse, and afterward, when he had nearly forgotten the prose, turning them back again.*

Careful composition of any kind, on any subject, in prose or poetry, will have the effect of giving copiousness of expression and exactness of thought. To this must be added the habit of speaking upon any subjects on which pupils are to be addressed. This should be practised daily.

* Sparks's edition of the Works of Franklin, vol. i., 18, 19.

Stories should be told, historical events related, curious facts stated, and advice given, upon subjects of conduct, study, and character. If you find that you forget what you intended to say, it may be well to make short notes, the sight of which will recall what you have thought.

1. In preparation, make yourself master of the subject by study and meditation.

2. Arrange what you have to say in distinct heads. This will improve your powers of reasoning and of order.

3. It may be well to select subjects on which you ought to say something.

4. Take occasions as they present themselves in school, or make occasions.

While engaged in improving the power of expression, we must also endeavour to gain an acquaintance with the best writers in the English language. It is a privilege belonging to our calling, that it leaves us several hours each day for reading. And what can be a better or pleasanter way of spending these hours than in reading the admirable books of which our literature is full? But more of this hereafter.

Intimately connected with this department, and essential to its completeness, is the study of Rhetoric and Logic. Something of both these is essential to enable us to explain the words that occur in the common reading-books. But, more than this, Rhetoric is the art of persuading, Logic the art of convincing;—Who has occasion for all the resources of both more than he who is engaged in convincing children of the truth, and persuading them to obey it;—who is, at the same time, moulding the affections, and training the powers of the understanding?

I would recommend to every teacher who has, or can create, an opportunity, to become acquainted with some other language besides the English. If possible, he should learn something of the Latin language. The reasons for so doing are briefly these: 1. It is one of the great sources of English, particularly of most of those words we call dictionary words. 2. It is the parent of all the languages of the South of Europe. 3. It has formed the study of nearly all the best writers in English, and with the knowledge of it we shall better understand their works. 4. All its forms of speech and idioms are extremely unlike those of our language, and we therefore get from it a better knowledge of language in general. 5. Translating from it is one of the best and surest ways of improving the style. 6. Its study gives an admirable discipline to the faculties.

If he have not time to learn the Latin, I would advise him to learn French. Several of the advantages of studying Latin may be obtained from this study, though I think in an inferior degree. It has, however, one advantage which the Latin has not. Books of great value, on all subjects, are continually making their appearance in this language.

That he may the more perfectly understand Arithmetic, he should study Algebra. Some parts of the former, the extraction of roots, for example, cannot be easily *understood* without, and it throws light upon every part.

He should, by all means, study Geometry. This is an excellent discipline to the reasoning powers, and is, moreover, essential to an understanding of the best treatises in Natural Philosophy and Astronomy. It is the foundation of Trigonometry, Surveying, and the other modes of measuring which he may be called to teach.

Another accomplishment which a highly-qualified teacher should have, is the art of Drawing. To all persons who are to have anything to do with machinery, this is of great importance. It would, indeed, be highly useful for every mechanic to be able to draw well enough to represent all the articles which he may be called upon to make. His employer often wants to see how a thing will look before he orders it. It would be well if all who have occasion to employ mechanics could draw. They could thus much more easily and perfectly show what they wanted done. To the planners of houses and other buildings it ought to be considered essential, and it is useful to travellers, to naturalists, and to many others.

On his own account the teacher ought to be able to draw. Every good teacher must use the black-board; and the more readily and skilfully he can draw upon it, the more frequently and successfully will he employ it.

Drawing should be communicated to females as a resource. What a pleasure is it to a benevolent lady to be able to carry home to her friends delineations of the beautiful prospects or remarkable objects she meets with on her travels! There are, moreover, a thousand solitary hours in the life of almost every female, which may be made pleasant by this art, and which would be monotonous or sad without. A highly-accomplished lady, whose excellent education had given her many resources, who was well read in English literature, and familiar with several other languages, has often told me that, of all her acquisitions, she valued none so highly as her power of drawing, on account of the resources it had given in the many solitary hours of a life, some portions of which had been passed in the seclusion of the country.

Another study is the Art of Teaching. On this subject he should be well read. There are several valuable books, written in this country, from which he may obtain very important aids.

"The Teacher," by Jacob Abbott, is full of ingenious devices, some of which are described in this volume, for accomplishing his objects in school, and especially for obtaining an influence over pupils. For its moral tone, this book is also of great value.

"Hall's Lectures" is a valuable book, made by a man of a great deal of experience.

"Hall's Lectures to Female Teachers" is a small but excellent work, addressed particularly to the teachers of primary schools.

The "Teacher Taught," by Emerson Davis, contains, in a small compass, useful practical directions for the management of a common school.

"The Teacher's Manual," by Thomas H. Palmer, obtained the prize offered by the American Institute of Instruction. It contains most valuable suggestions in regard to every part of a teacher's duty, and much important information, particularly in reference to teaching Arithmetic and Morality.

"Suggestions on Education," by Catharine E. Beecher, are admirable, especially in regard to the education of females. The shortness of the work is almost its only fault.

Still more is to be done by reflection. Every school is somewhat different from every other; and it is only by thinking much upon the peculiar circumstances of a school, and the individuals of which it is composed, that the best modes for its government and instruction can be devised. Still a teacher may be prepared for its duties by a previous knowledge of the regulations observed in other schools, and necessary in all.

In connexion with the study of the Art of Teaching, the study of the Philosophy of the Human Mind should command the attention of the teacher. This great subject has occupied some of the profoundest thinkers that have lived, men who have been the pioneers of human improvement, whose far-reaching eye has penetrated into futurity, and detected in its germe what would lead to the advancement of the race. They, more than any other class of men, have at all times drawn public attention to education in its various aspects. No well-read teacher should be ignorant of their writings.

CHAPTER V.

ADVANTAGES OF A TEACHER'S LIFE.

> "Turn your steps
> Wherever fancy leads, by day, by night—
> You walk, you live, you speculate
> With no incurious eye; and books are yours,
> Within whose silent chambers treasure lies,
> Preserved from age to age; more precious far
> Than that accumulated store of gold
> And orient gems, which, for a day of need,
> The sultan hides within ancestral tombs.
> And music waits upon your skilful touch.
>   Furnished thus,
> How can you droop, if willing to be raised?"
> WORDSWORTH.

SUCH are some of the endowments and some of the acquisitions which are necessary for distinguished usefulness as a teacher. If fully possessed, they will raise a man far above the level, as to intellect and acquirement, of common society. Yet all are but too little to enable you to do the good which may be done in the situation you are going to occupy. Still, some of you, regarding the low estimation in which the office is sometimes held, may be tempted to say, With these gifts and this education, with talents whereby I might distinguish myself before the world, shall I sacrifice myself in the seclusion of a schoolroom? If you have the poor ambition which makes you sigh for ephemeral distinction, go; there is no place for you within these quiet walls. But if you have something of that lofty spirit of devotion to duty, which led the poet Wolfe, with talents which could excite the envy of Byron, to bury himself in a remote and unknown parish, dare to live for others and for your own best good. Be ambitious of the power of being useful. Where will you have so much, or of so high a kind, as here? Where else can you do so much? The school is the great reforming and regenerating instrument. How many of the hopes of the improvement of the race cluster about it! You are surrounded by innocent childhood and generous youth, the hope of your native country, full of gentleness, docility, intelligence, uncorrupted by the world, open to all good thoughts and noble sentiments, full of warm affections, eager for improvement, burning with desires for excellence. To-day they are children, to-morrow they will be men and women, the fathers and mothers of the land. They crowd around you, waiting to receive the impress which your character shall give them.

The fair-haired girl before you may be the future mother of a Washington or a Marshall. By inspiring her heart with the highest principles, you will do something to advance humanity by forming a sublime specimen of a just man, a sage, and pure expounder of the great principles of law.

These boys are soon to fill the halls of legislation, the schools of philosophy, the ranks of literature, the workshops, the fields, the marts of trade, the pulpit, the desk of the editor, the chair of the teacher. Inspire them with a high sense of justice, and you will elevate jurisprudence and humanize the laws. Imbue them with a deep reverence for goodness, for the moral laws of God, and you raise the tone of society, and do something to purify the fountains of instruction. Give them a knowledge of the laws of physical nature, and you do much to improve agriculture and the useful arts. There is not a calling, however high and glorious, which some one of your pupils may not fill. If you have genius enough to enkindle his; if you have knowledge enough to give a right direction to his thoughts; if you have nobleness enough to give a higher aim to his young aspirations for excellence, you will have no mean agency in elevating the character of your country and mankind. Is not this enough for your ambition? What under heaven would you have higher?

The career of the teacher does not, it is true, lead to distinction or to wealth. It is not brilliant; but it leads to something better than distinction—to the heartfelt honour and affectionate respect of those who feel that they have been made wiser and better by its influence. Few men in their old age are looked upon with such reverential regard as faithful and intelligent teachers. I often converse with a gray-haired man, who had the good fortune to receive, when quite a child, instruction from a man of learning, and polished manners, and noble character; and, though he has been much in society, and seen familiarly all the most distinguished men of his day, he still looks back upon good master Pemberton as the model of an accomplished scholar and a finished gentleman; and there is no one whom he holds in higher respect than he cherishes for the memory of this venerable man. Would not such a remembrance be a higher and more enduring reward than the remembrance of popular favour?*

The life of a teacher has the advantage of perfect regularity. He has what most men in other occupations often sigh for, the entire disposal of his leisure hours. In nearly all places, the time spent in school is by custom limited to six or seven hours a day for four days of the week, and three or four for two other days. It never should be more

* "As time advances, and a new generation of well-educated men and women grows up, ... who have had no other association with their teacher but of the most able, wise, accomplished, and amiable man of their acquaintance, in whose society they have experienced only delight, and the chief delight of their lives, there will be less and less dependance on mere endowment, badges of honour, or examples of fashion, for securing to the educator that high place in public estimation which it will then be morally impossible to withhold from him."—SIMPSON.

than this. The health of the teacher and the welfare of the taught settle this limit. How many hours does this arrangement leave to the teacher to be employed as he pleases; how many pleasures it puts within his reach. If he be in the country, a few acres of land, or even a large garden, will give the recreation and exercise he needs, and, besides more substantial returns, will, if situated near the schoolhouse, give means for experiments, and lessons in horticulture, and the management of trees and fruits, a desirable addition to the course of instruction in the country towns. If he be also a botanist, he may transplant from the neighbouring fields and woods the plants in which he feels an interest, and enjoy the great satisfaction of studying their habits while he trains them with his own hand. Without extraordinary exertion or going to any expense, he might, in a few years, form about him, of our American wild flowers, the very flowers which are the pride of the gardens of the English and French—the most beautiful that grow in any temperate climate—a collection which would be worth a visit from a prince.

If he have a taste for Experimental Philosophy, he may, by means of a few instruments, a thermometer, barometer, and magnetical needles, at the expense of a few minutes devoted to observations daily, keep himself familiar with some of those great investigations of the laws of nature which are commanding the attention of the philosophical world; or he may combine with his walks interesting inquiries in Geology and Mineralogy; or form an acquaintance with the insects, the fishes, the shells, or the birds. Charming pursuits, enough to make the path of life pleasant and smooth, if it were roughened by many more asperities than are found on the way of the generous and faithful teacher. It is too late a day for the ignorant and frivolous to sneer at these delightful studies. Many a noble in the Old World values his princely fortune—many a retired gentleman values his competency, chiefly because it leaves him at liberty to devote his life to them. Thanks to God, his worshippers, and the votaries of the sciences that investigate his works, are become too numerous and too respectable for any of their number to suffer from scorn because he devotes himself to these elevating and dignified pursuits. The Newtons and Galileos, the Linnæuses and Cuviers, the Decandolles and Bowditches, are too large and mighty a band for one of their followers and associates, be he even no more than a village schoolmaster, to feel anything but an honest pride at being of the number.

Or, if he have no taste for any of the departments of Natural Science, he may still, if he have a love for reading, command resources which leave him little to desire, nothing certainly to envy, in the lot of any other man. Books, the best books that have been ever written, are so cheap that he must be very poor not to be able to surround himself with enough to occupy all his leisure. And in so doing, he exercises a power to which the fabled virtue of Aladdin's lamp made but a faint and distant approach. At his will, he summons about him the spirits of the wise and eloquent among the living and the dead. They come and sit down by his fireside, wait his questionings, and depart at his bidding; the poets, Halleck, Bryant with his wood-notes, the Danas, with Southey, Coleridge, Wordsworth, and Campbell, from the other side of the Atlantic; the historians, Bancroft, Prescott, Irving, Sparks, with Hallam, Turner, Mackintosh, and their brethren; the philosophers, Herschel, Arnott, Lyell; the naturalists, Audubon and Gray, with Wilson, and Hooker, and troops of others not less illustrious. And across the dark and wide ocean of time will come the sage, the gifted seer, the inspired prophet, and unfold the picture of times and men long past, and thoughts that can never pass away; the poet of the human heart, from the banks of Avon; the poet of Paradise, from his small garden-house in Westminster; Burns, from his cottage on the Ayr; and Scott, from his dwelling by the Tweed; and the blind old man of Scio, still blind but still eloquent, will sit down with him, and as he sang almost thirty centuries ago among the isles of Greece, sing the war of Troy or the wanderings of Ulysses.* Skill in music, with the little choir of his own pupils that he might always assemble about him, and who, as they passed from his tutelage, would not all break the tie which unites those who love the tuneful art, would be an added resource, and, with a talent for drawing, would make his habitation a point of attraction—a radiant centre of light and refinement.

May not a man be contented with his lot, who, after a few busy hours of useful labour, may spend his evenings in company and occupations such as these?

It may be considered a fortunate circumstance in an individual's life that he can make his duties and his pleasures one. This is your case.

You may have the satisfaction of thinking that, while indulging in these luxuries, you are, at the same time, preparing yourself for a better performance of your duties. To the purposes of the teacher no kind of knowledge comes amiss. He may find useful facts and apt illustrations in all sorts of books and in every variety of investigation; and, however highly he may be able to cultivate himself, he may be sure that his cultivation will not be merely selfish. In the school, the humblest intellect, with moderate attainments, with right views and earnest purposes, may do something; while the genius of an angel, united with all knowledge, all accomplishment, and all excellence, would not be

---

* Just as he was writing this, the author had occasion to address an audience at a school celebration. Having little time for preparation, he, almost in spite of himself, enlarged upon the thoughts above expressed. The reported address may possibly reach the eye of some who read this.

lost, but would find their true place and highest exercise, and, instead of being wasted in the poor office of advancing their possessor, would warm hosts of others with the love of knowledge, virtue, and excellence.

Another favourable circumstance in the life of a teacher is, that he is not subject to anxieties about the fluctuations of trade, like the merchant; the variations of a distant market, like the manufacturer; of the home market, like the mechanic; the vicissitudes of storms, like the mariner; or of weather and the seasons, like the farmer. He will sympathize with his neighbours in sufferings produced by these causes, but will not feel that personal solicitude which he has who realizes that events are likely to happen which his sagacity ought to have foreseen and his forecast to have provided against, and which, if not foreseen and provided for, may bring upon him inevitable ruin.

Such are some of the advantages which belong to the position of a teacher. If, with suitable character and talents, you devote yourself for life to the work, you may be able to realize them all, or, at least, so many of them as you prefer. Most of you will teach but a portion of each year, and that, perhaps, for only a few years. Yet you may, if you please, during the time you are so employed, enjoy, at least in a degree, the advantages which I point out as belonging to this pursuit. Faithful to your charge and to yourself, you may look back upon the time so spent as among the most profitable and happy of your life. What though yours be an humble lot:

> "The smoke ascends
> To heaven as lightly from the cottage hearth
> As from the haughtiest palace. He, whose soul
> Ponders this true equality, may walk
> The fields of earth with gratitude and hope."

BOOK III.
DUTIES.

"To watch over the associations which they form in infancy; to give them early habits of mental activity; to rouse their curiosity, and direct it to proper objects; to exercise their ingenuity and invention; to cultivate in their minds a turn for speculation, and, at the same time, preserve their attention alive to the objects around them; to awaken their sensibilities to the beauties of nature, and to inspire them with a relish for intellectual enjoyment,—these form but a part of the business of education."—STEWART.

THE duties of a teacher are fourfold:

I. To himself, the duty of self-culture, inasmuch as he is to teach by the influence of his character and example, as well as by giving direct instruction:

II. To his pupils, as he is bound,

1. To furnish them with the means of acquiring knowledge;

2. To contribute to the formation of their moral character;

3. To assist them in developing their various faculties, that they may have a healthy mind in a healthy body;

4. To give them knowledge, which shall prepare them for the proper discharge of all their duties in life:

III. To his fellow-teachers, as bound to elevate the calling in which he is engaged, and increase its usefulness:

IV. To the parents of his pupils, and to the community in which he lives.

These duties are intimately related, yet it will be convenient to treat of them in separate chapters, as thereby we may obtain clearer views of them.

In this book a plan of duties will be sketched, to the entire performance of which few, perhaps, will be able fully to attain. But it is to be remembered that it is only by setting our standard high that we shall accomplish the utmost in our power.

CHAPTER I.

A TEACHER'S PERSONAL DUTIES.

"The mind, impressible and soft, with ease
  Imbibes and copies what she hears and sees,
  And through life's labyrinth holds fast the clew
  That education gives her, false or true."
                                        COWPER.

"Yes, it is a grave responsibility which rests upon you. The great majority of the population of nations is confided to your direction. They become what you make of them. First impressions are all-powerful; they contain the germes of all virtues and of all vices."—*L'Instituteur Primaire.*

As is the teacher, so is the school. This has justly become almost a proverb. It recognises the great influence of a teacher, direct and indirect, upon the character and conduct, and present and future welfare of all who are in his school.

By *direct* influence is meant whatever a teacher exercises intentionally and expressly, in his labours, for the instruction and improvement of his school. By *indirect* influence is meant that which is exercised by every other expression of his character. All that is in a man speaks out in the tone of his voice, in his manners, his looks, his deportment. It often speaks more decidedly, and makes a deeper impression, than the words which he utters. Energy of character, for example, shows itself by marks not easily to be mistaken. It controls the eye, the voice, the step, every motion. It makes itself *felt*. It is the life of a school. In like manner, gentleness, which, in a well-balanced character, should always be combined with it, speaks in a language no less significant and intelligible. It diffuses an inexpressible charm over the whole conduct, and attracts to an imitation of itself. The combination of these, energy of action and gentleness in the mode of action, is most desirable in the character of a teacher. Both are insensibly, but rapidly, communicated to a school; so that a stranger, on going into one, would very soon discover, by the spirit of activity or of sluggishness, of good manners or of clownishness, which prevailed; whether it were under the direction of a person of energy and a gentleman, or a sluggard and a clown. Both these qualities are capable of being acquired, and must be, if they are not possessed already. Energy may be formed by a resolute purpose to do what we can, and with our might. Gentleness is the natural effect of the cultivation of the higher parts of our nature, and especially of habitual self-control.

What is true of these is also true, in a greater or less degree, of every other quality. All pass from the teacher into the character of the pupil, and contribute to form it. Thus a spirit of order diffuses itself, the love of application, of punctuality, of neatness, of labour, a spirit of courtesy, a cheerful and contented spirit. This is, of course, especially true of those qualities which find expression in language. Children learn language by hearing it spoken, and, with the words, they at the same time receive something of the feeling expressed by the words. If they could hear only pure, refined, and generous feelings expressed, they would derive only good from this source. The teacher should take care that, so far as relates to himself, this shall be the case. Children, even more than men, are the creatures of imitation. The qualities of which I have spoken are such as directly affect the language and actions. They are, therefore, objects of direct imitation. Children are also creatures of sympathy. This principle, so strong in all human beings, is most so in the unsophisticated heart of a child. What I have said, therefore, applies, with not less force, to those more inward sentiments, which, we are apt to think, are hidden in our inmost hearts. Love towards mankind, respect for truth, admiration of excellence, a sense of justice, the sentiment of veneration towards God and his laws,—all these speak in language often instinctively understood by a child. It is true that a person deeply read in the arts of deception may counterfeit them so as to impose upon others, but he is much more likely to impose on men than on children. No matter what pains he may take to conceal his real feelings, it is these which the hypocrite will be likely to impress upon the character of children. They will not detect his hypocrisy, but they will be bent to evil by his iniquity.

It is not, then, by our good qualities alone, of mind or heart, that we influence our pupils. They are hardly less prone, unfortunately, to sympathize with and imitate our vices than our virtues. It is in vain that we would give lessons of order if our affairs are in confusion; or enforce gentleness in words of violence; or inculcate the great lesson of self-control in tones of impatience or in the language of passion. Our abstract principles may be unintelligible, our words beyond their comprehension; but our voice, our look, our manner they will understand and feel.

These truths should serve as a caution to those who license teachers, as well as to teachers. The former should not introduce into a school any person whose qualities they are not willing to see wrought into the character and life of the future man. And for the latter,

You must not carry with you into school, principles, feelings, motives, or habits, the seeds of which you are not willing to sow in the susceptible heart of childhood.

Take care, then, what manner of men you are when you enter into the discharge of these high duties. "Whoso causeth one of these little ones to offend, it were better for him that a millstone were hanged about his neck, and he were drowned in the depth of the sea."

What motives are thus placed before you to elevate your own character by the cultivation of everything excellent, and the repression of everything bad! Who can tell what power you may exert, for good or for evil, over the whole future existence of the immortal beings confided to your care! Many of them will be committed to you at an age when their whole inward nature is capable of being moulded at your pleasure. In the unhesitating confidence of childhood they will trust entirely to you. Some of them will look upon you with a respect which they feel only for their parents; or, if you have the excellences of character which you ought to have, the learning, taste, eloquence, and sincerity, and their parents are the poor, ignorant, besotted things that but too many are, they will look upon you with a respect almost unbounded; they will learn from you their earliest lessons in truth, justice, and the fear of God; they will receive from you their first impressions of the laws of nature and the wisdom of God's providence. It will depend on you whether they grow up to virtue, usefulness, piety, and happiness, or in ignorance, bitterness, worthlessness, and wretchedness. If you are yourselves just, disinterested, and benevolent, you will awaken the elements of these qualities in them; if you are patient, orderly, industrious, so will they be; if your own heart burns with reverence, it will kindle a flame in theirs.

You thus see your duty. It is to examine yourselves, and remove from your character what will have a pernicious or a doubtful effect on theirs, and to cultivate, in the highest degree possible, the noblest of your faculties and sentiments.

CHAPTER II.

THE TEACHER'S DIRECT DUTIES TO HIS PUPILS. MEANS OF KNOWLEDGE.

> "Binding herself by statute to secure,
> For all the children whom her soil maintains,
> The *rudiments* of letters, and inform
> The mind with moral and religious truth,
> Both understood and practised; so that none,
> However destitute, be left to droop,
> By timely culture unsustained; or run
> Into a wild disorder; or be forced
> To drudge through weary life without the help
> Of intellectual *implements* and *tools*."
>
> WORDSWORTH.

THE teacher is bound to furnish his pupils with the means of acquiring knowledge. This is the particular business of every school. Whatever else is done or left undone, this must be accomplished. Every common school is established for the express purpose of communicating the arts of reading, writing, and calculation. These arts are not knowledge; they are something better; they are the keys of knowledge. One of them, the art of Reading, opens the door to all the accumulated learning, wisdom, science, and art of mankind,—the wealth of all time locked up in books. Writing bestows the power of communicating with all other persons, distant and future, as well as present. It opens the door between this and future ages. Calculation gives the means of doing perfect justice to ourselves, and to all other men in our transactions with them. These, therefore, are properly considered the fundamental branches, and of more essential importance than any others. If he fail in them, he fails altogether of the purpose for which he entered school.

"It is the duty, therefore, of every teacher, who commences a common district school for a single season, to make, when he commences, an estimate of the state of his pupils in reference to these three branches. How do they all write? How do they all read? How do they calculate? It would be well if he would make a careful examination of the school in this respect. Let them all write a specimen. Let all read, and let him make a memorandum of the manner, noticing how many read fluently, how many with difficulty, how many know only their letters, and how many are to be taught these. Let him ascertain, also, what progress they have made in Arithmetic; how many can readily perform the elementary processes, and what number need instruction in these. After thus surveying the ground, let him form his plan, and lay out his whole strength in carrying forward, as rapidly as possible, the *whole school* in these studies. By this means he is acting, most directly and powerfully, on the intelligence of the whole future community in that place. He is opening to fifty or a hundred minds stores of knowledge, which they will go on exploring for years to come."*

Grammar should be considered subsidiary to reading and writing. Its great use is to enable the pupil more perfectly to understand what he reads, and more correctly and distinctly to express what he writes. It is extremely difficult to make a very good reader without showing him the dependance of the parts of a sentence on each other, which belongs to Grammar. Properly taught, it may be also made a most valuable means of exercising some of the powers of the mind at every stage of the child's progress. It should be thoroughly understood by the teacher.

Connected with writing is Drawing. It should be taught when it can. It will be a valuable exercise in training the eye and the hand. Both may, by means of it, be trained to

---

* The Teacher, p. 65, 66.

great accuracy of perception and execution. It may also be oftentimes of use in furnishing employment to such pupils as have nothing else to do. I will not speak of it as an essential qualification in a teacher, but as a most desirable acquisition, which he should make if it is in his power.

The third important art to be communicated is Arithmetic, connected with which should always be something of book-keeping.

Of all these I shall speak more at large hereafter.

CHAPTER III.

DIRECT DUTIES. FORMATION OF MORAL HABITS.

"To instruct youth in the languages and in the sciences is comparatively of little importance, if we are inattentive to the habits they acquire, and are not careful in giving to all their different faculties and all their different principles of action a proper degree of employment."—STEWART.

A TEACHER should do what he can to form the moral character of his pupils. I have spoken of his indirect influence in this respect. That will chiefly affect their feelings, by giving them the love of excellence. I am now to speak of what he is to endeavour to do to form their *habits* of right action.

The great object to be kept always in view is to establish the dominion of conscience, to make it quick and active, and to connect with its action the formation of habit. We speak of conscience and habit separately, but they should, as far as possible, be constantly and inseparably associated.

Conscience is that power within us which approves of what is thought to be right, and disapproves of what is thought to be wrong. Beginning to act in infancy, as soon as a child is capable of the ideas of right and wrong, at first, like all the other faculties at their earliest dawn, its action is obscure, and its decisions indistinct. Like every other faculty, it is improved by exercise, and weakened by inaction. It should be enlightened by reflection upon those relations to God and man from which duties spring, by the truths revealed in the Scriptures, and by a knowledge of the laws of our nature, and of the creation in which we are placed. The enlightened conscience should be constantly exercised, from the beginning to the end of life. In this way only does it become, what it is doubtless intended by our Maker to be, the supreme and controlling power. It is exercised by deliberately asking, in regard to every action which is presented, "Is this right or wrong?" And in this way only will be established the most important of all habits, that of *acting conscientiously*.

The habits over which the teacher has most control, and which he may do much to form in his pupils, are;

The habits of punctuality and regularity; of diligence and love of labour; of economy; of perseverance; of forethought;

Of kindness and courtesy; of mercy to inferior animals; of forgiveness of injuries; of charitableness;

Of justice and respect for property; of respect for superiors; of submission to the authority of laws; of truth; of reverence for God, and obedience to his laws.

I shall endeavour to show very concisely, otherwise these remarks would become a volume of sermons, how the duties on which each of these rests may be explained and enforced, and how the habit may be formed. In regard to all of them, it should, however, be said, that there are individuals in whom it is nearly impossible for them to be formed. We must not, on that account, be discouraged. Our efforts may, and will, be successful in reference to the great majority. Let us not be disheartened that we cannot do all things.

The habit of *punctuality* at school will be strengthened by everything which makes school pleasant. If a story is told at the morning hour, which the children like to hear, they will be induced to exert themselves to be present. If a song or a hymn is sung, some laggard will be led to come early to enjoy the pleasure of joining in it. Kind commendation of those who are punctual, and kind expostulation with the tardy, will have their effect. Appeal to the example of good men. General Washington was always punctual, and required others to be so. Explain to a child that, by being tardy, he loses time which he cannot recall, disappoints his friends of the improvement he ought to make, and, what he has no *right* to do, sacrifices the time of others as well as his own.

The habit of *Regularity* is formed by the natural action of a good system. This depends on yourself. A child who has long been in the habit of doing things in a settled order, will feel the pleasantness and advantage of the course, and will be likely to adhere to it.

Love of Labour and *Diligence.*—Whatever makes labour or study pleasant will lead to this habit. The studies must be adapted to the capacity; they must be made clear and practicable, but not too easy. It is altogether false that children are naturally indolent. On the contrary, they are naturally active, and fond of exercising their faculties; and if we can find out how to lead them to exercise their minds upon appropriate objects, such as are suited to their state and strength, we shall easily form this habit. Indeed, our principal care is to see that we do not break this natural habit by absurd and unreasonable regulations.

Economy may be enforced by requiring children to be careful of their books and other articles of property, and by explaining to them the folly and wickedness of waste, in that it diminishes their power of doing good to those in want. It would be well to make economy the subject occasionally of remarks to the school, laying down and proving the principle that no one ought, in any case, to spend more than his income; and stating the pernicious consequences of borrowing, and then living on the property of others.

Forethought may be taught by our regulations. At the time of an exercise which is assigned beforehand, every pupil should be required to be prepared or to lose the lesson, or something else which he values. This is the natural penalty for want of forethought. Let us take care that we do not prevent its action by our own mistaken kindness. But remember that much forethought is not to be expected in a child.

Perseverance may also be taught by adherence to a good system. A child who, every day, at a certain hour, is called upon to perform a certain exercise, who is encouraged to do more and more without aid, and who, by our system, is led to persevere in it regularly for months together, and then is led to look back and see how much he has accomplished, has taken a lesson in perseverance and regularity which he cannot soon forget.

The law of *Kindness* is best taught in the language of our Saviour. His commands on the subject should be often read, and explained or enforced. Active kindness, *doing* good, is taught by his whole life and death more powerfully than it was ever taught before or since his time. The Christian law of love should be written on the heart of every follower of Christ,—should be often repeated and constantly appealed to. If you are not a follower of Jesus, still, if you will examine the records of his instruction, you will, if there is a strong feeling of humanity in your heart, be willing to admit that his great doctrine of peace on earth and good-will to all mankind is *worthy* of being divine, and that on this point, if on no other, no man ever spake like him. If you will calmly and impartially examine this question, you will probably be inclined to agree with Lord Bacon, in thinking " that there never was found, in any age of the world, either religion, or law, or discipline that did so highly exalt the public good as the Christian faith." The feeling and the practice of kindness are to be taught, also, by example. This is intelligible when words are not. Courtesy is the natural fruit of the principle of kindness. It needs no great eloquence or acuteness to show that whatever is rude, harsh, unfeeling, or discourteous, is no less offensive to Christian feelings or principles than it is unbecoming the character and manners of a gentleman.

Every act observed in school, which is a violation of courtesy or kindness, should be remarked upon to the offending individual, not openly, unless it be very public and offensive, but privately, and in the kindest manner possible. Nothing can be more absurdly inconsistent than to reprove a violation of this virtue in unkind and discourteous language. It not only fails of its effect, but it gives an example of the opposite vice. An excellent and practicable mode of forming the habit of kindness is to place one of the younger children in school under the particular charge of one of the older. They are to sit together, and the elder is, in every way in his power, to aid and encourage the younger. He is to show him the use of his slate, to explain his difficulties, and stimulate him to exertion. The benefit will be mutual, in so far as the studies are concerned; and in this way, each one of the more advanced will have one individual on whom constantly to exercise his kind affections, and each of the least advanced will feel that he has one friend in school.

We should also take occasion to excite sympathy for the wretched. The following example, from the work of an eminent teacher,* will show how we may avail ourselves of such incidents as occur: "It was a chilly day in winter, and we were seated in a comfortable schoolroom, when a man of wretched appearance was seen passing by, drawing a hand-sled, on which were several bundles of rags, the remnants of worn-out garments. He was clad in those

* S. R. Hall, Lectures on School-keeping, p. 103, slightly altered.

that were little better, and was apparently so weak as to be scarcely able to draw his sled. Some looked out of the window and began to laugh. The instructer told the school they might all rise and look at the wretched man who was passing by. All did so, and nearly all were excited to laughter. After all had seen him, the master told them they might take their seats, and then said, 'I was willing that you should look at that man, but possibly my object was different from yours, as I see the effect on your feelings was very unlike that which was produced on mine. That miserable man, you perceive, is crazy. His bundles of rags, which perhaps he values, can be of no use to him. You see that he looks pale and emaciated, and so weak that he is scarcely able to draw his load. He is very poorly shielded from the cold of winter, and will probably perish in the snow. Now tell me, should this man excite your laughter? He was once a schoolboy, as bright and active as any of you. His return from school was welcomed by joyful parents, and his presence gave pleasure to the youthful throng who met each other for merriment in a winter evening. Look at him now; and can you sport with him who has lost his reason, and, in losing that, has lost all? Should I point to one of you, and be able, by looking down into future years, to say to the rest, your associate will be hereafter, like this man, a roaming, wretched maniac, would you not rather weep than laugh? You saw me affected when I began to speak. I once had a friend; he was dear to me as a brother; he was everything I could wish in a friend. I have, indeed, seldom seen his equal. He could grasp any subject, and what others found difficult only served as amusement for him. I saw him after an absence of two years. He was a maniac—in a cage, and chained. The moment he saw me he seized my hand.—I have known sorrow; have seen friends die that were as near as friends could be; but the hour that I sat by poor Bernet was an hour of the greatest anguish I ever knew.'"

Mercy to inferior animals is an extension of the principle of kindness. There is this to be said of cruelty, that it proceeds from ignorance of the feelings of dumb creatures as often as from indifference to them. When the amount of suffering endured by these animals is pointed out, and the imagination is awakened to realize it, the way is prepared for the removal of the cruelty which is so often exercised towards them.

Forgiveness of injuries is the first and natural application of the Christian rule, and the seventy times seven of the Gospel are not an exaggeration of the extent and universality of its application. Another principle of Christian doctrine comes in here, in the words of Christ: "If ye forgive not men their trespasses, neither will your Father forgive your trespasses."* It is our only condition of forgiveness. Then comes the example of the Saviour in the very moment of his agony: "Father, forgive them, they know not what they do."† To this we must add our own practice. How many times ought we to forgive the violations of our own poor and imperfect laws!

Charitableness is a far higher, more comprehensive, and more difficult duty; more difficult, because it requires a lowliness of spirit entirely at variance with the pride which almost universally belongs to the human heart. Charitableness is the highest attainment of the Christian.‡ Many occasions will occur of doing something to recommend this virtue. It will often happen that children of different religious denominations are in the same school, all of whom, under the influence of the bigoted and intolerant spirit so natural to ignorance, will take it for granted that they are right, and those who differ from them are wrong. Nothing will diffuse a right spirit among such discordant materials

---

* Matthew, vi., 15. † Luke, xxiii., 34.
‡ "The greatest of these is charity."—1 Corinthians, xiii., 13.

but the recommendations of charity and the enforcement of the Christian command, "Judge not."

In all these instances we must, I think, teach Christian morality. All other codes of morals fall so infinitely short of this, that if we, who have been taught of Christ, who have read his doctrines and studied his life, would teach morality at all, it must be Christian morality. This we may do, if we are earnestly desirous of doing our duty, without interfering with the subject of religious opinions, upon which, by universal consent, it is agreed that the teacher of the common school should not encroach.

Justice, and respect for the rights of property. Justice, in its true meaning, is not less comprehensive than charity. It embraces what is due to ourselves and what is due to others. It demands of me that I should respect the property, the opinions, and the feelings of others. It teaches me that I have a right that others should respect my property, my opinions, and my feelings. In this comprehensive sense, it is second to no duty in importance.

It should be taught and enforced in school, both on account of its intrinsic excellence, and because it can be taught nowhere else so well. A school is a miniature community. Events are daily occurring in it similar to those which occur in society in after-life. It gives wider scope for duty than a family, because it embraces a greater variety of relations, and thus creates a greater variety of rights. All of these are liable to be infringed, and each infringement gives occasion for a lesson in justice. It may, moreover, be better taught than in a family, because there is one person in a school who should always be ready to attend to it. The teacher has no higher duty than this. He must not let the occasion pass by without taking advantage of it. Besides, he is, or ought to be, better qualified to teach this virtue than many parents.

It may be better taught in school than from the pulpit,

because it is most naturally and effectually taught by instances such as are continually presenting themselves in school, and because it should form part of the earliest lessons of children, of an age not commonly touched by the instructions from the pulpit.

It rests on the same foundation as the duty of charity,—on the great Christian law, "Whatsoever ye would that men should do to you, do ye even so to them;" and to this it should always be referred.

The simplest and most comprehensible application of this law is to the rights of property. "Thou shalt not steal," should be explained, not only to signify what, in its limited sense, it is commonly taken to mean, but to forbid all injury done to property.

Let me give a single instance.

A teacher often heard complaints of the injury done to bonnets, hats, and cloaks, in the entry where they were deposited when the children entered school. Not unfrequently a cloak was taken down from its peg, or carelessly thrown down, and afterward trampled on, dirtied, and sometimes torn. To present the matter in its proper light, he took occasion, in one of the general lessons, immediately after an injury of this kind had been done, to speak of the crime of theft. He showed that this consisted in taking, without leave, an article belonging to another. "This form of the offence," he said, "most of you are in little danger of committing; but a part of the evil of this violation of the rights of property is in the injury done to a person by depriving him of his property, and a part in the disappointment or vexation which it causes him. Now I have observed that injury is often done,—not a very great injury, to be sure, but an injury which is of some consequence,—to the cloaks and hats in the entry. You do not mean to injure each others' property; but, by your carelessness and thoughtlessness, you do actually violate the spirit of the command,

"'Thou shalt not steal.' Maria's cloak, which was thrown down and trampled on, is injured. She left it in its place; it was taken away, and she had to lose her time in searching for it. When she found it, instead of finding it neat and clean as she left it, she found it dirty and torn. She must have had her feelings hurt. Her property had not been taken away, but it had been injured, and she is subjected to the mortification of wearing home a dirty and trampled garment. If it had been my own cloak which was so much injured, I should certainly have preferred that money should have been taken from my pocket. It would have cost me money to have it mended; and, besides, I should have had the additional pain of seeing its beauty destroyed. None of you will think of taking my money; and yet, whoever throws down and tramples on my cloak, does me more harm than if he had taken some of my money. Can this be right? Is not this violating the spirit of the command of which I have been speaking?"

In a similar manner may we show that justice requires us to respect the *feelings* of others.

The greatest defect in the American character, in reference to others, seems to be want of respect for superiors. This leads to ill manners of every kind; for children ought rather to regard all as their superiors, and to be taught to respect them; and such, doubtless, is the spirit of the morality of the Gospel. Every teacher may do much to inculcate a right feeling in children towards their superiors, and a simple and modest habit of expressing it. There is no difficulty in the matter, except the proneness among teachers to consider it as something not belonging to them. But it is the duty of a teacher to do what he can for the benefit of his pupils in every respect, in manners as well as morals. They are intimately connected. Good manners are merely the outward expression of good feelings and good morals, and there must be some great defect in the latter when there is so much that is wrong in the former. The real defect at bottom is inordinate conceit and want of modesty. Much may be done towards correcting this by the example and instructions of a teacher who is himself modest. He should inculcate obedience to parents, and respect for the aged and for the stranger.

Submission to the *authority* of *Law*. In no part of the world is this so important as in these United States. Ours is a government of laws. All our people should therefore be accustomed, from their earliest years, to submit to the authority of law; to submit, not by compulsion, but voluntarily. This is one strong reason why authority should be established, and laws strictly observed, in every school. In this respect, school *must be* a preparation for the society of the world. It should be the object of the instructer, in his system of government, to form the habit of obeying the law because it is just law, and because it is for the common good. Such reasoning as the following may be employed: You see that, if every boy in school be allowed to leave his seat, speak, or whisper whenever he pleases, it will be impossible for any one to study. The purpose for which you came here will be defeated, and school will be of no use. Order and quiet must therefore prevail; and that they may, and that all may enjoy the great advantages which follow from them, each one must consent to give up a portion of his liberty. He will gain much more by it than he loses. He only gives up the privilege of making a noise when he ought to be quiet, and in exchange, he gains the privilege of not being interrupted by every one of forty others when they please to interrupt him.

A more fundamental principle to be inculcated is *love of Truth*, and the habit of respecting it. Children should be taught, as early as possible, to feel how mean, base, loathsome, cowardly, and wicked a thing falsehood is, and how noble, generous, and glorious it is always to tell the truth. Nothing is so important to the future character of a child as that he should have the right feeling, and, built upon the feeling, and growing out of it, the right habit in regard to truth and falsehood. The first requisite is that the teacher should himself have an abhorrence of falsehood. This must be modified only by his compassion for the weakness of childhood, so that he may be able to pardon even a lie. Children are made liars by the examples set them from their earliest days. They are coaxed by falsehood, by what are called white lies, to get up and to go to bed, to go to play and to give up their playthings, to give up food and to take medicine. They are even coaxed by falsehood into being good! They should never be deceived. No matter whether the thing in question be of small or of great consequence, they should never be deceived. A promise made to a child, like every other promise, should always be religiously kept. There is no such a thing as a white lie. Every deception is a lie, and, if practised upon a child, injures and tends to destroy, his moral sense. Such a deception is a lie of the blackest hue.

Another way in which children are made liars is being allowed, and even encouraged, by the example of others, to use exaggeration, to speak in extravagant language. This should be checked whenever the occasion occurs, and the falseness and dangerous tendency of it pointed out. Persons of little conscientiousness will be likely to think such practices of slight consequence. But, in forming the conscience of a child, they are of very great; and the susceptible conscience of most children may be easily led so to regard them.

Another way of teaching falsehood is by allowing and even encouraging children to make promises. On this point, the only safe course is that pointed out in the command of Jesus Christ, "Swear not at all," which, as is obvious from its connexion, was intended to forbid light promises, and has not, as is commonly supposed, anything to do with profane language. The author of this command knew the weakness of the heart; and the more we examine the subject, the more fully shall we be convinced that he was right. It is very questionable whether children should ever be allowed to promise—even to be better.

Children are often driven to falsehood by fear. That must be a bad system of government, in a family or in a school, which urges children to have recourse to falsehood to avoid punishment. The teacher should avoid any approach to it, as he should uniformly teach that falsehood is worse than any other offence of which children can be guilty.

The most distinguishing characteristic of man is his possession of the power of reverencing and worshipping the invisible Being who has created and who preserves him. No approach to this power seems to be possessed by the brute animals. To raise ourselves still higher in the scale of being, we must cultivate this power; and with it is connected a reverence for those laws which the Creator has impressed on all his works. It is the highest conception that we can have of the Creator, that he governs this vast creation, with all the innumerable classes of beings with which it seems to be populous, by wise, just, and merciful laws, all made with a perfect knowledge of the infinitely diversified relations which connect these beings, and all made with a view to the highest good and happiness of each creature. And it is the noblest and most elevating idea that we can form of man, that he is so created as to be able to find out and understand these laws, at least so far as they relate to himself and the portion of the universe in which he is placed, that he may gradually comprehend their wisdom, beauty, and beneficence, can perceive them to be worthy of the Infinite Being who has appointed them, and, observing and respecting them all as His laws, may rise, through them and by means of them, to the spiritual worship of Him who is a spirit, and to be worshipped in spirit and in truth. It is, therefore, the highest distinction and the most precious privilege of man, to be able to worship God, and to do something to lead others to worship him and to reverence his laws. This distinction and this privilege, in their widest extent, belong to the teacher. It is for him to do and to teach. How is he to exercise this great privilege—to perform this high duty?

First, by the strong and constant influence of his example. He must fill his soul with adoration of the Infinite Father. He must begin every day with God. He must endeavour to live with an habitual sense of his presence, and to be a servant of God. This, however really, he may do secretly.* He need make no pretensions to sanctity. If he feel himself not to be as religious as he ought, he need make no professions. In his own heart he may fear and reverence him, and strive daily to serve him better. If he can conscientiously do it, he ought to commence his daily labours in school with an act of worship. If he have no gift of language, he can at least utter the Lord's Prayer; or he may use some of the excellent prayers which are prepared, and which form part of the worship of many fraternities of Christians; or, if he feel that it would be sacrilege in him to do so much as this, and he yet feels a reverence for God, and acknowledges that it is his duty to express that feeling for the sake of others who are looking to him for guidance, let him select appropriate passages from the New and Old Testament, and read them as an introduction to his labours. In that vast treasure-house of rapt thought and devout aspirations, he may easily find an expression for his feelings.

If he be so disposed, and can do it reverently, let him add his own thoughts and the expression of his feelings in his

* "But thou, when thou prayest, enter into thy closet."

own words, or in those which he may have selected as expressive of his own. By daily doing or attempting this, he will best cultivate his own sentiment of reverence, and, at the same time, that of those who hear him. But all this must be done seriously and in earnest, else let it not be done at all. The deadliest offence against Heaven, against his own soul, and against the souls of his pupils, is hypocrisy.

Every occasion that presents itself in the course of the day must be used to awaken and strengthen the sentiment of reverence. Formal lectures do no good. There must be the *feeling* of reverence in what is said. The wickedness of profane language must be pointed out. To do this will be enough in the case of the conscientious pupil, in whom a reverential feeling is already excited. But there are those who are below this state, but who have yet what is called a sense of honour. To them the vulgarity of profaneness must be shown, and how despicable those are who indulge in such language. Besides this, the institutions of religion should always be spoken of with respect,—the Sabbath, the pulpit, and all that is connected with religious opinion; not only what we ourselves hold to be sacred, but what any others deem so. On the subject of religion, we should respect the opinions of others even when we differ from them.

The feeling of reverence is now extended to the moral laws. It should be also extended to the laws of the intellect and of the body. If we acknowledge God to be the author of both, they are all His laws, and to be obeyed as such. Here opens a new series of duties for the teacher. He is to study these laws, and to observe and teach them. He is to explain them to his pupils, and thus enlighten their conscience in regard to them, so that they shall consider it no less really a part of duty to keep the body in health, and to exercise and improve all the faculties of the mind, than to observe the laws of the Decalogue. I say that a new series of duties here opens to the teacher, because most persons now speak and act as if they thought that the laws that relate to the body and the mind were not God's laws, and to violate them were not disobedience to him. What is this but saying that the laws of God do not extend over his whole creation? that they do not embrace the mind and body, but the soul only? Is it not equivalent to saying that the command of Jesus, " Thou shalt love the Lord thy God with all thy heart, and with all thy soul, and with all thy strength, and with all thy mind,"* should be understood as extending only to the soul, and embracing neither the strength of the body nor the faculties of the mind?

I have spoken very seriously, in this chapter, of our duties as moral teachers. This I am bound to do. I am not at liberty to do less. To multitudes of our pupils we are the only teachers of moral truth. Unless they get a sense of their moral duties from us, they will not get it at all. And holding, as I do, that man's moral and religious nature is the highest part of his nature, I must hold that a teacher has no right to neglect the cultivation of this part of the nature of his pupils. This is vastly the most important part of their education; the most important to themselves and to the community, and for their whole future existence. It is more important to a man's self that he should be an upright and conscientious man, than that he should be an intelligent, a skilful, or a learned man. And it is, beyond measure, more important to the community, and especially to a community like ours.

A government of laws, such as ours is, must in reality be founded on the moral sense of the whole community. This, then, *must* be cultivated and enlightened, or as a people we are lost. The common schools are established by the people for the greatest good of the people. In in-

* Luke, x., 27.

numerable instances, I repeat it, the teachers of the common schools are the only persons who have access to the young, who can cultivate their moral sense. If this great duty be rightly and truly performed, the schools *will prevent the crimes* which the courts of justice are established to punish. To this the system established in our country must lead.

Every teacher of a common school should understand that one chief end for which the schools are instituted, and for which he is placed in one of them, is *to prevent crime by putting an end to moral ignorance and depravity;*

> "Needful instruction; not alone in arts
> Which to his humble duties appertain,
> But in the lore of right and wrong, the rule
> Of human kindness, in the peaceful ways
> Of honesty and holiness severe."

CHAPTER IV.

CULTIVATION OF THE POWERS OF MIND AND BODY.

"Bodily pain forms a large proportion of the amount of human misery. It is, therefore, of the highest importance that a child should grow up sound and healthful in body, and with the utmost degree of muscular strength that education can communicate."—LALOR

"The most essential objects of education are the two following: first, to cultivate all the various principles of our natures, both speculative and active, in such a manner as to bring them to the greatest perfection of which they are susceptible; and, secondly, by watching over the impressions and associations which the mind receives in early life, to secure it against the influence of prevailing errors, and, as far as possible, engage its prepossessions on the side of truth."—STEWART.

THE next aspect of the teacher's direct duties to his pupils is that which regards the cultivation of their powers of mind and of body. I say of body as well as of mind; not that the teacher of a common school can often do much directly towards the strengthening and improving of the bodily powers, but because it is important for him to keep them in view, otherwise he may sometimes allow them to be neglected, with injurious, and even fatal consequences. Forward and tractable children, especially those of great susceptibility and of a delicate constitution, are apt, in every stage, at school, as well as at the academy or college, to become so much interested in their studies as to be tempted entirely to neglect exercise, to forego the enjoyment of the air and light, and to abridge their hours of sleep. Here are natural laws violated; and no natural laws are ever violated with impunity. Whose business is it to prevent this? The children, as yet, know nothing of the natural laws; and their parents are often as ignorant as themselves. The teacher must, for he only can, interpose. He *is* responsible for the right education of the whole nature of his pupils, and he cannot shift his responsibility to other shoulders.*

Let me, at the risk of being charged with repeating what I have already said, state the particular laws which the teacher must see to it that his pupils shall not, so far as depends on him, violate.

The first is that which requires active exercise, for two or more hours each day, in the open air and by the sun's light.

The second is that which requires that, while the mind

* Numbers of the most promising young men in our country are annually offered up as sacrifices to atone for the violation of God's physical and organic laws. In most instances they are innocent sacrifices—innocent as Iphigenia. They know not the existence of the laws which they violate. Who is to blame for this? Who, but the teachers of the schools and colleges at which the dreadful immolation is made? An enlightened public opinion will hereafter, if it has not heretofore, hold them responsible.

is employed, the body should be at ease, with the feet resting fully on the floor, and the back supported.

The third, that the room occupied by children should be at all times supplied with an abundance of fresh air.

The fourth, that the body of a child should not be kept long in one unvaried position; that he should not only not be enjoined, but not be allowed to sit still for more than fifteen minutes at a time if under the age of seven, or thirty if under the age of twelve, or an hour at any age.

The fifth, that the skin should be kept constantly clean.

The sixth is that which requires for every child seven, or eight, or nine hours of undisturbed sleep in the early part of every night, in a well-ventilated chamber.

The seventh, that an abundance of simple, well-cooked food should be allowed every child during the whole period of his growth, that is, from birth till the age of sixteen or twenty.

The eighth, that the clothes should be clean and sufficient, and that the feet, particularly, should be kept warm.

It may perhaps be said, that in regard to the last three the teacher often has no control. True; but he has always an influence, and the observation of these laws will be secured by making them familiarly known to the child. If he understands that they are laws of God's enactment, founded upon the nature of his bodily constitution, and essential to the welfare of the moral and mental faculties as well as those of the body, he will learn to respect and keep them, and grow up in obedience to them. Thus only will society be pervaded with a knowledge of them.

But the teacher has to do more directly and entirely with the mind; and whatever may be the opinion of men as to his influence upon the other parts of the nature of a child, all agree that it is his particular province to educate the mind; to unfold, as far as he is able, all its powers; to give them their appropriate exercise, so that they may have all the activity and energy of which they are capable, and to place them under the control of their possessor.

To do this fully would require a complete knowledge of the powers of the mind and of the whole art of education. This, perhaps, would transcend the power of any man now living. Nevertheless, we may each do something, and some one, to rise up hereafter, may accomplish all. That one may be among our pupils, and it may be our business to give him the first impulse which shall carry him towards this most desirable end.

I shall not pretend to do more than to sketch a faint outline of what ought to be done, and leave it to be filled up by others more competent to the work.

If, with a full and philosophical scheme of the several faculties of the mind before us, we aim directly at bringing out and educating each of them, separately or in combination, we shall certainly accomplish more than now is usually done. It will soon be seen that there is, in every mind, such a thing as the pleasure of exercising its faculties, independently of the end for which they are exercised. In regard to many of the faculties, this is very obvious in little children, and has frequently been remarked. When they are beginning to talk, they evidently delight in the mere utterance of words, without knowing what they say; just as, when they are learning to walk, they delight to walk, without knowing whither they are to go. How diligently we sometimes see them exercising their vocabulary of numbers, when they have just learned to count! Now we may enlarge a little upon these indications, and show both the pleasure of exercising the faculties, and the means which have been found useful in training them.

In particularizing and arranging the several powers of the mind, I cannot follow any of the discordant, and often contradictory systems of the metaphysicians, but incline rather to that suggested by the phrenologists, without, however, venturing to pronounce upon the truth or falsity of the physiological theory with which it is associated.

There is, I think, such a faculty or mode of action of the mind as that called individuality. It helps us to examine individual things without reference to their use. We see that children usually delight to exercise their minds upon the objects about them. Indeed, it seems to be, in their earliest years, a great part of their occupation. At the same time that they are thus occupied, they usually take notice of the form, size, weight, and colour of objects, and, if there be several of them, observe their situation, number, and order. Now it is certain that children differ considerably, and sometimes extremely, in their disposition to examine one or another, or all of these particulars; and as it is in these particulars that objects differ from each other, it is certainly very important that children should not only be permitted, but encouraged, to observe them attentively and separately. Most children are much interested in any employment which requires the action of the mind in one or more of these ways, and I have certainly no doubt that the tendency of the mind to these various actions is all natural and right; yet most of what we call idleness and inattention in children, is owing to their choosing to occupy their mind thus, instead of giving their attention to something which we have prescribed, and which is less palatable to them. A little pains will enable us to turn this tendency to a practical use.

Geometrical models are interesting to young children, and have been recommended by writers on education as playthings for them. They may be used as something better than playthings, and at once exercise very agreeably the faculties which judge of form and size, and be the means of giving an acquaintance with important names and shapes of things. For this purpose they should be labelled; and an innocent and useful diversion for children would be drawing their figures on a slate. If models cannot be obtained, representations of them on paper may be used as a substitute; but these are of much less value.

Still better, especially for children somewhat more advanced, would be mineralogical specimens; and a useful exercise would be to direct the attention to their forms and angles; to their weight, in which they remarkably differ; to their hardness, and to their colours; and to ask separate questions in reference to each of these qualities. It would be a suitable reward for good behaviour, in elementary schools, to be allowed to examine specimens, and ask and answer questions upon them.

Drawing, on a slate or on paper, figures of any kind, or only straight and curved lines, is a pleasant and useful occupation and exercise, and one which is often a great favourite. I have been told by an intelligent teacher that he found no other reward necessary in the management of a number of boys of various ages, than the privilege of being allowed to remain after school, and take lessons of him in drawing. He, however, drew with taste and skill. How much better such a reward than a medal! He found no other punishment necessary than to deprive them of this lesson! The threat was usually sufficient to bring a rebellious boy to submission, or an inattentive one to order. Each desk should be furnished with a slate, and, if there are seats without desks, slates should be provided for the occupants, so that, when they have nothing else to do, they may employ themselves in drawing or cyphering. Much idleness, and vexation of spirit in master and pupil, would be prevented, and something might be gained, even if no pains were taken to direct the child how to use his slate. But if he were furnished with objects to copy, and assisted and encouraged to copy them, many useful ideas and some skill might be gained in time which is now worse than lost.

There are many occasions in which the power of judging

of the comparative size and different shapes of bodies is of considerable value. Is it not, therefore, worth the while to cultivate it? This may be done, and a familiar knowledge of inches, feet, and other dimensions, in lines and surfaces, be communicated, by setting children to draw lines, one, two, or any number of inches long, and dividing into halves, thirds, quarters, or any other portions, and doubling, trebling, or quadrupling them; and by setting them to draw squares of one, two, or any number of inches. To do this, it is only necessary to encourage them to use their eyes and pencils, and to furnish them with lines and squares of the necessary dimensions, or with rules wherewith to compare or measure their work.

Love of bright colours is natural to nearly all persons. There seems to be an absolute pleasure, independent of association or any ideas of utility, in looking at the blue of the sky, the white expanse of snow, the green of foliage, and the beautiful colours of flowers. Children that have never seen the sky, and that cannot possibly have any associations with most colours, often testify the liveliest delight in looking at flowers and other bright objects. Ought not this faculty to be cultivated? One object of instruction should be to teach the correct use of all common words, especially those of frequent occurrence. Such instruction is rarely given in regard to the names of colours. Yet it is very necessary; for any one who will take the trouble to observe, will find that there are many colours to which different persons would give different names, and that there are some to which many persons would be able to assign no name at all. This defect can only be corrected by making a considerable variety of colours familiar, and associating them habitually with their appropriate names. The list should contain not only black and white, and what are called the primary colours, red, orange, yellow, green, blue, indigo, violet, but many of the common shades. Of whites, for example, the difference between snow-white, milk-white, silver-white, greenish-white, and grayish-white, and other varieties, might be pointed out; and among the grays, ash-gray, smoke-gray, pearl-gray, bluish-gray, leaden-gray, steel-gray, and greenish-gray; among the reds, brick-red, scarlet, vermilion, flesh-red, rose-red, peach-blossom, carmine, lake, crimson, cochineal, cherry-red, blood-red, and chocolate-red; among the shades of orange, buff, brownish, and reddish orange; among the yellows, golden, sulphur, wax, lemon or citron, gamboge, saffron, honey, straw, and ochre; among the greens, leek, verdigris, apple, emerald, grass, sap, bottle, and olive-green; the difference between verditer, ultramarine, azure, Prussian, and indigo blues; among the violets or purples, lilach, pansy, lavender; and the various tints called browns, orange-brown, reddish-brown, chestnut-brown, yellowish-brown, wood-brown, liver, and clove-brown.* Where the teacher has the perception and the name of the colours, what an agreeable and useful exercise this discriminating of colours, and giving each its precise name would be! It would doubtless enhance the pleasure of seeing, and give precision to language.

In regard to the talent for reckoning, and its cultivation, I shall have occasion to speak much at large in another place. It is here only necessary to say that, among many hundreds of pupils of both sexes, I have never met with an individual who could not be taught most of the difficult mental processes in Colburn's First Lessons, and afterward most of the sections in his Sequel. If the admirable methods which are the foundation of these works were generally adopted, I believe that nearly all persons could be easily taught the science of numbers, though it must be confessed that some children find them always difficult.

Order and method are taught by the general arrange-

* See Barton's Flora of North America, Advertisement, p. xii.-xix.

ments of the school, by the regularity of the course in which studies are made to succeed each other, and by requiring the observance of exact neatness in the disposition of the contents of the pupil's desk, and the placing of his hat and coat. These may be regarded as trifling things, but they are not unimportant in reference to the habits to be formed. Method in business of every kind, on a farm, in trades, in commerce, and in studies, is so valuable, that whatever tends to communicate it is worthy of attention. Love of order should therefore be constantly inculcated, and the practice of it in every way enforced. Each study and exercise of school should have a particular time assigned it, which should not be departed from without sufficient cause. It is comparatively easy for a pupil to be prepared for a task which comes as regularly and as certainly as the clock strikes the hour; while all uncertainty is a temptation to him to defer preparing himself, and thus tends to form the dangerous habit of procrastination. It is on account of the importance of these consequences of order, or the want of it, that I have insisted upon love of order as an essential qualification in a teacher. The want of it is a great want, and costs himself and his pupils great and continual loss and trouble.

Some extremely valuable suggestions as to the mode of exercising the powers of observation and expression may be obtained from the account given in Professor Stowe's Report on Elementary Instruction in Europe. The following is his account of the occupations in the Prussian schools during the first six months, of children from six to eight years of age:

" The teacher brings the children around him, and engages them in familiar conversation with himself. He generally addresses them altogether, and they reply simultaneously; but, whenever necessary, he addresses an individual, and requires the individual to answer alone. He directs their attention to the different objects in the schoolroom, their position, form, colour, size, the materials of which they are made, &c., and requires precise and accurate descriptions. He then requires them to notice the various objects that meet their eye in their way to their respective homes; and a description of these objects, and the circumstances under which they saw them, will form the subject of the next morning's lesson. Then the house in which they live; the shop in which their father works; the garden in which they walk, &c., will be the subject of the successive lessons: and in this way, for six months or a year, the children are taught to study *things*, to use their own powers of observation, and speak with readiness and accuracy, before books are put into their hands at all."*

The following may serve as a specimen of the kind of accounts to be expected from little children in such a lesson as this: When I leave my father's house, on my way to school, I come through the gate into the Belleville road. Then I turn to the left, and walk under the trees which my father has set out before our garden. They are maple and hickory trees. The garden fence is very high, so that I cannot climb over it. It is made of pieces of wood sharpened at top and nailed to joists. The joists have a spike driven into them to fasten them to the posts, and the posts go into the ground. When I have passed by the garden, I come along by the orchard. There are apple-trees and cherry-trees in the orchard. Then I come to my Uncle James's house, and my cousin comes out to meet me. My Uncle James's house is two stories high, and painted white. It has four elm-trees before it, and soft grass underneath, where we play sometimes, but there is no fence. Nearly opposite to Uncle James's, I see the new meeting-house. It has a high belfry and a bell. The bell rings at seven

---

* **Professor Stowe's Report, p. 32, 33.**

o'clock to call people to breakfast, and at twelve o'clock to call them home to dinner; and on Sundays it rings to tell people when to go to meeting. Then I come down the hill to the bridge. Above the bridge I see the dam and the beautiful water falling over, and on one end of the dam I see the long flume that carries water to the sawmill. The sawmill is on the other side of the bridge. There are a great many logs before the mill, and the men roll some of them into the mill, and the saw cuts them into boards. Then I come up the hill, and walk along before Mr. Stevens's house, and then I get to school.

"If a garden is given to a class for a lesson, they are asked the size of the garden—its shape, which they may draw on the slate with a pencil—whether there are trees in it—what the different parts of a tree are—what parts grow in the spring, and what parts decay in autumn, and what parts remain the same throughout the winter—whether any of the trees are fruit-trees—what fruits they bear—when they ripen—how they look and taste—whether the fruit be wholesome or otherwise—whether it is prudent to eat much of it—what plants and roots there are in the garden, and what use is made of them—what flowers there are, and how they look," of what colour they are, and how they smell, " &c. The teacher may then read to them the description of the garden of Eden, in the second chapter of Genesis; sing a hymn with them, the imagery of which is taken from the fruits and blossoms of a garden; and explain to them how kind and bountiful God is, who gives us such wholesome plants and fruits, and such beautiful flowers, for our nourishment and gratification."

"The external heavens also make an interesting lesson. The sky, its appearance and colour at different times—the clouds, their colour," especially towards evening or early in the morning; " their varying form and movements," their appearance before rain—" the sun, its rising and setting; its concealment by clouds; its warming the earth, and giving it life and fertility; its great heat in summer, and the danger of being exposed to it unprotected—the moon, its appearance by night, horned, gibbous, full; its occasional absence from the heavens—the stars, their shining, difference among them; their number, distance from us, &c. In this connexion the teacher may read to them" portions of the eighteenth or the whole of "the nineteenth Psalm, or other passages of Scripture of that kind, sing with them a hymn celebrating the glory of God in the creation, and enforce the moral bearing of such contemplations by appropriate remarks. A very common lesson is the family and family duties, love to parents, love to brothers and sisters, concluding with appropriate passages from Scripture, and singing a family hymn."*

By lessons of this kind, the young pupil will not only be led to exercise his powers of observation and description, but he will be led to form pleasant associations with school, and to feel that it is connected, as it ought to be, with his life elsewhere and his preparation for the future. A farther exercise of the observing powers, and of those by which we form ideas of objects and events, is provided by the study of Geography and History, and requiring the pupil to give an account of what he learns, in his own language. These studies, to be interesting and useful, should always, as far as possible, be pursued in connexion. The study of Mineralogy or Botany, or any other branch of Natural History, exercises the powers of observation and comparison, at the same time that it cultivates habits of method.

Music. It is a matter of rejoicing to all who are interested in the progress of instruction in this country, that Music has already been introduced into so many of the schools.

* Professor Stowe's Report, p. 33, 34.

As was anticipated, the effects are of the most favourable character. An art by which so much can be done to soften the asperity of the temper, to cheer the heart, and to bring the faculties into a condition favourable to their best action, —an art which adds so much to the warmth of devotion, and affords an amusement so innocent and elevating, richly deserves cultivation. It may not be possible to introduce it into every school, but, when introduced, it affords a most useful exercise for the lungs, a delightful resource, and an opportunity of unbending from severe and wearying study, and resuming it with renewed vigour. If the teacher be sufficiently acquainted with music himself, he should teach it to his pupils, at least so far as to enable them to join with him in a hymn. It would be well, indeed, if every child could be taught music. There are few who have not some capacity for it, if trained early enough; and those children who have a decided taste and talent for it, learn so readily that they will soon become teachers to the rest. There are, however, some who are so wanting in the faculty that all instruction is thrown away upon them. In all others, so delightful a faculty should not be allowed to remain unimproved. If accustomed to sing together in school, children will continue the practice elsewhere. A beginning is made which will lead to a higher taste, and which will ever after be a source of enjoyment. How gladdening, in the poor man's cottage or in the rich man's house, is the sound of that sweetest of all instruments, the human voice, tuned to the wild and simple melodies of childhood's songs, or to the rapt strains of devotion!

" The loftiest conceptions of the divinity,—the profoundest adoration,—the ideas struggling out of the depths of the soul, of the power, and beauty, and goodness of God and creation, to which language, made up by the senses, seems so weak and inadequate, burst forth with the fulness of inspiration in the music of Handel; and who, with even the rudest power of appreciation, can listen to those immortal strains without being raised into sympathy with the eternal aspirations of the highest minds for the spiritual and infinite?"

"In teaching children to sing, the simplest combinations, both of poetry and music, should be presented, but they should be beautiful as well as simple. The early associations are the most lasting. We ought to make them beautiful. The songs of childhood should be such as may be loved in after life, and may contribute to form a pure taste."—LALOR, p. 16.

The power of expression may be exercised and improved by methods already spoken of, and also by the study of language, by committing to memory passages in poetry or prose, and by learning rules. Of verbal memory it is not necessary to speak very particularly, as it is frequently cultivated to the detriment of higher powers of the mind. Still it is valuable, and should receive a degree of attention. It should be a principle, to be observed as far as possible in teaching language, not to allow a word to be used before the object, action, or idea which it represents is known. The study of a foreign or ancient language is not, as is usually thought, the mere exercise of the faculty of language or expression,—the mere acquisition of words. On the contrary, the study of a language, rightly pursued, is a most improving exercise of several of the perceptive faculties—of the faculty of comparison, on which, in a great measure, depend judgment, and discrimination, and taste,—and of the faculty which traces causes. It gives constant exercise to the power of arrangement, obliges one to get the most precise ideas of the object or event he is reading about, in order to render it in the most appropriate language, and habituates the mind to look before and after. It would be difficult, and I have hitherto found it impossible, to find any study so well adapted to discipline thoroughly so great a variety of faculties.

The superior thoroughness of education, and the readier and deeper insight, not into words only, but things, and the more complete command of the faculties exhibited by young persons who have been faithfully drilled in the languages, in comparison with those who have had any other elementary education, sufficiently indicates their value; and we accordingly find, that in the Prussian schools they are very generally introduced as a discipline and preparation for other studies.

But as the study of languages, especially of the most valuable ones—the ancient languages—is perhaps necessarily excluded from a majority of our public schools, it becomes us to find the best substitute for it we can. To the teacher who has the opportunity and the time, I would again most earnestly recommend the study of the ancient languages as one of the best possible preparations for an office whose exercise so constantly requires an exact understanding of the various meaning of words, and readiness in the use of them.

Next to the powers of observation and expression, the powers of reflection and reasoning are to be exercised, as indeed they must necessarily be, in some measure, in every part of the course. One of the best subjects for the exercise of these powers is, at the same time, one of the greatest importance to the future welfare of the child. This is the knowledge of the structure and laws of his own body. This should be communicated to every child, and should therefore be an essential part of every course of education, in every school except those for the youngest children. The omission of this study in schools heretofore seems to be one of the strangest and most surprising facts in the history of human absurdity. What can be more absurd than to require a boy to be familiar with the constitution of the British Empire, when he is ignorant of the constitution of his own body? Or to teach him the course of the Gulf Stream, when he knows nothing of the course of his own blood? Or to make him familiar with mountains on the face of the moon, when he knows not that there are such things as pores in his own face? The study is as interesting as it is important, and equally to children of both sexes. Nothing, indeed, is so interesting to girls; for they feel, while studying it, that they are preparing themselves for their own place and duties in life, to be the educators and nurses of children, not only in illness, but in health. And they see at once what advantages this study gives them in forming and securing their own health, and providing for the health and welfare, bodily, mental, and moral, of those to be dependant on them.

The points to be communicated to them, on which they should be led to exercise their minds, to reason, ask questions, trace effects to causes and causes to effects, are the laws already laid down for physical health. To enable them to comprehend these, they should be taught, by familiar conversation, the course of the food after being taken into the mouth, the function of digestion, the action of the lacteals, the course of the blood,—in the lungs, the action of air upon it,—through the system, the action of the capillaries,—renovation of the substance of the body, respiration and the necessity of abundant air, the action of the skin, of the pores in insensible perspiration, the constitution of the muscles and the necessity of their exercise, the nature of the bones, and the necessity of strengthening them by exercise, the functions of the brain and nervous system, and the action and importance of light and air upon its health; then the action of the five external senses, and the manner in which we obtain ideas through them.

As a discipline to the reasoning powers, Geometry has from ancient times been recommended. Few persons capable of geometrical reasoning have failed to observe the advantages to be derived from this exercise. It obliges, and thus habituates us to fix the attention, and to follow a train of reasoning from beginning to end. Every one may derive this benefit from it. A few, perhaps one in a hundred, or a thousand, require its aid as an introduction to the higher mathematics.

Another good exercise for the discriminating and reasoning powers is Grammar, properly pursued. The common process of parsing has little or none of this effect. Indeed, it would be difficult to see what good effect it has.

Natural Philosophy, judiciously taught, gives a great variety of exercise for the reasoning powers, by showing the way in which truths are established and proved, and especially for the faculty that looks into the causes of things, by tracing back the innumerable phenomena of nature to a few great facts and laws.

A still higher exercise for these faculties will be furnished by turning the attention of the child to the powers of his own mind, and the processes which are going on within it. By observing the operation of his senses, he may be led to understand something of the formation of ideas. After having seen a book, for example, he may be made to perceive that he has the image of a book, or the *idea* of a book, in his mind, and that he can thus *conceive* of a book vastly larger or smaller than any that he has seen. By being led to think how an object or person looked that he had seen some time before, he will be made to comprehend that ideas formed in the mind may be remembered, and compared with each other. By being led to notice, in winter, that his recollection of summer is a recollection of warm, long days, of making hay, of the singing of birds, and a number of other particulars, he may be made to understand something of the association of ideas. He may be shown that he can imagine a country fuller of pleasant, wild hills, of sunny fields, of waving woods, of beautiful flowers and birds, than any that he has seen, and thus get the idea of the power by which he so imagines, and which is called *imagination*. In similar ways, many processes of his mind may be made familiar to him, and he may be shown that he possesses various intellectual powers. In like manner may he be made aware of the existence within him of propensities, appetites, and passions, which are impelling him to action, and that he has the power of controlling them all, and bringing them into subjection to reason and his sense of right; that a propensity to deceive may tempt him to falsehood, but that he has the power of resisting, and, notwithstanding the temptation, frankly telling the truth; that appetite for food leads him to eat, still that he has power to deny the appetite, to moderate it, or to refuse to eat altogether; that the passion of anger may tempt him to injure another, but that his better feelings may overcome this, and lead him to abstain from injuring. He may thus be convinced that he has an inward power, called conscience whose office it is to control the lower part of his nature; that, connected with this, he has a sentiment which leads him to reverence the Supreme Being and to observe his laws, and a power of resisting evil and persevering in virtue; that he has a faculty which makes him delight in contributing to the happiness of those about him, a faculty which attaches him to his friends, a faculty which is gratified by their approval, and another which leads him to value himself. By thus leading him to reflect on his passions, motives, and mental and moral powers, we may do much to form habits of self-examination and self-control. And we may not only exercise the reflecting powers, but lead the child to a sense of duty, the duty of counteracting and repressing whatsoever is evil in his nature, and of strengthening, and enlightening, and yielding to what his conscience approves as being right. It may be farther shown, and thus a new source of elevating exercises be opened to him, that the voice of Heaven, as spoken by Christ, confirms in a wonderful manner the decisions of the inward voice of conscience.

The imagination and the love of the beautiful are to be

cultivated by the study of the works of the poets and the best of the prose writers. Or, if these be not accessible, the teacher who has the elements of taste within himself, finds in the many-coloured woods of summer and autumn, in the flowers that deck the meadows, the numberless colours, shapes, and motions of the morning or evening clouds, the stars, the ocean, the waterfall,

> "The warbling woodland, the resounding shore,
> The pomp of groves and garniture of fields;
> All that the genial ray of morning gilds,
> And all that echoes to the song of even—
> All that the mountain's sheltering bosom shields,
> And all the dread magnificence of Heaven,"

enough to give play to the wildest imagination—to exercise, to form, to mature, the taste for the beautiful and the sublime. Some of the sublimest strains of poetry that have ever been written are to be found among the sacred books of the Old Testament. And native to the language are Milton, Shakspeare, Goldsmith, Gray, Young, Thompson, and a host of others in England, and Bryant, Percival, Willis, Longfellow, Alston, Sprague, and how many more Americans. Select portions of the best of these should be committed to memory; but, before it is done, the teacher should take care that his pupils understand the sense and feel the beauty of what they are to learn, that the exercise may not be one of mere words. Farther development will be given to the faculty by practice in composition.

CHAPTER V.

COMMUNICATION OF KNOWLEDGE.

"In truth, exact *knowledge*, science, is the last and noblest fruit of all this activity of intelligence, of all these acts of thought."—*L'Instituteur Primaire*.

THE teacher is bound, in the next place, to communicate to his pupils, so far as he can, the knowledge which shall prepare them for the proper performance of their duties in life.

The statement itself shows that the most essential thing for the teacher to do is, to point out to his pupils what those duties are, their nature, extent, and obligation. I have attempted to express, in another chapter, my sense of the magnitude and importance of this part of a teacher's duty. I shall, in this place, therefore, only recommend a method by which a teacher, who has not paid much attention to this subject, and who considers himself imperfectly qualified to perform it, may, notwithstanding, by devoting a little time to it daily, do great good to his pupils.

Let him begin each day with reading a portion of the Scriptures. If he read in course, the most suitable portions to read, as simpler and more intelligible and interesting to children than the rest, are the Gospels. If he do not choose to read in course, the passage for each day should be selected, if possible, with reference to the observations he is going to make. A person well acquainted with the Bible will always find this possible, for there is no point of human duty upon which light is not thrown by some part of the Sacred Volume, though some familiarity with it is necessary to enable him to find the most suitable passage. After reading this, I would have him make a few remarks on some particular duty. If he cannot do it without premeditation, let him take Dr. Wayland's Elements of Moral Science, or some other suitable book, and, by careful and attentive reading, possess himself of the substance of the portion he is about to teach. If he cannot do this, let him study it, and read the portion to his pupils, explaining what is not already sufficiently clear. He will find that he may explain it all in sixty lessons,—that is, in five lessons each week for twelve weeks, leaving one morning each week for instruction on some subject of duty which presents itself in the course of the week. I have generally assigned a single section for each lesson, but less than a whole section where it is long. For the first, then, he may give, in his own language, or read, the first section on Moral Law, and ask the questions at the end of the section, or such others as occur to him. This first section he will probably find the hardest in the volume, both for himself and for his pupils. Several new words occur in it, and the idea of a *law*, in the sense there given it, is not familiar to children or easy to communicate.* It is quite important, then, for him to make himself master of this first lesson, so as to give it in his own words, and let them be as simple and familiar as possible. For the second, he may show the importance of exercise; for the third, of cleanliness. For the fourth, he may give the substance of the second section in Dr. Wayland's book, on Intention. 5th, 6th, and 7th, Conscience. 8. Rules for moral conduct. 9. The conscience which does not reprove. 10. Rules for happiness. 11. Enlightening the conscience.

* The teacher should show that the word *law* is used in two very different senses: first, to mean a principle which is binding upon our conduct, which imposes upon us an obligation to act or not to act; and, second, to express a general fact. The command, "Thou shalt not steal," is a *moral law*, binding upon us; the fact that all heavy bodies fall towards the earth, is a *physical law*.

12. Defects of natural religion. 13. The New Testament. 14. How to enlighten the conscience. 15, 16, 17. Duties to God. 18. Nature of prayer. 19. The duty of prayer. 20. Utility of Prayer. If the teacher does not assent to these doctrines, he ought not to teach them, but may give some other lessons in their place. I say not this as dissenting myself, for I do not; but to guard the teacher against teaching anything formally when he is not sincere in it himself. 21. The Sabbath. 22. Christian Sabbath. 23. How to observe the Sabbath. 24. Reciprocity of duties. 25. Love to our neighbour. 26. Personal liberty. 27. Violation of it; 28. by society. 29. Nature of property. 30. Violation of it. 31 and 32. Law of property. 33, 34. Loans. 35. Insurance. 36. Exchanges. If these last subjects, or any others, are too difficult for his pupils, and he find he cannot explain them so as to make them intelligible, he may substitute something else for them. He will find, however, that when he perfectly understands these subjects himself, he may, by familiar instances, make them understood by his pupils. 37. Character. 38, 39. Reputation. 40. Veracity. This is so important a duty that it must be brought up often, and earnestly insisted on. 41, 42. Assertions. 43. Promises. 44. Contracts. 45, 46. Duties and rights of parents. 47. Duties of children. 48. Rights. 49, 50, 51. Duties of citizens. 52. Forms of government. This should be enlarged upon in teaching Geography. 53. Government of the United States. This, also, is to be explained in the same connexion. 54, 55, 56. Benevolence. 57. To the needy. 58. Education. 59. Benevolence to the wicked and injurious. 60. To brutes.*

* If the teacher prefer to connect his teaching with the readings from the Scriptures, and thus to give them their highest possible confirmation and authority, he may use the text-book referred to, or others, only to assist him in his thoughts, while he draws his instructions from meditation on the following or similar passages of

He will thus have gone over all the most important parts of Moral Philosophy, and, if he has succeeded in gaining the attention and reaching the hearts of his pupils, he will have given them a connected outline of their duties. This, be it understood, is *instruction* in morals,—it is knowledge of duty. It is not to take the place of that constant and effectual teaching, by example and influence, of which I have spoken elsewhere, and which alone can give a deep and abiding *sentiment* of duty.

A great deal of information may be, and ought to be, com-

Scripture; the observations on each passage serving as one lesson, to precede which the chapter, or a part of it, may be read. For the 4th lesson, on Intention, Matthew, xv., 19. 5th, 6th, and 7th. Romans, ii., 13; Luke, xii., 57. What was the authority spoken of, Matthew, vii., 29? For the 9th, 1 Timothy, iv., 2. 10th. Ecclesiastes, xi., 9. 11th. All or any of the teachings of Christ. 15th, 16th, and 17th, Matthew, xxii., 37; Mark, xii., 30; Deuteronomy, vi., 5. 18th. Matthew, vi., 6. 19th. Luke, xviii., 1. 20th. Luke, xi., 9. 21st. Exodus, xx., 8, in connexion with Luke, xiii., 15. 23d. Matthew, xii., 1–8. 24th. Matthew, vii., 12. 25th. Luke, x., 27–37. 26th. Matthew, xix., 19. Instead of those that follow in the text, some of the personal duties may be substituted, if it be thought best. 27th. Reconciliation, Matthew, v., 23, 24. 28th. Make no promises, Matthew, v., 34–37. 29th. Forgiveness, Matthew, vi., 14, 15, and xviii., 21–35. 30th. Primary importance of religion, Matthew, vi., 19–21, &c. 31st. Charitableness, Matthew, vii., 1–5. 32d. Righteous judgment, Matthew, vii., 16–23. 33d. The duty of cultivating all our talents, Matthew, xxv., 14–30. 34th. Economy, John, vi., 12. 35th. Courtesy, 1 Peter, iii., 8. 36th. Giving, Luke, vi., 30–38. 37th. Causing to offend, Luke, xvii., 2. 38th and 39th. James, iv., 11. 40th. 1 Timothy, i., 9, 10, where liars are associated with the worst criminals possible; John, viii., 44. 41st. Exodus, xx., 16. 42d. Self-righteousness, with contempt of others, Luke, xviii., 9–14 43d. Humility, Luke, xiv., 7–11. 44th. Purity, 1 Corinthians, iii., 16, 17. 45th. Theft, Exodus, xx., 15. 46th. Sinning in thought, Exodus, xx., 17. 47th. Ephesians, vi., 1. 48th. Charitableness, 1 Corinthians, xiii. 54th. Luke, vi., 32–36. 55th. Matthew, v., 43–48. 56th. Matthew, xxv., 31–46. 57th. Psalm xli., 1. 58th. God the author of good, and not of evil, James, i., 13–17. 59th. Luke, v., 35. 60th. Proverbs, xii., 10.

municated in connexion with the reading lessons, and especially with Geography. The most suitable for this last purpose is knowledge of history and antiquities, and of the productions, customs, and other peculiarities of various nations and countries. Of that I shall speak hereafter. Besides these, there is a great deal of useful, practical knowledge, which cannot so easily be introduced incidentally, and for giving which some provision should be made. For this purpose I would recommend the first exercise in the afternoon, or immediately after recess in the forenoon, or at such other time as may be found most convenient, to be a general lesson, in which the teacher shall speak for a few minutes on some interesting subject, whereon he shall be prepared beforehand. The following is a list of subjects for sixty lessons. For preparing these, any common book of Chemistry, as, for example, The First Principles of Chemistry, by Professor Renwick, in the third series of the School District Library,* and any one upon Mechanics, like the Illustrations of Mechanics, in the second series, will be sufficient.

In the first lesson he may speak of air, its nature, the height of the atmosphere, its motion and composition. In the second, of oxygen, its importance to life, its action on metals, its entering into the composition of many of the rocks. In the third, of nitrogen. Before each of these lessons, some questions should be asked in reference to the preceding. The fourth may be upon water, its great reservoirs in the ocean and in lakes, its sources in the clouds, to which it is raised by evaporation, and from which, descending, it forms rills, brooks, and rivers, and its composition of two gases or airs. 5. Hydrogen, the lightest of things. 6. Carbon, the essential portion of all wood, and of vegetable and animal bodies. 7. Heat, its sources; the sun, artificial fire, animal life, fermentation. 8. The effects of heat, expanding all things, changing ice into water, and water into va-

* Of New York.

pour. 9. Light, its sources; the sun, stars, fire, violent action of solids, its velocity. 10. Its effects on animals, vegetables, on man, on his nervous system, and on his spirits. 11. Iron, its sources and uses. 12. Copper. 13. Lead. 14. Tin. 15. Mercury. 16. Gold. 17. Silver. 18. Zinc, and any other metals. 19. The general properties and great uses of metals. In each of these the metal itself should be shown, and the pupils questioned in regard to its colour, brilliancy, hardness, weight, &c. In the 20th lesson he might speak of acids, of which vinegar may serve as an instance, in a diluted state, and show how it turns vegetable blues to reds. In the 21st and 22d, he may describe the powerful action of the nitric and sulphuric acids. 23. Common salt, its sources, composition, and uses. 24. Animal and vegetable oils. 25. Alkali, potash or soda, or both. 26. Soap, hard and soft. 27. Glass, its composition of sand and an alkali, with or without metallic ores. 28. Ink. 29. Dyes. 30. Paints. 31. The saccharine fermentation, the formation of sugar in the ripening of fruits. 32. Vinous fermentation, illustrated by the making of beer or of cider. 33. The acetous fermentation, succeeded by the putrefactive. Six lessons upon Soils: 34. Silex, flint, or sand, or gravel, the basis of soils; 35. Clay, importance and uses; 36. Lime; 37. Vegetable remains; 38. Bog earth; 39. Animal manure. Four on Meteorology: 40. Clouds; 41. Dew, rain; 42. Snow, hail, and ice, their causes and uses; 43. Thunder and lightning; 44. Winds, storms. Seven on Vegetables, for which the materials may be obtained from the 19th or 59th volume of the School District Library: 45. Stem and bark of trees; 46. Circulation of the sap and juices; 47. The leaves; 48. The flower; 49. The fruit; 50. Grains and roots; 51. Uses of trees for fuel, shade, ornament, and the arts; 52. Planting trees. Eight upon Mechanics: 53. First law of motion; 54. The second; 55. The third

56. The three kinds of lever; 57. The wheel and axle; 58. The inclined plane, a plank, a railroad; 59. The screw, a cider-press; 60. The rope, the pulleys. In speaking upon the last fifteen, constant use must be made of the blackboard, unless real machinery can be procured.

Such are specimens of the kind of information that should be given. It is not that which is peculiar to any trade, but those general truths which are of use in all trades and pursuits. It would be well if a book upon such subjects could be introduced as a reading book into schools. If there be none, this course of lessons may be a substitute.

A similar course of lessons of very great value, might be made from Andrew Combe's book on Health; and a third from George Combe's book, the Constitution of Man.

It cannot be too distinctly kept in view that our pupils are to be citizens of a free state. They should, therefore, be prepared for their duties as citizens by a knowledge of the forms of government, of the rights and duties of voters, of the formation and action of juries, of the administration of justice, of the great importance to liberty of an absolute independence on each other of the legislative, judicial, and executive departments of civil government, and of some of the most important of the laws. A similar course of lessons should therefore be given from Story on the Constitution, when a teacher remains from year to year in the same school, and has pupils, as he always will have some, capable of being benefited by them.

CHAPTER VI.

OF THE RELATION OF A TEACHER TO HIS FELLOW-TEACHERS AND TO THE CALLING.

"Conferences of teachers would suffer no man's experience to be lost. Every hint would be taken up and followed out by investigation. The resources of each would be drawn out; and men would learn the command of their powers, and the manner of keeping their position in society."—LALOR.

EVERY man is bound to do something for his calling, something to raise its respectability and advance its usefulness. Every teacher can do, and must do something for his. If, of the generation now coming upon the stage, each individual could number among his friends but one instructer who should be a man of learning and of worth,—intelligent, cultivated, and refined, just and generous; one to whom, in prosperity, he would go for the pleasure of his society, in difficulty for counsel, and in adversity for sympathy and aid,—the public feeling towards the teachers of the next generation would be very different from what it is now, in many parts even of this country. If every individual could feel that there was something of great value in his own character which he owed directly to the influence of a teacher, something which made him a more energetic, and a higher and happier being, he would feel a respect for that teacher which would naturally be extended to the class to which the teacher belonged. If he could remember that the happiest days of a happy childhood were spent under the eye of a gentle, wise, father-like friend, that remembrance of happiness would be associated with the image of that venerated friend. If the successful man of business could trace the germe of his love of order, of his exactness and his despatch, to the habits instilled by a teacher, he could hardly fail to associate him with the sources of his prosperity. If the ripe scholar could ascribe to the faithful discipline and influential example of a learned master his having made a right beginning, he would not fail to share with him something of the praise of his maturity and distinction. If the devoted man of God could remember that his early piety had received an upward impulse from the earnest and affectionate urging of a kindred spirit; if the Christian mother, leading her children in the right way, could look back to the time when the clear line of her duty was pointed out by one who felt that it was a part of his duty to prepare her for the holy office of maternity, would that man of God or that Christian mother regard teachers with indifference?

Is it not, my friends, because we do so little of what we ought, because we fall so far short of our duty, because we do not leave our mark deeply engraved on the character of our pupils, that we are not more highly esteemed?

To the motives for self-improvement which act on other persons, should be superadded, in the teacher, the consideration that every real advancement in himself will be a benefit to all who are to be instructed by him. He is to be, whether he wishes it or not, an object of imitation. He lives not for himself alone. If he do wrong, he necessarily teaches others to do wrong; if he accomplish all that he should, if he live up to his standard of duty, he leads others to do so. Every virtue which he cherishes and strengthens in himself is the prolific seed growing up into a harvest of virtues in the hearts of his pupils; every vice he indulges will be a sprinkling of tares among the wheat. From among his pupils will rise up teachers, who will be, in a greater or less degree, what he makes them. The first service, then, that he can render his fellow-teachers and his calling, is the setting to himself a high mark, and pressing forward constantly towards it.

His object should especially be to make himself an accomplished teacher. To this end every instructer should, if it be in his power, attend some course of instruction particularly adapted to educate the teacher,—some normal school. At present, this, with most teachers, is impossible, as it is only in Massachusetts that schools for teachers have yet been successfully established in this country. From the department for this purpose successfully attached to many of the academies in New-York, he may derive great advantages, and, in some favourable instances, most of those to be expected from a normal school. But it is only in an institution of this last kind, under a teacher whose whole time and energies are given exclusively to this object, and who has under his control a model school, in which every principle of instruction can be illustrated, that all the advantages of a school for teachers can be enjoyed. It is to be hoped that the time will come when many such shall be established in this and in every state of the Union. That will certainly be the case when the people shall generally understand that the education of their children is their dearest interest, and that children can be educated in the best possible manner only by teachers of the highest possible education.

Meanwhile, the teacher must make up for the defects in his education in the best manner he can. Much may be done by a resolute purpose to make his school what it should be. Some of the books by which he may be aided have been already spoken of. Much benefit may be derived from journals of education, such as the Common School Journal, edited by Horace Mann, of Boston, Massachusetts; the District School Journal, by Francis Dwight, of Albany; and the Connecticut Common School Journal, by Henry Barnard, of Hartford. The character and intelligence of these gentlemen, and their devotion to the cause of education, are a guarantee that these journals will continue to be of the highest value; and they will probably continue to receive communications from some of the most skilful and experienced teachers.

A means of great mutual improvement and not a little social enjoyment is presented in the meetings of teachers who live near enough to make this practicable. Those living within five or six miles might agree to meet, and spend an evening together, once a week, or twice a month. To make the meeting profitable, a plan like the following might be pursued. The first half hour might be spent in general conversation. Then, for the despatch of business, a chairman and secretary might be chosen, the one to regulate the discussions, the other to keep such a record of what was discussed, or agreed upon for future discussion, as might seem most useful. At each meeting, the following questions, or some of them, or similar ones, might be asked by the chairman, immediately after the meeting was called to order. "Have you, since the last meeting, read anything likely to benefit the teachers here assembled? What experiments have you made in managing or in teaching? With what success? If any school within your knowledge has been unsuccessful, what do you take to be the cause? Is there anything wrong in the present modes of teaching? What substitute would you propose? Has any new plan of teaching or governing occurred to you? How do you teach Arithmetic? How long do you drill your pupils in mental Arithmetic before taking the slate? Have you tried the abbreviations in Division recommended in the Teacher's Manual, page 158? Have you tried the experiment of teaching to read by words previous to letters? With what success? Cannot elementary reading be so taught as not to give habits of neglecting the thought? How do you teach your pupils to enunciate perfectly? How to pronounce? How to give the spirit of a passage? Such a person succeeds well in teaching to read; what is his method? How do you begin to teach writing? Do you use the blackboard in teaching to write? How do you teach spelling? Cannot the nonsense columns in spelling-books be dispensed with? Are they of any other use than to furnish exercises in enunciation? Cannot the blackboard and slate be substituted for other modes in teaching to spell? Ought any word ever to be spelt before its meaning is known? Cannot Grammar be best taught at first orally? Have you a general lesson? What hour do you find best for it? Ought not Physiology to be introduced? What ways have you to check tardiness? Can we dispense with corporal punishment in school, and yet secure perfectly good order? How can we check emulation in school, and substitute some other ways of exciting to activity not liable to objection? What are the best modes of lending the books from the library? You, Mr. A., are said to have excellent order in school, without severity; what is your secret? Have you any difficulties in school? Can any one present suggest a way of getting over them? Have you any difficulty with the parents? What ought to be done in the case?"

It may not be desirable or possible to ask all these questions at a single meeting. If not, it may be agreed to begin at the next meeting with the unfinished questions. Some of them may give rise to discussions of great interest, which may occupy several successive meetings. Or it may be thought desirable for some one or more to write an essay upon some of these questions. Let it be remembered, that the business of teaching has yet to be reduced to philosophical principles, and that the experience of every one is valuable, and his suggestions may lead to improved methods. If communications should be made to a teacher's meeting, which they find valuable to themselves, and think will be valuable to others, they should be transmitted to the Deputy Superintendent, or sent to the editor of some School Journal We are engaged in a common cause, and all our efforts should be for the common good.

CHAPTER VII.

THE TEACHER'S RELATION TO THE PARENTS OF HIS PUPILS.

"What has the teacher to do? To unfold intellect in varieties of character, to harmonize passion with moral principle,—work for the most powerful mind, even with the encouragement and co-operation of society. But the educator must carry it on, over a thousand obstacles, and in the face of perpetual opposition. He must resist the prejudices of parents, desiring evil things for their children; counteract the tremendous influence of bad example at home, and be able, in the short period of his power, to awaken a love of knowledge and a sense of right, vigorous enough to live and struggle when the aids of his sympathy and direction are withdrawn."— LALOR.

A TEACHER's success and usefulness in school, and the pleasantness of his position in society, often depend on the terms of his intercourse with the parents of his pupils. After a day spent amid the noise, and in the harassing and exhausting cares of school, a sensitive teacher is apt to feel little inclination for society. His solitary walk or his quiet fireside, his garden or his book, is wont to seem more congenial and attractive. In most cases this is a natural and reasonable feeling, and he may yield to it until he shall have recovered from his exhaustion by seclusion and rest, or an employment entirely unlike what has occupied him through the day. But he should not shun society. He must sometimes meet those with whom he can associate on equal terms, and those whom he cannot help regarding as his superiors, if he would avoid in himself the offensive arrogance, pedantry, and self-conceit which are so often the ridiculous characteristics of an old schoolmaster. And it is only in promiscuous society that his social qualities can be exercised, and his manners be refined, and he can learn to sink the peculiarities of the teacher in the better qualities of common humanity.

There are thus great advantages to be derived from society which the teacher should not be willing to forego. There are others, still more nearly related to his pursuits, of which he should never lose sight. Parents are often ignorant of what is best for their children, or thwart his plans for their good from thoughtlessness or inattention. In such a case a teacher has a duty to perform. By showing that he feels a sincere interest in their children, he may often, modestly and without undue assumption, induce them to take a nearer and juster view of their children's welfare, and to accede to his plans for their benefit. A few questions to a parent may sometimes be sufficient to give his thoughts a right direction: "Would it not be better, as your son is to attend school but a few months longer, that he should be more regular and more punctual? He now loses one or two days a week, and sometimes one hour a day, even when he is present. Does he know enough to leave school yet? Might he not do something more in preparation for the duties of life?" Such questions would come with an ill grace from one who was pursuing a mere dull routine, which left it doubtful with the parent whether the child were really making any preparation for active life; but very suitably from a teacher, who was using every exertion to improve his pupils' habits, and store their minds with useful knowledge. The expression of real interest in a child will never be without its effect upon a parent. He will be very likely to say to himself, "This teacher is my child's true friend; I certainly must not interfere to prevent his doing him good." All genuine feelings are easily communicated. The parent will feel, if not say, "Shall this teacher, this stranger, feel more and do more for my child than I myself?" The very fact that you express a strong desire to have his children come more punctually, will be a reason why they should come.

If you have difficulty in school, and know or have reason to suspect, that certain parents encourage their children to insubordination, a kind visit, evincing a regard for them and an interest in their children, will often completely disarm hostility, and change it to a favourable feeling. Sit down with them; laugh, and talk, and make yourself agreeable; show your friendly feelings towards them, and you will hardly fail to make them your friends.

They have sometimes a disinclination to get books for their children. Take pains to show them, as you easily can, what poor economy this is; how it wastes the time of the child, and deprives him of advantages.

Parents are often favourably influenced by what their children are doing. Many a vicious parent has been reclaimed by hearing, from the mouth of a child, the lessons brought home from a Sunday-school. For all good influences, your school ought to be as good as any Sunday-school whatever. Take care that the influence of the children in your school shall have a tendency to reform whatever is wrong about them.

Honour your calling. A teacher should not affect to be what he is not. Let him be content to be a teacher, and in that capacity do what he can. He will find enough to do in his own domain, in learning the character and circumstances of his pupils, and in adapting his instructions to their wants, without interfering in the duties or business of others. A source of great mischief throughout our country is the common disposition to aspire to places for which one is not qualified. Be modest. Guard yourselves against the besetting sin of those who have to do only with children, an undue estimation of yourselves. Be religious. "Those who consent to live for the service of men who neither know nor can appreciate them, must keep their eyes steadfastly fixed on Heaven; that witness is necessary for those who have no other."—Cousin.

BOOK IV.

THE SCHOOL.

"Thus, duties rising out of good possess'd,
And prudent caution needful to avert
Impending evil, equally require
That the whole people should be taught and trained."

"Earth's universal frame shall feel the effect;
Even till the smallest habitable rock,
Beaten by lonely billows, hear the songs
Of humanized society; and bloom
With civil arts, that send their fragrance forth,
A grateful tribute to all-ruling Heaven.
From culture, unexclusively bestowed,
Expect these mighty issues; from the pains
And faithful care of unambitious schools,
Instructing simple childhood's ready ear;
Thence look for these magnificent results!"
WORDSWORTH.

IN the previous chapters I have spoken of the general qualifications and duties of teachers, and of the objects at which they should aim in the discipline and instruction of any school whatever.

In the chapters which follow I shall speak particularly of the duties of the teacher of a district school, of the qualifications which are to be deemed essential to their performance, and of the manner in which each should be performed.

There are four distinct things, or, rather, classes of operations, which will command the teacher's attention on first entering a school: these are,

1. Organization;
2. Teaching the great essential branches, Reading, Wri-

ting, Arithmetic, Grammar, Geography, History, Composition, and Accounts;

3. Instruction, or the communication of knowledge;
4. Government.

With these must be combined, in as great a degree as possible,

Discipline,—the training of all the higher powers and faculties, moral, mental, and physical; and

The formation of proper habits and associations.

CHAPTER I.

ORGANIZATION.

"The general counsels, and the plots and marshalling of affairs, come best from those that are learned."—BACON.

THE teacher is to establish a system or organization, the object of which is to prevent irregularities, and to save time; to enable him to do as much for each, and for all, as possible; and to exercise each pupil according to his capacity and advancement, not overtasking him, nor leaving him unoccupied. This system should be comprehensive enough to embrace all the operations of the school, and so simple that all the children may be able to understand it; so that, when once established, it shall almost keep itself in operation, leaving the teacher his whole time for other duties.

To this end it will be a great advantage to a teacher to be familiar with the plans pursued in one or more well-organized schools. If he be so, he may at once adopt some known system, and leave it to be modified by his future experience. If he be not familiar with any, except such as he knows to be bad, he must consider the matter, and form one for him-

ORGANIZATION. 395

self. The following are some of the things to be provided for: 1. General exercises; 2. The time, order, and length of the exercises of the several classes; 3. Interruptions; 4. Recesses; 5. The punishment of offences.

I. There should be at least one general exercise, in which the whole school should give their attention to the teacher, and be instructed by him in those things in which it is possible for him to instruct all at once. And as there are always some children at school who cannot listen long without growing weary, it would be well that there should be two such general exercises, both of them short, at one of which instruction should be given in *duties,* and at the other, *useful practical knowledge* should be communicated. In the first of these, all the usual delinquencies and faults of children at school should be noticed in the most serious and deliberate manner,—in such a manner, if possible, as to bring the conscience of the children to act upon them. At this exercise, also, should be announced the general regulations of the school. Of both of these exercises I have already spoken in Chap. V. of the previous Book.

The best time for these must be determined by the experience of the teacher. As it is important that all should be present at them, an hour should be chosen at which all, or nearly all, are at school. If tardiness can be prevented, the opening of school in the morning is the best time for the first, and the opening of school in the afternoon for the second. I have found the first hour of the morning best. Other teachers have found the time immediately after recess most suitable.

II. In determining the time to be given to each particular class, in each study, it will be well for a teacher who goes into a school for the first time, to direct his pupils to come up in such order and in such classes as were formed by his predecessor. He will make them understand that this is only to enable him to become acquainted with the progress they have already made, and that he shall afterward arrange them as he finds it best. It should then be his object to divide them into as few classes in each study as possible. This is of the highest importance, as it is only by this course that he will be able to find time to give them much valuable instruction, or even to do them justice. Exact justice must be the basis of his arrangement. If he have fifty scholars, he will find that, allowing for the general exercise, for recess, and for necessary interruptions, he will not have, in a session of three hours, more than 150 minutes for all the classes. This would be, if they recited separately, only three minutes each. If the classes contain, on an average, ten each, he will be able to give thirty minutes to each pupil; and if they contain fifteen on an average, the time to each pupil will be forty-five minutes. All good instruction is thorough. Time must be taken to explain the difficulties in each lesson, and to see that each pupil masters them. But the difficulties may be explained to a large class in the same time as to an individual. The number of subjects to which the attention of each pupil should be given on the same day, should therefore be few, and the classes as large as they can conveniently be made.

Suppose that Geography, Writing, Reading, Grammar, Arithmetic, and Accounts, are to be attended to the same day: forty are attending to Geography, all are writing, all read, all attend to Grammar, all to Arithmetic, twenty to Accounts,—and that all these lessons are to be heard, and all the instruction is to be given, by one teacher. He finds that he can give an hour to Geography, half an hour to Writing, an hour to Reading, an hour to Grammar, an hour to Arithmetic, half an hour to Accounts. He divides those learning Geography into two classes, and gives half an hour to each class; the whole school may be engaged in writing at once; the whole may read in four classes, nearly equal, and have fifteen minutes each. In Grammar they may be divided into two classes, and have half an hour each; in Arithmetic, all in four classes, fifteen minutes each; in Accounts, all may be in one class, and have ten minutes; there are a few who must read a second time; for each of these classes a particular time must be set, so that all may be prepared, and take their places on the floor when the signal is given. I do not propose this as an arrangement to be actually made, but only as an illustration of the principle on which the time to be assigned for each exercise should be graduated.

III. The next thing to be provided for in the general plan of organization, is *interruptions*. These, in most schools, are, 1. Mending pens; 2. Giving leave to whisper or leave seats; 3. Explaining sums, and answering questions in regard to studies; 4. Tardiness, and hearing excuses for tardiness; 5. Punishing offences as they occur. Unless these are provided for on general principles, they will be continually occurring to harass the teacher, distract his attention from the proper exercises of the school, to overwhelm his faculties, and wear out his spirits. " Hundreds and hundreds of teachers," says Mr. Abbott, in his chapter upon this subject, " in every part of our country, there is no doubt, have all these crowding upon them from morning to night, without cessation, except perhaps some accidental and momentary respite. During the winter months, while the principal common schools in our country are in operation, it is sad to reflect how many teachers come home, every evening, with bewildered and aching heads, having been vainly trying all the day to do six things at a time, while He who made the human mind has determined that it shall do but one. How many become discouraged and disheartened by what they consider the unavoidable trials of a teacher's life, and give up in despair, just because their faculties will not sustain a sixfold task."*

* For many of the ideas in regard to irregularities, I am indebted to the chapter above referred to.

1. *Mending pens.* The teacher should never take school-time to make or mend pens. If he choose to do this for the whole school, he should do it out of school hours, and should bring with him a sufficient number to serve the school. These should be distributed just before the time for writing, by one or more persons appointed for the purpose. Children should not be allowed to be very particular in regard to their pens, but be made to understand that it is important that they should early accustom themselves to be content with tolerable pens.

Every pupil sufficiently advanced should be taught to make and mend pens. This is almost as important as the use of them. Some time should therefore be assigned for lessons in pen-making; and to give them the practice which alone makes perfect, the duty of making and mending pens for the whole school should be assigned to a sufficient number of competent pupils, who, after having served a stated time, should be succeeded by another set. The pen-makers for the time might be allowed to pass among the writers at intervals, and mend such pens as absolutely required it.

2. *Whispering and leaving seats.* Some intercourse among children in school must be allowed, and occasionally it is necessary for them to leave their seats. "How, then," asks Mr. Abbott, "can the teacher regulate this practice so as to prevent the evils which will otherwise flow from it, without being continually interrupted by the request for permission? By a very simple method. *Appropriate particular times at which all this business is to be done, and forbid it altogether at every other time.* It is well, on other accounts, to give the pupils of a school a little respite, at least every hour; and if this is done, an intermission of study for two minutes each time will be sufficient. During this time, general permission should be given to speak or to leave seats, provided they do nothing at such a time to disturb the studies of others." "It, of course, will require some little time,

and no little firmness, to establish the new order of things, where a school has been accustomed to another course; but where this is once done, I know no one plan so simple and so easily put into execution, which will do so much towards relieving the teacher of the distraction and perplexity of his pursuits."

In making the change, Mr. Abbott thinks it essential to get the co-operation of the majority of the school. This may be done by stating to them the difficulty, embarrassment, and loss of time occasioned by the common course, and proposing to them the new plan, if they are willing to aid him in introducing it. He recommends a rest of two minutes at the end of every half hour, during which they may leave their seats and whisper; or it may be three minutes at the end of every hour.

If a majority be in favour of it, success may be relied on, notwithstanding a minority which will probably be against it, and which must be dealt with by other methods. A great recommendation of thus inviting the co-operation of the students themselves, in this as in many other cases, is, that it exercises them in the habit of self-government; a habit which we should, in every way, endeavour to establish in our pupils.

" You cannot reasonably expect, however, that your plan will at once go into full and complete operation. Even those who are firmly determined to keep the rule, will, from inadvertence, for a day or two, hold communication with each other. They must be *trained*, not by threatening and punishment, but by your good-humoured assistance, to their new duties." " In my own school, it required two or three weeks to exclude whispering and communication by signs. The period necessary to effect the revolution will be longer or shorter, according to the circumstances of the school and the dexterity of the teacher. And, after all, the teacher must not hope entirely to exclude it. Approximation to excellence is all that we can expect."

"In order to mark more definitely the times for communication, I wrote, in large letters, on a piece of pasteboard, 'STUDY HOURS,' and making a hole over the centre of it, I hung it upon a nail over my desk. At the close of each half hour, a little bell was to be struck, and this card was to be taken down. When it was up, they were, on no occasion whatever, except some such occurrence as sickness, to speak to each other, but were to wait, whatever they wanted, until the *Study-card*, as they called it, was taken down."

"The following simple apparatus has been used in several schools where this principle has been adopted:

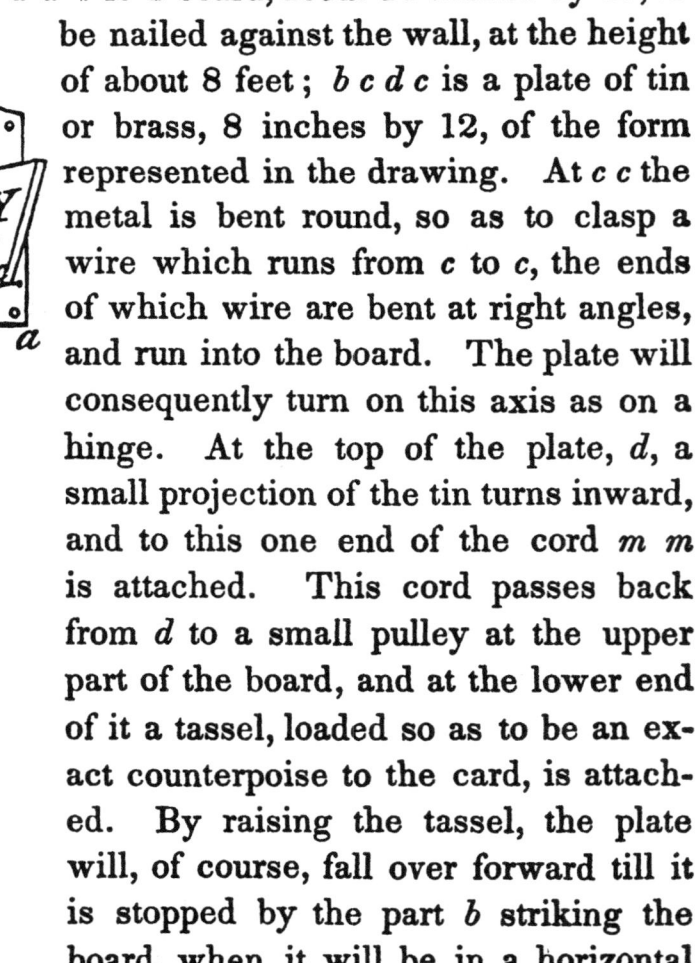

"The figure $a\ a\ a\ a$ is a board, about 18 inches by 12, to be nailed against the wall, at the height of about 8 feet; $b\ c\ d\ c$ is a plate of tin or brass, 8 inches by 12, of the form represented in the drawing. At $c\ c$ the metal is bent round, so as to clasp a wire which runs from c to c, the ends of which wire are bent at right angles, and run into the board. The plate will consequently turn on this axis as on a hinge. At the top of the plate, d, a small projection of the tin turns inward, and to this one end of the cord $m\ m$ is attached. This cord passes back from d to a small pulley at the upper part of the board, and at the lower end of it a tassel, loaded so as to be an exact counterpoise to the card, is attached. By raising the tassel, the plate will, of course, fall over forward till it is stopped by the part b striking the board, when it will be in a horizontal position. On the other hand, by pulling down the tassel, the plate will be raised and drawn upward against the board, so as to present its convex surface, with the words STUDY HOURS upon it, distinctly to the school. In the drawing it is represented in an inclined position, being not quite drawn up, that the parts might more easily be seen. At d there is a small projection of the tin upward, which touches the clapper of the bell suspended above every time the plate passes up or down, and thus gives notice of its motions."

The above is recommended as an expedient, the excellence of which has been tested by experience, to reduce to system the necessary communication between children at school, and to prevent its being a source of interruption and confusion. It may doubtless be introduced with great advantage into many schools, especially large ones.

In an advanced school of a limited number of pupils, seldom exceeding fifty in one room, I have found no serious inconvenience from allowing two engaged in the same studies to sit side by side, and to converse in whisper when no class was reciting. The penalty, seldom enforced, of abuse of the privilege, was separation. My system, however, has been to impose no restraints except such as were necessary, and to make school, as far as I could, in all respects a preparation for life, and, therefore, to induce habits of self-control in the midst of temptation.

3. *Explaining sums, and answering questions in regard to lessons.* If children are at all times allowed to ask any questions they please, the teacher will be able to do little else than answer them. Some system must therefore be adopted in regard to questions. The following directions may serve to prevent, in a considerable degree, interruptions of this kind. Before assigning any lesson, you should have learned it perfectly yourself. You will then easily anticipate the difficulties that are likely to occur, and explain them at the time of setting the lesson. For classes in Arithmetic, and often in other things, they should be done on the blackboard. Still some difficulties remain which you did

not anticipate. These must be allowed to remain till the time of recitation; and the first part of the time assigned for each recitation may be spent in answering questions. In this, however, discretion must be used, and the pupils must be made to understand how much better it is to surmount difficulties themselves than to have them removed. While a class is reciting, no questions should be allowed to be asked by the rest of the school; but between each two recitations there may be an interval for that purpose.

To prevent the necessity of answering questions in regard to the length of lessons, all the lessons for a week may be assigned at once, and the pupils be directed to mark them, each in his own book.

4. Tardiness, and hearing excuses for tardiness. To prevent tardiness, it may often be sufficient to require the individual to remain after school a length of time equal to his tardiness. Excuses for tardiness should be heard only after school is done. That the tardy may not escape, some trusty pupil should be charged with the office of noting all instances of tardiness, and reporting them at a suitable stated time.

In some schools in Boston, tardiness is prevented by subjecting a child who is tardy to the loss of all his credit marks, as if he were absent. In some other towns in Massachusetts, rules have been adopted by the school committee to close the door at five minutes past the hour for beginning school, refusing admission to all who come afterward. To prevent tardiness, however, falls within the province of committees and parents. Washington's maxim should be imprinted on the mind of all. "Appointments are debts. I owe punctuality if I have made an appointment, and have no *right* to throw away another's time, if I do my own."

It would, perhaps, be well to allow the door to be opened only every half hour. Those who come late would thus be prevented from disturbing the classes. An exact record of tardiness and absence should be kept, and exhibited to the committee or superintendent.

5. *Punishing offences as they occur.* This should seldom be done. The teacher should have a record-book or note-book always near him, and should only note the offence, and indicate to the offender that he does so. He must take occasion at one of the general lessons to speak upon it if it be a general offence; and if it be one that requires specific punishment, he should deal with the offender alone, and some time after the offence is committed. The time immediately after school, morning or evening, may be assigned for this purpose.

Another source of interruption occurs in some places, in the entrance of visiters. If possible, this should never be allowed to prove an interruption, but the business of the school should go on as usual.

IV. The fourth thing to be foreseen and provided for in the organization is the Recesses. These should equally divide the session, and should be made long enough for all the children, each sex in its turn, to go deliberately out, take a little air, and return. The shortest time to be allowed is five minutes for each sex. Ten would be better, as the time need not be lost, but may be employed by the teacher in attending to matters that need not the presence of the whole school. In schools which have a session of five hours or more, half an hour's recess is not too long. Advantage should be taken of this time to ventilate the room by throwing open the windows, unless the room be thoroughly ventilated by some other process.

V. The fifth thing is Government, and the punishment for offences. Of the principles of government we shall have occasion to speak hereafter.

In regard to these several points, the teacher should have the principles of his course arranged beforehand. I propose the following plan, to be followed or to be modified, according to the views and experience of the teacher.

8 o'clock. Children to be in their places at the hour assigned. The exercises to begin with reading a few verses from the Gospels or some other part of the Bible, a few serious words upon the duty taught, followed by a short prayer.

8h. 10′. First lessons of the morning, prepared the evening previous, to continue each 10′, 15′, or 30′, according to the importance of the lesson and the number of the class.

8h. 40′. Two minutes for whispering, leaving seats, and asking and answering questions.

8h. 42′. Lessons for 28′.

9h. 10′. Two minutes rest.

9h. 12′. Lesson for 28′.

9h. 40′. Recess for 10′.

9h. 50′. General lesson on duties and natural laws, 10′ to 20′.

10h. or 10h. 10′. Lessons for 30′.

10h. 30′ or 40′. Two minutes rest.

10h. 32′ or 42′. Lessons till 11. 10′ for settling difficulties with individuals.

A similar course for the afternoon.

I cannot advise a rigid adherence to any exact course. The successive lessons in every branch vary in difficulty and in interest. One may be despatched in fifteen minutes, and the next will require half an hour. It often happens that a class has just become engaged in a lesson when the usual time to conclude it arrives. In such a case, it will be better to omit the succeeding exercise altogether than to cut the one before you short. Valuable instruction is a thing rather to be weighed than measured. Still, method and regularity are so important in a school, that they should in no case be departed from without necessity.

CHAPTER II.

INSTRUCTION. GENERAL PRINCIPLES.

"'The Art of Education, that noblest but least studied of all the arts."—Brown.

The first inquiries you are to make on entering a school are, as has been said, What is the state of this school? Of each of the classes, and of each individual? How well does he read, write, and cipher now? What are his habits of mind? What is his character? What can I do for him in the time he is to remain under my care? How shall I teach him to read so readily, fluently, and intelligently, as to excite a love of reading, which will open to him an inexhaustible source of good, and of enjoyment for his whole future life? How shall I teach him the art of Writing, so that it shall be ever after a pleasure to him to write,—both to form the letters, and to express his thoughts? How shall I give him such a practical familiarity with the essential rules of Arithmetic as shall enable and induce him to apply them constantly in his business? And in performing these essential parts of a schoolmaster's duty, how shall I give him the greatest amount in my power of useful information; bring the faculties of his mind into action, and elevate his moral character? How, in short, shall I best prepare him for his station in life, and do what in me lies to make him a useful citizen, and a good and happy man? These things are to be accomplished, not for one only, but for all.

Consider, then, the ground before you, and lay your plans for doing as much and as well for each and all as can be done in the time allotted you. One great object in executing your plans is to discover how to act most efficiently *on the greatest number at a time.* Your power of useful action is increased just in proportion to the number on whom you can act at once. Hear what our experienced and sagacious friend says upon this point:

"The extent to which a teacher may multiply his power, by acting on numbers at a time, is very great. In order to estimate it, we must consider carefully what it is, when carried to the greatest extent to which it is capable of being carried, under the most favourable circumstances. Now it is possible for a teacher to speak so as to be easily heard by three hundred persons, and three hundred pupils can be easily so seated as to see his illustrations or diagrams. Now suppose that three hundred pupils, all ignorant of the method of reducing fractions to a common denominator, and yet all old enough to learn, are collected in one room. Suppose they are all attentive and desirous of learning, it is very plain that the process may be explained to the whole at once, so that half an hour spent in that exercise would enable a very large proportion of them to understand the subject. So, if a teacher is explaining to a class in Grammar the difference between a noun and a verb, the explanation would do as well for several hundred as for the dozen who constitute the class, if arrangements could only be made to have the hundreds hear it." "Now, so far as we fall short of this full benefit, so far there is, of course, waste; and it is not difficult or impossible to make such arrangements as will avoid the waste, in this manner, of a large portion of every effort which the teacher makes."

"Always bear in mind, then, when you are devoting your time to two or three individuals in a class, that you are losing a very large part of your labour. Your instructions are conducive to good effect only to the one tenth or one twentieth of the extent to which, under more favourable circumstances, they might be made available. And though you cannot always avoid this loss, you ought always to be aware of it and so to shape your measures as to diminish it as much as possible."—ABBOTT'S TEACHER.

There are several general principles, founded in nature and deduced from observation, but too often overlooked, which should be our guides in teaching, and of which we should never lose sight.

1. *Whatever we are teaching, the attention should be aroused and fixed, the faculties of the mind occupied, and as many of them as possible brought into action.* Nothing is learned unless the attention is gained, and the habit of commanding it throughout a lesson is more important than the lesson itself, whatever that may be. Moreover, the greater the number of faculties engaged upon an object, the deeper and more permanent will be the impression. At the end of a child's very first lesson, he should be asked, " What have you been reading about?" and should be made to answer. This should be uniformly done at every lesson. It turns the child's faculties to the lesson, and prevents its becoming what it will otherwise be likely to become, almost a merely mechanical exercise.

In order to command the attention, you must awaken the interest of the child, and to do this you must *first be interested yourself.* If you feel interested, your manner will express it, and you will have that *vivacity* of mind and of manner which are essential to successful teaching. Your interest will thus communicate itself to your pupil. You must also awaken his interest by beginning with what he knows and what interests his feelings, and connecting gradually with it what is new or difficult in the subject to be taught. You will thus clothe it with agreeable associations, and make him desire to know what he feels will be pleasant, and enable him easily to remember what has already taken some hold of his affections.

Then you must contrive to give a child something to do himself. Engage him in conversation; lead him to ask, as well as answer, questions; and be careful not to let your own words lose their animation, and become mere lecturing.

2. "*Divide and subdivide a difficult process, until your steps are so short that the pupil can easily take them.*"* This is the secret of that best of all schoolbooks, Colburn's First Lessons. It was the great discovery of Pestalozzi. It may be applied to every study which is necessary for children; and teachers differ in no one particular so strikingly as in a talent for applying this principle. Some possess it almost by intuition. They sit down by a child, and make him comprehend almost anything they please, by reducing it to its simplest elements, and presenting them one by one, in their natural order. This talent may be acquired. It depends on a complete knowledge of the subject to be taught, in all its bearings, and of the capacity of the child. Any one, therefore, who will take the pains to make himself master of what he wants to teach, and to enter into the character of the pupil, may be able to attain it. The possession of this talent is what we call *aptness to teach*. Its exercise requires patience, and a willingness to adapt our explanations to the imperfect capacity and limited vocabulary of the child. When, in our explanations, we want to use a word which the child does not know, we may do it without hesitation if we do it so as to show the child, at the time, what the word does mean.

Suppose you wished to explain to a class this sentence in Worcester's Geography, which I select purposely because it is the most difficult in the volume for a child to understand, and which, therefore, instead of being, as it sometimes is, part of a lesson, is quite sufficient for a whole lesson, or even several. It affords a very suitable lesson for one, or perhaps two or three, of the general exercises.

"The annual revolution of the earth round the sun, in

---

* Abbott's Teacher, p. 94.

connexion with the obliquity of the ecliptic, occasions the succession of the four seasons."

The class are supposed to be totally ignorant of whatever relates to Astronomy; everything must therefore be communicated. Those things only can be asked with which some of the pupils are probably acquainted.

Here are several distinct circumstances to be explained separately and in simple language. Use must also be made of some apparatus; of two balls to represent the sun and earth; or, if there are none to be had, an orange and an apple may take their place.

The distinct things to be explained are,

1. What is the succession of the seasons;
2. What is the obliquity of the ecliptic;
3. What is annual revolution;
4. The meaning of *occasions* and the other unusual words.

"What are the seasons?" you may ask. "All who know may hold up their hands." All hands are up. Some individual is told to answer, and says, "Spring, Summer, Autumn, and Winter."

"What is meant by the succession of the seasons?"

"First comes Spring; then Summer; then Autumn; then Winter."

"What is the difference in the seasons?"

"In Summer it is very hot."

"And what is it in Autumn?"

"Then it begins to be cold. In Winter it is very cold; in Spring it begins to be warm again."

"What makes it hot in Summer?"

"The sun."

"Is it nearer to us in Summer?" Some of the children answer "yes," some say nothing.

The teacher would say "No. The sun is not nearer then than in winter, but he shines more directly upon that side of the earth on which we live, which is called the northern half of the earth. It is that which makes it hotter. If I hold my hand to the fire thus, directly, you see that it is warmed much more than when I hold it thus, obliquely. Now in Summer the sun shines on our side of the earth more directly, which makes it hotter, and in Winter he shines more obliquely, which leaves it cold.

"Now, if I thrust a wire through this apple, thus, it may represent the earth. The wire projects, as you see, at each end, and I can make the apple turn thus on the wire. Just so turns the earth round and round continually on its axis, only the axis of the earth is not real,—there is no wire thrust through it. The hand of God makes it turn on its axis; but the axis is imaginary,—it cannot be seen,—it is not real. These ends of the wire represent the poles, only there are no real poles to the earth.

"Let that orange, which is still or *stationary* on the table, represent the sun. As I move the earth round it, you see the wire points always in one direction. Just so the imaginary axis of our real earth points always in one direction. Now, in this position, this end, which I call the northern, is turned from the sun, so that the heat and light from the sun fall obliquely upon this part, which represents the side of the earth on which we live. This position represents Winter; our side is turned somewhat away from the sun, and it is cold here, because less heat falls upon us. Now, again, in this position, the north pole is turned just as much towards the sun as the south, and it begins to be warm, because the heat begins to fall more directly on that part on which we live.

"And now, in this position, when the earth has gone half round the sun, you see the north side most turned towards the sun, and it is warmer on our side, because the heat of the sun is more direct. Now it is Summer.

"Now, again, in this position, the north and south side are turned equally towards the sun. It begins to be cold, because the heat of the sun comes less directly, and this is Autumn. So, you see, the turning of the earth round the sun once in a year, with its axis turned part of the time a little from the sun and part of the time a little towards it, but always directed to the same part of the heavens, makes first the Winter, then the Spring, then the Summer, then the Autumn: and that is what Mr. Worcester means when he says, ' The annual revolution of the earth round the sun, in connexion with the obliquity of the ecliptic, occasions the succession of the four seasons.' For this circle (moving the earth round the sun) is called the path of the earth in the ecliptic."

At the next general lesson precisely the same course may be gone through, except that now the teacher calls upon the pupils to state, as he proceeds, what is the position, and what are the consequences of it. For example, having reached the point where the children were at a loss on the previous day, he asks, " Is the sun nearer to us in Summer?" They are now prepared to say " No; but his heat falls more directly upon us:" and so on to the end of the lesson.

On the third day, if he choose to give another lesson to this subject (and it is well worth it), he lets one of the pupils take the apple and go through the positions, or several of them in succession, asking still the same questions, and now expecting the whole class to join in the answers. This repetition is an illustration of the third rule, which is,

3. *Whatever is learned, let it be made familiar by repetition, until it is deeply and permanently fixed in the mind.* This is an old rule, well known, from the most ancient times, to faithful teachers and careful learners. It is, nevertheless, liable to be neglected, from a feeling that there is so much more to learn which will be entirely new. The faithful application of this principle makes *thorough* teaching,—the best kind of teaching, certainly, since a few things well

known are of more use than many things superficially glanced at. It is of the utmost importance in the beginning of a study, when everything about it is new; the thoughts are new, and require an unaccustomed use of the faculties of the mind; and the language is new as the words of a foreign tongue. The progress of the learner may seem slow at first, and so indeed it is, and so it should be. But the complete command of the elementary and leading ideas of the subject which is thus gained, ensures a rapid, easy, and satisfactory progress afterward. When the elementary truths and first principles are well-learned and made familiar, they should be constantly referred to, and the learner should be accustomed to trace back to them whatever he afterward learns.

"The exercises which have for their object this rendering familiar what has been learned, may be so varied as to interest the pupil very much, instead of being tiresome, as it might at first be supposed.

"Suppose, for instance, a teacher has explained to a large class in Grammar the difference between an adjective and an adverb. If he leave it here, in a fortnight one half would have forgotten the distinction, but by dwelling upon it a few lessons he may fix it forever. The first lesson might be to write twenty short sentences containing only adjectives; the second to write twenty containing only adverbs; the third to write sentences in two forms, one containing the adjective, and the other expressing the same idea by means of the adverb, arranging them in two columns, thus:

He writes well. | His writing is good.

"Again, they may make out a list of adjectives, with the adverbs derived from each, in another column. Then they may classify adverbs on the principle of their meaning, or according to their termination. The exercise may be infinitely varied, and yet the object of the whole may be to make *perfectly familiar*, and to **fix forever** in the mind the distinction explained."

Nearly allied to this, and the best method of enforcing it in many studies, is the rule,

4. *Insist upon every lesson's being learned so perfectly that it shall be repeated*, as everything in a large school should be *done, without the least hesitation.* This must be insisted upon in lessons to be repeated from memory, as in lessons in the Tables, in Geometry, or lines in poetry. The observance of this rule is an incalculable saving of time. It is only by insisting strenuously upon it that a single teacher can accomplish much in a large school. It cannot, however, be safely applied in the case of very young scholars, or beginners, at any age, as in them the organs and the faculties are untrained and necessarily slow.

A contrasted case may suffice to illustrate its value. In a school where the practice is allowed of learning lessons and doing things *pretty well*, a class is called to recite a lesson in Geometry. They come straggling along, and at last form a line before the blackboard, if that can be called a line which is neither straight nor regular. One is called on to draw the figure. He has to look into the book to see what figure it is, to pause to consider how it is to be drawn, and to reflect as to what letters he shall attach to it. A second is called to state the proposition. He does not remember how it begins; begins wrong, is corrected, and obliged to begin again; observes modestly to his teacher, that, if he will just give him the first word, he believes he knows what comes next. After several blunders, he succeeds in stating something like the truth to be proved. A third begins the demonstration, and stammers on in uncertainty and confusion, apologizing by saying, that if he had begun the lesson, he could have gone on very well, but that he was confused by beginning where he did. Thus they limp on tediously, and with great loss of time and patience, and often with a hearty hatred of the study.

What happens in a school where this rule is carried into

practice? A class is called to recite this same lesson. They are at their places at once, and arranged in order and silence. One is called at random. He knows what he is to do, and draws the figure and makes the letters without a moment's delay. A second is called. He repeats the theorem. A third, with the same alacrity, proves the first case. A fourth is called, and proves the second. A fifth states one corollary, a sixth another. Each one, knowing he is to be in readiness, and that he must know what he is to do, takes up the recitation at once where his predecessor had left it, and the lesson is gone through with thoroughly in less time than would have been spent, under the other system, in drawing the figure or stating the theorem; and they go to their seats delighted with this stirring exercise in a most interesting study.

The practice of this rule requires *energy* in a teacher, and creates it in a school.

5. *Present the practical bearings and uses of the thing taught,* so that the hope of an actual advantage, and the desire of preparation for the future, may be brought to act as motives. As soon as a child has learned three words, he should be set to read, or to make a sentence containing them. Dwell upon the advantages of a love of reading, the resources it gives in a life of leisure and in the weariness of old age,—the delights of learning, the value of knowledge. The learner will read well in order to reap these fruits, and will thus be prepared to enjoy them. In lessons in writing, speak sometimes of the advantage of communicating with friends in a distant part of the world,—of the delights of a correspondence,—the exquisite pleasure of receiving a letter from home.

This principle is often neglected. I have known whole books of Geometry to be taught, and even a long series of lessons in Trigonometry to be given, without one word of the beautiful applications of this science in measuring land, ascertaining the heights and distances of inaccessible objects, and obtaining many of the conclusions of Astronomy. For want of observing this rule, it is very common to find a person who has been one or two years engaged in the business of life, look back with regret to the neglect of opportunities which are gone forever.

6. *Follow the order of Nature in teaching, whenever it can be discovered.* This is only admitting that God is wiser than man, and that all our processes may be improved by the study of his works. The method hereafter recommended, of learning to read by words first instead of letters, is suggested by this rule.

7. *Where difficulties present themselves to the learner, diminish and shorten rather than remove them; lead him, by questions, to overcome them himself.* This gives action to his mind, and puts him in possession of its powers. A study which has no difficulties soon becomes wearisome, even to the indolent, and leaves very faint impressions on the mind. What we obtain by a strong effort, we value and retain. It is not, therefore, what you do for the child, so much as what you lead him to do for himself, which is valuable to him.

This principle should be more and more practised upon as the pupil is farther advanced. Where there are not sufficient difficulties in a subject to excite the action of the mind, the teacher may suggest difficulties and raise questions, which he may leave to be met and answered at a future lesson. By pursuing this course he will be led to,

8. *Teach the subject rather than the book.* Remember that it is not Colburn's Arithmetic, or Davies's, which you are to teach, but Arithmetic, the science of numbers. Take care, therefore, to make yourself familiar with the principles, and with their various applications, as you may find them in several authors, or by reflecting on them yourself. For in this way, and in this way only, you will at last get

a complete mastery of the science and art in all its forms; and, while you are engaged in the acquisition, it will be in the highest degree interesting to you.

9. *Teach one thing at a time.* In teaching Grammar, for example, show first what a noun is, and let the pupil be exercised in this, in various ways, until it becomes perfectly familiar, before he is even taught the difference between a common and proper noun. Advance thus, step by step, making sure of the ground you stand on before a new step is taken.

After all the pains we can take, it will still often happen that much which a child is learning he can understand but imperfectly. There will still be some things which he cannot understand at all. In these cases he should be led to distinguish what he understands from what he does not, and be encouraged to hope that he will, by reviewing and farther study, be enabled to understand better hereafter.

The following suggestions, under the name of *general cautions*, are taken from the excellent work so often referred to.*

" 1. Never get out of patience with dulness. Perhaps I ought to say, never get out of patience with anything. That would, perhaps, be the wisest rule. But, above all things, remember that dulness and stupidity (and you will certainly find them in every school) are the very last things to get out of patience with. If the Creator has so formed the mind of a boy that he must go through life slowly and with difficulty, impeded by obstructions which others do not feel, and depressed by discouragements which others never know, his lot is surely hard enough, without having you to add to it, the trials and suffering which sarcasm and reproach from you can heap upon him. Look over your schoolroom, therefore, and, wherever you find one whom you perceive the Creator to have endowed with less intel-

* The Teacher.

lectual power than others, fix your eye upon him with an expression of kindness and sympathy. Such a boy will have suffering enough from the selfish tyranny of his companions; he ought to find in you a protector and friend. One of the greatest pleasures which a teacher's life affords is the interest of seeking out such a one, bowed down with burdens of depression and discouragement—unaccustomed to sympathy and kindness, and expecting nothing for the future but a weary continuation of the cheerless toils which have imbittered the past; and the pleasure of taking off the burden,—of surprising the timid, disheartened sufferer by kind words and cheering looks, and of seeing in his countenance the expression of ease, and even of happiness, gradually returning.

"2. The teacher should be interested in *all* his scholars, and aim equally to secure the progress of all. Let there be no neglected ones in the schoolroom. We should always remember that, however unpleasant in countenance and manners that bashful boy in the corner may be, or however repulsive in appearance or unhappy in disposition that girl, seeming to be interested in nobody, and nobody appearing interested in her, they still have, each of them, a mother, who loves her own child, and takes a deep and constant interest in its history. Those mothers have a right, too, that their children should receive their full share of attention in a school which has been established for the common and equal benefit of all.

"3. Do not hope or attempt to make all your pupils alike. Providence has determined that human minds should differ from each other, for the very purpose of giving variety and interest to this busy scene of life. Now if it were possible for a teacher so to plan his operations as to send his pupils forth upon the community, formed on the same model, as if they were made by machinery, he would do so much towards spoiling one of the wisest of the plans which the

Almighty has formed for making this world **a happy scene.** Let it be the teacher's aim to co-operate with, not vainly to attempt to thwart, the designs of Providence. We should bring out those powers with which the Creator has endued the minds placed under our control. We must open our garden to such influences as shall bring forward all the plants, each in a way corresponding to its own nature. It is impossible if it were wise, and it would be foolish if it were possible, to stimulate, by artificial means, the rose, in hope of its reaching the size and magnitude of the apple-tree, or to try to cultivate the fig and the orange where wheat only will grow. No; it should be the teacher's main design to shelter his pupils from every deleterious influence, and to bring everything to bear upon the community of minds before him which will encourage, in each one, the development of its own native powers. For the rest, he must remember that his province is to cultivate, not to create.

"4. Do not allow the faults or obliquities of character, or the intellectual or moral wants of any individual of your pupils, to engross a disproportionate share of your time. I have already said that those who are peculiarly in need of sympathy or help should receive the special attention they seem to require; what I mean to say now is, do not carry this to an extreme. When a parent sends you a pupil, who, in consequence of neglect or of mismanagement at home, has become wild and ungovernable, and full of all sorts of wickedness, he has no right to expect that you shall turn your attention away from the wide field which, in your whole schoolroom, lies before you, to spend your time, and exhaust your spirits and strength, in endeavouring to repair the injuries which his own neglect has occasioned. When you open a school, you do not engage, either openly or tacitly, to make every pupil who may be sent to you a learned or a virtuous man. You do engage to give them all faithful instruction, and to bestow upon each such a degree of attention as is consistent with the claims of the rest. But it is both unwise and unjust to neglect the many trees in your nursery, which, by ordinary attention, may be made to grow straight and tall, and to bear good fruit, that you may waste your labour upon a crooked stick, from which all your toil can secure very little beauty or fruitfulness.

"The school, the whole school, is your field,—the elevation *of the mass*, in knowledge and virtue, and no individual instance, either of dulness or precocity, should draw you away from its steady pursuit."

CHAPTER III.

INSTRUCTION.

SECTION I. READING.

"Learning to read is the most difficult of human attainments."—EDGEWORTH.

A COMMON mode of teaching the letters has been to point them all out in succession, at each lesson, until they were learned. This is a slow and bad way. The impression of each letter on the mind is erased by that which is shown next. A better way is to show a child only one or two letters at a lesson, give their names very distinctly, speak about their appearance, and let him look at them until he can distinguish them and call their names. They may be on blocks of wood or on pieces of pasteboard, and the child may be sent to bring them to you, directed by the name, until he is familiar with them. One may be added at each lesson, but care must be taken that he *does not forget* either of those he has already learned. Each child should be furnished with a slate and pencil, and when he has learned a letter, he may try to draw it on the slate; and he should be encouraged to persevere until he can make something like it. When he has learned the small letters, he may learn the capitals, and afterward the italics.

If no blocks or printed letters on pasteboard are to be had, the letters may be drawn, an inch or more long, on a blackboard or slate, and the child be allowed to learn and copy them. When he has learned a letter, he should be encouraged to find it in a book. What are called the *abs* should never be allowed to be learned, as they mean nothing, are of no use, and have a tendency to accustom a child to read without using his understanding.

A better way of learning to read, much and successfully practised of late, is to let children learn words first, and afterward the letters of which they are made up. This is Nature's method. A child learns to know his mother's face before he knows the several features of which it is composed. He learns what a dog is, before he learns what ears, hair, teeth, and paws are; and what a cradle is, before he knows what the sides, back, and rockers are.

The following excellent directions as to the first steps in reading by this method are from the Teacher's Manual, page 113:

"Worcester's Primer is an admirable little book for beginners. We shall use it, therefore, as our *First Book*. Commencing with a child ignorant of his letters, we should turn to page 15, where we find pictures of a man, a cat, a hat, and a dog, opposite the corresponding names, in capitals as well as in small letters. The teacher may commence thus:*

"*Teacher*. What is that?

* "In order that what follows may be fully understood, the reader should have a copy of the Primer before him, and turn to the pages indicated."

"*Child.* A man.

"*T.* That is the *picture* of a man. Would you not like to know the *word* man?

"*C.* Yes.

"*T.* (*pointing to the word*). There it is. Look at it well, that you may know it again. Now do you think you shall know it?

"To this question the child generally answers yes.

"*T.* (*turning to page* 17). Which of these words (pointing to man, dog, cat) is man?

"Unless the child has been brought up in habits of attention by his parents, his heedlessness will be apparent by his ignorance of the word. And this will generally be the case. So, turning back to page 15, the teacher can say,

"*T.* You are wrong. See, it does not look like that. You should give more attention. Look at it again (page 15; trace the form of the word with a pointer). Are you sure you will know it now?

"*C.* Yes.

"Most children will now know the word. But a few will be found so heedless as still not to have given *any* attention. With these there will be some difficulty. But, as soon as their attention can be caught, the instant one word is known, the spell is broken, and all will go smooth. Persevere with the first word. If you cannot succeed in the first lesson, give him two, three, four. Have a little patience. In some favourable moment you will gain his attention, and the difficulty then is over. Such is the testimony of many teachers.

"*One* word is enough for the first lesson. And now comes an exercise which must ALWAYS, *without one solitary exception*, follow reading. There must be no excuse for want of time. The teacher must *take* time, whatever else he may slight.

"*T.* What have you been reading about?

"*C.* About a man.

"At the second lesson, see if he can still point out the word man (page 17); if not, repeat, as before. But if he knows it, show him the next word, and say, that is cat. There is no occasion to make farther use of pictures for the present. Turning again to page 17,

"*T.* Which of these words (man, cat, hat) is cat?

"When he knows this word, conclude, as before:

"*T.* What have you been reading about to-day?

"*C.* A cat.

"*T.* Nothing else?

"*C.* Yes, a man.

"By a similar process, the other seven words will readily be learned by the child. But it is scarcely possible to repeat too often, in this stage of education, that a minute examination of the child as to what he has read must be gone into at the close of *every* lesson. No excuse can be admitted unless the house be on fire, or tumbling about your ears. Should the teacher find there is not time, the lessons may be made shorter, or fewer given per day. Three a week, with questioning, are of far more value than twenty without. The development of the faculty of *attention*, the formation of a *habit*, is all-important. If that be done *early*, there will be no difficulty in educating the child. It ought, then, to be commenced at the *first* lesson, and never, for a moment, be lost sight of during the whole course of education."

Common significant words should be selected, such as *dog, my, dear,* and repeated in different arrangements, *dear, dog, my,—dog, dear, my,* until he can distinguish them perfectly, and put them together to make sense. He should, at the same time, be taught to pronounce the words distinctly. He has thus the satisfaction of reading,—of seeing the use of his learning, from the beginning. To make them still more familiar, he should be set to look for the words in a page where they are to be found, and to copy them on his slate. A word may be added each day; and he should be led to amuse himself and exercise his ingenuity by making as many sentences or parts of sentences as possible of his words, and by writing them on his slate. When he has become familiar with a good number of words, and is convinced of the usefulness and pleasantness of reading, he may be set to learn the letters. This he will do with interest when he knows that by means of them he will soon be able to learn to read by himself, without help.

He should not yet, if ever, be set to learn words which he cannot understand, but only such as will occupy at the same time his mind and his eyes. Various books for children may be found, made according to this method. Such are Worcester's Primer, now much used in Massachusetts, and My First School-Book, by Mr. Bumstead, of Boston, and Mr. Gallaudet's. In these, and such as these, his reading by means of words should be continued; and he should never be allowed to spell the words, by sounding the names of their letters, for the purpose of finding out the pronunciation.* If a child be never allowed to read what he cannot un-

---

* The absurdity of this course is placed in a very striking light by the author of the Teacher's Manual: "Let us, then, candidly inquire whether it be really necessary 'to spell before we can read;' whether, in fact, spelling, that is, naming the letters, be of any assistance whatever.

"Commencing with the elementary *syllables*, then, ab, eb, ib, &c., let us carefully note the sounds of their constituent letters, and, joining them, observe whether they have any resemblance to the sounds of the syllables: thus, a, b, will be found to make *aibee*; e, b, to make *eebee*; i, b, *eyebee*; o, b, *obee*; and u, b, *youbee*. Now what resemblance is there between the sounds *aibee* and *ab*; *eebee* and *eb*, &c.? Evidently none.

"The same discrepancy will be found to exist on comparing the sounds of *words* with those of *their* constituents. For instance: before a child is allowed to read the word bat, he is directed to say *bee-ai-tee*; before cat, *see-ai-tee*; mat, *emm-ai-tee*; rat, *ar-ai-tee*; sat,

derstand, he will never form those bad habits of reading, called school reading, now so nearly universal. I have known several children, taught to read by their mothers on the principle of never reading what they did not understand, who always, from the beginning, read naturally and beautifully; for good reading seems to be the natural habit, and bad the acquired.

Reading intelligible books should alternate with writing on a slate. This is the best possible substitute for spelling, which, therefore, as a separate exercise, should not be yet begun. Time must not be wasted on spelling yet, as it is important, as early as practicable, to let a child learn to read fluently, that he may be able to occupy himself with reading, and be prepared for all the other parts of his education.

At this period in his progress, that is, when he can read easy books readily, and even before, columns of words may be sometimes placed before him, not to be studied, much less to be spelt, but to furnish him with words of which to make sentences on a slate. The words hen, men, pen,

ess-ai-tee; and, before he is allowed to pronounce *which*, he is required to say *doubleyou-aitch-eye-see-aitch!* But, lest it should be supposed that an unfair selection of words has been made, in order to place the subject in a ludicrous point of view, let us examine a line with which we are all familiar—the initiatory sentence in Webster's old spelling-book:

"' No man may put off the law of God.'

"The manner in which we were taught to read this—and this manner still prevails in most of the schools—was as follows:

"*En-no,* no, *emm-ai-en,* man, *emm-ai-wy,* may, *pee-you-tee,* put, *o-double-eff,* off, *tee-aitch-ee,* the, *ell-ai-doubleyou,* law, *o-eff,* of, *gee-o-dee,* God.

"What can be more absurd than this? Can we wonder that the progress of a child should be slow, when we place such unnecessary impediments as these in his way?

"The fallacy on this subject lies within a nutshell. It arises wholly from confounding the *names* with the *powers* of the letters."

ten, for example, may be introduced into such sentences as, my hen has chickens; I put her in a pen; there were ten men in the house. If, at every step of reading, the use of the slate and pencil be allowed, writing, and reading, and composition will go on, hand in hand, in natural progress, and will be gradually acquired, improved, and perfected together. There is one caution, however, to be observed in the use of the slate and pencil. They should be always taken away from a child before he becomes weary of them; and their use should daily be granted as a privilege.

If all persons about a child habitually enunciated distinctly and pronounced correctly, he would seldom have occasion to learn either enunciation or pronunciation as a separate exercise. This, however, is far from being the case, and lessons should now be given for the double purpose of exercising the organs of the voice, and of teaching full and perfect enunciation. These may safely be pursued for a short time at once, without danger of inducing the habit of reading without thought, as the effort to enunciate perfectly will sufficiently occupy the mind.

There are two excellent works containing suitable exercises for this purpose; one is Russell's Lessons on Enunciation; the other, Tower's Gradual Reader. The former has long been tested. The latter has been recently introduced into the Boston schools with the best effects. The teacher ought to be furnished with one or both of these From them, with the aid of the blackboard, he might give all the requisite instruction. It would be still better if the pupils also could be furnished with them.*

The first series of exercises should be all the sounds of the vowels and consonants, uttered separately, and afterward in combination, and continued until each should be

---

* If the teacher have neither of these, an excellent substitute may be furnished by the Key in Worcester's Dictionary, which he *must have*.

most fully and distinctly enunciated. These exercises may be conducted somewhat in this manner: A word containing the sound to be practised upon, fāte, for example, may be written on the board, and fully sounded, first by the teacher, then by one or more individuals, then by the whole class simultaneously, uttering a sound as loud and full as possible. Then the letter ā may be written by itself, after fāte, and sounded in the same manner. Then a series of words, āle, nāme, sāve, māte, &c., may be written, and each of them sounded in the same strong, full manner. Next, let a word containing a second sound, măn, be written, and sounded by the whole class; then ă by itself, and a series of words containing the sound, măt, căn, plăn, begăn, &c., to be sounded as before. Care should be taken that, in sounding the ă, the true sound, as heard in man, be given, and not the *name* sound as heard in fate. And afterward, wherever it occurs, the pupil should be taught to call it ă, and not ā. This principle, carried out with all the sounds of all the vowels, will much improve and simplify the process of spelling.

When the class shall have gone through all the vowel sounds, a similar exercise may be given on the consonants. This is still more important in reference to the two objects now in view, viz., training the vocal and enunciative organs, and forming the habit of perfectly distinct enunciation. Write the word *rob*, and after requiring all to utter it forcibly, utter, and make them utter, as forcibly as possible, the final consonant sound, *b*, distinct from the vowel sound. This, in the case of several of the consonants, is very difficult, but becomes more easy as the organs become accustomed to the effort; so that it rarely happens that, of a whole school, any one is incapable of sounding each of the consonants by itself.* Care should be taken, as before,

* The assertion that the consonants cannot be sounded without a vowel, is simply, as was long ago shown by Dr. Rush, false. In

that the name of the letter be not mistaken for its sound. In *c*, for example, the sound is sometimes the initial sound of *key*, and sometimes the initial sound of *see*, but never the name *see*. After all the sounds of the letters are thus obtained, and can be distinctly and correctly given, the class should be practised almost daily in a table formed by taking the short sound of each of the vowels, next combining it with each of the consonants in succession, and next uttering the consonant sound by itself. Thus,

ă, ăb, b ; ĕ, ĕb, b ; ĭ, ĭb, b ; ŏ, ŏb, b ; ŭ, ŭb, b.
ă, ăk, k ; ĕ, ĕk, k ; ĭ, ĭk, k ; ŏ, ŏk, k ; ŭ, ŭk, k, &c.

The most difficult of the vowel sounds to get perfectly are the delicate sound of *a* in branch, fast, &c., which should be an intermediate sound between the *a* in far and the *a* in man ; the true sound of *e* in fern and of *i* in virtue ; and the full compound sound of *u* in tune, similar to that in situation, which may be easily uttered by making it a separate syllable.

The most difficult of the consonants to utter distinctly without a vowel sound, are *k*, *p*, and *t*. But even these may form separate sounds. The next most difficult are *b*, *d*, and *g*.

After the class has become accustomed to utter the sounds of the letters instead of their names, they may be accustomed to spell in this manner. This will make the business of spelling incomparably more easy and natural. It must not, however, even in this improved form, be allowed to take the place of many other things more important Let the learner never, at any period of his progress, waste his time upon spelling-lessons. The proper, and the only

the final syllables of such words as hidden, sickle, &c., there is no vowel sound. See the Philosophy of the Human Voice, by James Rush, M.D., for a very full and philosophical analysis of the sounds of the language, and the functions and powers of the voice.

perfectly proper way of learning to spell, is by writing the words on slates or on paper.

After the simple sounds, exercises should follow in the most difficult combinations of consonants; such as those in didst, width, rafts, mangl'dst, shak'st, prompt, canst, return'dst, and similar words, on which an excellent series of lessons may be found in the Gradual Reader already referred to. It is by such exercises, daily resumed, but never continued long at once, that the organs of the voice are trained, and perfect enunciation, the most important element of reading, speaking, and, in no slight degree, of thinking, is gradually acquired.

Correct pronunciation is to be gained only from a teacher who understands the principles, and from a good dictionary. As soon as the pupil is old enough to use a dictionary for this purpose, he should be furnished with Worcester's. The marks used to indicate the sounds of the letters should be explained to him, and he should be encouraged to consult it in every case of doubt.

If, through all the exercises that have been described, care has been taken always to examine the pupil upon the meaning of what he has read, the foundation will have been laid for reading in a natural and intelligent manner. Many of the faults will thus have been avoided which it is usually a considerable part of the duty of the teacher to correct. Still, very much more is necessary to make an accomplished reader. The teacher must be a good reader himself. If he be so, and endowed with a clear understanding, good taste, and quick feelings, he will be able to make good readers of his pupils. In any case, he will derive much assistance from a good treatise on Reading, such as Dr. Porter's in the Rhetorical Reader. From some such source he must obtain a knowledge of the rules of emphasis, and the inflection and modulation of the voice. Having made this preparation to teach, he must give the class an idea of the manner in which a passage is to be read by reading it himself. Good reading is a commentary upon a passage, and is oftentimes the only thing necessary to explain its meaning. When, however, a passage is difficult to understand, and the class not far advanced, the teacher should give them the substance of it in his own familiar language, and when they understand it, read it properly in the language of the passage. Such an explanation is usually better than merely explaining the words singly.

The reading lessons should be the vehicle of vastly more of information than they commonly convey. The well-prepared teacher may make them the occasion of much useful instruction, by talking to his pupils upon subjects suggested by the reading-lesson, and, by interesting them, may lead them to desire to read for themselves upon the subjects, and induce them to pay more attention to the lessons. It would be well if the teacher would daily look forward to the reading exercises of his classes, and ask himself what useful fact, or interesting narrative or anecdote, he can call up, to arrest their attention or to supply them with materials for thought. Our common reading-books contain selections from orations. How much additional interest will the teacher give, by telling something of the occasion on which one of them was delivered, and the effect it produced. Some of the selections are from histories. By a few introductory words, he may show what was the state of things to which the passage refers, and by putting them into the current of history, prevent it from being to them a mere insulated fact. Satan's Address to the Sun loses half its sublimity to one who has not read the previous portions of the Paradise Lost; and how much more moving does the beautiful passage beginning "Hail! holy light!" become to the child who knows that they were uttered by one who had worn out his eyes and his health in noble exertions for liberty and truth.

It must be admitted that many of the selections in **our reading-books,**—vapid Fourth of July oratory, extracts from deep treatises, philosophical discussions, and refined criticism,—are poorly adapted to prepare the children of citizens for the great duties of their situation in life. But, unfitting as they seem, they may be made far more useful than they commonly are, by suitable explanations from an intelligent and well-informed teacher.

It is not uncommon to find children who have been taught to read at home, in books which they could perfectly understand, and who consequently read naturally, giving all the intonations of animated conversation, change this habit for the stiff, monotonous, lifeless style called *school-reading*, in a short time after being sent to school. This they do from being set to read lessons which they do not understand. This the teacher should take pains to avoid; and if there be pieces in the reading-book, as must often be the case, which his pupils cannot understand, and which he has no time to explain, pass them by, and read again and again the intelligible and useful lessons. Books that have few such should be exchanged for better. The reading-lessons should be such as not only to form the voice, to educate the taste, and serve as suitable models for composition, but to furnish food for the mind, materials for present thought and future action. In how many instances, in our schoolbooks, might the vagaries, speculations, and declamations of scholars, philosophers, and politicians, be exchanged for descriptions of the useful and essential things in God's great and beautiful creation.

SECTION II. SPELLING.

" The pupils ought not to be tasked and annoyed with the absurdity of that laborious and generally abortive exercise, LEARNING TO SPELL."—SIMPSON.

I HAVE already spoken of the manner in which this should be taught, in the early stage of learning to read. In every stage we should avoid, as the bane of good habits of thought, the common use of the nonsense columns of a spelling-book. Nothing more pernicious could be contrived. The use of them prevents thinking, without teaching to spell.

Still there are numerous anomalies in English which must be learned from a spelling-book. After the child has learned to read well and fluently, a spelling-book should be placed in his hands, and his attention particularly directed to the difficult combinations. These are admirably well presented in Wm. B. Fowle's spelling-book.* The simple words will have already become familiar, and time need not be wasted upon them. The whole attention should be given to the difficulties. What these are every teacher must judge for himself. It will depend upon the skill with which the pupils have been taught to use their slates in learning to read and write. When a lesson has been assigned, a few minutes may be appropriated for reading it over carefully. Examination in it should be conducted in various ways. One is putting out words successively to different individuals. When this is practised, care should be taken never to begin twice in succession with the same individual, and to keep all on the lookout by calling on those who are in different parts of the class, leaving it always uncertain who will be called next. This mode, however practised, costs much time. An agreeable mode of varying it will be to let the whole class spell simultaneously, in measured time. This is good for the voice, and, if care be taken to detect those who spell wrong, and such as depend on the rest, may be often very useful.

A much better way is for each child to have a slate before him, and write each word as it is put out. When all the words are written, the slates may be passed up, one of

* THE COMMON SCHOOL SPELLER, in which about 14,000 words of the English language are carefully arranged according to their sound, form, or other characteristics, so that the difficulties of English orthography are greatly diminished, and the memory of the pupil is greatly aided by classification and association. Published by Fowle & Capen, 184 Washington St. Boston.

them be examined by the teacher, and the others by the class, no one examining his own slate.

A still better way is to give out sentences to be written containing the difficult words, or, rather, to give out the words, and require the pupil to make sentences including them. They thus become fixed in the memory so as never to be erased. The objection that will be made to this course is the time which it takes. When, however, it is considered that by this exercise not only is spelling taught, but writing and composition, and all of them in the way in which they ought to be taught, that is, in the way in which they will be used, the objection loses its weight. As spelling is usually taught, it is of no practical use; and every observer must have met with many instances of persons who had been drilled in spelling nonsense columns for years, who misspelt the most common words as soon as they were set to write them; whereas, a person taught in the way here recommended, may not, in a given time, go over so much ground, but he will be prepared to apply everything he has learned to practice, and he will have gained the invaluable habit of always associating every word with a thought, or an idea, or a thing.

SECTION III. GRAMMAR.

"We think we shall do the public preceptor an acceptable service if we point out the means by which parents may, without much labour to themselves, render the first principles of grammar intelligible and familiar to their children."—EDGEWORTH.

In connexion with reading and spelling, Grammar may be taught; but, if taught to any except the most advanced pupils, it must be taught orally. The following method, suggested many years ago by Warren Colburn, whose talent for teaching other things was almost as remarkable as that shown in his works on Arithmetic, has been tried with eminent success in very many schools in Massachusetts particularly in the excellent schools of the city of Lowell

It is incorporated into his series of elementary reading-books,* among the very best, certainly, for teaching Grammar and Reading that have ever been made. Mr. Colburn did not make the use, here about to be recommended, of the slate in teaching Grammar. This is an obvious advance upon his method, which must have suggested itself to any one who had long made much use of the blackboard.

Mr. Colburn thus introduces the subject, in the Preface to his First Lessons in Reading and Grammar. "When the scholars have read this book through two or three times, and are able to read it with considerable fluency, the teacher may explain to them what a noun is, in a familiar, easy way, like the following: '*Every word that is the name of anything is a noun.* The words John, Mary, man, woman, boy, girl, horse, dog, chair, table, book, &c., are nouns: not the things themselves, but their names, are nouns.'

"Children will very soon understand this. They may then be required to select the nouns in some of the sentences which they have read during the day. They will soon do this readily, and be interested in it. They will be likely, at first, to call some of the pronouns nouns. If they do so, they may be allowed to do it. They will easily learn the distinction at the proper time. They should be exercised in this way for several days, or even weeks, if necessary, until they can readily tell all the nouns in any sentence in the book without mistake."

It will be more interesting to them, and, in the end, shorter and more effectual, to set them to write these words on their slates, making thus a practical exercise in writing, spelling, and grammar. They may also be encouraged to make a list of nouns from the names of the objects about them, or from the things elsewhere, and thoughts with which

---

* "First Lessons, Second Lessons, Third Lessons, Fourth Lessons in Reading and Grammar, &c. By Warren Colburn." Boston. Published by Hilliard, Gray, & Co.

they are familiar. This elementary exercise in composition will be found a useful one.

"When they are able to do this," proceeds Mr. Colburn, "some of the distinctions may be explained as follows: 'Names of particular persons or things are called *proper nouns*; as Thomas, David, Sarah, Jane, Lightfoot, Towser, &c. Names applied to sorts or kinds of things, comprising several individuals, are called *common nouns*; as man, woman, boy, girl, fish, tree, stone,' &c. Let them be exercised in this distinction," both in their books and on their slates, "until they are familiar with it, and then teach the distinction of *number* in a way like the following:

"Observe that we say '*one* boy.' What do we say when there are two of them? Do we say '*two* boy?' The scholar will probably answer 'No; we say two boys.' Then say, 'Write *boy*; write *boys*. What difference do you observe?' Again, we say, '*one* hat.' Do we say '*two* hat?' Write *hat*; write *hats*. What difference do you observe? Do you make any difference between *two hats* and *three hats?*"

"Propose several words in the same way. Then make them observe that it may be adopted as a general rule, that when a noun expresses more than one thing, the letter *s* must be added in spelling it.

"Then tell them that, when the noun expresses one single thing, it is said to be in the *singular number*; and when it expresses more than one, it is said to be in the *plural number*."

A similar course may be pursued with all the parts of Grammar, taking care to observe our 9th rule, *Teach one thing at a time.*

The blackboard is a valuable auxiliary in this process. In teaching the formation of the plural, for example, the following rule may be written distinctly on the blackboard: "When the noun ends in *x*, *ch* soft, *sh*, or *s*, and sometimes in *o*, add *es* to form the plural, as *fox, foxes*,' &c. With this before them, let them write on their slates all the words they can think of or find to which this rule applies. The same may be done with the other rules for forming the plural. *Gender* may be explained and rendered familiar in a similar manner, and, next, the use of *s* with an apostrophe, as John's hat, to signify possession. But nothing needs ever be said of cases.

Mr. Colburn next recommends that children should be taught to parse thus: "'Frank went into his father's garden.' *Frank* is a proper noun, of the singular number and masculine gender. *Father's* is a common noun, of the singular number and masculine gender. It has an apostrophe with the letter *s* added to it, to express that the garden belongs to the father. *Garden* is a common noun, of the singular number, and of neither gender. The scholars should be made to parse briskly, and to tell all the distinctions without being questioned. The teacher should frequently ask the reasons for the distinctions, but seldom more than one at a time."

The pupil may next be taught, orally, what an adjective is, and then the degrees of comparison, being made to practise on his slate, on each thing taught, till it becomes perfectly familiar. Next in order are the article, the pronoun, its various kinds, with exercises on the slate to render familiar the use of all the kinds, and all of what we call the cases.

Next the verb may be explained. Write on the blackboard any sentence containing several verbs; point them out; show that they all signify action or being; and then say that "*a verb* is a word which *signifies doing something, or sometimes simply being*."

In the sentence, 'David *rides* upon his horse, and *holds* his reins in his left hand, and *carries* his stick in his right hand, and his little dog *runs* along by his side,' the words in italics are verbs. They signify action; that is, they represent David and his dog as doing something.

"Whenever Frank *did* anything wrong, he always told his father and mother of it; and when anybody *asked* him about anything which he *had done* or *said*, he always *told* the truth. For Frank *was* a brave boy, and *dared* always to tell the truth. But Robert *was* a coward, and *lied*."

In this sentence, the words in italics are verbs, as they signify *doing* something, or *being*.

When, by exercises on the slate, the class has become perfectly familiar with verbs, so as to be able to distinguish them in every sentence read or uttered, what is meant by agent or actor may be explained. They must then be required to tell the agent of the verbs in their reading lessons, and to write sentences in which the verbs have agents. In the sentence, " Frank ran for his basket and began to pluck the pods," *ran* is a verb, because it signifies doing something, and *Frank* is the agent, because he is the one that does it. *Began* is a verb, and Frank is the agent for the same reasons. *Pluck* is a verb, because it signifies doing something, but it has no agent. N.B.—When a verb has the word *to* standing before it, it has no agent.

The difference between transitive and intransitive verbs may next be explained. This may easily be shown, together with the fact that the transitive has an object, while the intransitive usually has none, or it requires some word between it and its object. In the sentence, " The water flows," the verb *flows* has no object. In " George rides upon a horse," the word *upon* shows the relation between the verb *rides* and the noun *horse*.

The learner may then be set to select the transitive verbs in a page and write them on his slate; and, next, the intransitive verbs in like manner. He may afterward be directed to make up sentences containing the agent, transitive verb, and object, and others; at separate exercises, con taining agents and intransitive verbs. Much time, many days, and perhaps weeks, may be required to be given to these exercises, on account of their great importance.

Prepositions may be then explained, and similar exercises be given to make their use familiar. These may be followed by exercises on the various *times* of verbs; distinguishing at first only the three great divisions, past, present, and future, but in subsequent lessons marking the times particularly.

At this point in the progress of the learner, a book may be introduced containing a catalogue of the irregular verbs, and the variations of mood, number, and person, which, however, must be made familiar by appropriate exercises on the slate. Adverbs, conjunctions, interjections, will form the subject of subsequent exercises; after which may be introduced punctuation, and the use of marks and capital letters.

The above is not offered as a system of Grammar, but only as indicating the true natural method by which any system of Grammar may be taught. Neither is it intended to take the place of that instruction in the analysis of sentences,* which must be given as a complement of the rules of Grammar, for the purpose of showing the dependance of the parts of a sentence on each other. Something of this may be found essential to the best instruction in reading.

The whole time occupied in these exercises will not be so great as that commonly devoted to the acquisition of adroitness in the process of parsing. The difference will be obvious. The most adroit *parser* is often unable to write a single sentence grammatically. The pupil who has gone through with a course of such exercises as have been described, will have a familiar practical acquaintance with every principle of Grammar.

* Valuable hints in the analysis of sentences will be found in Hazen's Grammar.

SECTION IV. WRITING.

"Writing must be zealously practised according to the briefest and best system yet adopted, and the pupil habituated gradually to write down words on his slate."—SIMPSON.

IF the directions above given for learning to read be followed, the pupil will, from almost the very beginning of his course, have occasion to write. He must therefore be taught as early as practicable the written characters. This will be a natural and almost necessary step with the teacher, who makes the use he ought of the blackboard. For this purpose, the child must be taught the italic letters, and shown that the written characters differ from them only in certain particulars, and that more convenient forms are substituted for *f*, *g*, *s*, and *z*. The constant use of the pencil and slate will be the best possible preparation for the use of the pen. And the pupil, long accustomed to their use, will acquire almost necessarily those most important requisites in writing, legibility, rapidity, and compactness.

When paper and a pen are substituted for the slate and pencil, pains should be taken to form correct habits of holding the pen. The following directions, from the Teacher's Manual, are worthy of being observed. "Every child should be shown how to hold and move his pencil, and how to sit at his desk while writing, as soon as he enters school. The body should have a regular slope from the seat to the crown of the head; *no bend*. The seat should be so far back as to allow of this position. The left arm should rest on the desk. The right should rest on a point a little below the elbow, the little finger slightly touching the desk, but not pressing on it. The pen or pencil should lie on the second finger, and be held, not too firmly, by that finger and the thumb. The forefinger should rest on the pen or pencil, to keep it steady. . . . . The motions should be" principally "made with the forearm. The downward motions should be all parallel. . . . . The ends of the *r, o, v*, and *w* should not descend, lest they degenerate, as they are very apt to do with rapid writers, into *n, a*, and *u*. For the first week or two, the teacher, standing or sitting where he can see all the writers, should keep a constant eye upon them, to see that all the positions and movements are steadily kept.

"The first beauty in writing is *legibility*. Everything should give way to this. Flourishes may be useful in giving freedom of hand, but they should be practised by themselves, and never introduced into writing, least of all in a signature. The plainer the writing, the more difficult to counterfeit it."

The next beauty is compactness. So far as is consistent with perfect legibility, the greater the number of letters taken in by the eye at a single glance, the better for the writer and for the reader.

The style of writing should, in the next place, be such as is capable of great rapidity of execution. The round text hand, formerly so common, and so beautiful as an object of art, is objectionable on account of the time required to execute it well. For the purposes of the man of business and of the scholar, a ready, simple, and swift running hand is very important. Such a style will be the natural consequence of the constant use of slate and pencil in writing.

If to this quality it be thought advisable to superadd that of elegance of shape in the letters, they may be analyzed, and the elements given in distinct lessons. These should be carefully formed on the blackboard, to be imitated by the class in their books. The first lesson may be the straight line, the important element in the letters *h, k, p*, and *q*. The second may be the straight line with the curve at the bottom, the most important element, as it occurs in fourteen or fifteen letters. The straight line with the curve at the top is an element in three letters; that with the curve at top and at bottom, of seven. The *o* is also an element of seven; the end of the *r* of four; the *j* of three. Then there are the irregular characters *c, f, k, s, x*, and *z*.

In giving lessons in writing on the blackboard, it is well to represent several characters, one giving the letter and its element just as it should be, the others exemplifying the usual mistakes that are made in forming it. The comparison of these will teach the pupil how to avoid what is faulty, and form his eye and his hand to what is most correct and beautiful. When all the letters can be correctly formed and joined together in current hand, practice only is necessary to make good writers. This may be given in copying well-written or engraved slips, and still better, by requiring all written exercises to be neatly and carefully performed. In using a copy-book, let them write at first only on the left-hand page, and after having gone through the book, begin again, and write on the opposite page. They can hardly help desiring to make this better than what they had written some weeks, perhaps, before.

SECTION V. DRAWING.

"Drawing is no more than writing down objects."—SIMPSON.

I HAVE already spoken of ability to draw as a desirable qualification for a teacher. One who has this talent will, almost as a matter of course, desire to communicate it to his pupils. And one who cannot draw himself, may do something towards forming a taste for it by allowing and encouraging his pupils to use the pencil in drawing horizontal, vertical, and oblique lines, and various regular geometrical figures, such as triangles, squares, and circles, and copying pictures of any kind.

Every child should be taught the elements of drawing in lines, or linear drawing, if for no other reason than the advantage it gives in learning geography. But there are several other advantages in it, even in childhood. It affords an innocent and interesting occupation for children during many hours not otherwise occupied in school; and if acquired there, will serve the same purpose at home. It gives exactness to the eye, and the power of judging correctly of the dimensions of magnitude. It gives skill to the hand, and to the mind the power of appreciating beauty of form; and is thus an element in a cultivated taste. Its after uses are still more numerous. It enables one to understand at once all drawings of tools, utensils, furniture, and machinery; and plans, sections, and views of buildings; and it gives the power of representing all these. It is essential to the skilful execution of the plots, plans, and drawings of the surveyor and engineer. It enables the naturalist to represent the plants or animals of which he wishes to convey a correct idea, and the traveller of taste to bring home to his friends a vivid image of the natural objects or striking views which have presented themselves to him. By the help of a little skill in drawing which he had acquired at school, but which he had never taken an hour from more imperative duties to cultivate, a missionary returning from Palestine brought back, among other things, in a thin portfolio, a view of Mount Lebanon as seen at a distance; a plan of Jerusalem as it now appears; rock scenery near the Dead Sea; a view of the fishing-boats used on the Lake of Genesareth; of the small merchant vessels that ply along the coast of Syria; of some of the cedars of Lebanon; of the beautiful lily-like flower that grows abundantly on the hill from which the Sermon on the Mount is supposed to have been delivered; a plan of an inner court in an Oriental house, such as they have been ever since the times of the Saviour. These cost him but a few moments at a time, yet how pleasant were they to look upon, to his children and friends at home.

The following are some of the exercises which even a person unacquainted with drawing may require, and have well executed. Parallel lines; perpendicular, horizontal, and oblique; the division of such lines into halves, thirds, fourths, &c.; geometrical figures; plans of the schoolroom, yard, play-ground, and vicinity; drawings of tables, benches, chairs, bookcases, stoves, globes, copies of any drawings or pictures.

SECTION VI. ARITHMETIC.

"If a man's wit be wandering, let him study the mathematics."
BACON.

COLBURN's "First Lessons," the only faultless school-book that we have, has made a great change in the mode of teaching arithmetic, and is destined to make a still greater. It should be made the basis of instruction in this department.

The following method is recommended by a most intelligent writer* to teach beginners who have not yet learned to count. A numeral frame should be procured, and, if one made expressly for the purpose cannot be had, an old slate frame will answer. "The vertical sides should be pierced for eleven wires, ten of which should be at equal distances, the eleventh farther apart,—say double the distance. On each wire should be placed ten beads, half of one colour and half of another,—say blue and yellow,—arranged as follows: three yellow, two blue, two yellow, three blue. Thus we shall have one hundred beads on ten wires to represent units, and ten on the eleventh to represent hundreds; and so arranged, by twos, threes, fives, and tens, that any number not exceeding one thousand can be read off as easily as by the use of ciphers.

"Let us now take a class who cannot count. The teacher, holding the frame so that the beads are all on one side, and passing one of those on the upper wire across to the opposite side, says, 'There is one bead. Repeat, after

---

* Thomas A. Palmer, author of the Teacher's Manual, from which work much in this section is, by his permission, taken

me, one bead (passing another across), two beads,' &c., till all the ten are passed across and named. Then repeat the operation, omitting the word *bead*, till all can readily count from one to ten. This is enough for the first lesson. The second lesson should be a repetition of the first, with this addition: When the three yellow beads are passed across, say, 'Now try to recollect three.' Then pass three across on another wire, and ask how many there are. If they do not know, count the first three again, and repeat, on different wires, till they know three at a glance. In like manner, make them familiar with four, five, six, seven; and for eight, nine, ten, direct their attention to the other side, as eight on one side may be known by two being on the other; nine by one, and ten by none. This may probably be too much for the second lesson. The teacher must take care not to fatigue the little pupils by too long exertion.

"As soon as the class has become familiar with the first ten numbers, and able to name them on the frame at a glance, the difficulty is pretty much over, as the others are chiefly a repetition of the first ten. In teaching them, we should take the same pains with the second ten as with the first, since the words *eleven*, *twelve*, *thirteen*, &c. are learnt in precisely the same way in which the first are learnt, and should be made just as familiar. After the first ten are familiarly learnt, and have been gone over readily, we pass the ten beads on the first wire across, and then say, 'There are *ten*.' Now, one bead being passed across on the second wire, 'There are *eleven*; another will make *twelve*,' and so on to nineteen; and passing the last across, 'We have *two tens*, or *twenty*.' Here it will be well to exercise the class until, seeing all the beads on the first wire passed across, they will fix their attention on the second, and give the names which belong to the second ten, without each time counting over the first ten. Here also they must be taught that *teen* in the names of the numbers from twelve to twenty is the same as *ten*, and that the syllable *ty*, in the numbers from nineteen to one hundred, is used instead of *ten*. Then, by passing the beads on the third wire singly across, we have *twenty-one*, *twenty-two;* and so on with the other wires, the last bead on the tenth wire making *ten tens*, or *one hundred*. " We have seen classes who have gone at once from ten to one hundred, and at the next lesson could name any number required, on the frame, not exceeding one hundred; and, by telling them that each bead on the eleventh wire stood for one hundred, their knowledge extended to one thousand. These minute explanations are necessary for those only who know nothing of arithmetic. " But it would be profitable for the whole school to go over the frame once or twice, as there are few who have clear notions of the meaning of *ty* and *teen*." It is desirable also to exercise all upon the frame, to teach them to judge of numbers from one to ten by the eye. If all the beads on the first seven wires, for example, are passed across, and three on the eighth, they may be made so quick in judging as to say *seventy-three* as readily, on seeing the frame, as we do on seeing the characters 73.

" Our little pupils, having thus acquired the nomenclature of numbers, the fundamental processes of addition, subtraction, multiplication, and division, may now be commenced. The first two should be taught simultaneously on the frame: thus, passing two beads and two beads, the class will see they make four; and, if two be taken from four, two will remain. If this be practised a very few minutes every day, in a week or two the class will add or subtract instantly any two numbers not exceeding one thousand. Multiplication and division should also proceed simultaneously. Thus, taking eight beads, ask how many twos they contain; and, if one of the class separate them on the wire into twos, all will see there are four; consequently, four twos make eight, and eight contains four twos. It will not be necessary to go farther than the fifth line in multiplication and division, as the higher numbers will be more readily taught from Colburn's 'First Lessons.' The frame need now be no longer used as a regular exercise, but should always be near to the teacher's desk; as, if properly used, it will be of much advantage to the class."

If the teacher finds he can more easily teach his pupils to count by reckoning on their fingers, or in any other way, he may employ that mode. It is very desirable, however, that the three names of ten should be taught and made familiar, whatever method is used.

" For very small children, Fowle's 'Mental Arithmetic' should precede Colburn's ' Lessons ;' but those of seven or eight years of age may pass at once into Colburn. Of these books, there should be only one copy in school. Any intelligent teacher can use them, even though unpractised in mental arithmetic. When this is the case, however, he should work out every question mentally along with the class. The main advantage of mental arithmetic is, the wonderful manner in which it disciplines some of the most important faculties of the mind, particularly those of attention, abstraction, and reasoning. But, to gain these advantages in any considerable degree, the pupils should distinctly know that the questions are never to be repeated. They must give their *whole* attention while the question is reading, and they must retain the whole in their minds until they have found the answer, and explained the process by which it was discovered. The books ought to be used thus : The teacher reads, ' Your brother William gave you nineteen cents, your brother John ten, and your cousin Mary two. How many have been given to you in all ?'

" C. (*after consideration*). Thirty-one.

" T. How do you know ?

" C. Because brother William gave me nineteen, brother John ten ; now ten and nineteen make twenty-nine ; and cousin Mary gave me two; twenty-nine and two make thirty-one.

"*T.* Very well. Twelve men are to have ninety-six dollars for performing a piece of work. How much is due to each?

"*C.* Eight dollars.

"*T.* Why?

"*C.* Because, as the twelve men were to have ninety-six for their work, and as there are eight twelves in ninety-six, of course each man would have eight.

"I now give a question in a more advanced stage.

"*T.* A cistern has two cocks; the first will fill it in three hours, the second in six hours; how long would it take both to fill it?

"*C.* Two hours.

"*T.* Why?

"*C.* Because, if the first can fill it in three hours, it will fill one third of it in one hour; and if the second will fill it in six hours, it will fill one sixth in one hour; but one third is equal to two sixths; therefore, both will fill three sixths, or one half, in one hour; or the whole in two hours.

"Some of the exercises in addition, in Colburn's 'First Lessons,' are so easy, though not the less important, that there is some danger of the class allowing their minds to wander, and yet answering correctly. This may be checked by varying the questions as follows: Instead of Nine and four? Nineteen and four? Twenty-nine and four? Thirty-nine and four? regularly increasing the number of *ty*, let them be varied thus: Twenty-nine and four? Forty-nine and four? Thirty-nine and four? Fifty-nine and four? &c.

"It requires some tact to gain the utmost advantage from mental arithmetic, but it is easily acquired. The main point is, that the attention of the teacher be kept *wide awake*. The dull and slow must be allowed time; the bright must not be suffered to monopolize the answers. At the same time, it will not do for the answers to be received in the order in which the pupils stand in the class, for in this case only one child would be occupied at once. Each pupil would attend only to his own question; whereas all should be occupied, and should actually solve every question put to the class. The best plan, then, is for each to hold up a finger when ready to answer, leaving the teacher to select whose turn it shall be. Thus every one might have an equal chance. The dull and the bright, however, ought not to be together, but in different classes. In fact, it would be well to have the classes differently arranged for each separate study. Some are bright at reading and dull in arithmetic, and *vice versa*. To chain the dull to the bright has bad effects on both."

"*Abbreviations in Mental Arithmetic.*—The following abbreviations may probably not only be useful to the student, but lead to the invention of others equally profitable.

" To multiply by 5. Take half the number, and multiply by 10. We take half, because multiplying by 10 gives double of multiplying by 5. Thus, $5 \times 64 = \frac{64}{2} \times 10 =$ 32 tens, or 320. When the number is odd, halving leaves a remainder of 1, which, of course, is one 5. Thus, $73 \times 5 = \frac{73}{2} \times 10 = 36$ tens and five, or 365.

" Let us next proceed to 15, 20, 25, 30, &c., and afterward take up the intervening numbers.

" Fifteen is 10 and half of 10; therefore, increasing any number a half, and multiplying by 10, is the same as multiplying by 15. Thus, as 64 and half of 64 make 96, $64 \times 15 = 96$ tens, or 960. When the number is odd, proceed as above in speaking of 5. Thus, $75 \times 15 = 112$ tens and five, or 1125, and the square of 15 is 22 tens and five, or 225.

" Twenty being two tens, to multiply by 20, double the number, and multiply by 10. Thus, $20 \times 45 = 90$ tens, or 900.

" Twenty-five is one fourth of 100; therefore, to multiply

by 25, take ¼ of the number for hundreds: **every unit in the remainder is one twenty-five.** Thus:

$$24 \times 25 = \tfrac{24}{4} \times 100 = 600.$$
$$25 \times 25 = \tfrac{25}{4} \times 100 = 625.$$
$$26 \times 25 = \tfrac{26}{4} \times 100 = 650.$$
$$27 \times 25 = \tfrac{27}{4} \times 100 = 675, \text{ \&c.}$$

"Fifty is half of 100; therefore, to multiply by 50, take ½ the number for hundreds. Thus, $24 \times 50 = \tfrac{24}{2} \times 100 = 1200$.

"Thirty is thrice ten; therefore, to multiply by 30, take thrice the number, and multiply by 10. Thus, $24 \times 30 = 72$ tens, or 720.

"Let us now examine the intermediate numbers, which are all done on one principle. Fourteen times any number are 15 times that number less once the number, and 13 times any number are 15 times the number less twice the number. Thus, $14 \times 24 = 15 \times 24$ less once 24; and $13 \times 24 = 15 \times 24$ less twice 24. Again, $16 \times 24 = 15 \times 24$ more once 24; and $17 \times 24 = 15 \times 24$ more twice 24. Thus, by connecting two numbers less and two numbers more with our 15, 20, 25, 30, &c., we have all the intermediate numbers.

"Division is performed by reversing these processes; that is, multiplying where division is shown above, and dividing where multiplication is indicated. Though not so easy as multiplication, some practice in it will be useful.

"This system of abbreviations may seem obscure or difficult, perhaps, to those who have never practised mental arithmetic. But nothing is hazarded in the assertion that, where Colburn's Arithmetic is used as pointed out above, the class will understand and apply it with ease and rapidity before they have gone half through that work. The teacher may exemplify the abbreviations for himself on the slate, but they should be performed by the school exclusively in the mind.*

---

* In schools in which these abbreviations have been practised, the most striking and valuable effects have been produced.

"It is a matter of the first importance that the teacher should have a distinct idea of the objects to be gained by the practice of mental arithmetic, as otherwise the main advantages that might result from it will assuredly be lost. Let it be constantly borne in mind, then, by the teacher, that the knowledge of arithmetic is *not* the chief benefit to be derived from it, but one of secondary importance. It is the mental discipline, the power of abstraction, the habit of attention and of reasoning which it develops, that constitute its chief value. But all these advantages are lost if the child is allowed to study the book, more especially by working out the questions on the slate. They can only be completely attained by calling on the class to solve each question *mentally*, merely from hearing it *once* read, and then to give a clear account of his mental operations. And so beautifully are the questions arranged, so completely does the knowledge gained in each question come into requisition in those that follow, that, if the plan of study be commenced right, and strictly followed, the most intricate and difficult questions will give no trouble to the class.

"It may, perhaps, be incredible to some, but it is not the less true, that Colburn's book may be gone through, and correct notions be attained of the principles of arithmetic, without the knowledge of a single character. A child who can neither write nor read, who has never even seen a figure, will probably acquire this knowledge more correctly than those who fully understand them. Notwithstanding this, however, as the knowledge of figures is an indispensable part of education, and as its acquisition is much the easiest in early youth, as soon as a child can hold his pencil correctly, and can write the ten characters, he should proceed to the practice of written arithmetic."

The inexperienced teacher will find the key very useful in explaining the mode in which each section is to be taught. He must not, however, depend too much on these explanations, as better ones will often occur to himself. The plates are of very doubtful utility. They may be employed if the teacher, after carefully studying them, can make good use of them. Many of the best teachers have found them of no use.

A pupil who has been faithfully taught Colburn's First Lessons will very seldom find any difficulty in the management of fractions. It may sometimes be necessary to produce the apple and cut it in parts, to illustrate the meaning of the names, when they are first used. Afterward it will usually be sufficient to imagine the apple to be divided and subdivided; and this has been found better than the use of any plate or frame whatever.

Some of the kinds of questions may be enlarged upon and multiplied to great advantage. The questions 132 to 143 of the Miscellaneous Examples contain all the principles of Simple Interest. If similar questions are repeated until these principles are made perfectly familiar, most questions of Simple Interest may be solved mentally with great facility; and precisely these principles are applicable, without rules, to all cases of interest that can occur.

The method of Mental Arithmetic is capable of far greater extension than is given it in this little volume. The following are some of the things done by this process in a school in England. The age of the moon is determined at any given time; the day of the week found, which corresponds with any day of any month and year; any number not exceeding a thousand may be squared; the square root of a number of not more than five figures extracted; the space through which a body falls in a given time calculated; and the circumferences and areas of circles determined from their diameters, and many other similar problems solved.*

* See "Plans for the Government and Liberal Instruction of Boys in large numbers, drawn from experience," p. 17.

ARITHMETIC. 451

WRITTEN ARITHMETIC.

The Roman numerals are so frequently used, that all children at the primary schools should be made familiar with them.

"The following are supposed to be the original forms of the Arabic characters:

1	2	3	4	5	6	7	8	9
I	=	≡	□	5	6	9	8	♌

"These nine characters have each two values, viz., their *simple* value, as one, two, three, &c., and their *local* value, which depends on their distance from the place of units, which is always the first on the right hand, unless otherwise indicated by a mark, which shall be explained presently. Thus, in the following number, 6666, we have six four times repeated, but every time the character represents a different value—the first on the right hand representing the units (or *ones*), and, therefore, simply six; the second, 6 ty, or tens; the third, 6 tens of tens, or hundreds; the fourth, 6 tens of tens of tens, or thousands; and if there were more, they would still go on increasing tenfold to infinity. Thus we perceive that the fundamental law of the Arabic system is, that *a removal of a figure one place towards the left increases its value tenfold; and, on the contrary, its removal towards the right decreases it tenfold.*

"In addition to the nine characters mentioned above, there is one which does not consist of *lines*, like the *significant figures*, but, on the contrary, is entirely round, to express that it has, in itself, *no value*, its sole use being to occupy the *place* of some denomination which may be wanting, and which, therefore, instead of its customary name of *cipher*, may be appropriately termed *figure of place*. Thus, to represent six hundred and five (605), it is necessary to have a character that has no value in itself, to stand in the place of tens; otherwise the 6 would be 6 tens, in place of 6 hundred."

It is of great importance that the learners should become perfectly familiar with the numeration table. For this purpose, let a series of figures be written on the blackboard; let one of the class divide them into periods of threes, and let the class be exercised in naming them, irregularly, until all are familiar with them. Then write a series of figures of the same kind, thus,

$$4\ 4\ 4\ 4\ 4\ 4$$

and ask how many times is the second 4 greater than the first? how many times is the third greater than the second? how many times is the third greater than the first? the fourth than the third? &c. Again, how many times is the first *contained* in the second? the first in the third? &c.

When the class have become sufficiently familiar with whole numbers, they should be immediately introduced to a knowledge of decimals, by being shown that the same law prevails on the right of the decimal point as on the left. Having been taught to estimate the value of a figure by observing its distance from the place of units, they may be shown that, by placing a dot on the right of units, the figures on the right of units have the same names as those on the left, with the addition to each of *th*, and a value continually decreasing in tenfold proportion. Thus,

$$444.444:$$

the 4 on the right of the dot represents 4 tenths, the next 4 hundredths, &c. This being made familiar, the effect of moving the decimal point to the right or left may be shown: that to divide by 100, for example, we remove the decimal point two places to the left; to multiply by 100, we move it two places to the right. It may require some care and repetition to render these things *perfectly* plain, but when they are made so, many of the difficulties of arithmetic are entirely prevented. The only reason why decimals should ever be considered, as they often are, more difficult than whole numbers, is, that they are separated from them, and treated of in a different section, as if they had some peculiar difficulties. As they have not, the student is bewildered, and is led to suppose that he does not understand decimals, while they certainly are just as easy to understand as anything else in Arithmetic. To prevent this, exercises in decimals should be given interchangeably with those on whole numbers, in practice upon all the rules.

Here the use of the cipher or zero, 0, should be shown, by writing the same figure with several zeros before and after it, and pointing out their effect. Thus, 30, 300, 3, .03, 003, or any other combinations, may be written, and the class exercised in reading them, writing similar numbers from dictation, and *showing* the effect of the zero.

When the class perfectly understand notation, so far, at least, as thousands and thousandths, *and not before*, they should proceed to addition.* And in this the object should be, first, to make them understand the simple fact that one is carried from a lower to a higher column for every ten, merely because more than nine units cannot be expressed by a single figure in the unit column; and, secondly, to teach to add rapidly, not only by single figures at a time but by taking two or more at once. In order to this, the class may be exercised by such questions as the following: How many does 6 want of 10? How many 7? 8? &c. How many are wanting to 7 of 11? 6? 8? &c. How many to 12?

"When the class can answer such questions instantly, they should be made to observe that adding 10 to a number

---

* With young classes, it may be well to confine notation, at first, to numbers as small as thousands or tens of thousands. They should be made perfectly to comprehend such numbers before they are introduced to millions. Most teachers are not aware how slowly the idea of such large numbers is comprehended by children. One great excellence of Colburn's First Lessons is, that small numbers only are used in it.

does not change its units; that adding 11 or 12 increases them by 1 or 2; and that adding 8 or 9 decreases them by 2 or 1.

Columns should then be constructed, for practice, like the following:

1st.	2d.	3d.
$a\ b\ c$	$d\ e\ f$	$g\ h\ i$
1 3 5	2 1 8	3 4 2
9 8 7	3 2 3	4 3 3
7 7 4	5 8 1	7 7 4
3 4 8	3 7 2	6 6 1
4 5 5	4 3 4	8 1 2
6 6 7	3 1 6	5 2 3
2 2 3	2 4 8	2 8 4
8 9 9	7 4 3	5 9 5
5 8 4	1 3 1	3 7 6
5 3 8	4 5 4	9 6 7
3 7 5	2 1 5	7 4 8
7 4 7	4 5 3	1 3 9

In the column a, every two figures make 10; in b, every two make 11; in c, every two make 12. In d, every three figures make 10; in e, every three make 11; in f, every three make 12. In g, every two alternate figures, viz., first and third, and second and fourth, &c., make 10; in h, the first and fourth, second and third, fifth and eighth, seventh and sixth, &c., make 10; the column i goes on a different principle, which is, that whenever three figures follow in regular order, their sum is equal to three times the middle one; that is, the sum of 9, 8, and 7 is 3 times 8; $4+5+6=3\times 5$; because, if 1 be taken from the largest and added to the smallest, all three would be equal. Let the teacher point out to the school, or to a class, the different combinations in the columns a, b, c, d, &c., and then write some columns of figures at random, and he will be surprised how quickly the little pupils will catch the different combinations, and add them together."

In teaching subtraction, the practice of borrowing should be thus explained:

>From 635
Take 476
Remain 159

We cannot take 6 from 5, but 35 may be considered as 20 and 15, and 6 taken from 15 leaves 9. So, we cannot take 70 from 20, or 7 in the column of tens from 2, but 62 may be considered 50 and 12, and 7 from 12 leaves 5. Then, as 5 remains in place of 6 in the column of hundreds, 4 from 5 leaves 1.

MULTIPLICATION.—The student having been taught, by mental arithmetic, to form the multiplication table, it will be well to let it be perfectly learned as far as 20 by 20. This is earnestly recommended, as it will be found a great saving of time. But if it be not thought advisable, he should at least be perfectly familiar with it as far as 12 by 12; and care should be taken that he know it as well in one order of the factors as in another, that 9 times 7, for instance, should come as readily as 7 times 9. When it is well learned, the student should be exercised in multiplying by each of the digits separately, and afterward by larger numbers. Care should be taken that he do not lose the real value of the numbers. This may be done by some exercises of this kind:

Multiply 439
By   37
———
3073
1317
———
16243

Say 7 times 9 are 63; set down 3 and carry 6 tens: 7 times 3 tens are 21 tens, to which add 6 tens, and you have 27 tens; set down 7 and carry 200, &c.; in the next line, 30 times 9 are 270; set down 7 in the ten's place, and carry 200, &c.

Much time may be saved by abbreviated modes of multiplying, some of which are the following: to multiply by 5, consider the multiplicand to be multiplied by 10, by annexing 0, and divide it by 2. To multiply by 9, consider the multiplicand as multiplied by 10, by annexing 0, and, as this is once too many, subtract the multiplicand from it, thus:

$$\begin{array}{r} 9245 \\ 9 \\ \hline 83205 \end{array}$$

5 from 0, 4 from the 4 which would be left, 2 from 4, &c.

To multiply by 11, suppose the operation to be performed as in No. 1, and so exhibit it on the blackboard, and explain No. 2 as if No. 1 were before you, thus:

No. 1.
$$\begin{array}{r} 426{,}389 \\ 11 \\ \hline 426{,}389 \\ 4{,}263{,}89 \\ \hline 4{,}690{,}279 \end{array}$$

No. 2.
$$\begin{array}{r} 426{,}389 \\ 11 \\ \hline 4{,}690{,}279 \end{array}$$

9 are 9; 9 and 8 are 17; 1 added to 3 are 4 and 8 are 12; 1 and 6 are 7 and 3 are 10, &c. That is, first set down the figure on the right, then add each figure to the one next it on the left, and lastly set down the last figure on the left by itself.

To multiply by any number between 12 and 20: multiply by the units' figure of the multiplier, continually adding in the next right-hand figure of the multiplicand, and on the left setting down the highest figure of the multiplicand, increased by what was to be carried.

To multiply by 25, conceive two zeros, 00, to be added to the multiplicand, and divide by 4.

DIVISION.—After the pupil has become familiar with division by one or more numbers, he should be taught the Italian method, as follows. In this, as in all cases of long division, the divisor, as well as the quotient, should be placed on the *right* of the dividend.

ARITHMETIC.

```
17589|39
  198 |451
   39|
```

Having found that 39 are contained 4 times in 175, say 4 times 9 are 36, which cannot be taken from 5, but, taken from 45, leave 9; then 4 times 3 are 12, which, taken from the 13 which remain of the 17 after 4 are borrowed, leave 1. To the 19 bring down 8, and proceed as before.

The following abbreviations are too obvious to need explanation:

"To divide by 5, 15, 35, 45, or 55, multiply by 2 and divide by twice 5, &c. To divide by 75, 175, 275, multiply by 4 and divide by four times the number. To divide by 125, 375, 625, 875, 1125, or 1375, multiply by 8 and divide by 8 times the number, or 1, 3, 5, 7, 9, and 11 thousand.

By reversing these processes we obtain modes of abbreviating multiplication, thus:

"To multiply by 175, multiply by 700 and divide by 4, &c."

Division of decimals should be explained in connexion with that by whole numbers. To the student familiar with Colburn's First Lessons, the matter is perfectly simple and easy. Suppose 24 are to be divided by 8. If both are whole numbers, the quotient is at once seen to be the whole number 3. But suppose 2·4 are to be divided by 8. An eighth part of 24 tenths is 3 tenths. The quotient is therefore ·3; or a third part of 24 tenths is 8 tenths, or ·8. Suppose the dividend to be ·24; then an eighth part of 24 hundredths is 3 hundredths, or ·03, and a third part of 24 hundredths is 8 hundredths—that is ·24÷3=·08. Lastly, suppose 24 are to be divided by ·8: 24 are 240 tenths, and 8 tenths are contained in 240 tenths 30 times. The quotient, therefore, of 24·0 divided by ·8 is 30. A few explanations of this kind on the blackboard would be sufficient to show that the principles of division of decimals are identical with those for division of whole numbers, and that the only difficulty is the place of the decimal point.

FRACTIONS.—All the difficulties of managing fractions vanish before the processes of Colburn's First Lessons. If the student be familiar with these, therefore, he has only to refer to the section in which they are contained, and to perform on the blackboard or slate the processes which he has been in the habit of performing mentally. If he were required, for example, to multiply one fraction by another, he would only have to recall the mental process of finding $\frac{3}{5}$ths of $\frac{4}{7}$ths, and work it out on the slate or blackboard: $\frac{1}{5}$th of $\frac{1}{7}$th is $\frac{1}{35}$th, $\frac{1}{5}$th of $\frac{4}{7}$ths is $\frac{4}{35}$ths, and therefore $\frac{3}{5}$ths of $\frac{4}{7}$ths are $\frac{12}{35}$ths. This may then be represented on the blackboard thus: $\frac{3}{5} \times \frac{4}{7} = \frac{12}{35}$; and he may be made to observe that he has multiplied the numerators for a new numerator, and the denominators for a new denominator. In this manner he will find that all the rules or principles of fractions are contained in the last three sections of the " First Lessons."

In reducing a fraction to its lowest terms, the learner will be often much assisted by the following facts, which should therefore be pointed out to him, with the reason:

Every even number is divisible by 2.

Every number whose two right-hand figures are divisible by 4 or by 25, is itself divisible by 4 or by 25; because both these numbers will divide *one* hundred without a remainder, and therefore any number of hundreds.

Every number whose three right-hand figures are divisible by 8 or by 125, is itself divisible by 8 or by 125; because, as *one* thousand is divisible by these numbers, any number of thousands must be so likewise.

Every number ending in 0 or 5 is divisible by 5.

Every number, the sum of whose significant figures is divisible by 3 or by 9, is itself divisible by 3 or by 9; because, as 10, 100, 1000, &c., are equal to 9, 99, 999, &c., and 1 over, so 3, 4, or any other number of 10s, 100s, &c., are equal to 3, 4, or any number of 9s, 99s, &c., with 3, 4, &c., over.

The process of multiplying a series of fractions may often be much shortened by cancelling such factors as are at the same time in the numerator and denominator, or above and below the line; since, if a number is first multiplied and then divided by the same factor, its value remains the same: thus, in the question, What is the value of $\frac{3}{4}$ths of $\frac{4}{5}$ths of $\frac{5}{6}$ths of $\frac{6}{7}$ths of $\frac{7}{8}$ths? we cancel first,

$$\frac{3}{\cancel{4}} \times \frac{\cancel{4}}{\cancel{5}} \times \frac{\cancel{5}}{\cancel{6}} \times \frac{\cancel{6}}{\cancel{7}} \times \frac{\cancel{7}}{8} = \frac{3}{8},$$

4 above and below the line, because, otherwise, we first divide and then multiply by 4. For the same reason, we cancel, successively, 5, 6, and 7, and find the value of the fraction to be $\frac{3}{8}$ths.

In the same manner, we may sometimes cancel several factors of the same number, when the same factors are found at the same time on the opposite sides of the line. In the case

$$\frac{\cancel{4}}{\cancel{7}} \times \frac{\overset{4}{\cancel{28}}}{\underset{\underset{2}{\cancel{8}}}{\cancel{32}}} \times \frac{3}{5} = \frac{3}{10},$$

we first cancel 4 above, and the factor 4 in 32 below the line, reducing the latter to 8; then 7 below, and the factor 7 in 28 above, reducing the latter to 4; then this 4 above and 4 in the 8 below, reducing this last to 2. There remain 3 above and 2×5 below the line.

This process of cancelling admits of numerous and important applications in the solution of practical questions. Of these I shall give various instances hereafter.

Whenever a new principle is to be explained, it should

first be introduced by instances, in numbers so small as to be easily comprehended by the mind of the learner. *Proportion* may be thus explained: ask, How much larger is the number 4 than 2? Twice as large. How much larger is the number 8 than 4? Twice as large. Then you see that 4 is as much larger than 2 as 8 is than 4. These four numbers form what is called a proportion. They may be written thus: $2:4::4:8$; and when so written, may be read, 2 is to 4 as 4 is to 8; or, 2 is as much smaller than 4 as 4 is than 8. Or they may be written thus: $2:4=4:8$, and read as before. In each case, these numbers so arranged form a *proportion*. So $3:5=9:15$. What four numbers can you find which will form a proportion? (The class should be exercised in forming proportions, until the word and the thing expressed by it are perfectly familiar. The explanation may then proceed.) When one number is twice as large as another, as 4 and 2, or 8 and 4, we say that they have the *ratio* of 2 to 1, or that one is $\frac{1}{2}$ of the other. In like manner, when one is three times as large as another, as 6 and 2, we say it has the ratio of 3 to 1, or that one is $\frac{1}{3}$d of the other. What other numbers have the ratio of 3 to 1? What have the ratio of 4 to 1? What have that of 5 to 1? Observe that of any two pairs of the numbers that have the same ratio, you may form a proportion; for example: $2:10=4:20$. Form a proportion of numbers that have the ratio of 4 to 1, 6 to 1, &c., &c. Most numbers have not so simple a ratio to each other: 3 is $\frac{3}{5}$ths of 5, and 5 is $\frac{5}{3}$ds of 3. Form a proportion in which the ratio shall be $\frac{3}{5}$ths. $3:5=9:15$. Another in which the ratio shall be $\frac{4}{9}$ths. $4:9=12:27$, &c. The four numbers which form a proportion are called the *terms* of the proportion; the first and last are called the *extremes*, and the second and third are called the middle terms, or the *means*. Now examine all the proportions that you have formed, or can form, and you will find that *the product of the extremes is always equal to the product of the means* This is called the rule of proportion.

By means of this rule, we may always find any one term of a proportion when the other three are known. "For, if one of the *means* be wanting, we have only to take the product of the extremes, and, as that is equal to the product of the means, if we divide by the given mean, the quotient will be the other. In like manner, if one of the *extremes* be wanting, it can be found by dividing the product of the means by the given extreme. Thus, in the two following proportions, in which x stands for the unknown number:

No. 1. $4:6=x:18$.   No. 2. $x:4=3:6$.

"1. The product of the extremes $4 \times 18 = 72$, which, being also the product of the means, dividing by the given mean 6, will give the other 12, which here is represented by x.

"2. The product of the means $4 \times 3 = 12$, divided by the extreme 6, gives the other, 2.

"It appears, from the above, that it is of no consequence which term of the proportion is wanting. If any three are given, the fourth can be found. But, as it will be more *convenient* for the student always to place the unknown term last, we shall regularly pursue that course."

Most practical questions are capable of solution by the rule of proportion, which is the foundation of what is called the *Rule of Three*.

"1.* If a piece of cloth, 4 yards long, cost 12 dollars, *what will be the cost* of a piece of the same cloth 7 yards long?

"Our first business is to ascertain what it is that is wanted, which will be known *from the words asking the question.* In the above, we know it to be *money*, because the question is, 'what will be the cost?' Therefore, 12 dollars is one of the terms of the imperfect ratio. Accordingly, we write

* These questions are taken from Adams's **New Arithmetic**

it thus : 12 : *x* ; the *x* representing the unknown number. The other ratio is one of *yards*, and the numbers are 4 and 7. To know in what *order* to place them, we read the question, and say, *More* or *less ?* As 7 yards will evidently cost more than 4, the answer is, *More.* Having thus ascertained that the consequent *x* is more than 12, the other ratio must be placed in the same order, that is, making its largest term the consequent :

$$4 : 7 = 12 : x.$$

" We might now proceed to take the product of the means 7×12, and dividing by the given extreme 4, would show the amount of the other, represented by *x* ; but as this, and almost all other questions, can readily be abbreviated, it will be proper to examine the proportion more particularly with that view. At a glance, then, it will be perceived that the 7 and 12 are factors, according to the rule, and 4 a divisor." But as, when there are the same factors in the multipliers and the divisors, the result is the same if we cancel the equal factors in both, " it appears that, if we divide 4 and 12 by 4, we shall have the same proportion,

$$1 : 7 = 3 : x,$$

in which *x*, the answer, is seen, by inspection, to be **21**."

" 2. At $54 for 9 barrels of flour, *how many barrels* may be purchased for $186 ? (*More* or *less ?*)

$$54 : 186 = 9 : x$$

Dividing by 9, $6 : 186 = 1 : x$

"   " 6, $1 : 31 = 1 : x = 31$, by inspection.

" Many of these questions may be still farther shortened by abbreviating, mentally, while first stating them. Thus ·

" 3. If three men perform a certain piece of work in 10 days, *how long* will it take 6 men to do the same ?

Dividing by 3, $2 : 1 = 10 : x = 5$, by inspection.

" FELLOWSHIP.—4. Two men own a ticket ; the first owns $\frac{1}{4}$th, the second $\frac{3}{4}$ths of it. The ticket draws a prize of **$40** What is each man's share ?

First man, 1 fourth.
Second man, 3 fourths.
$$\overline{4}$$

First man's proportion, $4 : 1 = 40 : x = 10$, by inspection.
Second "   " $4 : 3 = 40 : x$
Dividing by 4, $1 : 3 = 10 : x = 30$ "   "
$$\overline{40}, \text{ proof.}$$

"5. Two persons have a joint stock in trade. A puts in $250, and B $350; they gain $400. What is each man's share?

A.'s stock, 250
B.'s   "   350
$$\overline{600}$$

Dividing by 200, mentally,

$3 : 250 = 2 : x =$ evidently $\frac{1}{3}$d of $500 = \$166\frac{2}{3}$ds.
$3 : 350 = 2 : x = \frac{1}{3}$d of $700 = \$233\frac{1}{3}$d.
$$\text{Proof, } \overline{\$400}$$

"FRACTIONS.—6. If $\frac{11}{30}$ths lb. of sugar cost $\frac{7}{15}$ths of a shilling, what will $\frac{33}{43}$ds of a lb. cost?

$$\frac{11}{30} : \frac{33}{43} = \frac{7}{15} : \frac{x}{x}.$$

By reversing our divisor, $\frac{11}{30}$, the whole proportion is changed into *multiplication of fractions*.

Reversing, $$\frac{30}{11} \times \frac{33}{43} \times \frac{7}{15} = \frac{x}{x}.$$

Dividing by 11 and by 15, $\frac{2}{1} \times \frac{3}{43} \times \frac{7}{1} = \frac{42}{43}$ of a shilling.

"*Every* question is not susceptible of such abbreviations; but a vast majority may be thus considerably shortened, and a large number entirely so, as above, so as to require no multiplication. The pupil should be encouraged even still farther to shorten such questions, by resolving all the abbreviating processes into one, mentally, while stating the question. Such a habit is easily acquired. Children of both sexes, under nine years of age, have solved questions like the above without writing them down at all, merely by inspecting the book. Where questions cannot be sufficiently abbreviated to be solved by inspection, recourse must be had to the rule, *Product of means=product of extremes.*

"COMPOUND PROPORTION.—Proportion is said to be compound when the ratio of the unknown number is not equal to another given ratio, but is compounded of *several* ratios. Take, for instance, the following question:

"7. If a man travel 273 miles in 13 days, travelling only 7 hours in a day, *how many miles* will he travel in 12 days, travelling ten hours in a day?

"Here it will be perceived that the question, *How many miles?* depends neither entirely on the number of days, nor on the number of hours travelled in each day, but is influenced by both. It might be resolved into two questions of simple proportion, but it is more easily and simply treated as one of compound proportion, solved, however, on the same principles.

$$\begin{array}{l}\text{Days,}\\ \text{Hours,}\end{array} \left.\begin{array}{l}13:12\\ 7:10\end{array}\right\} \overset{\text{Miles. Miles.}}{273:x.}$$

Dividing 273 by 13 and by 7, or by their product, 91,

$$\left.\begin{array}{l}1:12\\ 1:10\end{array}\right\} 3:x=360,\text{ by inspection.}$$

"8. If 6 men build a wall 20 feet long, 6 feet high, and 4 feet thick, in 16 days, *in what time* will 24 men build one 200 feet long, 8 feet high, and 6 feet thick?

$$\left.\begin{array}{l}24:6\\ 20:200\\ 6:8\\ 4:6\end{array}\right\} 16:x. \quad \text{Contracting,} \left.\begin{array}{l}\cancel{3}\ \cancel{24}:\cancel{6}\ 2\\ \cancel{20}:\cancel{200}\ 10\\ \cancel{6}:\cancel{8}\\ \cancel{4}:\cancel{6}\end{array}\right\} \left.\begin{array}{l}4\\ \cancel{16}:x=80,\\ \text{by inspect.}\end{array}\right.$$

"This was done by dividing 24 and 8 by 8; 20 and 200 by 20; 3 and 6 (first ratio) by 3; 6 and 6 by 6; 4 and 16 by 4. It is hardly necessary to observe, that in these abbreviations all the 1s have been omitted, as the multiplying or dividing by that number can produce no change.

"There being a greater variety of numbers in compound

proportion, it admits of contractions more frequently than simple proportion, though there may be *some* questions which are not susceptible of any. When multiplication *has* to be performed, it should be recollected that the left-hand extreme and the first mean consist of several numbers, the product of which being severally taken, we proceed as in simple proportion. The teacher should be careful to impress on his pupils the necessity of asking the question, *More or less?* previously to the writing down of *every ratio*.

" 9. If $100 gain $6 in one year, what will $400 gain in 9 months?

$$\left.\begin{array}{l} 100:400 \\ 12:9 \end{array}\right\} 6:x. \quad \text{Dividing by 100,} \left.\begin{array}{l} 1:2 \\ 1:9 \end{array}\right\} 1:x=18.$$

" INTEREST.—Let the subject of interest be explained from any of the popular books on Arithmetic; adding, the words *per cent.*, *per ann.*, are either expressed or understood, in every question respecting interest, immediately after the rate. *Per cent.* means *for every hundred.* *Per ann.* means *for every year.* When the rate is not expressed, *six* is always understood.

" For instance, in the following question, What is the interest of $11.04 for 1 year, at 3 per cent.? the words *per annum* are understood. And in the question, What is the interest of $150 for 16 days? the words *at 6 per cent. per ann.* are understood, and must be supplied in stating the question. From the want of a clear understanding of the terms employed, many pupils find the subject of interest exceedingly difficult. Let the teacher repeatedly question his class, till he is sure they are thoroughly understood.

" *Case I.*—Principal, time, and rate, given, to find the interest or amount.

" 10. What is the interest of $11.04 for 1 year, at 3 per cent.?

$$\left.\begin{array}{l} 100:11.04 \\ 1\text{ yr.}:1\text{ yr.} \end{array}\right\} 3:x.$$

Dividing by 100, $\left.\begin{array}{l} 1:.1104 \\ 1:1 \end{array}\right\} 3:x=.3312$, by inspection.

"11. What is the *interest* of $150 for 16 days?

$$\left.\begin{array}{l}100:150\\360:\ 16\end{array}\right\}6:x. \quad \text{Divide by 100,} \left\{\begin{array}{l}1:.15\\6:16\end{array}\right\}1:x.$$

Divide by 6; that is, the upper by 3, the lower by 2.

$$\left.\begin{array}{l}1:.05\\1:\ 8\end{array}\right\}x=.4,\text{ by inspection.}$$

"*Case II.*—The time, rate per cent., and amount, given, to find the principal.

"12. What *sum* of money, put at interest at 6 per cent., will *amount* to $61.02 in 1 year and 4 months?

"Here, as we have only one amount given, we must find another, at the same rate and time, to complete the ratio. Let us find the amount of $100.

$$\left.\begin{array}{l}100:100\\12:16\end{array}\right\}6:x.$$

Divide by 100 and 12, $\left\{\begin{array}{l}1:1\\1:8\end{array}\right\}$ 1 : $x=$8, interest.
$$\underline{100}\text{, principal.}$$
$$\$108\text{, amount.}$$

Amt.   Amt.   Princ.
108 : 61.02 = 100 : x.

Removing the dot, viz., multiplying by 100, and dividing by 108, gives $x=$ $56.50."

"*Case III.*—Time, rate, and interest given, to find the principal.

"13. What sum of money, put at interest 16 months, will gain $10.50 at 6 per cent.?

$$\left.\begin{array}{l}6:10.50\\16:12\end{array}\right\}100:x.$$

Divide by 12, and remove the dot, $\left\{\begin{array}{l}1:1050\\8:1\end{array}\right\}$ 1 : $x=$131.25, by inspect'n."

"*Case IV.*—Principal, interest, and time given, to find the rate per cent.

"14. If I pay $3.78 interest for the use of $36 for 18 months, what is the rate per cent.?

$$\left.\begin{array}{l}\cancel{36}:\cancel{100}\\\cancel{18}:\cancel{12}\end{array}\right\}\cancel{3.78}:x=7.$$

"Here we suppress the dot and strike out 100; divide 36 and 12 by 12; and divide 378 by $3\times 18 = 54$.

"*Case V.*—Principal, rate per cent., and interest, given, to find the time.

"15. The interest on a note of $36, at 7 per cent., was $3.78. What was the time?

$$\left.\begin{array}{r}\cancel{\$}\\ \cancel{36}:\cancel{100}\\ 7:\$.\cancel{78}\\ 18\end{array}\right\} \cancel{12}:x=18 \text{ months.}$$

"A very few questions, worked out on the blackboard by an intelligent teacher, will give his pupils a practical knowledge of the whole system of arithmetic, which could not be easily attained by any other means; and they will be able to perform such questions as the above, after a little practice, with still fewer figures."

Most of the questions just solved by the Rule of Three, admit of easy solution by Mental Arithmetic; and all of them may be readily solved by the method of fractions, which is the shape which the mental processes of Colburn's First Lessons take, when wrought out on the slate. The teacher should make himself familiarly acquainted with all these methods. He may then adopt in teaching whichever he finds best suited to his pupils, or whichever he prefers; or he may communicate all to his classes, and enable them, in the solution of each problem, to apply such of the methods as is best adapted to its particular conditions. The solutions are given below. The questions are referred to by their numbers.

1. If a piece 4 yards long cost 12 dollars, one yard will cost one fourth of 12, or 3, and 7 yards will cost 7 times 3 dollars, or 21 : indicated thus, $\frac{12\times 7}{4} =$ (by cancelling the factor 4 above and below the line) $\frac{3\times 7}{1} = 21$.

2. If 9 bbls. cost $54, 1 will cost one ninth of 54, or $6,

and for $186 may be purchased as many bbls. as 6 are contained times in 186, which is 31.

$$\frac{186 \times \cancel{9}}{\underset{6}{\cancel{54}}} = 31.$$

3. If 3 men perform the work in 10 days, it will take 6 men half as long, or 5 days.

4. One fourth of 40 is 10, three fourths, 30.

5. A's and B's stocks together are $600. They gain $400. Each dollar gains $\frac{400}{600}$ths or $\frac{4}{6}$ths or $\frac{2}{3}$ds of 1 dollar. 250 gain 250 times $\frac{2}{3} = \frac{500}{3} = \$166\frac{2}{3}$. 350 gain 350 times $\frac{2}{3} = \frac{700}{3} = \$233\frac{1}{3}$.

The 6th has a solution essentially the same by both methods.

7. If a man travel 273 miles in 13 days, at 7 hours a day, in 1 day he will travel $\frac{1}{13}$th of 273, or 21, and in 1 hour $\frac{1}{7}$th of 21, or 3 miles. In 10 hours he will travel 10 times 3, or 30 miles; and in 12 days, 12 times 30, or 360 miles. This may be indicated thus, placing the numbers to be divided by, *below*, and those to be multiplied by, *above* the line, and indicating the successive steps by the letters taken alphabetically:

$$\frac{a \overset{f\ \cancel{21}\ g\ 3}{\cancel{273}} \times d\ 10 \times e\ 12}{b\ \cancel{13} \times c\ \cancel{7}} = 360.$$

In every case, the numbers used to divide by should be placed below the line, and those used to multiply by, above it.

8. If 6 men build such a wall in (*a*) 16 days, 1 man will require (*b*) 6 times as long, or 96 days, and (*c*) 24 men will do it in $\frac{1}{24}$th part of the time, or 4 days. If the wall were 1 foot thick, it would require (*d*) $\frac{1}{4}$th part of that time, or 1 day to build it; if it were but 1 foot long, it would require

but (e) $\frac{1}{20}$th part of that time to build it; and if 1 foot only high, (f) $\frac{1}{8}$th part of *that* time, namely, $\frac{1}{120}$th of 1 day. But as it is to be (g) 6 feet thick, it will require $\frac{6}{120}$ths, or $\frac{1}{20}$th; as it is to be 8 feet high, it will require (h) $\frac{8}{20}$ths; and as it is to be 200 feet long, it will require (i) 200 times $\frac{8}{20}$ths, or 80 days. This process may be represented thus, and the cancelling be performed afterward.

$$\frac{a\cancel{1}\cancel{6} \times b\cancel{6} \times g\cancel{6} \times h8 \times i\cancel{2}\cancel{0}\cancel{0}}{c\cancel{2}\cancel{4} \times d\cancel{4} \times e\cancel{2}\cancel{0} \times f\cancel{6}}\overset{m10}{}=80,$$ by cancelling 6 in f and g, 6 in b and c, 16 in a, and in d and k, and 20 in e and i.

9. If $100 gain $6 in one year, $400 will gain 4×6, or $24, in 1 year, and three fourths as much, or $18, in 9 months.

$$\frac{6 \times \cancel{400} \times 3}{\cancel{100} \times \cancel{4}}=18.$$

10. Interest at 3 per cent. is $\frac{3}{100}$ths of the principal, therefore $\frac{11.04\times 3}{100}=.3312$ is the interest of $11.04. Here 11.04 is divided by 100, by removing the decimal point two places to the left.

11. If the interest is 6 per cent. for 1 year, or 12 months, it is 1 per cent. for 2 months, or 60 days: that is, for $150, the interest is $1.50 for 60 days. For 12 days it is one fifth of that, or .30, and for 4 days, one third of that, or .10; for 16 days it is therefore $.30 + .10 = .40$.

$$\begin{array}{r|l} 5 & 1.50 \\ \hline 3 & .30 \\ & 10 \\ \hline & .40 \end{array}$$

12. At 6 per cent., $100 will amount in 1 year and 4 months to $108: $61.02 is, therefore, $\frac{100}{108}$ths of the sum to be put on interest.

$$\frac{61.02 \times 100}{108}=56.50.$$

Multiply by 100 by removing the dot two places to the right.

13. In 16 months, or 1 year and 1 third, the interest of $100 will amount to $8. The sum ought, therefore, to be $\frac{100}{8}$ths of $10.50.

$$\frac{10.50 \times 100}{8} = \$131.25.$$

14. As $3.78 is the interest for 18 months, two thirds of that sum, $2.52, must be the interest for 12 months, or 1 year; and as 6 per cent. is six dollars on a hundred, so the rate per cent. here must be 2.52 on 36., or $\frac{2.52}{36.}$ths, which, reduced to a whole number or decimal, must give the rate per cent.

$$\frac{\overset{7}{\cancel{\$3.78}} \times \cancel{2}}{\cancel{\$36.} \times \cancel{3}} = .07, \text{ or } 7 \text{ per cent.}$$

15. The interest on $36, at 7 per cent., for 1 year, is $2.52; therefore the time is $\frac{378}{252}$ds of 1 year.

$$\frac{378}{252} = \text{(cancelling 9)} \ \frac{42}{28} = \text{(cancelling 14)} \ \frac{3}{2} = 1\tfrac{1}{2} \text{ year.}$$

If the teacher wish to communicate intelligibly a knowledge of the roots, and of progression, he may give, in a few lessons on the blackboard, enough of Algebra to enable his pupils to comprehend them. Sherwin's or Colburn's Algebra will furnish the means.

SECTION VII. ACCOUNTS.

CONNECTED with Arithmetic, and the great practical end for which it should be studied, is the knowledge of Accounts. This has been greatly neglected. It seems almost absurd to spend so much time as is usually devoted to Arithmetic, and especially to the subject of Interest, in preparation for the management of Accounts, and yet not to teach the very thing for which all this preparation is made. Many parts of Arithmetic commonly taught at school are, to most persons, matters of mere curiosity. It is very well to learn them, if there be time enough, but to omit them would be no serious loss. While a knowledge of Accounts is necessary to every person who is likely ever to have property of his own, or the management of the property of another.

It is necessary to thrift. The merchant or dealer, on a large or small scale, cannot tell definitely whether the business he is engaged in is productive or not, unless he keeps an exact account of his payments and receipts. The farmer cannot be sure how much more or less productive one branch of husbandry is than another, without an account of the outlay and income of both.

It is necessary to economy. The minister, or clerk, or teacher on a salary, the head of a family with a limited income, or the mechanic with a fixed rate of wages, cannot tell what he can or ought to afford, what expenses he may allow, and what he must deny himself, unless he knows, from month to month, what is his income and what are his expenses.

It is necessary to justice. Whoever deals on credit, even for a limited period, whoever receives or parts with money, goods, labour, or time, for which an equivalent is to be given or received hereafter, must keep an exact account with every person with whom he deals, or have a memory from which no particular of time, place, quantity, or value can be erased, or he will necessarily run the risk of doing injustice to himself or his neighbour. If I have given my note or my promise to pay, I am bound to make timely provision beforehand for the resumption of my note and the redemption of my promise. This I *must do;* and this I cannot do with absolute certainty, unless I know precisely how much I may lay aside for the purpose each week or month, until the day of payment comes. If I look upon what I have as the gift of God, and myself as his steward, and therefore bound to devote what I can spare from the claims of family, kindred, and friends, to the relief of the sufferings, the wants, or the ignorance of His children, I cannot, without exactness in my accounts, be sure that I am opening my hand in charity without a violation of the more imperative demands of justice.

Every one, therefore, should be taught accounts; and the teacher should be prepared to explain such modes of keeping them as are best suited to the probable future condition of his pupils. This is not the place for a system of Book-keeping: it may be sufficient to say, that every person, male and female, should be taught how to keep personal accounts, and an account of the expenses of a family; that, in addition to these, the future farmer should be shown how to keep accounts of a field or a particular crop, as well as of his whole operations; that the mechanic should be taught to keep an account of the expenses and income of his shop or trade; and the future merchant or trader should be taught book-keeping by double entry.

Personal accounts may be taught on the blackboard to a class or the whole school at once. Care should be taken to explain familiarly what is meant by Dr. and Cr.; a specimen like the following should be given, and then each pupil be required, according to his capacity, to form similar accounts on his slate, and afterward on paper.

Dr. John Thompson.		Contra Cr.	
1842.		1842.	
May 20. To cash,	$1 50	May 24. By 1 day's labour,	$1 25
21. To 2 bushels corn,	1 30	25. By 1 day's labour,	1 25
23. To 3 yds. br'dcloth,	6 60	27. By ½ ton hay,	4 00
		28. By cash to balance,	2 90
	$9 40		$9 40

SPECIMEN OF A FARMER'S FIELD ACCOUNT.

Dr. The Five-acre Lot.		Contra Cr.	
1842.		1842.	
Apr. 11. To 3 days' ploughing,	$6 00	Oct. 21, By 74 bushels wheat,	$74 00
12, 13. To 30 loads of manure,	30 00	By straw,	4 00
14. To 1½ days' harrowing,	3 00	By feeding,	5 00
To 5 bush. seed wh.,	5 50		
Aug. To 3 days' reaping,	4 50		
To binding & carting,	4 00		
Sept. To threshing,	6 00		
To interest on land,	5 00		
To balance gain,	19 00		
	$83 00		$83 00

SECTION VIII. GEOGRAPHY.

"To the reading of history, chronology and geography are absolutely necessary."—LOCKE.

THE first lesson in Geography should be, to set the class to draw a plan, as well as they can, of the schoolroom. This every one will do readily who has been encouraged to use his slate, and many a child of eight or ten years will do it accurately, and even beautifully. It is only *necessary* that it should be done. Then the cardinal points, in reference to the plan, should be shown. "This side, with the window, into which the sun shines in the morning, is the East side; the opposite one is the West side. This side, where the sun shines straight in at noon, is the South side; and the opposite side, where the master's desk is, is North. Let this north side be at the top of the plan. Now this is a map of the room. I have directed you all to have the north side at the top of your map, that all may be alike, and you may always know, when you look at it, which is north." Any other explanations may be made that are necessary; as, that the seats in the northeast corner of the room are to be represented towards the top and towards the right side of the plan, &c.

The next lesson may be a plan of the lot on which the schoolhouse stands, with a part of the road running near it, care being taken, now and at all times, to represent the north side by the top of the plan. The fences may be represented by lines, and trees and other objects may be drawn, as well as they can draw them, in the places they occupy.

For a third lesson, the teachers may draw on the blackboard a plan or map of the vicinity of the schoolhouse, with the roads for a quarter of a mile in each direction, and houses, streams, or any other remarkable object. This the class may copy.

If there be a map of the town accessible, the next lesson should be an explanation of that; showing how all the roads, buildings, forests, hills, and other objects with which the pupils are acquainted, are represented, and giving an idea of distance.

The next step should be, if possible, a map of the county, showing how much less space the town now necessarily occupies, and what towns are north, east, &c., from it. The next step should be a map of the state; and thence the progress should be to that of the country, of the continent, and the world as represented on a globe.

It may not always be possible to take this course. If not, the nearest approach to it possible should be made. It is the natural method,—from the known and familiar, to the unknown. It is of the utmost importance that the first ideas and impressions should be correct and clear. This will throw light upon every future step, and do more than anything else to render the study intelligible and delightful. I tried a similar method with one of my children with complete success. When I had taken him, then four or five years old and just able to read, to walk with me in the streets of Boston, I pointed out, at our return, on a map of the city, our path, the streets we had passed through, and the course we had taken. This was done after walks to all parts of the town. I then took him with me in my drives; first to Brookline on one side of the town, and, successively, to Cambridge on another side, and to Chelsea Beach on a third; pointing out each time, on our return, upon a map of Boston and its vicinity, the roads we had taken and the places we had visited. He afterward accompanied me on a journey to Maine, and I showed him, as before, on a map of New-England, the road and course we had taken, the towns we had passed through, and the rivers we had crossed. The same was done after a journey to the western part of Massachusetts. He in this way obtained, from the beginning, correct impressions of the objects which maps represent. He has always been, up to the present time, extremely fond of maps, pores over them for hours for his amusement, and always chooses to have one open before him as he reads history, which is one of his favourite occupations. It will rarely happen that a teacher of a school can have so favourable opportunities for his pupils. But a parent who has the happiness of teaching his own children, may often have.

When correct impressions have been given of the objects represented by maps, the geography of the state may be learned. Great care should be taken to give an idea of the motion of the earth on its axis, and thence of longitude and latitude, as there is nothing in geography of which children are so apt to get false ideas. For this purpose, a globe should be considered an essential part of the apparatus of a school. Much time is usually spent, to little purpose, in learning the names of unknown, and, therefore, speedily-forgotten places; and still more in studying and trying to remember the climate, soil, cities, &c., of countries. It is nearly impossible for a child to remember, by an absolute effort, that with which he has no associations. It should, then, be the object of the teacher to connect what is learned with what is already known, and to give agreeable associations to be connected with things unknown.

The learner should from the beginning, if possible, be set to copy the maps he is studying. This act impresses on the mind the outlines, boundaries, rivers, hills, lakes, and position of towns, better than any other exercise, and it is far more agreeable to the learner. Out of a large number of pupils who have been taught in this way, not one has been found incapable of making pretty correct representations, not one who did not take great pleasure in the exercise, and not one who did not improve in it very rapidly. When each one of a class has drawn a map without any names, a satisfactory examination as to how much they know of the objects represented, may be made in a very short time. This may be conducted either individually, each looking at his own map, or by means of the excellent out line maps of Mather, prepared for this purpose.

For each lesson in Geography the teacher should make special preparation. If he will do this, he may always render the exercise very interesting, and he may make it the vehicle of a great deal of instruction in history, morals, and civilization. Suppose, to give an instance or two, the lesson included Iceland. He may take the occasion to speak of its extraordinary natural features—a small land, and yet traversed by almost impassable mountains and deserts; of its icebergs, and of the immense eruptions of its volcanoes. He may dwell upon that phenomenon in the history of mankind, that while learning hardly dared to lift her head in the rest of Europe, she had her home in the ice-encircled and half-subterranean huts of the Icelanders; that they had poets and historians when the names poet and historian were hardly elsewhere known; and he may tell of its colonization by the sea-kings, its early history, and the state of things at that time in the north of Europe. All this he may get by an evening's reading of the interesting volume on Iceland, which forms the 155th No. of the School District Library.

If the lesson is upon Greece,* he may give, in a few words, some idea of the remarkable people who occupied that country in ancient times, the fathers of the arts, sciences, and literature, the remarkable institutions, the immense and beautiful structures, the perfect language, the famous men.

In the Geography of New-England, he may speak of the early acts of the Revolution at Lexington or Charlestown, and the earlier events at Plymouth or Mount Hope; on New-York, of Ticonderoga, West Point, &c. In speaking of our early history or late, he should not fail to speak a word for humanity in pointing out the cruelty and injustice of our ancestors and their descendants to the present day towards the original possessors of the soil.

There is scarcely anything which a studious person picks up in voyages and travels, histories, books of geology and natural history,† which may not be naturally introduced to give variety and interest to the lessons in geography. After he has talked himself, he should question his pupils upon what he has said, both to quicken their attention and to get access to their understanding. The lessons may be varied by sometimes setting the class to find out from what parts of the world come the various articles employed for food, dress, furniture, and the several arts; making an imaginary voyage round the world or to a particular port, and noting the objects which would present themselves, and the articles which would be found and those which it would be necessary to carry. Another lesson, or

---

* See Goldsmith's Greece, in the 81st No. of School District Library, or the 3d and 4th volumes of Rollin's Ancient History.

† Many curious facts on the subjects of Natural History may be found in that delightful work, White's History of Selborne, School District Library, No. 166.

several, may be given upon the government of different countries; upon their religion, their intelligence, their commerce, and other pursuits. The comparative value of gold and silver, on the one hand, and iron and industry on the other, may be shown by pointing out the fact that there is scarcely an instance in history of a country having grown rich from the possession of mines of what are called the precious metals, and none naturally so sterile as not to have become independent and wealthy, with industry and such resources as iron, coal, and salt. Mexico, Peru, and Old Spain are wretched and poor, with streams of gold and silver flowing into them for hundreds of years; and Scotland, New-England, and Old England, comparatively barren originally, have become rich, and the happy abodes of free and intelligent men, by the industry and energy of their inhabitants acting upon such productions as nothing but skill and slow labour can work out for the necessities and convenience of men

A more difficult exercise than copying maps, and one suited to a higher state of progress, is requiring a class to be prepared to draw a map, from recollection, on the slate or blackboard. In this exercise, which is strongly to be recommended, at its proper time, much allowance must be made for the difference that exists between individuals otherwise equal, as to the power of representing from memory. Unless regard be had to this difference, injustice will be done to the best intentions and efforts.

A method used with great success by Professor Newman at the normal school at Barre, was to call on one of the class to draw an outline of the country on the blackboard. A second was to draw the river courses and lakes; a third the mountains. A fourth mentioned some large place; a fifth gave its position by writing 1 on the blackboard; a sixth named a second place, which a seventh indicated by 2. In this way all the important places were represented by numbers, and the examination of the topography was concluded by calling individuals at random to name the several places so indicated.

SECTION IX. HISTORY.

"Histories make men wise."—BACON.

HISTORY cannot be fully taught at any school. All that can be accomplished in regard to the history of any other country than our own, is to give sketches or pictures of certain important periods or events. The abridgments and compends of history often used, do little more than disgust children with the study. The teacher's object should be to give them such pictures as will win them to it.

Some idea of the most important periods of history might be given in connexion with the lives of certain individuals. Such are the following. After the interesting events recorded in the first chapters of Genesis:

The patriarchal period, as given in the lives of Abraham, Isaac, Jacob, and Joseph, of which a portion only should be read in school. The personal history of Moses, of David, and of Solomon. All these are to be found only in the Old Testament.

The life of Hector and that of Ulysses, as given by Homer, in Pope's Homer. The life of Xerxes.* Pericles.* Alexander of Macedon.†

Romulus and Numa.‡ Brutus, the first consul.‡ Hannibal and Scipio Africanus.‡ Pompey, Cæsar, Cicero.‡ Augustus.‡

The coming of Jesus Christ. Constantine.§ Attila.§ Mohammed.‖ Clovis.¶ Charlemagne.¶ Alfred. Haroun

---

* Goldsmith, 81st No. School District Library, or Plutarch's Lives
† Rev. J. Williams, 32d No. School District Library.   ‡ Goldsmith, 87th No. School District Library, or Plutarch's Lives.   § History of Italy, Family Library, No. 79.   ‖ Bush's Life of Mohammed, Family Library, No. 10, or the History of Arabia, No. 68.   ¶ James. Family Library, No. 60, School District Library, No. 176.

al Raschid. Peter the Hermit.* Richard the Lion-hearted.* Saladin.* William the Conqueror.† Cosmo de Medici. Columbus.‡ Luther.§ Cromwell.‖ William the Third. Peter the Great,¶ and others for later times.

The life of Washington, which may be found, fully enough delineated, in the volumes of Paulding in the School District Library, or with much more of detail in Marshall, will suffice to give an outline of the history of our country immediately previous to and during the Revolution; as the life of Napoleon Bonaparte, also contained in the first series of the School District Library, may give of the French Revolution. But there is no one volume which contains all, or even the greater part of the lives above enumerated. They must be collected from various sources, and the teacher must take pains to prepare such accounts as he can either read, or give in his own language. History, for the use of the young especially, is still to be written. As it now stands, it is occupied, in an absurdly undue proportion, with wars, and the ambition and dissensions of the falsely-called great. What relates to the advancement of society, what shows the progress of the sciences and the useful and the fine arts, and the records of the various stages in the personal liberty, rights, and enjoyments of individual man, must be laboriously gleaned from distant sources.** You will find

---

* See "Chivalry," an interesting work by James, School District Library, No. 26. † For the life of William the Conqueror, and the other characters referred to belonging to English history, see Keightley, School District Library, 102, 3, 4, 5, 6. ‡ Irving; or Belknap, in 146th No. School District Library. § See Luther's Life and Times. ‖ See his life, by Rev. M. Russell, in the 36th and 37th numbers of the School District Library. ¶ See Barrow's life of him, in the 35th No. of the School District Library.

** In order to enable him to understand and explain many things in History and Geography, the teacher should have some acquaintance with political economy. This he may get from Dr. Potter's work on that subject, School District Library, No. 124.

some very interesting periods in the history of science and literature sketched in the Lives of the Philosophers, by Fenelon;* Brewster's Life of Sir Isaac Newton;† in the Martyrs of Science, by the same author;‡ in Franklin's Life;§ and in the lives of Johnson‖ and Goldsmith.¶

History is usually taught by assigning a certain number of pages in some text-book, and requiring the class to answer questions in them. The questions are either prepared and known beforehand to the pupil, or are such as the teacher pleases to ask at the time of recitation. The danger incident to the use of prepared questions is, that the pupil will commit to memory just such a portion of the text-book as furnishes answers. This process gives no exercise to discrimination, judgment, taste, or language. It is a mere exercise of memory. The other mode is apt to be so too. The faithful and ambitious pupil will be tempted to commit the whole lesson to memory, and to answer in the words of the author. To prevent this waste of time, the teacher should encourage his pupils to answer in their own language. He should also ask questions of a general nature, such as, What is the subject of this lesson? or this chapter? State, in a few words, the events recorded in it. What should we think of this measure? What of that character? Questions of right and wrong should be constantly brought up in lessons in history.

As we can teach so little of History at school, one object should be to show how it should be studied; another, as I have already said, to create an interest in the study. It may serve, at the same time, to exercise the attention, the power of orderly arrangement, the moral judgment, and the use of language in narration. To answer these ends, it is best taught without a text-book, the teacher himself

---

* School District Library, No. 156.   † Ibid., No. 27.
‡ Ibid., No. 152.   § Ibid., No. 51.   ‖ Ibid., No. 122.
¶ Ibid., No. 109.

making the whole preparation. The pupils should be furnished with maps, or a large map should be suspended before them by the side of the blackboard. If the pupils have no suitable maps, and that of the teacher be on too small a scale for exhibition to a class, he should draw on the blackboard a magnified outline of the seat of the event

Care should first be taken to give an idea of the remoteness of the event to be described, by tracing a line on the blackboard, to represent two or more years, and showing how long it would be necessarry to draw it to represent the period which has elapsed since the event occurred. The date may be given on the blackboard, and the place may be pointed out on the map, or mentioned, and the pupil allowed to find it for himself. The teacher may then read, or, what is far better, narrate in familiar language, and in the manner of conversation, the event, or series of events, which he intends to make the subject of the lesson. If his pupils are beginners, he should not speak long before asking questions as to what he has been telling. If these are made frequent, the pupil will be encouraged to give his attention to the end. The questions, who? and where? and when? as well as what? should be asked. When the teacher's narrative is finished, he should ask if some one will not undertake to tell the whole story in his own language. Those who have the best talent for narrative will be ready to do this, and, after some little practice, nearly the whole class. Or the teacher may say, "I wish you all to write upon your slates or paper, and bring to me to-morrow, what you can remember of the story I have just told you." Questions should also be asked as to the moral right or wrong of the characters of the actors in the event.

Let not the teacher be discouraged by the slow progress he seems to make. In the usual mode of teaching History, two or three hours are often spent by the pupil out of school, and half an hour, or an hour, at the recitation in school, upon a single lesson of six or eight pages; and, after all, very little is learned except mere facts, and those perhaps indistinct and barren; while in this way, in half an hour, two or three pages at first, and afterward five or six, or even ten, will be learned, and at the same time the power of attention be improved, the moral taste elevated, the power of narration exercised, and the connexion between History, and Chronology and Geography will be shown.

In the introduction to the excellent School History of the United States, by Hall and Baker, are some judicious directions as to teaching History by means of text-books, which are deserving of great attention.

SECTION X. PHYSIOLOGY.

"There is no mystery into which mankind are more curious to pry, than into that of their internal structure; and certainly there is none on earth which so nearly concerns them."—E. JOHNSON.

NEXT in importance to the indispensable arts which are at the base of all instruction, and before Geography and History, is Physiology, the laws of our own constitution. In some form it should be taught in every school. I have already shown how it may be taught in the general lessons. When it can be done, it should be introduced as a regular study. As in importance, so in interest and in the exercise it gives to the observant and reflecting powers, it is second to no other.

There are several good works upon the subject published in this country,—Hayward, Coates, and Andrew Combe. Neither of these is complete. The last seems best suited for study in school, although the first is most elementary. The teacher should have the two; and if he uses one as his class-book, should take the other to help him supply its deficiencies.

Physiology may be taught in the same way as history,

the teacher only having the book and requiring attention, and asking all the necessary questions; or, if there be not time for this, all may have books, and come prepared for examination in an assigned portion. Take care that they learn not words only. Insist upon answers in their own language. In the case of muscles, and bones, and in whatever else it can with perfect delicacy be done, let the learner find what is described in his own body. The great principles should be frequently brought up, and made familiar by daily repetition. If so, they will become an integrant part of the pupil's knowledge; and none is more essential, or more fruitful of beneficial effects.

A useful exercise in composition is an enumeration of the most important principles on a particular part of Physiology, in the learner's own language; or his inferences from one or more; or a more general enumeration of the leading principles of the science.

SECTION XI. COMPOSITION.

"What is this power which puts us in possession of the future,—transports us to all distances,—makes us conceive objects invisible to sense,—introduces us to what is merely possible,—sustains our strength by hope,—extends the narrow sphere of our existence beyond the limits of the present? May it not, by deepening the sources of our sensibility, fertilize the field of our virtue?"—DEGERANDO.

THE modes recommended for teaching reading, spelling, English Grammar, History, and Physiology, all furnish exercises in composition. If those modes be faithfully and fairly tried, there will be little difficulty, to the pupil sufficiently advanced, in the essay or theme as usually required. But, for the benefit of those teachers who are unable or unwilling to depart so far from usual methods as to adopt these, a few observations upon composition will be given, and exercises or steps pointed out which have been inferred from, and have stood the test of experience. 1. Simple sentences are to be written. Several words are given, and the pupils are required to write a sentence so as to bring in one or more of them. Phrases are given for the same purpose, or sentences in which several words are omitted, which the pupil is to supply. 2. Variety of arrangement is taught by arranging a sentence in several different ways, and assigning others for practice. 3. Variety of expression is taught by showing how the participle may be substituted for a conjunction, by changing an active verb into a passive, and the reverse, by the substitution of nearly synonymous words, by circumlocution, and by softened expressions. 4. Compound sentences are reduced to simple ones, and these united into compound ones. 5. Poetical sentences are given, to be expressed in prose. 6. The definition of words may be given in a sentence, and several sentences may be written to show the difference in the meaning of two words. 7. A short story is told, which the pupil must write in his own language. The heads of a story only are given, which the learner is to make into a connected narrative, or to amplify from his own imagination. 8. Objects are assigned, to be described. 9. The figures of speech, tropes, metaphors, allegories, hyperbole, personification, apostrophe, simile, antithesis, climax, &c., are successively explained, and suitable sentences or subjects are suggested, on which they may be exemplified. 10. Simple and compound themes and essays are explained, models are given, and exercises are required. The above is a rapid outline of "Parker's Progressive Exercises in English Composition," a valuable aid, even where the teacher is only disposed to take hints from it.

A very useful exercise in composition, after the pupil can make sentences, is writing abstracts of sermons or lectures. In this, attention, the power of arrangement, and the use of language are exercised, while the thoughts are furnished. It is adapted to one who is almost a beginner, and is at the same time an excellent practice for an accomplished writer.

Descriptions of objects in nature or art, of the mill or the manufactory, the village, a walk in the forest, the rising of the sun, the stillness of night, a storm, a sunny day, a drive, of any object or event which is calculated to interest the feelings or awaken thought, are obvious and suitable exercises. Familiar letters to friends, imaginary ones to the birds or the stars, to characters in history or in distant parts of the earth; journals of occurring events; criticism upon works that have been read; opinions upon subjects that have been discussed in school; upon those suggested by the daily studies;—these will be interesting to children, will be felt to be within their capacity, and will exercise their judgment and their imagination. There are usually several in every school who have a talent for versification, and nearly all may be made to measure syllables and collect rhymes. Such trials should be encouraged, chiefly on account of the greater pleasure they give to the reading of poetry.*

The above are offered as methods of teaching which have been found successful; not as the best possible, but as somewhat better than many of those now in common use. They are all susceptible of improvement, and the attention of all teachers is invited to the subject of improving them.

Whoever examines schools, will see at once that they may be elevated to a much higher rank than they now hold.

* It may be asked why I say nothing in regard to the study of Logic and Metaphysics, so common in many schools: I answer, in the words of Milton, that "I deem it to be an old error of universities" (and it would be a much greater in schools) "not yet well recovered from the scholastic grossness of barbarous ages, that, instead of beginning with arts most easy, they present their young unmatriculated novices at first coming with the most intellective abstractions of Logic and Metaphysics."

By the introduction of improved methods of teaching; by the employment of qualified and devoted teachers, especially, of highly qualified and endowed female teachers for the lower schools; by a better selection of studies and the omission of those which have hitherto occupied much time to little purpose; by a greater interest on the part of the community, and the consequent improvement of the schoolhouses and the apparatus of teaching, all the schools in the state may be made much better than the best at present are. I see no reason why the public schools should not be better than any private now are; why the children of the great body of the people of the state should not have as good an education as the most favoured have. This may be done. The schools may all be improved. Step by step, they may rise higher than any one now dreams.

CHAPTER IV.

SECTION I. GOVERNMENT.

"The construction of a system of education cannot be a creative, but an imitative process, which must be founded only on the lessons of experience. Here, as in the cultivation of every other science, it is not by the exercise of a sublime and speculative ingenuity that man arrives at truth, but it is by letting himself down to simple observation;—in short, by following only the lights of observation and induction."—SPURZHEIM.

THE art of governing a school naturally divides itself into, 1. The preservation of order; 2. The prevention of wrong; 3. Incitement to study.

Towards the accomplishment of all these the first requisite is *to render your school pleasant*. How is this to be done?

There are some mistakes upon this point, which must be corrected. The unpleasantness of a schoolroom is sometimes attributed to the order, silence, and study which are made to prevail there. 1. Order is not unpleasant. The orderly proceeding of a well-regulated school, the quiet succession of one thing to another at its proper time, the seeing everything in its place,—all these are pleasant. To most persons, order is pleasant. 2. Silence is not unpleasant. On the contrary, as it is beneficial to all, it is suitable, and therefore pleasant. 3. Study is not unpleasant. When the thing studied is understood, nothing is more pleasant. It is the exercise of one or more faculty, which is the very essence of happiness. It is unpleasant only when long continued on one subject. It should therefore be varied; for little children, as often, perhaps, as every half hour; for older ones, as often as every hour. Day after day, at the same hour, the same study should be resumed, but should not be allowed to be continued too long at once. If so resumed, it becomes daily more easy. Just as, in any manual operation, the fingers or the hands gradually get accustomed to exercise, and perform it more readily the longer it has been pursued, so does any faculty of the mind. Children are variously constituted in this respect; some grow weary much sooner than others. An exercise should cease before any one has become weary.

Restraint, unnecessary or too long continued, becomes wearisome. Every young person is impatient of it; the law of his whole nature requires action. The younger the child, the greater the impatience of restraint and confinement. There must therefore be breaks and recesses; for very young children as often as once in an hour; for all, as often as once in two or two and a half hours.

Uneasy positions are and ought to be unpleasant. Care should therefore be taken that the seats be convenient, of a proper height, and provided with a back. An ill-ventilated room is unpleasant. Take care that yours be well ventilated. Harshness is unpleasant; scolding, in man or woman, is excessively unpleasant. Avoid both, and learn to govern yourself, and to win by kindness and by reason. Mere repetition of lessons is monotonous; break its dullness by introducing variety. Study the lesson of the class, and make it pleasanter by making it clearer.

The first work of a teacher, when preparing to go into school, is with himself. The success of the day and the happiness of the school depend in a great degree upon the temper he carries into school. This is particularly important on the opening of the school. Let him be careful to make, if possible, an agreeable impression then. His pupils, full of expectation and curiosity, are watching every motion and look, and listening to every word, to gather omens of their future fortune, hoping or fearing, as these elements predominate in their character, but almost sure to like or dislike according to the first impression. Let the teacher take care that their first impression be, that he is a kind and generous person, who feels a great interest in their welfare, but one of firmness and resolution, who will not allow anything wrong. Many years ago the mastership of a public school in a town in New-England became vacant by the dismission of a worthless teacher. A successor was appointed and introduced into his new office with some ceremony, an address from the chairman of the school committee, one from himself, and other formalities. The boys, who had long been accustomed to the loosest discipline, and many of whom had learned to like the state of anarchy which had prevailed, determined, as soon as the company and the committee should retire, to try the spirit of their new master. Accordingly, as the door was shut, they began to make a noise with their feet, in preparation for more decided measures. Mr. G., the new master, who had waited upon the company to the door, turned towards them, and in a perfectly kind manner, but with a tone of authority which every boy in the room felt and understood, tapped slightly upon the floor and said, "Order, boys." The effect was instantaneous. Unaffected kindness and firmness not to be trifled with were so clearly expressed, that every one felt that the reign of anarchy had ceased.

One of a teacher's first duties is cheerfulness. If he can enter upon his labours with cheerful alacrity, he will do much towards success. The cheerfulness of the master, like the sun, fills everything with warmth, and he will see it reflected from every face. The first word he utters, the first look he casts upon many a child, gives the tone to its feelings for the day. What matter the storm and the drift without, if he can meet the sunshine of a cheerful teacher's face within? That warms and makes pleasant the room, for it warms the hearts of the little company. Hence, I repeat it, health, the essential prerequisite of cheerfulness, is a duty, and all which is necessary to secure it is a law which he must obey. God loveth a cheerful giver; and nowhere is this more true than where the gift is moral guidance and the light of intelligence.

It is a difficult thing to enter upon the scene of so much labour, anxiety, and disappointment as a school often is, with a cheerful temper. There are some there, he thinks, who are cold and indifferent, who care nothing for him or any of his plans for their good. There may be those whom he knows to be adverse to him, to hate him, and to be seeking to thwart his plans and prevent his success. To go among such with confidence, and kindness, and cheerfulness; to leave behind all resentment, all selfishness, all despondency, is very difficult. But so must we overcome evil with good. They are children. There is something at the bottom of their hearts which will respond to all our kindness. There is something which will take sides with us against whatever is wrong in themselves. If we go in the true spirit of our calling, we shall be able to turn aver sion into favour, hate into love, and indifference into interest. And in doing this, we not only accomplish our immediate ends, we work out the higher good of repressing the evil and awakening the good tendencies of their character, while we do this in a still greater degree for ourselves.

Order should be secured by the general arrangements of the school. Children must not be left unemployed. When so left, they are almost sure to fall into mischief, or what a teacher calls such, to relieve themselves from the listlessness of idleness. If they cannot be employed, they should be dismissed, or allowed to take a recess. Children are often confined in school after their lessons are learned and said, from a feeling that it is a waste of time to let them go. It should be understood that it is a much greater waste to oblige them to remain unoccupied. When it can be done, the lower classes should be dismissed at an earlier hour than the upper, that a portion of time may be given uninterruptedly to the latter.

The following excellent observations are from a teacher* who was distinguished for his success in obtaining a moral influence over his pupils:

"In endeavouring to correct the faults of your pupils, do not, as many teachers do, seize only upon *those particular cases* of transgression which may happen to come under your notice. These individual instances are very few, probably, compared with the whole number of faults against which you ought to exert an influence. And though you, perhaps, ought not to neglect those which may accidentally come under your notice, yet the observing and punishing such cases is a very small part of your duty.

"You accidentally hear, I will suppose, as you are walking home from school, two of your boys in earnest conversation, and one of them uses profane language. Now the course to be pursued in such a case is most evidently not

* Mr. Abbott, the author of "The Teacher."

to call the boy to you the next day and punish him, and there let the matter rest. This would perhaps be better than nothing. But the chief impression which it would make upon the individual, and upon the other scholars, would be, 'I must take care how I *let the master hear me* use such language again.' A wise teacher, who takes enlarged and extended views of his duty in regard to the moral progress of his pupils, would act very differently. He would look at the whole subject. 'Does this fault,' he would say to himself, 'prevail among my pupils? If so, how extensively?' It is comparatively of little consequence to punish the particular transgression. The great point is to devise some plan to reach the whole evil, and to correct it, if possible.

"In one case, where such a circumstance occurred, the teacher managed it most successfully in the following way:

"He said nothing to the boy, and, in fact, the boy did not know that he was overheard. He allowed a day or two to elapse, so that the conversation might be forgotten, and then took an opportunity, one day after school, when all things had gone on pleasantly, and the school was about to be closed, to bring forward the whole subject. He told the boys that he had something to say to them, after they had laid by their books and were ready to go. The desks were soon closed, and every face in the room was turned towards the master with a look of fixed attention. It was almost evening. The sun had gone down. The boys' labours were over. The day was done, and their minds were at rest, and everything was favourable for making a deep and permanent impression.

"'A few days ago,' says the teacher, when all was still, 'I accidentally overheard some conversation between two of the boys of this school, and one of them swore.'

"There was a pause.

"'Perhaps you expect that I am now going to call the boy out and punish him. Is that what I ought to do?'

"There was no answer.

"'I think a boy who uses bad language of any kind does what he knows is wrong. He breaks God's commands. He does what he knows would be displeasing to his parents, and he sets a bad example. He does wrong, therefore, and justly deserves punishment.'

"There were, of course, many boys who felt that they were in danger. Every one who had used profane language was aware that he might be the one who had been overheard, and, of course, all were deeply interested in what the teacher was saying.

"'He might, I say,' continues the teacher, 'justly be punished, but I am not going to punish him; for, if I should, I am afraid that it would only make him a little more careful hereafter not to commit this sin when I could possibly be within hearing, instead of persuading him, as I wish to, to avoid such a sin in future altogether. I am satisfied that that boy would be far happier, even in this world, if he would make it a principle always to do his duty, and never, in any case, to do wrong. And then, when I think how soon he and all of us will be in another world, where we shall all be judged for what we do here, I feel strongly desirous of persuading him to abandon entirely this practice I am afraid that punishing him now would not do that.

"'Besides,' continues the teacher, 'I think it very probable that there are many other boys in this school who are sometimes guilty of this fault, and I have thought that it would be a great deal better and happier for us all, if, instead of punishing this particular boy, whom I have accidentally overheard, and who, probably, is not more to blame than many other boys in school, I should bring up the whole subject, and endeavour to persuade all to reform.'

"I am aware that there are, unfortunately, in our country a great many teachers from whose lips such an appeal as this would be wholly in vain. The man who is accustomed to scold, and storm, and punish, with unsparing severity, every transgression, under the influence of irritation and anger, must not expect that he can win over his pupils to confidence in him, and to the principles of duty, by a word. But such an appeal will not be lost when it comes from a man whose daily and habitual management corresponds with it. But to return to the story.

"The teacher made some farther remarks, explaining the nature of the sin, not in the language of execration and affected abhorrence, but calmly, temperately, and without any disposition to make the worst of the occurrence which had taken place. In concluding what he said, he addressed the boys as follows:

"'Now, boys, the question is, do you wish to abandon this habit, or not? if you do, all is well. I shall immediately forget all the past, and will do all I can to help you resist and overcome temptation in future. But all I can do is only to help you; and the first thing to be done, if you wish to engage in this work of reform, is to acknowledge your fault; and I should like to know how many are willing to do this.

"'I wish all those who are willing to tell me whether they use profane language, would rise.'

"Every individual but one rose.

"'I am very glad to see so large a number,' said the teacher; 'and I hope you will find that the work of confessing and forsaking your faults is, on the whole, pleasant, not painful business. Now, those who can truly and honestly say that they never do use profane language of any kind may take their seats.'

"Three only of the whole number, which consisted of not far from 20, sat down. It was in a seaport town, where the temptation to yield to this vice is even greater than would be, in the interior of our country, supposed possible.

"'Those who are now standing,' pursued the teacher, 'admit that they do, sometimes at least, commit this sin I suppose all, however, are determined to reform; for I do not know what else should induce you to rise and acknowl edge it here, unless it is a desire hereafter to break yourselves of the habit. But do you suppose that it will be enough for you merely to resolve here that you will reform?'

"'No, sir,' said the boys.

"'Why? If you now sincerely determine never more to use a profane word, will you not easily avoid it?'

"The boys were silent. Some said faintly, 'No, sir.'

"'It will not be easy for you to avoid the sin hereafter,' continued the teacher, 'even if you do now sincerely and resolutely determine to do so. You have formed the habit of sin, and the habit will not be easily overcome. But I have detained you long enough now. I will try to devise some method by which you may carry your plan into effect, and to-morrow I will tell you what it is.'

"So they were dismissed for the day; the pleasant countenance and cheerful tone of the teacher conveying to them the impression that they were engaging in the common effort to accomplish a most desirable purpose, in which they were to receive the teacher's help; not that he was pursuing them, with threatening and punishment, into the forbidden practices into which they had wickedly strayed. Great caution is, however, in such a case, necessary to guard against the danger, that the teacher, in attempting to avoid the tones of irritation and anger, should so speak of the sin as to blunt their sense of its guilt, and lull their consciences into a slumber.

"At the appointed time on the following day, the subject was again brought before the school, and some plans proposed, by which the resolutions now formed might be more certainly kept. These plans were readily and cheerfully adopted by the boys, and in a short time the vice of profaneness was, in a great degree, banished from the school. This whole account is substantially fact.

"I hope the reader will keep in mind the object of the above illustration, which is to show that it is the true policy of the teacher not to waste his time and strength in contending against *such accidental instances* of transgression as may chance to fall under his notice, but to take an enlarged and extended view of the whole ground, endeavouring to remove *whole classes of faults*,—to elevate and improve *multitudes together*.

"By these means, his labours will not only be more effectual, but far more pleasant. You cannot come into collision with an individual scholar, to punish him for a mischievous spirit, or even to rebuke him for some single act by which he has given you trouble, without an uncomfortable and uneasy feeling, which makes, in ordinary cases, the discipline of a school the most unpleasant part of a teacher's duty. But you can plan a campaign against a whole class of faults, and put into operation a system of measures to correct them, and watch from day to day the operation of that system, with all the spirit and interest of a game. It is, in fact, a game where your ingenuity and moral power are brought into the field, in opposition to the evil tendencies of the hearts which are under your influence.

"Remember, then, as, for the first time, you take your new station, that it is not your duty simply to watch with an eagle eye for those accidental instances of trangression which may chance to fall under your notice. You are to look over the whole ground. You are to make yourself acquainted, as soon as possible, with the classes of character and classes of faults which may prevail in your dominions, and to form deliberate and well-digested plans for improving the one and correcting the other.

"And this is to be the course pursued, not only with

great delinquencies, such as those to which I have already alluded, but to every little transgression against the rules of order and propriety. You can correct them far more easily and pleasantly in the mass than in detail.

"You avoid, by this means, a vast amount of irritation and impatience, both on your own part and on the part of your scholars, and you produce at least twenty times the usual effect."

"Everything which is unpleasant in the discipline of the school should be attended to, as far as possible, privately. Sometimes it is necessary to bring a case forward in public for reproof or punishment, but this is seldom. In some schools it is the custom to postpone cases of discipline till the close of the day, and then, just before the boys are dismissed at night, all the difficulties are settled. Thus, day after day, the impression which is last made upon their minds is received from a season of suffering, and terror, and tears.

"Now such a practice may be attended with many advantages, but it seems to be, on the whole, unwise. Awing the pupils by showing them the consequences of doing wrong should be very seldom resorted to. It is far better to allure them by showing them the pleasures of doing right. Doing right is pleasant to everybody, and no persons are so easily convinced of this, or, rather, so easily led to see it, as children. Now the true policy is, to let them experience the pleasure of doing their duty, and they will easily be allured to it.

"I am next to consider what course is to be taken with *individual* offenders, whom the general influences of the schoolroom will not control.

"The first point to be attended to is to ascertain who they are. Not by appearing suspiciously to watch any individuals, for this would be almost sufficient to make them bad, if they were not so before. Observe, however; notice, from day to day, the conduct of individuals, not for tne purpose of reproving or punishing their faults, but to enable you to understand their characters. This work will often require great adroitness and very close scrutiny; and you will find, as the results of it, a considerable variety of character, which the general influences above described will not be sufficient to control. The number of individuals will not be great, but the diversity of character comprised in it will be such as to call into exercise all your powers of vigilance and discrimination.

"Now all these characters must be studied. It is true that the caution given in a preceding part of this chapter, against devoting undue and disproportionate attention to such persons, must not be forgotten. Still, these individuals will require, and it is right that they should receive, a far greater degree of attention, so far as the moral administration of the school is concerned, than their mere numbers would appear to justify. This is the field in which the teacher is to study human nature, for here it shows itself without disguise. It is through this class, too, that a very powerful moral influence is to be exerted upon the rest of the school. The manner in which such individuals are managed; the tone the teacher assumes towards them; the gentleness with which he speaks of their faults; and the unbending decision with which he restrains them from wrong, will have a most powerful effect upon the rest of the school. That he may occupy this field, therefore, to the best advantage, it is necessary that he should first thoroughly explore it.

"Every boy has something or other which is good in his disposition and character, which he is aware of, and on which he prides himself; find out what it is, for it may often be made the foundation on which you may build the superstructure of reform. Every one has his peculiar sources of enjoyment, and objects of pursuit which are before his mind from day to day; find out what they are, that by taking an interest in what interests him, and perhaps sometimes assisting him in his plans, you can bind him to you. Every boy is, from the circumstances in which he is placed at home, exposed to temptations, which have, perhaps, had a far greater influence in the formation of his character, than any deliberate and intentional depravity of his own. Ascertain what these temptations are, that you may know where to pity him and where to blame. The knowledge which such an examination of character will give you will not be confined to making you acquainted with the individual. It will be the most valuable knowledge which a man can possess, both to assist him in the general administration of the school, and in his intercourse among mankind in the business of life. Men are but boys, only with somewhat loftier objects of pursuit. Their principles, motives, and ruling passions are essentially the same. Extended commercial speculations are, so far as the human heart is concerned, substantially what trading in jackknives and toys is at school, and building a snow fort, to its own architects, the same as erecting a monument of marble.

"After exploring the ground, the first thing to be done, as a preparation for reforming individual character in school, is to secure the personal attachment of the individuals to be reformed. This must not be attempted by professions and affected smiles, and still less by that sort of obsequiousness common in such cases, which produces no effect but to make the bad boy suppose that his teacher is afraid of him; which, by-the-way, is, in fact, in such cases, usually true.

"A most effectual way to secure the good will of a scholar is to ask him to assist you. The Creator has so formed the human heart, that doing good must be a source of pleasure, and he who tastes this pleasure once will almost always wish to taste it again. To do good to any individual creates or increases the desire to do it."

"The teacher can awaken in the hearts of his pupils a personal attachment for him, by asking, in various ways, their assistance in school, and then appearing honestly gratified with the assistance rendered. Boys and girls are delighted to have what powers and attainments they possess brought out into action, especially where they can lead to useful results. They love to be of some consequence in the world, and will be especially gratified to be able to assist their teacher. Get a turbulent boy to co-operate with you in anything, and he will feel how much pleasanter it is to co-operate than to thwart and oppose; and by judicious measures of this kind almost any boy may be brought over to your side.

"Another means of securing the personal attachment of boys is to notice them; to take an interest in their pursuits, and the qualities and powers which they value in one another. It is astonishing what an influence is exerted by such little circumstances as stopping at a play-ground a moment, to notice with interest, though perhaps without saying a word, speed of running or exactness of aim; the force with which a ball is struck, or the dexterity with which it is caught or thrown.

"Whenever a boy has been guilty of an offence the best way is to go directly and frankly to the individual, and come at once to a full understanding. In nine cases out of ten this course will be effectual. For four years, and with a very large school, I have found this sufficient, in every case of discipline which has occurred, except in three or four instances, where something more was required. To make it successful, however, it must be done properly. Several things are necessary. It must be deliberate; generally better after a little delay. It must be indulgent, so far as the view which the teacher takes of the guilt of the pupil is concerned; every palliating consideration must be felt. It must be firm and decided in regard to the necessity of a change, and the determination of the teacher to effect it. It must also be open and frank; no insinuations, no hints, no surmises, but plain, honest, open dealing.

"In many cases, the communication may be made most delicately, and most successfully, in writing. The more delicately you touch the feelings of your pupils, the more tender these feelings will become. Many a teacher hardens and stupifies the moral sense of his pupils, by the harsh and rough exposures to which he drags out the private feelings of the heart. A man may easily produce such a state of feeling in his schoolroom, that to address even the gentlest reproof to any individual, in the hearing of the next, would be a most severe punishment; and, on the other hand, he may so destroy that sensitiveness, that his vociferated reproaches will be as unheeded as the idle wind."

The teacher should be particularly cautioned against partiality. He must be, as nearly as possible, just in his treatment of all. The older scholars must not be indulged in doing what would not be allowed to the younger, nor the reverse. There should be no favouritism. These things are not merely bad in themselves; they destroy the whole moral influence of the teacher.

There are two almost opposite courses which may be pursued for the maintenance of the daily order of school. One is, to have perfect order and absolute silence, except at stated periods, when whispering or leaving seats is allowed; the other is, to allow a certain liberty, to fix limits beyond which it is not permitted to pass, but within which whispering and other intercourse are, to a certain extent, allowed, and to rely upon the power of self-restraint in the pupils to keep them within those limits. The former is easy, and an economy of time; the latter is difficult, and costs time, but is more pleasant to pupils and to teacher. In the former case, the teacher must be always on the watch, and nothing must be suffered to escape his eye, and no offence its penalty. This seems best for a large school, where numbers are to be dealt with on general principles. The other may be pursued in a small or select school, and where a high moral tone has been made to prevail. It renders school a better preparation for the trials of life, but it supposes a considerable advancement already to have been made.

Is corporal punishment allowable and necessary? *Sometimes*, certainly. Order *must* exist. Obedience *must* be given. If the higher motives fail, recourse must be had to the lower; and if they fail, to this, the lowest of all. But the child on whom it is to be inflicted must be in a wretchedly low state; and the teacher who habitually has recourse to it, must be considered as not well understanding the principles or the duties of his calling.

SECTION II. OF THE MOTIVES TO BE APPEALED TO IN GOVERNMENT.

"Every bias, instinct, propension within, is a real part of our nature, but not the whole; add to these the superior faculty, whose office it is to adjust, manage, and preside over them, and take in this its natural superiority, and you complete the idea of human nature. And as in civil government the constitution is broken in upon and violated by power and strength prevailing over authority, so the constitution of man is broken in upon and violated by the lower faculties or principles within prevailing over that which is, in its nature, supreme over them all."—BUTLER.

The remaining object of discipline is to stimulate children to exertion in their studies, as well as to secure their good behaviour. The motives which are most frequently addressed, both in families and schools, are, 1. fear of pain, 2. fear of shame, and, 3. emulation, by which I mean the spirit of rivalry—the desire of outstripping others.*

The first to be considered is the fear of pain. This is not to be condemned altogether. The teacher ought al-

---

* Most of the views contained in this section have been laid before the public, in the Common School Journal.

ways to have the power, in case of absolute need, of inflicting corporal punishment. But the mere possession of the power is all that would be required. A boy who knew that the teacher had this power, and would use it, if obliged to do so, would be unwilling to drive him to the necessity. The great objection to corporal punishment is the fact that it excites angry passions, not only in the child, but in the master, and much more in the latter than the former. I very distinctly remember that corporal punishment, when inflicted in a school where I was a pupil, rarely excited a permanent ill-feeling in the pupil, because it was felt to be just. Certain laws had this penalty annexed to their infraction; and, as the master was really a kind and just man, there was no feeling of rebellion against a consequence which the offender brought on himself. In another instance which recurs to my mind, the only effect of a severe punishment of this kind, for neglecting a lesson, was a determination never again to deserve it. But my own experience teaches me that the effect is almost necessarily bad on the individual who inflicts the pain. It excites a horrible feeling in him,—a feeling which we might conceive to belong to evil spirits. But fear of pain does not necessarily pervert the character of the child.

Not so with the *fear of shame*. I believe its effects to be altogether bad. And the essence of its badness is, that it can be brought to bear upon what is excellent as readily as upon what is evil. Indeed, what is noble, and high-minded, and pure, can more easily be turned to ridicule than the contrary. Cruelty, hardness of heart, selfishness, the meanest of vices, can with difficulty be exposed to ridicule; while compassion, tender-heartedness, generosity, are particularly obnoxious to it.

Most children are, by nature, too susceptible of ridicule. How common it is to see children ashamed of poverty, or any appearance of poverty, or of any natural defect or peculiarity, and not ashamed of gluttony, or profaneness, or malice!

Children of delicate temperament, great generosity, and warmth of imagination,—those of the very character that needs not the influence of a severe punishment, would be made to suffer terribly from the fear of shame; while those of obtuse temperament, cowardly, and mean, and wanting in imagination, would suffer very little.

Besides, from whatever cause, our countrymen are most inordinately susceptible to the influence of ridicule already. Is not the great want of independence, which every observer must notice, owing to this? Are we not, in the highest and most absurd degree, sensitive to other people's opinions? And, if we are so, would it not be unphilosophical and wanting in patriotism to increase this national infirmity, by rendering individuals more sensitive by addressing the fear of shame?

The great objection to it, however, is what I have stated, that it operates with terrible inequality and injustice; giving great pain to the fine characters that ought to be dealt delicately with, and not touching those who are, if possible, to be taken hold of by influences of all kinds.

The same objection lies against *emulation*. It operates with great force upon noble natures that need no excitement, and passes over those dull ones whom it should be the business of discipline to move.

It must be admitted that it is a most powerful motive, perhaps the most powerful that can be put in action. To be at the head of a class can never be an object of indifference to a child of talent, if that is held out as the greatest good. Still less, to be at the head of a school. To gain a medal, when only one or a very few are given, and where the number of competitors is great, may be made to assume, to the eye of a child, an importance greater than any other object for which he can live. But it sacrifices the higher powers to the lower,—the moral to the intellectual. The object of the teacher ought not to be to make as good scholars as possible by any means whatsoever, but to elevate the being as highly as possible. If the scholar is made at the expense of the man, an incalculable injury is inflicted. The teacher capable of sacrificing the moral character of his pupil to his appearance at an exhibition or his triumph at an annual examination, is totally unworthy of his office.

Emulation, when exercised among companions and equals, almost necessarily excites the worst passions, envy, jealousy, hatred, malice. I say *almost*, because I believe that there are a few so noble in their nature, so raised above all selfishness, that they are able to see the prize for which they have been long striving, with all possible efforts, borne away by a rival, with no other feelings than gratification at his success, and resignation to their own disappointment. But these are *very few*. I might, therefore, without departing from the truth, leave out the qualifying expression, and say, that *emulation*, as it usually operates, *excites the worst passions of the human heart.*

As to the effect produced on the character by emulation, an obvious and important question to be asked is, whether the habits formed by it are most likely to lead to the regular, quiet, and conscientious discharge of the daily duties of life. Many of those who have at school been stimulated to great efforts by it, lay aside their books and their habits of study when they leave school. If it thus fails to produce permanent effects in the things about which it has been employed, is it likely to produce a healthy effect upon the whole character? Would a woman, whose character had been formed under the influence of this motive, be more likely than another to endeavour to form in her children simplicity of character, humility, the charity which does good for the sake of its object, the love of truth for its own sake, the principle of doing right because it is right? Would the desire of distinction, and of surpassing others, be most likely to suggest her highest duties as a wife? Will it best fit her for her duties to herself and her Maker? If they had any effect, would they not tend to lead her astray? And can those motives which are obviously wrong for children of one sex, be the best possible for those of the other? If these doubts are not wholly unfounded, what an infinite amount of unnecessary evil must be created by emulation! To say nothing of the envy and hatred it often engenders, cankering instead of purifying the heart of infancy and childhood,—to what cause more than this, acting so generally in schools, and even in families, can be attributed the insane desire, so prevailing among us, of outstripping each other in wealth, in houses, in dress, in everything which admits of external comparison? To what else, in an equal degree, can we attribute the notorious profligacy of so many political leaders? The desire of excelling has been, from childhood, so fostered, that it has become an irrepressible passion, rushing to its end, regardless of all principle and of all consequences.

It doubtless does good as well as harm. But the question is, whether we cannot secure the good from the action of higher motives, while we avoid the evil. The best men have been above its influence. Emulation may have formed such men as Cæsar and Napoleon. How little could it have done to form Washington! The noblest deeds and the highest works, those which have advanced society in civilization and truth, have been produced under the influence of entirely different and higher motives.

Of whom was Galileo *emulous*, when, having gone beyond what was already known, he stretched out, by the help of experiment and geometry, into the vast unexplored ocean of mechanical and astronomical truth? Of whom was Kepler *emulous*, when, from the collected observations of many years, he deduced those famous laws which he did not expect the minds of his own age even to comprehend, but which were to serve as a foundation for the system of the universe? What *rivalry* stimulated Newton, when, in the seclusion of his own study, he established those immortal principles of philosophy, which his friends could with difficulty persuade him to give to the world? What *emulation* taught Archimedes mechanics, or Pascal geometry, or Shakspeare poetry? What *rivalry* set George Fox or John Wesley to preach? or launched the Santa Maria or the Mayflower upon the waves of the Atlantic?

It must be admitted that we cannot entirely exclude the action of emulation. Children can hardly be assembled for any purpose without its showing itself. But nothing need be done to strengthen it. It is already a sufficiently powerful element in the character of every child; and the excessive prominence which is given to it by its being constantly addressed, destroys the balance of the powers, and sacrifices the moral being to the intellectual.

What other motives can be made to take the place of the powerful ones of which I have spoken?

I. The love of the approbation of friends and teachers.

The love of approbation is, in a greater or less degree, natural to every individual, and must have been implanted for some good purpose. It soon shows itself in the child, and, for several of the earliest years, affords the parent one of the most powerful means of control and influence. If appealed to constantly and simply, it may be made a genial and healthy element of the character. It is, however, often perverted by being associated with inferior motives. In stead of being satisfied with showing that, if their children do well, they will be rewarded with their love and approbation, parents too often bring in the meaner motives of appetite for delicacies, pecuniary rewards, or the desire of surpassing each other. A child may be made to feel that, by improper conduct, he will forfeit his parents' approbation, and, if he has been properly trained, he will feel this to be one of the greatest losses possible.

I suppose that all parents begin, instinctively, by appealing to this motive. The mischief is, that they too often degrade it by mean associations, and pervert it by giving it a wrong direction. 'What will people think?' is the common expression of parents without principle, and is sometimes thoughtlessly uttered even by those who would shrink from believing that they were themselves acting from a regard to the opinion of the world, and would justly condemn themselves for inculcating such a principle on their children. The love of indiscriminate approbation,—that of the bad, the worthless, the frivolous, equally with that of the intelligent and the just,—would be as likely to have an ill effect on the character as a good, to form a mere creature of the world as to form a person of high views and noble principles. It is obvious, therefore, that the good influence of this motive depends on its associations. It is perfectly safe only when it has reference to those who bestow approbation on what deserves it, and who are capable of judging.

In school, the love of approbation should be directed, first, to the parent at home; next, to the teacher; lastly and least, to the standard of action and opinion pervading the little community. In order that it may be directed to the parent, the teacher must either have constant intercourse with him, or he must statedly send him some report of the child's progress and deportment. The latter, where practicable, is the better course, since, when the reports are made on just principles, they come to operate regularly, and form habits of action in the child of the greatest importance.

In order that written reports should have a permanently good effect, they must be, as nearly as possible, just. I say as nearly as possible, because I hold it to be almost impossible that they should be quite just. To be so, the dullest child in a school, who has made uniform and faithful exertions, should have an expression of entire commendation; and to be able to say how faithful the exertions have been, we must have a complete knowledge of the capacity and character of the child. Now, as this is obviously very difficult, it is equally so to do absolute justice. An earnest desire, however, on the part of the teacher, to do exact justice, and to rectify any instance of injustice which is brought to his knowledge, has almost the effect of justice.

The reputation for justice and benevolence in the teacher is, of course, essential to his having a good influence in the bestowal of his own approbation. The expressed approbation of an able teacher will have its effect, doubtless, in stimulating to exertion, even when it is clearly unjust. But the influence of such approbation is pernicious, inasmuch as it sacrifices the child's love of justice to his progress in his studies; while, on the other hand, a teacher of moderate intellectual ability will be able to give great force to his approbation, and to exert an influence on his pupils higher far than belongs to his own mere intellect, if he takes care always to fortify his opinions by an appeal to their natural sense of justice.

This sense of justice, however, in children collected from families of all kinds, such as usually make up a miscellaneous school, needs continual correction. It is apt to be warped by too strong a feeling, in each individual, of his own rights, and a disregard of the rights of others. Occasionally you find a child who thinks that more than justice is done to himself. Much more frequently, each thinks he receives less than justice. When a teacher is sure he is himself just, at least in his intentions, he may correct the perceptions of justice in his pupils. Till this is done, he cannot safely appeal to their judgment to award the meed of approbation.

The love of approbation, then, with these limitations, may be appealed to as a powerful and harmless motive. Without these limitations it must be admitted to be unsafe, from the danger of its invading the province of those higher principles, which it should be the business of education to establish as umpires over all the parts of the mental and moral constitution.

II. The love of knowledge, and the pleasure of exercising the faculties in learning.

Any one who had never been inside of a school, but had acquired a knowledge of the things in the creation and of the history of man by observation, and converse, and reading, among men and women engaged in the usual occupations of life, would be surprised to be told that little advantage is taken, in the common course of instruction, of this universal and most powerful principle. What can be more universal or more powerful than curiosity?—this instinctive love of the soul for all the beautiful creation into the midst of which it has been born?—this innate yearning of every faculty towards the objects for which it was created? Observe how, in a child, every sound awakens it. See how every colour, every motion, every new form charms. See with what delight the young lord of the world handles, lifts, pulls, breaks, weighs, and measures the materials of his future power, the creatures of his empire. Mark the rapt attention with which he listens to the story of every one of his fellow-creatures, of the lower or the higher races,—the impatience with which he waits for your answer to his innumerable questions about ends, and causes, and mechanisms,—the how, and whence, and what for; and then be told that this almost irrepressible desire to learn *is repressed*, this powerful impulse is neglected and forgotten, and the noble boy is made to learn, not because knowledge is delightful, and *by the delight* with which the heart and mind spring outward to it, but by being mated against his brother, and by his desire of outstripping him,—by blows, and shame, and envy!

And how happens this? We mistake the means for the end. Instead of endeavouring to teach things of human life, the laws of the creation, the character of the infinitely benevolent Author, we act as if we thought that the great *ends* of teaching were how to spell and read, and cipher and parse. We imprison a child for hours, and condemn him to stillness at an age when he was never intended to be still, and put into his hands a book of columns and pages of nonsense, page after page of impenetrable, inexplicable nonsense, and then wonder that he is not as bright and gleesome as we have seen him in a garden, in the pursuit of flowers and butterflies. We approach him with an outstretched ferule, and stern look and voice, and are vexed that he is not as much delighted to see us as if we came with smiles and kindness. We carry on this process for some years, and then wonder that all his associations with a school are not pleasurable. The wonder should be, that any child should be susceptible of being moulded to our will to such a degree that any of these associations should be pleasant.

But how shall the love of knowledge be substituted for the usual motives? How shall a child be taught spelling, and reading, and parsing by the desire of knowledge? As to reading, it is now usually, when taught at home by kind and intelligent parents, taught through the love of knowledge, —or that and love of a parent's approbation. Put suitable, well-written children's books, such as they can perfectly understand, into the hands of children, and they will soon learn to read, from the desire of getting at what they contain. And they will learn to read, not in the drawling, monotonous tone so common in schools, but in a simple and natural man ner, with spirit and effect. I have now in my eye and in my heart two children, who, without a tear or a sigh, but with delight, learned, of a sensible and loving mother, how to read, and well too; and beautifully and naturally they did read, so that it was a pleasure to hear them, until they went to school. There, from books they could not understand, and befitting teachers, they soon learned to substitute for the natural method, in which feeling answered to feeling and thought to thought, the loud, boisterous, humdrum, school mode, which had nothing to do with sense or feeling.

Regard reading as an end, and you will not succeed in teaching it well. Consider it only as the means by which the heart and head of the writer may reach the heart and head of the reader, and it becomes an easy and natural thing. We often hear surprise expressed that there are so few good readers, when so much time is spent on the art. The wonder rather is, that there should be any; that a child should be carried through the long rigmarole of the spelling-book, such as we usually find it, and ever after be able to learn to read well at all.

If the object of a teacher were to communicate as much knowledge as possible, he would immediately find that the love of knowledge might be enlisted, and that much might be communicated, without having recourse to other stimulants. For this purpose, however, he must pursue one of two courses. He must either select simple, well-written books for the pupils to read, or he must make special preparation himself, that he may supply the place of books. In most schools, it would be difficult to introduce a sufficient variety of books to communicate information upon all the subjects upon which instruction should be given. In none would it be impossible for the teacher to impart a great amount of valuable knowledge to pupils in almost every stage of advancement. The subjects which will be found interesting to children are such as the following: the appearance, food, dress, manners, and customs of different nations, and whatever relates to the condition of man in all parts of the world; the air and its motions, and the cause of wind; water, what it is made of, how it is raised into the air, and falls, and flows into the sea,—how it freezes, and forms snow, and rends rocks; rocks, their uses, the fact that they are made of airs and combustible substances; heat and its effects; useful plants, such as are used for food, or fuel, or the arts, what makes them grow, and how beautiful they are; animals, their sagacity, habits, uses; the moon, its changes and action on the tides; ships, how they are made, how they sail, whither they go, what they carry; short histories, anecdotes of great or good men, and others without number.

Let a teacher make it a part of every day's duties to prepare himself *to communicate some particular piece of information*, and feel a strong interest in it himself, and I doubt whether he will find it difficult to excite interest in children. Let him, for example, tell his pupils that there is a country where, for some weeks in winter, the sun does not rise, and where the snow is often so deep that there is no travelling, and ask them how they think people can occupy themselves during these long nights; then let him give the beautiful picture we have of the domestic life and habits of the Icelanders, where every family is a school and a workshop, and the business and the instruction of life go on together. Or let him tell them how glass is made, or how a book is printed, and I have no fear that he will have to whip them to attention.

He must, however, learn to talk, not Latin, not from the dictionary, but in simple, downright, household Saxon English, such as men of sense talk on their farms and in their workshops, and women of sense in their kitchens or among their sisters. Let the end of talking be to interest and instruct, not to exhibit himself.

And let him not be discouraged if he do not succeed the first or second time. It will require some practice to enable him to do the thing well himself, and it will require some patience to break up the bad habits of inattention in children, and accustom them to listen and look. But what good thing is there that we can get without any trouble? And this art is well worth the pains.

III. The love of truth.

A love of truth must emanate from the teacher. It is in vain that he shall attempt to impress it upon his pupils, if he have it not in his own breast. And he will teach it more effectively, just in proportion as he has it more deeply and sincerely. Let him feel an entire reverence for the truth, and let him show this in his words and actions.

Many practices, common in school, have a tendency to destroy, or at least to weaken, the love of truth. A teacher should never distrust a pupil without cause. In doing so, he does what he can to teach him falsehood. A child is never so much tempted to lie as when he finds he is already considered a liar.

I need hardly say he should never tempt his pupils to lie. An obvious feeling and understanding of the command, *Swear not at all*, is, never make a promise. I believe it was given by him who knew what weakness is in man, to guard this sacred love of truth. A teacher should not require nor allow his pupil to promise not to repeat an act. If he do, he tempts him to break his promise. He tempts him to do a thing infinitely worse than the trifling offences which he would guard against. He ought to be satisfied with pointing out the evil and exacting the penalty. But let him never require the promise.

Much harm is done by attempting to induce children to tell of each other. Most children in school have a natural sense of honour in regard to this, which, so far from being violated, should be cherished and respected. It may be a mistaken sense of honour,—it usually is; but it is a noble feeling, and may be enlightened into a high principle. The detection of the author of little freaks of childish folly, or even of childish mischief, is, and should be considered, of infinitely less consequence than the preservation of this sense of honour. There is no great harm in the culprit's escaping; there is very great in children's learning to regard each other and themselves as informers.

If a teacher will look a little into his own motives, he will find that the anxious desire to bring to light and punishment a culprit who has been guilty of some practical joke or violation of school-law, has more of selfishness and pride in it, than love of justice or of the good of the offender. Let him have magnanimity enough to look upon his own laws as of little consequence, in comparison with the *real* good of his pupils, and he will be less galled at seeing them broken; and, if he persevere long enough, he will awaken a magnanimity in the pupil, which will be a surer protection of his laws than any selfish precaution. When the pupil sees that the master's anxiety for the execution of the laws comes from a consideration that they are *his* laws, he loses respect for the law and for the law-maker. But convince him that you have a higher regard for him than you have for your temporary laws, and you soon enlist the feelings of his better nature in favour of yourself and your regulations.

In a school at least, if not in society, how much might be gained on the score of justice and truth by constant reference to that code, according to which the most effectual punishment for one frail creature to inflict upon another equally frail is—*forgiveness?*

Another temptation to falsehood to be avoided, always, if possible, is the setting one child to be monitor or spy over others. I know that, in some schools and according to some systems, this is unavoidable. But I know, also, that it is liable to produce falsehood, injustice, and ill feeling. A child must be more than a child,—he must have, in abundant measure, all the best qualifications of a mature teacher, to be able to perform justly, truly, and kindly the duties of a monitor. Such there sometimes are, and such may be employed. But none others should.

I have adverted briefly to the common occasions of a departure from truth. I have done it from a conviction that the love and the habit of truth-telling are of infinitely more importance than any acquisition connected with studies which can ever be made in school, and for the sake of which the love of the truth is put at hazard.

The desire of attaining to the truth in matters of science or history will be found to be a natural consequence of the love of moral truth, of which I have been speaking. This is a strong inducement to thoroughness in investigation; but I admit that it comes into operation later, and supposes a higher degree of advancement, than any other of the motives of which I have had occasion to speak.

Its cultivation, however, is of such consequence, that it ought to receive far more attention than is usually given it. A teacher has many opportunities of inculcating it. The extravagant language that young persons are very prone to use, though possibly proceeding only from exuberant feelings, should be guarded and repressed. Over-statements naturally lead to falsehood. Good taste, as well as truth, is concerned in the restriction; exaggeration is a violation of both.

Exactness in statements, and in the performance of all school exercises, is chiefly important in its moral relations, as leading to scrupulous adherence to truth.

IV. The desire of advancement and progress is a natural and commendable motive. The only difficulty is, so to direct and control it, as to prevent the competition becoming personal. And it is so necessary an ingredient in every intelligent and active character, that it is of great importance that a right direction should be given to it in early life.

I shall suggest, in a few words, some modes in which this may be done.

1. The pupil may be led to desire to be more perfect in the study in which he is engaged. This is not so difficult as might at first be thought. Self-emulation may be easily excited. Show a child that what he is doing he may do better; have patience with his slow improvement; commend the slightest advance, and be just in marking that advance; you lead him to enter into judgment with himself. He compares what he is doing with what he had done; he sees that he has attained something; he becomes his own friend. But we must be careful to refer to the right standard. Let him not applaud himself for doing more, unless it be also better. Better should be ever the word.

2. He will need little excitement to be made to desire to rise to a higher class or division. Let him desire it; and let him be advanced, but only with the condition that all, as he goes, be learned thoroughly. The stimulus may act upon a whole division, consisting of many individuals. All may push on together, without ill-feeling, to a higher division This should be done as often as it can, in most schools, for another reason, that classes should be as few as is consistent with the progress of all. If the principle of self-judgment has been properly brought to act, some may be advanced without injury to the rights and feelings of those left behind. They, indeed, will prefer not to be advanced rather than to go unprepared.

3. There is a sufficiently strong desire always existing among children to go on to higher studies. It may be rendered useful by faithfully requiring thoroughness in the present study, as a condition of advancement to a new one. Curiosity thus stimulates love of progress. An examina-

tion may determine the qualification; or, if the same teacher have charge of both classes, he may decide, without special examination, that a part or the whole of one class is qualified to go on to a higher, or to pursue another study.

4. A school may be divided into several divisions, according to general progress and deportment. Let the grades be so numerous that the distance between contiguous divisions shall not be great. This arrangement may exist only on paper, in the record of the school. It need not affect the studies or the seats of the pupils. And it is much better that it should not. A child may be in the same division, on the book, with another, but be in a higher class in Arithmetic, a lower in Reading, and a different one in Geography. Personal competition is much weakened by these various arrangements according to progress, while better motives are brought to act more powerfully. It will be a strong inducement to a child to have a faultless character for three months, if the consequence is also to have a higher place on the weekly record of the school. And the contest is prevented from being a personal one, by the names in each division being arranged alphabetically. Fifteen, or any other number of pupils, may thus have the satisfaction of having raised themselves, from grade to grade, to the first division, without having any emulation, as no one of the number shall know which is highest or lowest of the fifteen.

5. If there be a system of several connected schools, examination for each higher one may be rendered a strong motive to study. Every one who has had any experience in preparing boys for college, knows how powerfully, as it draws near, the expectation of the examination for admission acts.* It seems very desirable and very practicable to in-

---

* Every college examiner who lowers the standard of requirement does a wrong to all the youth who are looking in that direc-

troduce a gradation of schools into all the large towns of New-England and New-York. A few, taught by masters of first-rate qualifications, might accomplish more than is effected by many under inferior teachers. Those of the second grade might be better taught than they now are, by females. If admission to the higher depended on a thorough examination, a strong and effectual motive would be brought to bear on a class that now stand in need of one;—tall boys, who think themselves too old for the dominion of a woman.

Nearly connected with this is

V. The desire of preparing for the business and duties of life.

It often happens that young men who have been idle during the course of their academical or collegiate education, become diligent and careful when they enter upon the study of a particular profession. This is not the consequence of maturer years only, but, rather, that the business of life is placed distinctly before them, and the necessity of specific preparation for it rendered evident. The same principle might have been appealed to with effect in every part of their previous course. The child learning his letters may oftentimes be urged to attention by being shown that he will thereby obtain the advantage of reading whatever and whenever he pleases. He will be induced to learn to spell and to write, by being convinced that writing will be an advantage and a pleasure to him in his future life. The boy who is to look only to his own exertions for support, will be stimulated to diligence from the beginning of his studies, if it can be made clear to him that success in life will depend on his excellence as a scholar. The generous boy of twelve, who is made to foresee that the support of a

---

tion. If all the colleges of the Northern and Middle States could be induced to unite, they could easily and rapidly raise all the preparatory schools to a far higher grade, by agreeing to insist on higher qualifications.

mother or a sister will depend on him, and that all he can have to rely on is his talents and his education, will press on with the resolution to get the best education and make the most of his talents. The future merchant will apply patiently to Arithmetic, Letter-writing, and Book-keeping, when he is convinced that these are necessary to his preparation for his future calling. Chemistry and Vegetable Physiology will recommend themselves to the future farmer on the same grounds; Geometry and Physics to the mechanic; and Physiology and the laws of the constitution to her who realizes that an important part of the duty of woman is to nurse the sick and to bring up children in health.

Such views should never be omitted in recommending a study to our pupils; and if there be a study in regard to which such statements cannot be made, we may reasonably hesitate whether we have a right to recommend it to them. We must take care, however, that the view we take of success in life be not the mean and ordinary one which measures everything by its pecuniary value, but the loftier one, based upon more just ideas of the worth of our existence, and the elevation, excellence, and happiness which should be its aim.

A lad of some talent, who had failed to be influenced by the rod, by medals, by the desire of pleasing his friends, or fear or love of his instructer, was awakened as from a sleep by a striking picture of the miserable condition of an old age spent without any of the resources which love of books can give. What was immediately before him did not touch him; but his imagination passed over youth and manhood, of which he felt secure, and dwelt upon old age; and the desire of being, at that period of his life, surrounded by friends and books, set him seriously at work.

VI. The generous affections.

Every school might be, in a much greater degree than is

often thought possible, governed and controlled by an appeal to the highest and most generous affections that belong to the human character. I admit that it would be often difficult, and, to some of us, impossible; but the fault would be with ourselves. It would be because we have not, in a sufficiently ample measure, the qualities that we would call up in our pupils; for, to avail himself of these principles the teacher must have them in his own character. How can he touch the spring of generous feeling in his pupils who, in his intercourse with them, is habitually influenced by low and selfish motives?

1. He should have a strong sympathy with childhood, and he should not be ashamed to feel and express it. The affections, as truly as genius, are always young. They never grow old. And if they did, life is so short, that the oldest of us have to look back but a very few years to enter again into the feelings of childhood. Without sympathy, the teacher cannot understand, much less direct, the feelings of the child. But a ready sympathy will enable him to understand the difficulties that a child meets with,—how obscure the plainest thing may appear to him; how long the shortest; and how soon his scanty stock of patience is exhausted. It is partly from their quicker sympathy that females are so much better qualified to teach young children than we are; partly, also, from the silly pride that is apt to prevail among men, particularly those of obtuse perceptions, and the savage idea that want of sympathy is not a want, that hardness is manliness; forgetting that the men of the best endowments have been always marked by the most extensive sympathies.

The most generous allowance should be made for the faults of children; the most lenient construction should be put upon every offence. We may easily remember, if we will, that our own faults, when children, were far more frequently those of ignorance, of thoughtlessness, of impulse, or of weakness, than of design or of malice. Such are always the sources of most of their faults; and it is unreasonable to expect to find children without faults. It is unreasonable, too, when these causes are so obvious, to look deeper and search for anything worse. Impute to children the best motives, and you create them, or, rather, you bring into action those principles which produce the best motives. We cannot doubt that the capacity for all that is good and noble exists in every child, and only needs to be roused and brought out by the teacher. His power of doing this will be in proportion to the elevation of his own character.

2. A teacher must show entire confidence in the child; and not only show, but feel it. Confidence begets confidence, as distrust begets distrust and falsehood. There is no other so ready way to produce falsehood in a child as to doubt his word. And it must be so. A doubter is a liar. One who was himself perfectly true could never suspect. It is true that there is a distrust produced by the experience of other men's falsehoods. But this belongs to the world. It cannot be felt by a teacher towards a child. Real truth, like charity, thinketh no evil. Distrust, therefore, to the whole extent of the influence a teacher has, corrupts the principle of truth, and generates falsehood. It is as if he said to the child, 'I distrust you, because I believe that you are like myself.' But a child who feels that his teacher confides in him has all the strength of the teacher's character on the side of his own good promptings and resolutions. He can, perhaps, resist the temptation from within, if all from without is removed. The teacher's smile gives him confidence in himself. He is safe, because he is in good company. But let the teacher meet him with the dark leer of suspicion, and the trembling flame of truth within him goes out. 'What am I to lose,' thinks the child, 'by this falsehood? He already looks upon me as a liar; and by a lie I may save myself from the consequences of this of-

fence.' For thus is falsehood always cowardly and full of fear. Let us remove the fear, if we would prevent the lie.

3. The teacher should take care to make it felt that he is on the side of his pupils. This is often difficult. In some schools the master has always been looked upon as an enemy, and the impression comes down by inheritance to all the children. The same, too, is the impression of parents, which makes the case still harder. But the difficulty will cease in the case of one who has a genuine sympathy for his pupils. They are quick to find out their friends; and if he is a true friend—a prudent, wise, and confiding friend, they cannot miss of sooner or later finding it out.

The common truth,—almost too common even for a proverb,—that we learn more from imitation than precept, is in everybody's mouth, and yet how much disregarded in practice. What higher object can be proposed than to teach the moral virtues, justice, liberality, charity, gentleness, generosity, humility? But how can he properly teach justice who is habitually unfair? or liberality, who is mean-spirited? or charity, who is close and suspicious? or gentleness, who is rough and overbearing? or generosity, who is overreaching and selfish? or humility, who is proud, and querulous, and self-sufficient?

VII. Conscientiousness, and the desire of obeying the laws of God.

The highest object of education, I repeat, is to establish the dominion of these principles, and to form the habit of acting under their influence. This is to be accomplished by exercising them, or, so far as it depends on the teacher, by constantly appealing to them, so as to call them into action.

The conscience, beginning to act in very early childhood, is, in many individuals, more active then than at any future period. The common course of education, both in school and out of school, is wrong in nothing else so much as in failing to give greater activity to the conscience. The child who is once habituated, as under a conscientious mother he may be, to ask the question " Is it right ?" in regard to every proposed action, might easily be led to continue to do this, and would then grow up, seeking always, and first of all, to do his duty. But how often are his scruples laughed at. How constantly does he see those about him acting from appetite, from malice, from passion, from self-interest, from desire of the approval of the world, from the wish to outstrip others, and from the other ordinary low motives. How constantly are these presented to himself. No wonder that the still, small voice of conscience is never heard, or, if heard, that it is stifled by the confused sounds about him. It should be our endeavour to change this state of things, to take the side of conscience, to point out what is wrong and what is right, and to suggest constantly the question, Is it right ?—not always in so many words, but in such a manner that it shall really be asked within. With pupils of all ages, I have from no other source seen such satisfactory effects produced, as from the action of this principle and affection alone. I have never known a young person insensible to the simple statement, " You can do better than this, and you *ought*;" nor any form of reward which produced its effect more clearly and certainly than being able to say, " You have done well"—" that is right"—" that is very well !"

But the conscience is to be enlightened. This is to be done by teaching the child his relation to God, as his Author and the Creator of his conscience, as of everything else, thus showing the authority of the laws of God, and then showing what the laws of God are. The laws of the spiritual and moral nature are to be learned from the Bible,— most distinctly and fully from the instructions of Jesus

Christ. For this purpose, a portion of the Gospels, or a selection from other parts, should, as I have repeatedly said, be read each day, and such assistance given, in pointing out and explaining the laws, as the teacher may be able to give. The two highest principles,—the sentiment of duty and reverence for God and his laws,—are thus made to act together.

The sphere of conscientiousness is enlarged by enlarging our views of the Creator's laws. When the body is admitted to be his workmanship, the laws of the structure of the body are his laws, and whatever is necessary to secure health becomes a part of duty. The parable of the talents, explained to signify *all the talents*, the powers of mind and of body, as well as the moral and religious faculties, will show that every part of our nature is to be conscientiously cultivated, improved, and perfected, according to the obvious purpose of its Creator.

I have placed this class of motives last, because it is the highest. It would, perhaps, be more proper to place it first, as it comprehends all others; and if we could teach and govern perfectly, it would take the place of all others. As we advance in knowledge of our duties and in skill, we shall approach more and more nearly to this end.

BOOK V.
THE SCHOOLHOUSE

CHAPTER I.

SITUATION.

"The outside of the building is as agreeable as the inside is convenient; it is situated on the prettiest side of the town, and has no communication with any other building. It has a magnificent view over a delightful country, a large kitchen-garden, a commodious court, and two flower-gardens."—COUSIN, *The School at Bruhl.*

So much do the future health, vigour, taste, and moral principles of the pupil depend upon the position, arrangement, and construction of the schoolhouse, that everything about it is important. When the most desirable situation can be selected, and the laws of health and the dictates of taste may be consulted, it should be placed on firm ground, on the southern declivity of a gently-sloping hill, open to the southwest, from which quarter come the pleasantest winds in summer, and protected on the northeast by the top of the hill or by a thick wood. From the road it should be remote enough to escape the noise, and dust, and danger, and yet near enough to be easily accessible by a path or walk, always dry. About it should be ample space, a part open for a play-ground, a part to be laid out in plots for flowers and shrubs, with winding alleys for walks. Damp places, in the vicinity of stagnant pools or unwholesome marshes, and bleak hilltops or dusty plains, should be carefully avoided. Tall trees should partially shade the grounds, not in stiff rows or heavy clumps, but scattered irregularly as if by the hand of Nature. Our native forests present such a choice of beautiful trees, that the grounds must be very extensive to afford room for even a single fine specimen of each; yet this should, if possible, be done, for children ought early to become familiar with the names, appearance, and properties of these noblest of inanimate things. The border of a natural wood may often be chosen for the site of a school; but if it is to be thinned out, or if trees are to be planted, and, from limited space, a selection is to be made, the kingly, magnificent oaks, the stately hickories, the spreading beech for its deep mass of shade, the maples for their rich and abundant foliage, the majestic elm, the useful ash, the soft and graceful birches, and the towering, columnar sycamore, claim precedence.* Next may come the picturesque locusts, with their hanging, fragrant flowers; the tulip-tree; the hemlock, best of evergreens; the celtis, or sweet gum; the nyssa, or tupelo, with horizontal branches and polished leaves; the walnut and butternut, the native poplar, and the aspen.

Of extremely beautiful American shrubs, the number is so great that I have no room for a list. What place intended to form the taste of the young, should be without the kalmias, rhododendrons, cornels, roses, viburnums, magnolias, clethras, honeysuckles, and spiræas? And whoever goes into the woods to gather these, will find a multitude of others which he will hardly consent to leave behind. The hilltop should be planted with evergreens, forming at all seasons a barrier against the winds from the north and east.

Of the flower-plots little need be said. They must be left to the taste of the teacher and of cultivated persons in the district. I can only recommend our wild American plants, and again remind the reader that there is hardly a country town in New-York or New-England from whose woods and meadows a hundred kinds of flowers might not

---

* There are at least ten oaks, four hickories, three or four maples, and as many birches, native to our woods, and all deserving the character given above.

be transplanted, of beauty enough to form the chief ornament of a German or English garden, which are now neglected only because they are common and wild. Garden flowers need not be excluded; and if either these or the former are cultivated, the great object, to present something to refine and inform the taste, will be in some degree accomplished.

Where land is not excessively dear, not less than one fourth of an acre should be assigned for the school lot; so much being essential for the necessary play-grounds. If proper enclosed play-grounds are provided, the master may often be present at the sports, and thus become acquainted with the character of his pupils. If children are compelled to resort to the highway for their amusements, we ought not to wonder that they should be contaminated by the vices, brawlings, and profanity which belong to the frequenters of highways. If the additional purpose of improving the taste and giving information as to trees, shrubs, and flowers, and their management, be in view, an acre at least should be appropriated.

If the situation of the house is important, its structure and internal arrangement, its size, and the way in which it is warmed, lighted, and ventilated, are still more so. I shall state, as concisely as I can, the principles by which these particulars should be regulated.

CHAPTER II.

SIZE.

The room should be sufficiently large to allow every pupil, 1. to sit comfortably at his desk; 2. to leave it without disturbing any one else; 3. to see explanations on his lessons, and to recite, without being incommoded or incommoding others; 4. to breathe a wholesome atmosphere.

1. Each desk should be large enough to contain the books, maps, and slate of its occupant, and to allow them to be spread open before him; and each seat should be sufficient to give an easy position and freedom of motion. For these purposes, the desk should be from 21 to 24 inches long, and from 13 to 17 wide; and the seat from 10 to 12½ inches in each dimension, varying according to the size of the children.

2. Each seat should be accessible, at least on one side, by a passage of sufficient width to allow the pupil or the master to pass without touching those on either side; and there should be a space on one side, which, together with the passage, should be sufficient to allow the whole school to be standing at once.

3. There should be sufficient unoccupied space, in front or in the rear of the desks, to allow more than one class to be conveniently arranged while reciting, and to accommodate the blackboards and other apparatus necessary for the teacher; and in a large school, this space should be both in front and in rear, so that two or more classes may be reciting at one time without disturbing each other. Wherever arrangements can be made for them, there should be separate reciting rooms.

4. The room must be ventilated; but as this may not always be done, during the first hours of the morning, in cold weather, inasmuch as it must necessarily be done at the expense of some portion of heat, the room should be capacious enough to prevent the air becoming offensive and poisonous in the course of a single session. For this purpose, at least 150 cubic feet of air should be allowed for every occupant.

The atmosphere, it is well known, consists essentially of oxygen and nitrogen, in the proportion of about 1 part of the former to 4 of the latter. Of these two elements, **oxygen** alone is capable of sustaining life, the nitrogen serving merely as a medium in which the oxygen is diffused, but having in itself no vital property. By the process of breathing, the oxygen is rapidly consumed, and, in its place, carbonic acid gas, an air which is poisonous, is thrown into the atmosphere Besides this cause, which is continually operating to render the air unfit for respiration, the whole mass of the air around us is gradually rendered impure by the vapour which is breathed from the lungs, and by the matter which is constantly passing from the surface of the body in insensible perspiration. The amount of corruption produced by these sources is astonishing. From 1400 to 2000 cubic inches of oxygen are every hour withdrawn from the air by each pair of lungs. In the same space of time, from one to two ounces of foul matter, which has performed its office in the body and become effete and offensive, is thrown into the air by insensible perspiration from the surface of the body of each individual, besides a portion, amounting to one third as much, in the vapour from the lungs.*

The Creator has poured round the earth an ocean of air 40 or 50 miles in height, thus showing the importance of this element in the economy of nature. When the vital importance to the health of the body is considered of a full supply of perfectly fresh air, and the extent to which it is corrupted by the various sources mentioned above, we cease to be surprised at the loathsomeness of the foul, poisonous air with which a close, full room reeks, or at the headaches, languor, dullness, and ill-temper which are its immediate effects, or at the habitual feeling of weariness and the sure

* Suppose a schoolroom to be 30 feet square and 9 feet high; it will contain 13,996,000 cubic inches of atmospheric air. According to Davy and Thompson, two accurate and scientific chemists, one individual respires and contaminates 6500 cubic inches of air in a minute. Fifty scholars will respire (and contaminate) 325,000 cubic inches in the same time. In about 40 minutes all the air in such a room will have become contaminated, if fresh supplies are not provided.—*Dr. S. B. Woodward's Letter to H. Mann.*

exhaustion of the system which it so often entails upon him who is condemned to breathe it constantly for years in succession.

If the first three objects above mentioned are fully provided for, the space on the floor will be sufficient. But to secure the advantage of an adequate supply of air, the room must be not less than 10, and, if possible, 12 or 14 feet high.

CHAPTER III.

POSITION AND ARRANGEMENT.*

It is very desirable that the north end of the schoolhouse be occupied by the master's desk; that this end be a dead wall; that the front be towards the south; and that the

---

* *Arrangement.*—For the accommodation of 56 scholars, so as to give ample room for moving, for recitations, and for air, the dimensions of the house should be 38 feet by 25, and 10 feet in height within. This will allow an entry of 14 feet by 7½, lighted by a window, furnished with wooden pegs for the accommodation of clothes; a wood-room, 10 feet by 7½, to serve also as an entry for girls at recess, or as a recitation-room; a space behind the desks, 8 feet wide, for fireplace, passage, and recitations, with permanent seats against the walls 10 or 11 inches wide; a platform, 7 feet wide, for the teacher, with the library, blackboards, globes, and other apparatus for teaching: the remaining space to be occupied by the desks and seats of the scholars. For every additional 8 scholars the room may be lengthened 2½ feet. The desks and seats for scholars should be of different dimensions. A desk for two may be 3½ or 4 feet long. If the younger children are placed nearest the master's desk, the desks in the front range may be 13 inches wide, the two next 14, the two next 15, and the two most remote 16, with the height, respectively, of 24, 25, 26, and 27 inches. The seats should vary in like manner. Those in the front range should be 10 inches wide, in the two next 10½, in the two next 11, in the two last 11½ or 12; and 13½, 14, 15, and 16 inches, respectively, high. All edges and corners are to be carefully rounded.

desks be so placed that the pupils, as they sit at them, shall look towards the north. The advantages of this arrangement are, 1. That the scholars will obtain more correct ideas upon the elements of geography, as all maps suppose the reader to be looking northward; 2. The north wall, having no windows, will exclude the severest cold of winter; 3. The scholars will, in this case, look towards a dead wall, and thus avoid the great evil of facing a glare of light; or, if a window or two be allowed in the north wall, the light coming from that quarter is less vivid, and, therefore, less dangerous than that which comes from any other; 4. The door, being on the south, will open towards the winds which prevail in summer and *from* the cold winds of winter.

If, from necessity, the house must front northward, the master's desk should be still in the north end of the room, and the scholars, when seated, look in that direction.

The arrangement of the desks has often been made with special reference to the quiet of the school. There are other, higher objects, which should be also provided for. The first is the social nature of the child. Two seats should be contiguous, that friends may sit together, that a delicate child, when it first comes to school, may not be placed by itself or among strangers, but next to one that it already knows and loves; that one may help another, and that the most advanced may take care, each of one of the least advanced. Such arrangements have been sometimes thought unfavourable to the utmost amount of study. I have not found them so; and, even if they were, we are to remember that moral culture is of higher importance than mental.

The end of the room occupied by the master should be fitted with shelves for a library and for philosophical apparatus and collections of natural curiosities, such as rocks, minerals, plants, and shells, for globes and for blackboards. The books, apparatus, and collections should be concealed and protected by doors, which may be made perfectly plain and without panels, so as to be painted black and serve as blackboards. They may be conveniently divided by pilasters into three portions, the middle one for books, the others for apparatus and collections. On one of the pilasters may be the clock; on the other a barometer and thermometer; on shelves in the corners, the globes; and over the library, in the centre, the study card. One of the pilasters may form part of the ventilating tube. The master's platform may be raised eight inches. For all these purposes, the space in front of the ranges of scholars' desks should be not less than seven or eight feet wide; ten or twelve would be much better. The sides and front of this space should be furnished with seats, ten or eleven inches wide, for recitation. By means of a large movable blackboard, this space may be, in case of need, converted into two, so that two classes may recite at a time. In a school intended to accommodate more than 64 pupils, there ought also to be a space for recitation in the south end of the room, separable by movable blackboards into two.

The entry should be lighted by a window, and be furnished with wooden or iron pins for the accommodation of hats, bonnets, and cloaks; and there should be a wood closet large enough to contain two or three cords of wood This room may, in case of need, be used as a recitation-room.

By making the ceiling of the entry and wood-closet only seven feet high, two commodious rooms for recitation may be formed above them, lighted from the window over the front door, and accessible by stairs from within the school-room.

CHAPTER IV.

LIGHT—WARMING—VENTILATION.

1. LIGHT.—The windows should be on the east and west sides of the room, on the right and left of the pupils and teacher. Windows on the north admit too much cold in winter; on the south, too intense a light at the hour when it is greatest. The eye is often materially and permanently injured by being directly exposed to strong light; and if the light come from behind, the head and body interposed throw the book into their shadow. If windows open towards a road or any other object attractive to children, they should be so high that the pupil, sitting at his desk, cannot look out upon it. Windows set high give a more uninterrupted light, and are less liable to be broken than low ones, and are, therefore, on the whole, preferable. But if the house be situated at a distance from objects likely to draw the children's attention, the windows may be at the usual cheerful height. In any case, they should be furnished with blinds or green curtains. They should be made to open from the top as well as the bottom, so that, in the summer season, when the ventilator will not act, they may supply its place.

2. WARMING.—The usual mode of heating a room by means of an iron stove has no recommendation but its cheapness. It burns the air, and renders it disagreeable and unwholesome. The best mode with reference to health is by a common open fireplace. By a little pains in the construction, the advantages of the latter may be combined with the economy of the former, and the room be at the same time furnished with an ample supply of fresh, warm air from abroad. In a suitable position, pointed out in the plates, near the door, let a common brick fireplace be built. Let

this be enclosed, on the back and on each side, by a casing of brick, leaving, between the fireplace and the casing, a space of four or five inches, which will be heated through the back and jambs. Into this space let air be admitted from beneath by a box 24 inches wide and 6 or 8 deep, leading from the external atmosphere by an opening beneath the front door, or at some other convenient place. The brick casing should be continued up as high as six or eight inches above the top of the fireplace, where it may open into the room by lateral orifices, to be commanded by iron doors, through which the heated air will enter the room. If these are lower, part of the warm air will find its way into the fire place. The brick chimney should rise at least two or three feet above the hollow back, and may be surmounted by a flat iron, soap-stone, or brick top, with an opening for a smoke-pipe, which may be thence conducted to any part of the room. The smoke-pipe should rise a foot, then pass to one side, and then, over a passage, to the opposite extremity of the room, where it should ascend perpendicularly and issue above the roof. The fireplace should be provided with iron doors, by which it may be completely closed.

The advantages of this double fireplace are, 1. The fire, being made against brick, imparts to the air of the apartment none of the deleterious qualities which are produced by a common iron stove, but gives the pleasant heat of an open fireplace;* 2. None of the heat of the fuel will be lost, as the smoke-pipe may be extended far enough to communicate nearly all the heat contained in the smoke; 3. The current of air heated within the hollow back, and constantly pouring

---

* The poisonous effects of hot iron on air are not generally understood. There are always floating in the atmosphere minute particles, which are chiefly carbon. These, coming in contact with a hot iron surface, are partially converted into the poisonous carbonic acid gas. There seem to be some other deadening effects produced on the air not so easily explained.

into the room, will diffuse an equable heat throughout every part; 4. The pressure of the air of the room will be constantly outward, little cold will enter by cracks and windows, and the fireplace will have no tendency to smoke; 5. By means of the iron doors, the fire may be completely controlled,—increased or diminished at pleasure, with the advantages of an air-tight stove. For that purpose, there must be a valve or slide near the bottom of one of the doors.

If, instead of this fireplace, a common stove be adopted, it should be placed above the air-passage, which may be commanded by a valve or register in the floor, so as to admit or exclude air. Of the stoves in use, the best seems to be that called the "air-tight." A winter's trial of one of them in a teacher's room shows it to be far inferior to the double fireplace above recommended, and not essentially different in the consumption of fuel.

3. VENTILATION.—A room warmed by such a fireplace as that just described, may be easily ventilated. If a current of air is constantly pouring in, a current of the same size will rush out wherever it can find an outlet, and with it will carry the impurities wherewith the air of an occupied room is always charged. For the first part of the morning the open fireplace may suffice. But this, though a very effectual, is not an economical ventilator; and when the issue through this is closed, some other must be provided. The most effective ventilator for throwing out foul air, is one opening into a tube which encloses the smoke-flue at the point where it passes through the roof. Warm air naturally rises. If a portion of the smoke-flue be enclosed by a tin tube, it will warm the air within this tube, and give it a tendency to rise. If, then, a wooden tube, opening near the floor, be made to communicate, by its upper extremity, with the tin tube, an upward current will take place in it, which *will always act whenever the smoke-flue is warm.**

---

* There is a difficulty in ventilation as it is often managed

It is better, but not absolutely essential, that the opening into the wooden tube be near the floor. The carbonic acid thrown out by the lungs rises, with the warm breath, and the perspirable matter from the skin, with the warm, invisible vapour, to the top of the room. There both soon cool, and sink towards the floor; and both carbonic air and the vapour bearing the perspirable matter are pretty rapidly and equally diffused through every part of the room.* It matters not, therefore, from what part of the room the outlet is made, as from every part, probably, an equal amount of foul matter will be thrown out. If it be from a point near the floor, it will be accompanied with less heat, and it will, at the same time, increase the tendency of the warm air above to diffuse itself through the space below.

The best possible ventilator is an open fireplace. Many schoolrooms were originally constructed with a fireplace, which, from the superior economy of a stove, has been closed up, and the smoke-pipe has been made to enter into the upper part of the chimney. Where this is the case, a most efficient ventilator may be secured by partially opening the fireplace near the hearth, and commanding the orifice by a slide of wood or metal. The opening of the ven-

Where no warm air is admitted, an opening made for the purpose of letting out foul air is just as likely to let air in; or, if the opening is a single one, two currents will be established in it, one outward, the other inward, and neither of them active. A ventilator opening into an attic is often quite inefficient.

* This diffusion, from the mutual penetration of gases, is often lost sight of. Turner says, "One gas acts as a vacuum with respect to another; and, therefore, if a vessel full of carbonic acid gas be made to communicate with another of hydrogen, the particles of each gas insinuate themselves between the particles of the other, till they are equally diffused through both vessels. . . . . The ultimate effect . . . is the same as if the vessel of hydrogen had been a vacuum."—*See Turner's Chemistry, 4th Am. Edition,* p. 162. *See, also, Manchester's Memoirs,* vol. v., *for Dalton's original investigations on this subject.*

tilator should in any case be not less than 12 inches square, and, in the case in question, it should be near the master's seat, not far from the floor, two feet long and eight inches high, and open into a box in the wall of these dimensions, or at least 24 inches by six, extending to the ceiling, where it should communicate with the tin box enclosing the smoke-pipe. If the building have two stories, the ventilator tubes must be carried from the lower, upward, within the wall, and communicate in the upper ceiling with the tin box. The supply of fresh air for the upper room should then be brought in from the side of the house between two joists in the floor, and open beneath the stove or behind the fireplace.

This mode of ventilation will be found much more economical, as well as more certain, than a usual mode of making openings into an attic which has windows into the atmosphere. In the latter, you have a flight of stairs to the attic, an attic floor and two windows; in the other, a wooden tube 12 feet long, and a tin one four or five feet long: the attic being left unfinished, or, what would be better, having the ceiling of the schoolroom arched, to embrace a part of the space of the attic.

The details of construction will be given in the explanation of the plates

SCHOOL FOR FORTY-EIGHT PUPILS.

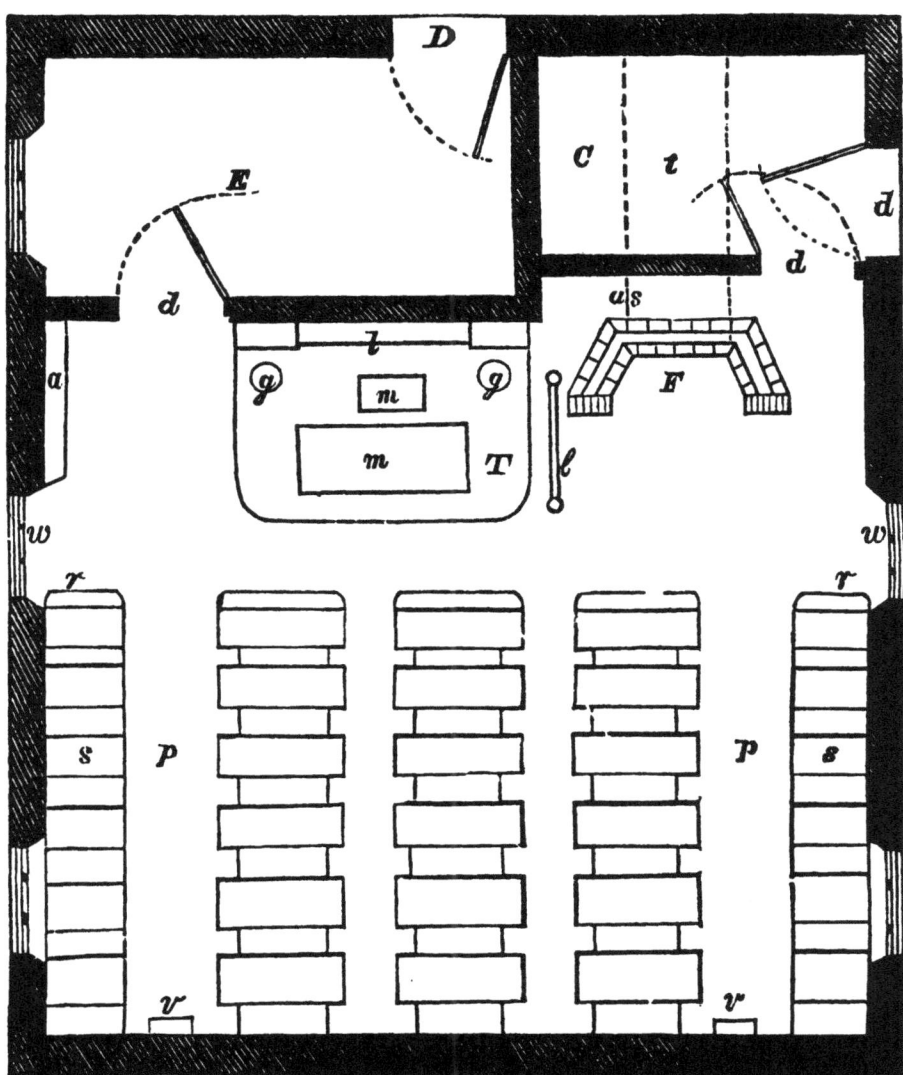

[24 feet by 28 feet outside.]   [Scale 8 feet to the inch.

- D. Entrance door.
- E. Entry.
- F. Fireplace.
- C. Wood closet, or recitation room.
- T. Teacher's platform.
- a. Apparatus shelves.
- t. Air tube beneath the floor.
- d. Doors.
- g. Globes
- l. Library shelves.
- m. Master's table and seat
- p. Passages.
- r. Recitation seats.
- s. Scholars' desks and seats.
- v. Ventilator.
- w. Windows.
- b. Movable blackboard.
- a s. Air space behind the fireplace

SCHOOL FOR ONE HUNDRED AND TWENTY PUPILS.

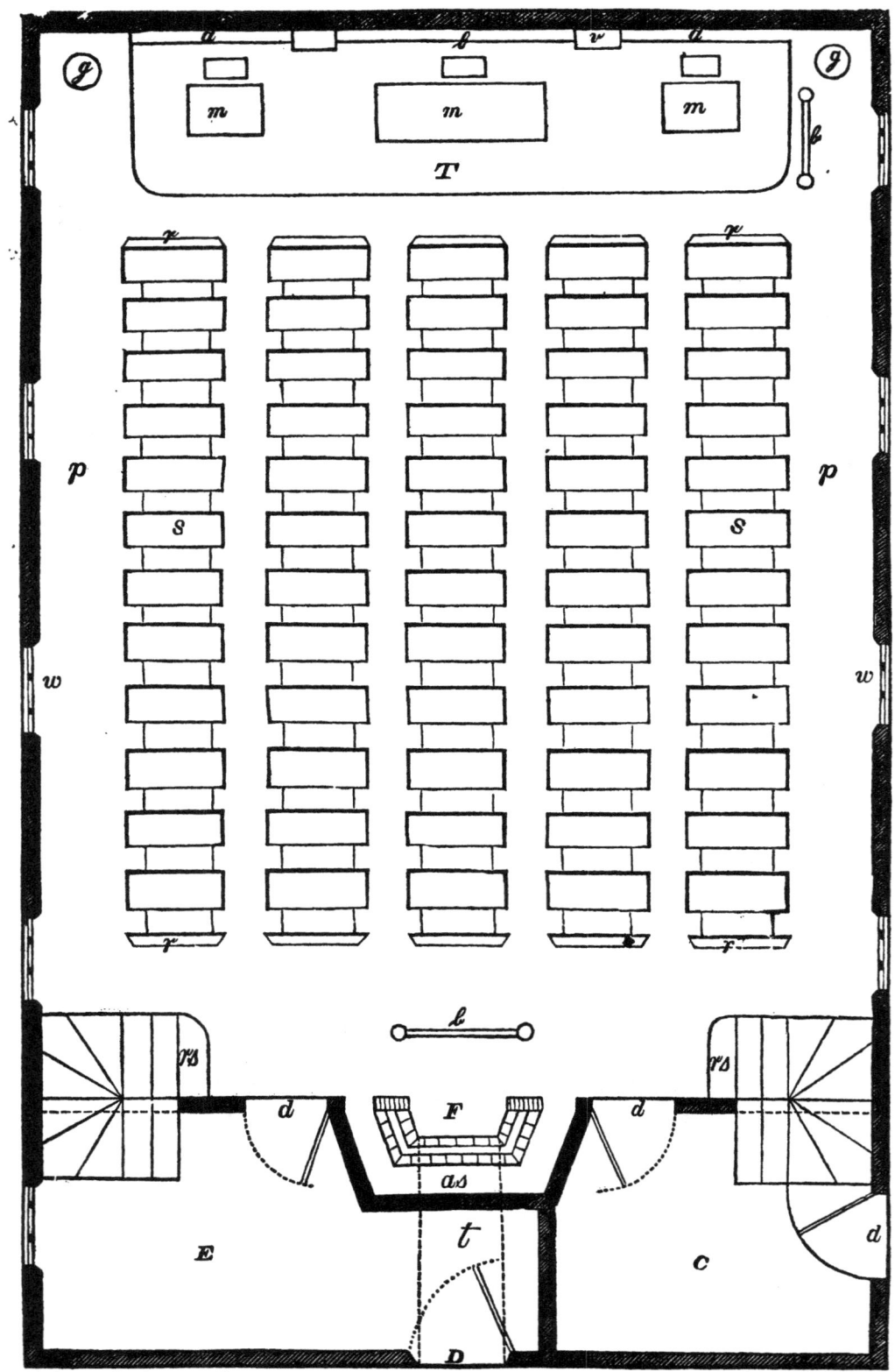

51 feet by 31 feet outside.]   [Scale 8 feet to the inch.

D. Entrance door. E. Entry. F. Fireplace. C. Wood closet. T. Teacher's platform. *a.* Apparatus shelves. *t.* Air tube beneath the floor. *d.* Doors. *g.* Globes. *l.* Library shelves. *m.* Master's table and seat. *p.* Passages. *r.* Recitation seats. *s.* Scholars' desks and seats. *r s.* Stairs to recitation rooms in the attic. *v.* Ventilator. *w.* Windows. *b.* Movable blackboard. *a s.* Air space behind the fireplace

FIREPLACE.

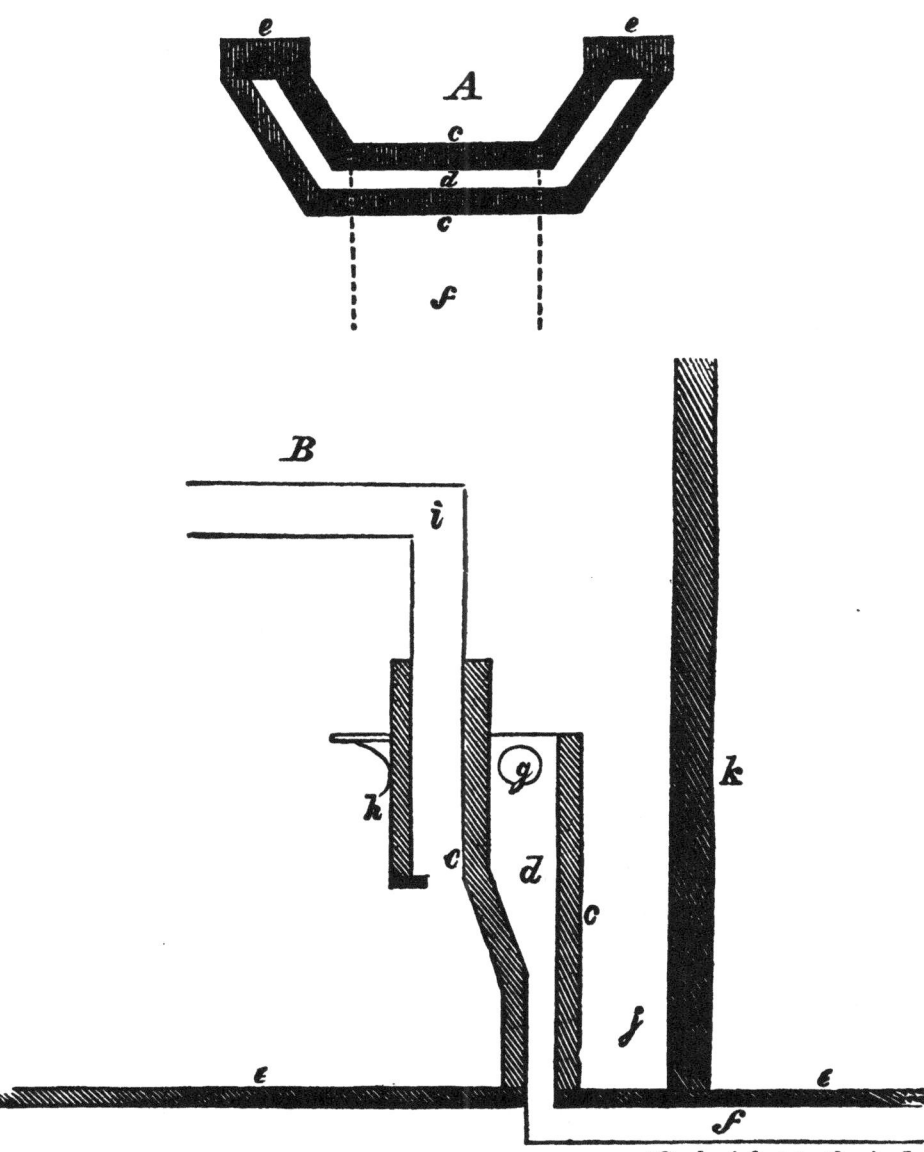

A. Horizontal section.
B. Perpendicular section.
c. Brick walls, 4 inches thick.
d. Air space between the walls.
e. Solid fronts of masonry.
f. Air box for supply of fresh air, extending beneath the floor to the front door.
g. Openings on the sides of the fireplace for the heated air to pass into the room.
h. Front of the fireplace and mantelpiece.
i. Iron smoke flue, 8 inches diameter.
j. Space between the fireplace and wall.
k. Partition wall.
l. Floor.

[Scale 4 feet to the inch.

Z z

VENTILATING APPARATUS

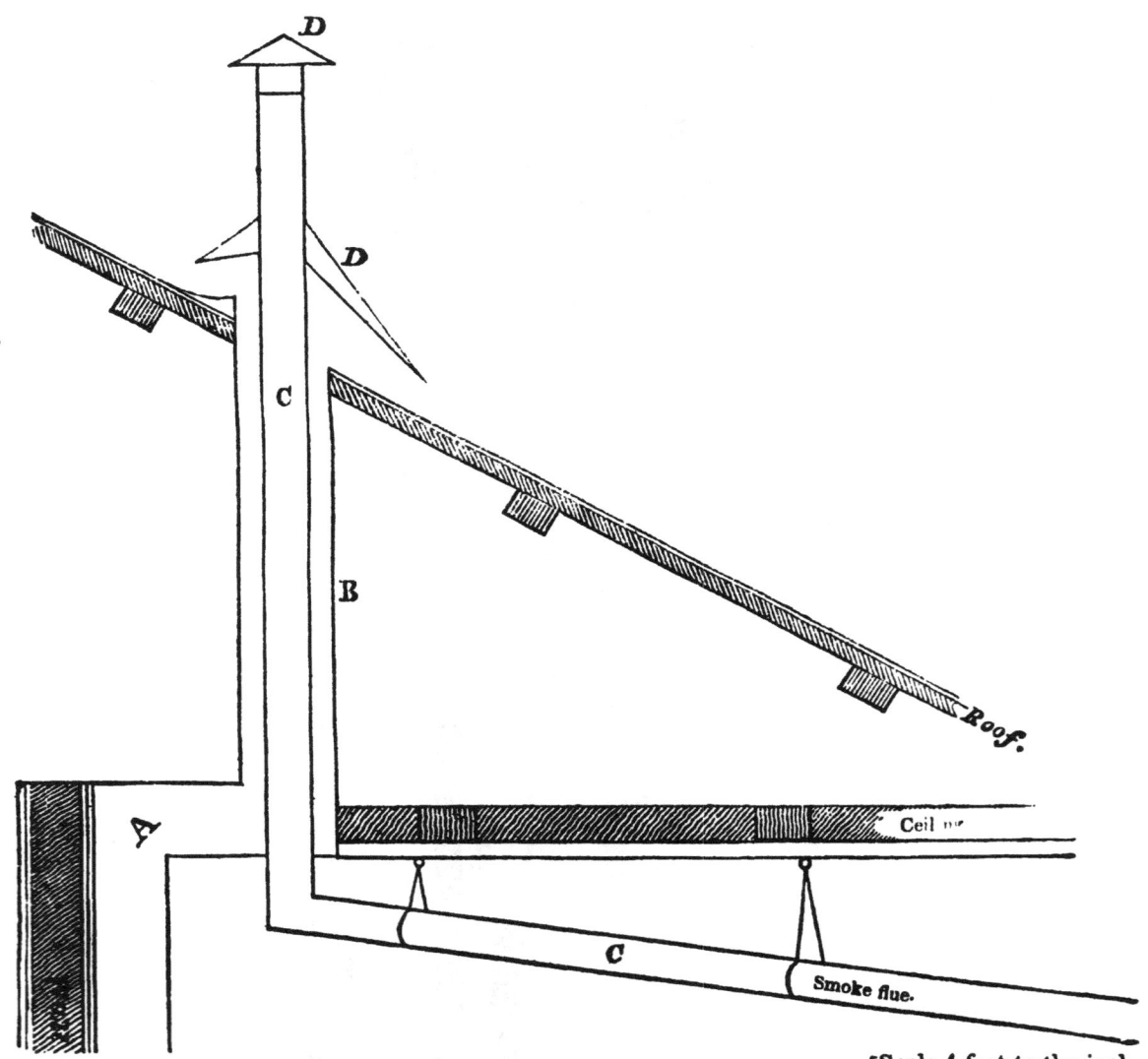

[Scale 4 feet to the inch.

A. Air box, 1 foot square, or 24 inches by 6, covered by the pilaster, and opening at the floor, in the base of the pilaster.
B. Round iron tube, 15½ inches in diameter, being a continuation of the air box, through the centre of which passes,
C. The smoke flue, 8 inches diameter
D Caps to keep out the rain

SECTION OF SCHOLARS' DESKS AND SEATS.

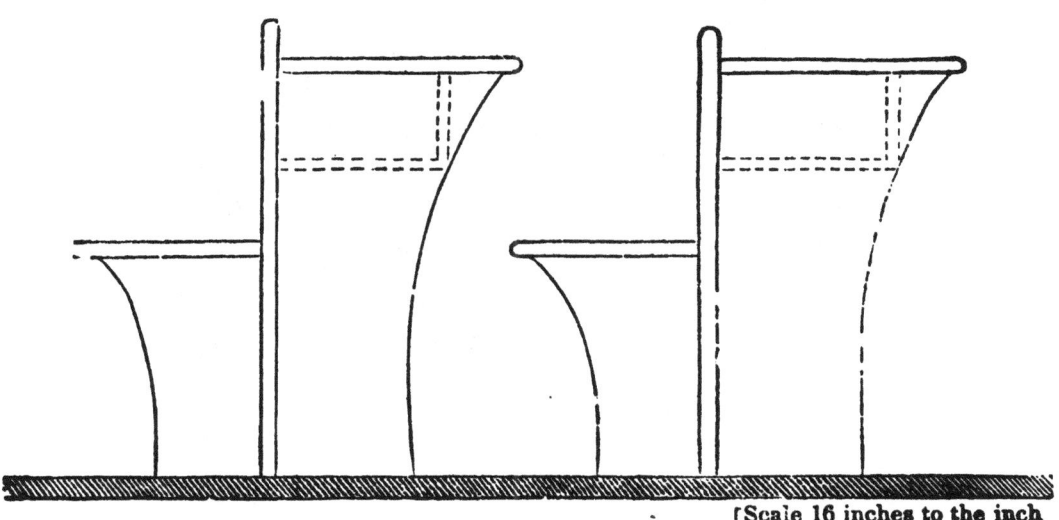

[Scale 16 inches to the inch

BLACKBOARD.

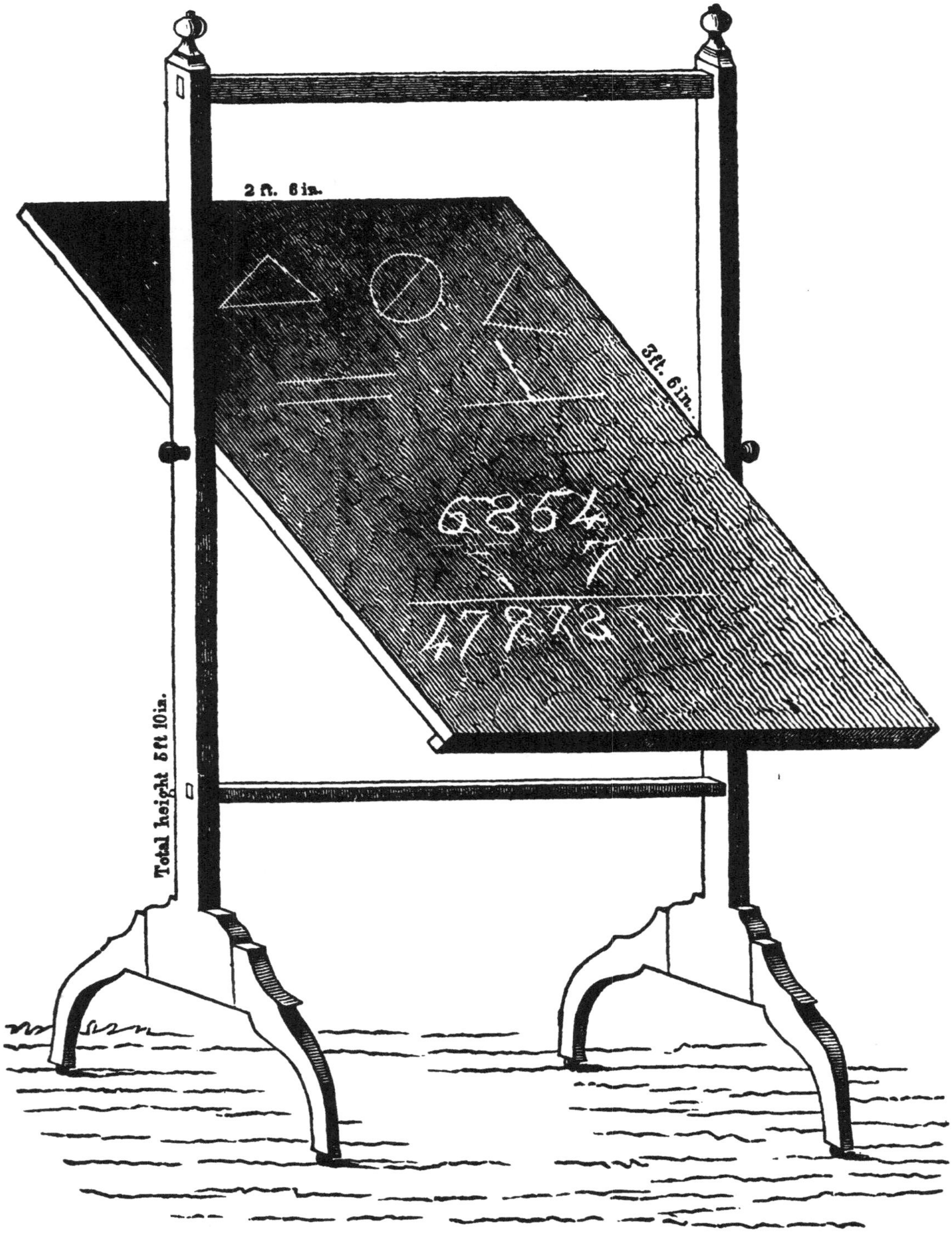

Octagonal Schoolhouse—Cost from $400 to $550.

APPENDIX.

DESCRIPTION OF AN OCTAGONAL SCHOOLHOUSE,

FURNISHED FOR THIS WORK BY MESSRS. TOWN AND DAVIS, ARCHITECTS, NEW-YORK.

This design for a schoolhouse intends to exhibit a model of fitness and close economy. It differs from a design published by the Common School Society of New-York, in being made more simple, without the belfry, and complete in the octagon form. It is also similar to a design published by the Connecticut Board of Commissioners of Common Schools. The principles of fitness are the same in both, viz.: 1. *Ample dimensions,* with very nearly *the least possible length of wall* for its enclosure, the roof being constructed without tie beams, the upper and lower ends of the rafters being held by the wall plates and frame at the foot of the lantern. The ceiling may show the timber-work of the roof, or it may be plastered. 2. *Light, a uniform temperature, and a free ventilation,* secured by a lantern light, thus avoiding lateral windows (except for air in summer), and gaining wall-room for blackboards, maps, models, and illustrations. Side windows are shown in the view, and may be made an *addition* by those who doubt the efficiency of the lantern light. (The lantern is not only best for light, but it is essential for a free ventilation.) With such a light, admitted equally to all the desks, there will be no inconvenience from shadows. The attention of the scholars will not be distracted by occurrences or objects out of doors. There will be less expense for broken glass, as the sashes will be removed from ordinary accidents. The room, according to this plan, is heated by a fire in the centre, either in a stove or grate, with a pipe going directly through the roof of the lantern, and finishing outside in a sheet-iron vase or other appropriate cap. The pipe can be tastefully fashioned, with a hot-air chamber near the floor, so as to afford a large radiating surface before the heat is allowed to escape. This will secure a uniform temperature in every part of the room, at the same time that the inconvenience from a pipe passing directly over the heads of children is avoided. The octagonal shape will admit of any number of seats and desks (according to the size of the room), arranged parallel with the sides, constructed as described in specification, or on such principles as may be preferred. The master's seat may be in the centre of the room, and the seats be so constructed that the scholars may sit with their backs to the centre, by which their attention will not be diverted by facing other scholars on the opposite side, and yet so that at times they may all face the master, and the whole school be formed into one class. The lobby next to the front door is made large (8 by 20), so that it may serve for a recitation-room. This lobby is to finish eight feet high, the inside wall to show like a screen, not rising to the roof, and the space above be open to the schoolroom, and used to put away or station school apparatus. This screen-like wall may be hung with hats and clothes, or the triangular space next the window may be enclosed for this purpose. The face of the octagon opposite to the porch has a woodhouse attached to it, serving as a sheltered way to a double privy beyond. This woodhouse is open on two sides, to admit of a cross draught of air, preventing the possibility of a nuisance. Other wing-rooms may be attached to the remaining sides of the octagon, if additional conveniences for closets, library, or recitation-rooms be desired.

The mode here suggested, of a lantern in the centre of the roof for lighting all common schoolhouses, is so great a change from common usage in our country, that it requires full and clear explanations for its execution, and plain and satisfactory reasons for its general adoption, and of its great excellence in preference to the common mode. They are as follows, viz.:

1. A skylight is well known to be far better and stronger than light from the sides of buildings in cloudy weather, and in morning and evening. The difference is of the greatest importance. In short days (the most used for schools) it is still more so.

2. The light is far better for all kinds of study than side light, from its quiet uniformity and equal distribution.

3. For smaller houses, the lantern may be square, a simple form easily constructed. The sides, whether square or octagonal, should incline like the drawing, but not so much as to allow water condensed on its inside to drop off, but run down on the inside to the bottom, which should be so formed as to conduct it out by a small aperture at each bottom pane of glass.

4. The glass required to light a schoolroom equally well with side lights would be double what would be required here, and the lantern would be secure from common accidents, by which a great part of the glass is every year broken.

5. The strong propensity which scholars have to look out by a side window would be mostly prevented, as the shutters to side apertures would only be opened when the warm weather would require it for air, but never in cool weather, and therefore no glass would be used. The shutters being made very tight, by corking, in winter, would make the schoolroom much warmer than has been common; and, being so well ventilated, and so high in the centre, it would be more healthy.

6. The stove, furnace, or open grate, being in the centre of the room, has great advantages, from diffusing the heat to all parts, and equally to all the scholars; it also admits the pipe to go perpendicularly up, without any inconvenience, and it greatly facilitates the ventilation, and the retention or escape of heat, by means of the sliding cap above.

Construction.—Foundation of hard stone, laid with mortar; the superstructure framed and covered with 1¼ plank, tongued, grooved, and put on vertically, with a fillet, chamfered at the edges, over the joint, as here shown. In our view, a rustic character is given to the design

by covering the sides with slabs; the curved side out, tongued, and grooved, without a fillet over the joint; or formed of logs placed vertically, and lathed and plastered on the inside. The sides diminish slightly upward. A rustic porch is also shown, the columns of cedar boles, with vines trained upon them. The door is battened, with braces upon the outside, curved as shown, with a strip around the edge. It is four feet wide, seven high, in two folds, one half to be used in inclement weather. The cornice projects two feet six inches, better to defend the boarding; and may show the ends of the rafters. Roof covered with tin, slate, or shingles. Dripping eaves are intended, without gutters. The roof of an octagonal building of ordinary dimensions may with ease and perfect safety be constructed without tie beams or a garret floor (which is, in all cases of schoolhouses, waste room, very much increasing the exposure to fire, as well as the expense). The wall-plates, in this case, become ties, and must be well secured, so as to form one connected *hoop*, capable of counteracting the pressure outward of the angular rafters. The sides of the roof will abut at top against a similar timber octagonal frame, immediately at the foot of the lantern cupola. This frame must be sufficient to resist the pressure inward of the roof (which is greater or less, as the roof is more or less inclined in its pitch), in the same manner as the tie-plates must resist the pressure outward. This security is given in an easy and cheap manner; and may be given entirely by the roof boarding, if it is properly nailed to the angular rafters, and runs horizontally round the roof. By this kind of roof, great additional height is given to the room by *camp-ceiling*; that is, by planing the rafters and roof-boards, or by lathing and plastering on a thin half-inch board ceiling, immediately on the underside of the rafters, as may be most economically performed This extra height in the centre will admit of low side-walls, from seven to ten feet in the clear, according to the size and importance of the building, and, at the same time, by the most simple principle of philosophy, conduct the heated foul air up to the central aperture, which should be left open quite round the pipe of the stove, or open grate standing in the centre of the room. This aperture and cap, with the ventilator, is shown by the figure adjoining, which is to a scale of half an inch to a foot. The ventilator is drawn raised, and the dotted lines show it let down upon the roof. It may be of any required size, say two feet wide and twelve inches high, sliding up and down between the stovepipe and an outward case, forming a cap to exclude water. This cap may be pushed up or let down by a rod affixed to the under edge, and lying against the smokepipe.

In the design given, the side-walls are ten feet high, and the lantern fifteen feet above the floor; eight feet in diameter, four feet high. The sashes may open for additional ventilation, if required, by turning on lateral pivots, regulated by cords attached to the edges above. The breadth of each desk is seventeen inches, with a shelf beneath for books, and an opening in the back to receive a slate. The highest desks are twenty-seven inches, inclined to thirty, and the front forms the back of the seat before it. The seat is ten to twelve inches wide, fifteen high, and each pupil is allowed a space of two feet side to side.

I. Town and Alex. J. Davis, *Architects*,
No. 93 Merchants' Exchange, N. Y.

For the sake of variety, we have given a design in the pointed style, revised from a sketch by ——, an amateur in architecture. Any rectangular plan will suit it; and the principles of light and ventilation dwelt upon in the description of the octagon design, may be adapted to this. The principal light is from one large mullioned window in the rear end. The side openings are for air in summer—not glazed, but closed with tight shutters. The same ventilating cap is shown, and height is gained in the roof by framing with collar beams set up four or five feet above the eaves. The sides, if not of brick or stone, may be boarded vertically, as before described. The porch may be of any convenient size to shelter the door of a recitation room, through which may be the passage to the schoolroom One end of the recitation room may be partitioned off for a book room, and one opening on each side may be glazed for light.

I. T. and A. J. D

THE END.

www.ingramcontent.com/pod-product-compliance
Lightning Source LLC
Chambersburg PA
CBHW062123160426
43191CB00013B/2176